THE ALBATROSS
OF DECISIVE VICTORY

**Recent Titles in
Contributions in Military Studies**

Desert Storm at Sea: What the Navy Really Did
Marvin Pokrant

A Peripheral Weapon? The Production and Employment of British Tanks in the First World War
David J. Childs

Where a Man Can Go: Major General William Phillips, British Royal Artillery, 1731–1781
Robert P. Davis

Truman, MacArthur, and the Korean War
Dennis D. Wainstock

Secret Soldiers of the Revolution: Soviet Military Intelligence, 1918–1933
Raymond W. Leonard

The Writing of Official Military History
Robin Higham, editor

Reorganizing the Joint Chiefs of Staff: The Goldwater-Nichols Act of 1986
Gordon Nathaniel Lederman

Bullies and Cowards: The West Point Hazing Scandal, 1898–1901
Philip W. Leon

The Bradley and How It Got That Way: Technology, Institutions, and the Problem of Mechanized Infantry in the United States Army
W. Blair Haworth, Jr.

Soldier and Warrior: French Attitudes Toward the Army and War on the Eve of the First World War
H. L. Wesseling

In the Shadow of Nelson: The Naval Leadership of Admiral Sir Charles Cotton, 1753–1812
Paul C. Krajeski

Iron Admirals: Naval Leadership in the Twentieth Century
Ronald Andidora

THE ALBATROSS OF DECISIVE VICTORY

War and Policy Between Egypt and Israel in the 1967 and 1973 Arab-Israeli Wars

GEORGE W. GAWRYCH

Contributions in Military Studies, Number 188

GREENWOOD PRESS
Westport, Connecticut • London

Library of Congress Cataloging-in-Publication Data

Gawrych, George W.
 The albatross of decisive victory : war and policy between Egypt and Israel in the 1967 and 1973 Arab-Israeli wars / by George W. Gawrych.
    p. cm.—(Contributions in military studies, ISSN 0883–6884 ; no. 188)
  Includes bibliographical references (p.   ) and index.
  ISBN 0–313–31302–4 (alk. paper)
  1. Israel-Arab War, 1967. 2. Israel-Arab War, 1973. 3. Israel—Foreign relations—Egypt.
 4. Egypt—Foreign relations—Israel. I. Title. II. Series.
 DS127.G28   2000
 327.5694062—dc21   99–044521

British Library Cataloguing in Publication Data is available.

Copyright © 2000 by George W. Gawrych

All rights reserved. No portion of this book may be
reproduced, by any process or technique, without the
express written consent of the publisher.

Library of Congress Catalog Card Number: 99–044521
ISBN: 0–313–31302–4
ISSN: 0883–6884

First published in 2000

Greenwood Press, 88 Post Road West, Westport, CT 06881
An imprint of Greenwood Publishing Group, Inc.
www.greenwood.com

Printed in the United States of America

The paper used in this book complies with the
Permanent Paper Standard issued by the National
Information Standards Organization (Z39.48–1984).

10 9 8 7 6 5 4 3 2 1

To my wife Joan,

son Andrew, and daughter Teresa

. . . even the ultimate outcome of a war is not always to be regarded as final. The defeated state often considers the outcome merely as a transitory evil, for which a remedy may still be found in political conditions at some later date.
—Carl von Clausewitz

The history of the twentieth century suffices to remind us that there are many ways to win a war, that the various ways are not equivalent, and that the final victory does not necessarily belong to the side that dictates the conditions of peace.
—Raymond Aron

CONTENTS

Maps ix

Key to Maps xi

Introduction xiii

Abbreviations xvii

1. Stumbling into War 1
2. Israel's Blitzkrieg 39
3. The Egyptian Phoenix 71
4. A Three-Year Border War 95
5. "No War, No Peace" 127
6. Egypt's Assault 163
7. Israel's Resurgence 199
8. Ascent of the Dove 239
9. Conclusion 257

Select Bibliography 263

Index 275

MAPS

1.	Plan *Qahir*	17
2.	Egyptian Deployments on 5 June 1967	20
3.	Israel's Strategic Depth	24
4.	Plan *Kilshon*	29
5.	Plan *Nahshonim*	32
6.	Operation *Moked*	40
7.	Battle for Rafah	45
8.	Battle for Abu Ageila	49
9.	Israel's Blitzkrieg	61
10.	Major IDF Raids, 1968–70	112
11.	Sinai Front, 6 October 1973	155
12.	Battle for Golan, 6–8 October	169
13.	Israeli Counterattack, 8 October	185
14.	Battles on 8 October	188
15.	Egyptian Attack on 14 October	207
16.	Operation Stouthearted Men	212
17.	Battle for the Chinese Farm, 15–17 October	218
18.	Israeli Breakout, 19–22 October	222
19.	Second Cease-Fire, 25 October	233

KEY TO MAPS

SIZE OF UNITS

XXXX	Field Army
XX	Division
III	Regiment
II	Battalion
I	Company

COMBAT BRANCHES

⊠	Infantry	⊗	Mechanized Infantry
◯	Armor	●	Artillery
⋂	Paratroopers	S	*Saiqa*, Egyptian Commandos
☐	Israeli Forces	▨	Egyptian or Syrian Forces

INTRODUCTION

Achieving a decisive military victory in a short war with minimum casualties stands as a noteworthy achievement in the annals of modern warfare. The Six Day War of 5–10 June 1967 saw the Israel Defense Forces accomplish such a triumph over the combined armies of Egypt, Jordan, and Syria. As a result of this remarkable feat, Israel emerged as *the* regional superpower in the Middle East, seemingly invincible in conducting maneuver warfare against any Arab coalition. Conventional wisdom, therefore, would counsel against challenging such a militarily superior foe in war, and Israel naturally expected some respite from hostilities as a result of its impressive victory. But such proved not to be the case.

Egypt refused to countenance military defeat and offered armed resistance to Israel's occupation of the Sinai. The next three years saw a border war between the two countries, with serious escalation occurring in the third year, followed by three years of relative calm. During this entire six-year period, the Egyptian Armed Forces sought to improve their combat effectiveness as they prepared to recapture territory through military means. Finally, frustrated by the lack of diplomatic progress, Egypt, in alliance with Syria, attacked Israel on 6 October 1973.

Virtually every Western pundit expected an early Israeli victory. Egyptian president Anwar Sadat was acutely aware of the Israeli army's marked superiority over his own; out of desperation, he crafted a war strategy designed to achieve political benefits *without* a military victory. His statesmanship proved successful. After five and a half years of negotiations following the October War, Egypt and Israel finally signed a peace treaty that ended their state of belligerency and returned the Sinai to the Egyptians. Sadat's political achievement is as remarkable as the Israeli army's military victory in 1967; the Egyptian example should give pause to Western armies, especially the US armed forces after their blitzkrieg-type victory on the ground in Desert Storm.

In analyzing the saga of warfare on the Egyptian-Israeli front from 1967 to 1973, this study relies on the theory of war of Carl von Clausewitz (1780–1831) as published in his classic work, *On War*. Clausewitz viewed war as "an act of policy," as "merely the continuation of policy by other means."[1] For him, policy (*Politik*) refers to "those political actss that lead to war, determine its purpose, influence its conduct, and bring about its termination.[2] He regarded policy as not something static, but it had to adjust in response to changing circumstances on the battlefield: "the political aim . . . must adapt itself to its chosen means, a process which can radically change it."[3] Thus, policy can never be studied in isolation of the violence on the battlefield, and vice versa. War and policy influence each other during the course of armed conflict.

Clausewitz saw the phenomenon of war as the interplay among three "dominant tendencies," which he referred to collectively as "the paradoxical (*wunderliche*) trinity." These three elements are policy; chance and probability; and primordial violence, hatred, and enmity. For him, policy is "the business of government (*Regierung*) alone," subject to the powers of reason. War also depends upon the passion of the people (*Volke*), making it a social act. Finally, the waging of war requires the creative energies and courage of the commander and his armed forces.[4] Commanders have to confront a combat environment filled with danger, fog (uncertainty), and friction (the errors, accidents, and technical problems that make waging war so difficult).[5] The Clausewitzian trinity provides an excellent analytical tool for studying war.

In light of Clausewitz's theory, this study adopts a broad approach to analyzing the 1967 and 1973 wars between Egypt and Israel. It analyzes campaigns and major battles within the context of competing political aims, diplomatic maneuvers, war strategies, and military doctrines. Put another way, this study links strategic, operational, and tactical events. In this regard, war is here treated more as a clash between opposing political and military cultures than a conflict between competing weapons systems and force structures. Finally, to gain an appreciation of the linkage between the 1967 and 1973 wars, this work devotes a chapter to the reform of the Egyptian army after its defeat in 1967 and another to the Three Years War (1967–70).

A study of this nature poses certain difficulties for the military historian. Both Israel and Egypt have kept their archives closed to foreign researchers. Thus, a good portion of the military literature on the two wars is of an impressionistic, journalistic nature, written in the aftermath of conflict. Subsequent analyses have tended to echo earlier descriptions and interpretations without critically reevaluating the data. This study retraces the military events with a more critical eye, drawing upon the small body of scholarly publications on the subject.

Much of the analysis relies on memoirs, interviews, and the press. Interviews with Israeli and Egyptian participants have been especially helpful in clarifying key aspects of both wars. Unlike most Western publications, this study incorporates Arabic works published by Egyptian participants. However, all the literature—whether Israeli, Egyptian, or Western—must be approached with healthy skepticism. The Arab-Israeli conflict has been a highly emotional subject, which amplifies problems of balance and objectivity in research. The reader should particularly note the author's approach to Israeli and Egyptians sources. I avoid using one side's sources to criticize the other's performance. Moreover, when critically evaluating one side in the conflict, whenever possible, I rely on sources from that side. This methodology is intended to achieve, as much as possible, balance and objectivity in the analysis.

Numerous individuals were instrumental in this study. Many thanks go to those American, Middle Eastern, and other international officers at the US Army Command and Staff College (Fort Leavenworth, Kansas) who participated in my course on the art of war in the modern Middle East. Their experiences and insights have truly fostered an intellectually stimulating environment for research and teaching, for which I am most indebted. Naturally, the views expressed in this study are those of the author and do not necessarily reflect the positions of any individual or institution.

Finally, I dedicate this book to my wife Joan, son Andrew, and daughter Teresa. Their love, support, and encouragement have made this endeavor possible.

NOTES

1. Carl von Clausewitz, *On War*, edited and translated by Michael Howard and Peter Paret (Princeton: Princeton University Press, 1984): 87.

2. Peter Paret, "Clausewitz," in *Makers of Modern Strategy from Machiavelli to the Nuclear Age*, edited by Peter Paret (Princeton: Princeton University Press, 1986): 210. The words quoted are those of Paret

3. Clausewitz, *On War*: 87.

4. Ibid.: 89.

5. Ibid.: 100-121.

ABBREVIATIONS

EAF	Egyptian Armed Forces
IDF	Israel Defense Forces
RPGM	Remotely-Piloted Guided Missile
SAF	Syrian Armed Forces
SAM	Surface-to-Air Missile
UAR	United Arab Republic, official name for Egypt during period of study
UN	United Nations
US	United States
USSR	the Soviet Union

1

STUMBLING INTO WAR

But at the level of the so-called higher civilizations, when states are legally organized, war can no longer be anything but a means if consciously desired, or a calamity if provoked for a cause unknown to the actors.
—Raymond Aron[1]

It was not hard to imagine, early in May of 1967, that the mounting tension in the Arab world would lead to some sort of violent outbreak. The conflict to which all signs seemed to point, however, was between Arab revolutionaries and conservatives. The old quarrel with Israel seemed irrelevant.
—Malcom H. Kerr[2]

During the period between 14 May and 4 June 1967, an unexpected rush of events heightened tensions between Israel and its Arab neighbors to such a degree that the outbreak of hostilities on 5 June should have found all the principal combatants fully prepared for war. By that date, Israel, Egypt, Jordan, and Syria had deployed their respective armies forward, placing them in a high state of alert. Though the immediate events leading to war had, in fact, begun on the Golan front, the Sinai theater became the main stage in the process of escalation. During the mushrooming crisis, Egypt, then officially known as the United Arab Republic (UAR), caught Israel off guard with its political decisions and military movements. However, by the eve of war, the initiative had clearly passed to the Israeli side. The Israel Defense Forces (IDF) were now poised, ready to launch a major offensive against the UAR, whereas the Egyptian Armed Forces (EAF) had been ordered onto the defensive in anticipation of a first strike from Israel. Despite the three weeks of steady increase in tensions leading toward war, both

Egypt's and Israel's political and military leadership experienced some difficulty in coordinating a military strategy with clear political objectives.

THE STRATEGIC ENVIRONMENT

At the beginning of 1967, the prospect of a general war in the near future appeared very low. Egypt, Israel, and Syria were all preoccupied with matters other than the Arab-Israeli conflict. The Israelis and Syrians were more focused on domestic matters, whereas the Egyptians were deep into the fifth year of their military involvement in a distant war down in North Yemen. Though the strategic environment made likely yet another year without a major conflagration, the Syrian border suddenly emerged as a major flash point, threatening to engulf other Arab states.

In 1967, Egypt was without doubt the most powerful Arab state. With a population of over thirty million, the UAR stood as the political and cultural center of the Arab world and the possessor of the region's largest army and population. President Gamal Abd al-Nasser (1918–70) was the country's undisputed leader. On 23 July 1952, Nasser, then a lieutenant colonel of humble background, had engineered a bloodless military coup that overthrew King Faruq and established a republic the following year. By 1955, Nasser had emerged as Egypt's strongman, although fate and talent destined him for even greater stature.

The Suez crisis of 1956 propelled Nasser onto center stage as a major figure in the Middle East and the third world. Hoping to take advantage of controversy created by Nasser's nationalization of the Suez Canal, Israel, France, and Great Britain formed a coalition and invaded Egypt, defeating the Egyptian army. Israel seized the Gaza Strip and the entire Sinai, while British and French forces occupied the port cities of Said and Fuad on the northern entrance to the Suez Canal. Though defeated militarily, Nasser won politically: American pressures and international condemnation forced all three invaders to withdraw their armies from captured Egyptian territory. Overnight, Nasser, by refusing to surrender to blatant foreign aggression by colonial powers of the West, became a political hero in the Arab world. Many Arabs embraced him as the symbol of their hopes and aspirations to earn dignity and pride vis-à-vis the more powerful and prosperous Western countries.

Nasser proved quite a charismatic leader, one who easily captivated Arab audiences with his oratorical powers. This gift of oratory served as an important source of Nasser's power and legitimacy. Once, in February 1966, Nasser revealed his reliance on mass appeal as a strategic weapon in response to President Lyndon Baines Johnson's request for secret diplomacy.

You [Johnson] have got money and atom bombs, riches and power without limit. These are your means. What have I got? The main weapon of the Revolution is its masses, the conviction of the masses and the mobilization of those masses to defend themselves against any danger. The weapon of the Arab Revolution is the masses. So perhaps quiet diplomacy would suit the United States. But quiet diplomacy would not suit us because I would be cut off from the support of my masses.[3]

Such dependence on personal magnetism, however, could easily backfire, making Nasser to some degree a prisoner of people's passions and his own public declarations, as would occur in May 1967.

The year 1967 found the Nasser regime in difficult straits. In September 1962, Nasser had committed military force to North Yemen in support of a military junta that had siezed power. Rather than gain a quick victory, the Egyptian army had become embroiled in a conflict that by 1965 had tied down some seventy to eighty thousand troops. Yemen thus turned into the Egypt's Vietnam, spawning a Cold War in the Arab world. Saudi Arabia led the conservative bloc in supporting the Yemeni royalists, while Egypt counted on assistance from progressive regimes to maintain the republicans in power. By 1967, the war had become an immense financial drain, requiring an expenditure of approximately one million dollars a day from Egyptian coffers. In May 1967, unable to maintain its debt payments to the International Monetary Fund, Cairo reluctantly agreed to implement a program of stringent economic reforms.[4] This agreement hurt Nasser's prestige.

Like Egypt, Israel was experiencing problems at the beginning of 1967. Strategically, this small country of over 2,600,000 was still in a unstable environment, as no Arab neighbor had yet seen fit to recognize the Israeli state. Economically, Israel was in the throes of a recession, with unemployment in the first quarter of 1967 hovering at an unacceptable rate of 12.4%. On 14 March 1967, twenty demonstrators were injured protesting against the high unemployment. The gross national product had fallen from an annual average growth of 10.3% between 1961 and 1965 to a mere 1% increase in 1966, with little indication of a quick turnaround. These economic woes had an adverse social impact: Israel was losing some of its magnetism as a land of opportunity for world Jewry. The number of immigrants to Israel fell from 66,465 in 1963 to 18,510 in 1966; many intellectuals and scientists were exiting the country for work abroad.

Politically, the country was under a weaker leadership than it had enjoyed. In 1963, David Ben-Gurion, the father of the modern state of Israel, had retired from politics in favor of his handpicked successor, Levi Eshkol (1895–1969). Eshkol, who lacked the charisma and decisiveness of Ben-Gurion, stood in sharp contrast to Nasser in both character and temperament. Born in the Ukraine, Eshkol had immigrated to Palestine in 1914 and helped found the now-ruling Labor Party. From 1952 to 1963, he served as finance minister, earning a reputation as an effective organizer. Yet, at the helm of the Israeli government, Eshkol proved too much a man of compromise, willing to procrastinate in order to explore all possibilities in a search for consensus. A popular Israeli joke of the time encapsulated his personality: "If you ask Eshkol whether he prefers tea or coffee, he'll have to think about it before he'll say 'Half and half.'"[5] During the May crisis, the Israeli leader preferred quiet diplomacy over confrontation. This leadership style would leave the appearance of an indecisive and tired man, unable to respond effectively to the challenges posed by the dynamic Nasser. As a result, the Egyptian leader scored numerous political points as the crisis unfolded, though these small victories would quickly evaporate in war.

While the charismatic Nasser led Egypt and the conciliator Eshkol steered Israel, Syria had fallen under the spell of the radical Salah Jadid. At the time, the kaleidoscope of Syrian politics reflected a political instability unparalleled in the Arab world. Twenty-one years of independence had witnessed six constitutions and twenty-three governments, including three successful military coups in 1949. In November 1963, junior officers, members of the Arab *Bath* (Renaissance) Party, seized power. As reward for his role in the military coup, Jadid, then an air force major, was made the chief of the General Staff by the end of the year. He came from the Alawite community, a religious minority that formed approximately 13% of the Syria's population of 5.6 million: the Sunni majority (60%) resented the growing Alawite influence in the government. On 23 February 1966, Jadid ousted his rivals in a bloody coup and emerged as Syria's new strongman.

Jadid, a committed leftist, embarked on radical policies that spawned domestic unrest. A new wave of nationalization alienated the business community. Meanwhile, the Sunni Muslims chafed under the secularist rule of the Alawite minority, and major sectarian tensions surfaced just prior to the 1967 war. On 25 April 1967, an article in the military journal *al-Jaysh al-Shaab* (People's Army) called for the creation of a new Arab socialist personality, while condemning Islam as a reactionary ideology. Such iconoclast thinking sparked religious demonstrations throughout the country on 5 May. Approximately twenty thousand demonstrators, including Christian clergy, protested the article, chanting anti-Bathist slogans while marching through the streets of Damascus. Arresting a number of religious leaders, the Jadid government also tried to defuse the explosive situation by establishing a military tribunal to investigate charges that the article undermined Islamic religious traditions and principles. On 11 May, the military court reached a guilty verdict and sentenced the author of the article, the editor of the journal, and the magazine's managing editor to life imprisonment and hard labor.[6]

Although confronted with the internal problem of legitimacy, the Bathist regimes adopted a hawkish policy toward Israel. Beginning in 1964, Damascus sponsored Palestinian guerrilla operations into Israel, often through Lebanon. Jadid, who seized power in February 1966, was quite willing to apply more military pressure on Israel. By the end of 1966, the Upper Jordan Valley had become Israel's most volatile front with numerous minor incidents of artillery and small arms exchanges. There now loomed the danger that the violence might escalate a dangerous notch.

A FALSE ALARM

Sporadic border clashes on the Golan front finally resulted in a major confrontation on 7 April 1967. The day began with an Israeli tractor moving into a disputed area in the demilitarized zone. Syrian troops opened fire on it, and Israeli forces responded in kind. At 11:30 A.M., Eshkol, after conferring with the chief of the General Staff, authorized the continuance of the civilian work in defiance of Syrian military opposition, no doubt as bait to teach the Syrians a tough lesson about Israeli deterrence. In the early afternoon, the ground clashes were transformed into air engagements. At 1:40 P.M., two Syrian MiG-21s faced off against Israeli Mirages. By the day's end, the Israeli air force had committed three squadrons and shot down six Syrian planes. To add a bit of salt to the Syrian wound, Israeli pilots followed up on their aerial success with a defiant buzzing of Damascus.[7] This incident, although embarrassing the Jadid regime, failed to intimidate it.

Israel could afford to press the border issues militarily. With twenty to thirty thousand Egyptian troops committed to the Yemeni civil war, Israeli military intelligence assessed that the EAF would be incapable of waging a major war against Israel before 1970.[8] Israel thus could conduct a military operation against Syria without fear of Egyptian participation. On 7 May, exactly one month after the downing of six Syrian fighter planes, the Israeli cabinet, frustrated by the continuing incidents on the northern front, authorized the IDF to conduct a limited retaliation raid if Damascus failed to heed Israel's public warnings to desist from military operations.[9] A few additional armor units were transferred to the Golan front in anticipation of such a strike. Meanwhile, Israel's political and military leaders began making public statements that force might be the only way to break the cycle of violence.[10] The Jadid regime defiantly responded with boasts that it would gladly meet any Israeli aggression with military resistance. Neither side seemed disposed to disengage from the war of words.

Meanwhile, back in Egypt, Nasser drew acerbic criticism from Arab capitals for failing to honor his defense pact with Syria. That agreement, initialed on 4 November 1966, obligated each country to provide military support should the other face attack from Israel. Now, at the beginning of May 1967, critics in the Arab world charged the Egyptian leader with hiding behind the United Nations (UN) peacekeeping force that had been placed on the Israeli-Egyptian border and at Sharm al-Shaykh shortly after the 1956 war. On 13 May, Dimitri Pozhiidaev, the Soviet ambassador in Cairo, informed the Egyptian government that Israel was massing ten to fifteen brigades on its northern front for a punitive strike against Syria. Anwar Sadat, the speaker of Egypt's National Assembly, received the same information from Soviet officials while departing from Moscow for Cairo.[11] That evening, Cairo received an official communiqué from Damascus that Israel had mobilized fifteen brigades for an attack on Syria scheduled to begin between 15 and 22 May.[12]

Several factors influenced Nasser in his calculations concerning an appropriate response. Though mired in an unpopular war in Yemen, the Egyptian leader felt pressure from his own people and from other Arab governments to support his Syrian brethren. There was also the possibility of using the crisis as an excuse for pulling out Egyptian troops from the Yemeni civil war. Finally,

Nasser was apprehensive about Israeli development of nuclear weapons. In the late fifties, with French assistance, Israel had begun its nuclear program, with the construction of the Dimona reactor in the Negev. By 1965, Arab leaders were regularly expressing concern and even threatening to use military force to arrest the program. In May 1967, Nasser might have been seeking to strengthen his strategic position with the militarization of the Sinai. Such a move would provide Egypt the option of using conventional forces to stop Israel's development of a nuclear bomb. Whether Nasser knew it or not, Israel apparently possessed two operational bombs.[13]

Whatever his exact calculations, Nasser decided to respond quickly and decisively. At a meeting with senior political and military figures on the night of 13/14 May, he ordered the dispatch of a sizable force to the Sinai as a clear demonstration of his solidarity with Syria. This show of force, Nasser hoped, would deter any aggressive action by Israel against Syria. Accordingly, at 11:30 on 14 May, Cairo commenced a general mobilization and sent additional troops to the Sinai.

Meanwhile, General Muhammad Fawzi, the chief of the General Staff, departed for Damascus to evaluate the situation there and discuss coordination of operations with senior Syrian officers.[14] A major surprise awaited him. He found no signs of an Israeli buildup against Syria. In fact, much to his chagrin, the Syrian regime appeared rather unconcerned about recent reports of Israel's massing troops on its border. Fawzi, therefore, returned to Cairo the following day (15 May) with the assessment that there existed no clear indication of an impending Israeli attack against Syria.[15]

Despite Fawzi's sobering report, Nasser had ventured out too far, too publicly, to exit gracefully. To prove to the Arab world his faithful commitment to Syria, the Egyptian leader had had troops dispatched to the Sinai with much fanfare, parading them through the streets of Cairo and other cities before thousands of spectators. Such conspicuous troop movements had been designed for domestic and regional consumption. Recalling these forces would have proved an embarrassing matter, indeed. Arab rivals would have gladly exploited such a retreat to the hilt; the immediate political and military consequences would have been serious for Nasser's standing in the Arab world. His decision had certainly raised tensions in the region. As Egypt had taken concrete steps in support of Syria, other Arab heads of state had found themselves on the defensive and had felt compelled to make military preparations of their own.

Israel eventually grew concerned about the developments around it. Initially, the atmosphere at general headquarters in Tel Aviv was quite relaxed. Despite the movement of Egyptian soldiers into the Sinai, Israeli military intelligence assessed the probability of war as very low, for several reasons. Mainly, the Israelis believed that Nasser would avoid risking a war while a sizable part of his regular army was tied down in Yemen. Furthermore, relations among a number of the Arab states had worsened over the last year, especially between Jordan and Syria, and thus it appeared highly improbable that the Arabs would suddenly bury their differences and unite against Israel. As Major General

Yitzhak Rabin, Israel's chief of the General Staff, noted in 1972, "In May 1967 there was no atmosphere of cooperation in the Arab world and it was impossible to suppose that in this setting the Arabs would strike against us."[16]

Nasser, however, now seemed disposed to throw caution to the wind and improve his sagging image in the Arab world with bold diplomatic moves. In the 1956 Arab-Israeli war, as mentioned earlier, the IDF had conquered the Sinai. As a price for Israel's pullout from the entire peninsula, Egypt had agreed to the stationing of UN peacekeeping troops along the Egyptian side of the border with Israel, as well as in the Gaza Strip and at Sharm al-Shaykh, on the extreme southern tip of the Sinai. These limitations on Egyptian sovereignty had wounded its national pride. Forcing the withdrawal of these soldiers of peace would raise Nasser's popularity in Egypt and the Arab world. Such a move would also silence critics who claimed that the Egyptian leader was hiding behind these international peacekeepers.

Thus on 16 May, General Fawzi sent a letter to Major General Indar Jit Rikye, the UN commander, requesting the withdrawal of his troops from the Egyptian-Israeli border. Rikye immediately informed U Thant, Secretary-General of the United Nations, who refused to comply without a formal request from the Egyptian government addressed directly to him. Moreover, U Thant would not countenance a partial withdrawal; it was all or nothing. Rather than back down, Cairo hardened its position and on 18 May demanded the removal of all 3,400 UN troops, including those stationed in Gaza and at Sharm al-Shaykh. In the interim, that is, from 16 to 18 May, Egyptian troops began occupying UN observation positions near the Israeli border.[17] Rather than attempt to solve the crisis through negotiations, the Secretary-General quickly acceded to the Egyptian demand for a complete pullout, and the UN commenced withdrawing all its forces on 19 May, leaving for the first time since 1957 no international force to separate Israel from Egypt.

Without such a buffer, Israeli military intelligence reassessed the possibility of war as having become more likely than a few days earlier. Not only were the UN troops departing, but according to intelligence estimates, the size of the Egyptian force in Sinai had increased from thirty thousand men and two hundred tanks before the crisis to some seventy thousand troops and six hundred tanks. On 19 May, the Israeli government reacted promptly with its own mobilization of sixty to seventy thousand reserves, most of these earmarked for the southern front. Eshkol also moved on the diplomatic front, calling upon international support to prevent Nasser from blockading the Gulf of Aqaba, Israel's only outlet to the Indian Ocean through the port of Eilat.[18]

The departure of the UN peacekeeping force removed a sore spot in Egypt. Egyptians could now claim complete sovereignty over their border with Israel, as well as over the Strait of Tiran. Although having gained much political capital from his crisis management so far, Nasser now chose to stretch the envelope even farther. He reached another important decision at a meeting at his home of the Arab Socialist Executive, a meeting that commenced at 9:00 P.M. on 21 May and dragged on into the early hours of the next day. There, the top political and military officials discussed closing the Strait of Tiran to Israeli shipping, a move that would establish a blockade of Eilat. Nasser cautioned that this action would increase the likelihood of war to 50 percent, but his senior military commanders assured him that the armed forces were prepared for war. Consequently, Nasser decided to announce the closure that evening at a meeting with air force pilots at Bir Gifgafa Airbase in the Sinai. Meanwhile, General Command prepared orders for the rapid deployment of troops to Sharm al-Shaykh.[19]

In the evening on 22 May, as planned earlier that morning, Nasser told the pilots stationed at Bir Gifgafa of the decision to prohibit the passage of the Israeli flag through the Gulf of Aqaba. Very early the next morning, Radio Cairo announced to the world the dramatic turn of events. Closing the body of water to Israeli vessels, a highly provocative and unnecessary step, constituted for Israel a casus belli; it also generated international sympathy for Israel, making the Arabs appear as warmongers in the Western press. By now, the Middle East crisis had taken on a decidedly international dimension. In 1957, President Dwight D. Eisenhower had promised that the United States wound ensure freedom of navigation through the Gulf of Aqaba, as part of the deal to convince Israel to withdraw all its forces from the entire Sinai and the Gaza Strip, captured in the 1956 war. What would the U.S. administration do now?

THE FINAL COUNTDOWN

With the evolution of the May crisis, Israel and Egypt turned to the United States and the Soviet Union, respectively, for support. Both Washington and Moscow wanted to avoid a major conflagration in the Middle East, and therefore they counseled a political solution. Yet neither superpower followed its words of caution with effective action to defuse tensions; instead, the United States and USSR reluctantly found themselves having to speak of standing behind their respective allies. Thus, on the eve of war, Egypt's and Israel's leaderships had both concluded that superpower support would be forthcoming in the event of the outbreak of hostilities. That conclusion came earlier in Egypt than in Israel.

On 25 May, Shems al-Din Badran, Egypt's war minister, departed for Moscow at the head of a delegation consisting of both military and political officials. In two special meetings held on 26 and 27 May, Premier Aleksei Kosygin offered diplomatic, financial, and material assistance but at the same time urged the exhaustion of every possible effort to avoid the outbreak of war. Badran, a hawk, ignored the cautionary statements and instead focused on Soviet guarantees of support, which for him translated into a green light for Egypt to take any actions it deemed in its national interest. In particular, just prior to boarding his plane for Cairo on 28 May, Badran heard encouraging words from Marshal Andrei Grechko, the USSR's new defense minister: "I want to make clear to you that if America enters the war, we will enter on your side. . . . I want to confirm to you that if something happens and you need us, simply send us a signal. We will come to your aid immediately in Port Said or elsewhere." Bolstered by these seemingly unequivocal words of full Soviet support, Badran returned to Cairo with the most positive report possible.[20] Nasser, in turn, in a speech delivered on 29 May, confidently assured Egypt's National Assembly of Soviet backing.

While the Egyptians looked to the Soviets, the Israelis sought help from the United States, fully expecting Nasser's declaration of a blockade to galvanize America into action. But like Moscow, Washington wanted to bring the crisis to an end through peaceful means. Johnson was deeply absorbed by the Vietnam War and the Great Society; so his administration, together with Congress, wanted to avoid any military involvement, especially one that might require unilateral action. Consequently, in his dealings with Israel throughout May, Johnson consistently advocated the use of diplomatic means to resolve the crisis. He promised to take all possible steps to ensure free transit through the Gulf of Aqaba, but he first wanted to work through the UN and other channels. Needing time for diplomacy, Johnson cautioned Israel against initiating war: "Israel will not be alone unless it decides to do it alone. We cannot imagine that Israel will make this decision."[21]

Washington's position held considerable sway in Israel as long as the Arabs were not poised to attack. On 27 May, Eban, who had just returned from a fact-finding mission to Paris, London, and Washington, joined the Israeli cabinet several hours into a secret session. The foreign minister reported that Johnson, although failing to offer anything concrete, had promised to press the issue for the opening of the Strait of Tiran. Eban recommended that the cabinet accept the American request for two to three weeks to resolve the crisis, especially since Israel had just asked for Johnson's intervention on 25 May. Despite pressure for a first strike by senior generals present at the meeting, the eighteen-member cabinet appeared evenly split on the issue of war or delay. Eshkol, therefore, recommended adjournment without a vote. Another session of the cabinet was scheduled for later that afternoon (28 May).[22]

In the interim, there was more American pressure on Israel to seek a diplomatic resolution. On 28 May, two letters arrived from the United States. In the first, Johnson restated his desire that Israel not initiate hostilities. The second letter carried a message from Secretary of State Dean Rusk summarizing Eban's talks in Washington. Rusk assured the Israeli government that the United States was attempting to mobilize an international naval escort to sail through the Strait of Tiran should all diplomatic efforts fail, but the American secretary of state still cautioned Israel against taking unilateral action. Fortified with these two letters, Eban went to the cabinet session at 3:00 P.M. recommending a two-week delay. This time, there was no indecision: seventeen members voted for giving the United States the additional time, with only Transportation Minister Moshe Carmel calling for immediate action. Meantime, Israel's reserves were to remain mobilized and in a high state of alert.[23] Now the Israeli government had to inform its people of its decision to give diplomacy a chance.

That same evening (28 May), Eshkol, having had very little sleep and near exhaustion, went on radio to deliver to the nation a live speech that increased anxiety among the Israeli public. Both the substance of his address and its tone were quite disconcerting. The government would wait, placing trust in the international community to secure free passage for all ships through the Strait of Tiran. Having had no time to read the text beforehand, Eshkol appeared unprepared: he stumbled through the presentation, his voice stammering and quaking. For a nation expecting some decisive action, or at least confident and defiant words, the address left Israelis with an impression of a tired man at the helm, a leader who lacked the confidence or will to lead the nation in a time of great peril. Consequently, over the next few days, domestic pressure from both the military and the public mounted for Eshkol, who held the positions of prime minister and defense minister, to give up the latter portfolio.

By the end of May, the strategic environment appeared quite threatening for Israel. Egyptian militarization of the Sinai had exceeded a mere demonstration of military support for an ally. At the beginning of May, Egypt had stationed two regular divisions or thirty-five thousand troops in Sinai and Gaza. This force had grown to six divisions and one hundred thousand troops by the end of the month. Moreover, developments in other Arab countries further raised the risk of war.

By the end of May, Syria had mobilized some sixty thousand troops on the Golan Heights. On 30 May, King Hussein of Jordan, whose relations with Nasser had been strained, suddenly surprised many observers by journeying to Cairo to initial a mutual defense pact with Egypt. Before the onset of the May crisis, Amman had played a major role in fueling the vociferous propaganda in the Arab world attacking Nasser for his inactivity. But as Nasser took decisive steps in support of Syria, the mood of the Jordanian people and elements within the country's armed forces shifted to support of Egypt and the Arab cause. When Nasser announced the closure of the Strait of Tiran, Hussein ordered Jordanian military units to parade down the main street in Amman en route to the West Bank as a demonstration of Jordan having sided with the Egyptians. Then, to save his throne from domestic unrest and possible mutiny within the armed forces, Hussein decided to join the Arab fold under Nasser's leadership by signing a defense pact with Egypt on 30 May that placed the Jordanian army under Egyptian control. On 2 June, Egyptian Lieutenant General Abd al-Munim Riyad arrived in Amman to assume command of some fifty-five thousand Jordanian forces; the next day, three Egyptian commando battalions followed him to Jordan. Upon his arrival in Amman, Riyad immediately changed Jordanian war plans and troop deployments for the purpose of forcing Israel to divert some of its armed forces away from the Egyptian and Syrian fronts.[24]

The Arab coalition expanded nearly with each passing day. Diplomatic relations between Jordan and Syria, which had been severed on 22 May 1967, were now restored. Damascus agreed to send a brigade to Jordan. On June 4, King Hussein announced that Iraqi forces would take up positions in Jordan. An Iraqi mechanized infantry brigade was already entering Jordan to deploy on the West Bank. Other Arab countries prepared to send their own token forces to the three confrontationist states as symbols of Arab solidarity. The noose around Israel's neck was tightening, although the Arabs suffered from mutual mistrust and an overall lack of unity of command and purpose among the coalition forces. Still, the sheer size of combat forces could compensate, to a degree, for military inefficiency.

Meanwhile, Israel moved closer to war as well. After his disastrous speech of 28 May, Eshkol decided to form a government of national unity. This step failed to placate public concern. More pressure mounted on Eshkol to relinquish his post of defense minister; public opinion favored the recall of Moshe Dayan, whose eye patch had come to symbolize Israeli military prowess. Eshkol finally succumbed to influence from within his own Labor Party and on 1 June, at 7:00 P.M., offered Dayan the post of defense minister. Dayan promptly accepted.[25] The new defense minister advocated a major attack on Egypt.

Before Dayan's appointment, Eshkol had initiated another attempt to assess the America's position. On 31 May, Meir Amit, the head of Mossad, the Israeli equivalent to the Central Intelligence Agency, departed for Washington to gauge American reaction to an Israeli first strike. By the end of May, the Johnson administration had softened its opposition to the idea of Israel initiating military action.[26] In the evening of 3 June, Amit returned to Israel and filed a report at a special meeting, held at Eshkol's Jerusalem home and attended by key figures in the new government and several senior military figures. According to Amit, the United States would do nothing to break the blockade; neither would it oppose Israel going to war. Washington might even help Israel in the UN Security Council or General Assembly. This assessment made the Israeli government's decision relatively easy; all present agreed to recommend to the cabinet the next day a decision to go to war against Egypt. In the afternoon of 4 June, the Israeli cabinet, after hearing all the arguments for war, gave the green light for hostilities to commence against Egypt the next day. The military was free to chose the time, place, and method.[27] The main political aim was to restore the strategic situation prior to the May crisis, especially the free navigation of the Strait of Tiran. Israel's waiting period (*hamtana*) had finally come to an end, having lasted from 23 May to 4 June.

Several major considerations brought the cabinet to war. First, cabinet members believed that neither help nor condemnation would come from the United States. Second, troop movements of various Arab countries, coupled with the aroused passions in the Arab world, might eventually lead to a combined attack against Israel. A special concern was expressed that the Arabs might launch air strikes on Israel's nuclear facility at Dimona.[28] Third, there was the grave danger that Nasser might engineer a political victory without war. On 31 May, the Egyptian leader had agreed to send his vice president, Zakariya Muhiy al-Din, to Washington for meetings on 7 June. Senior Israeli officials became alarmed that the United States and Egypt might reach, at Israel's expense, a compromise that would enhance Nasser's prestige in the Arab world. The IDF's deterrent capabilities would undoubtedly suffer a serious blow in this scenario. As Eban candidly noted, "For us the importance of denying Nasser political and psychological victory had become no less important than the concrete interest involved in the issue of navigation."[29]

Meanwhile, back in Cairo, Nasser grasped the significance of Dayan's appointment as defense minister. On 2 June, the Egyptian president held a key meeting with his senior military commanders.[30] He ordered them to prepare for an Israeli attack within seventy-two hours. Moreover, Egypt would not launch a preemptive strike. After having created an international crisis by his provocative actions during the month of May, Nasser was willing to let Israel appear the aggressor by attacking first. Perhaps there was some concern that if Israel had a nuclear bomb, it might use it in response to an Arab offensive on three fronts. Should war come, Nasser no doubt expected a repeat performance of the 1956 Suez Crisis, which had catapulted him on to the status of a pan-Arab leader, even though the EAF had been defeated.

In 1967, however, Nasser did not contemplate a military defeat, and he certainly sought a political victory. Unfortunately for Nasser, the EAF's performance would fall far short of expectation, owing, in part, to serious internal problems within the military.

CRACKS IN THE EGYPTIAN MILITARY

The revolution (*thawra*) of 23 July 1952 had brought major changes to modern Egypt, transforming society and the army's place in it. To legitimize the military putsch, Nasser promised the transformation of Egypt into a modern and just society. Over the next fifteen years, such reforms as land distribution, nationalization of industry, improvement of health care, and establishment of free universities were implemented to deliver on that promise.

With respect to his promised social transformation, Nasser relied on the military to be his primary engine of change. No longer was Egypt to have an army serving as the personal instrument of the king to control the people. The new military was a national (*qawmi*) institution and a people's (*al-shaab*) army. The armed forces assumed responsibilities for more than just national defense. They were also to be an instrument for controlling nonmilitary institutions of society and for modernizing Egypt, under the banner of Arab socialism. Thus, the military became involved in such projects as running agricultural farms, manning customs, and helping manage Cairo's traffic system.[31] Retired and active officers could count on second careers in politics, the bureaucracy, or the economy. Such policies blurred the military's boundary with civil society. As a result, the EAF suffered from having too many missions.

To ensure the army's absolute loyalty to the regime, Nasser entrusted control over the armed forces to a close friend, Muhammad Abd al-Hakim Amer, who rose from the rank of major to major general in 1953. From that year until 1967, Amer, a field marshal after 1958, directed the military, gradually transforming the institution into his own personal fiefdom, with cliques (*shilla*) that depended on him for patronage. In the process, Nasser lost effective control over the armed forces, effecting, for example, promotions only to the ranks of general and lieutenant general. Amer took advantage of this arrangement and surrounded himself with "people of trust" (*ahl al-thiqa*), in essence yes-men. In this politicized environment, personal loyalty took precedence over expertise and competence in promotions.[32] Amer's detrimental policy fostered careerism and favoritism, spawning a "deprofessionalization" of the officer corps.[33]

In the summer of 1966, Amer cemented his control over the military by pushing through the appointment of his crony, Colonel Shems al-Din Badran, as war minister. On paper, Amer was responsible for operations, training, and organization; Badran handled personnel assignments, promotions, intelligence, military police, and morale.[34] Such a division of responsibility between two political soldiers, one a commander in chief and the other a war minister, made little sense. But this arrangement gave Amer more freedom to engage in political activities. By the time of the Six Day War, Amer had become too engrossed in nonmilitary matters to appreciate the state of affairs in the armed forces. He held the positions of vice president of the republic, deputy supreme commander of the armed forces, president of the Higher Executive Committee, president of the Aswan High Dam, head of the Committee for the Liquidation of Feudalism, and president of the Soccer Federation.[35] With so many distractions, much of the running of the armed forces was left in Badran's hands.

Yet Badran lacked the credentials to be a war minister. A former intelligence officer without any higher education after graduating from the military academy in 1948, Badran had risen from captain to colonel by working in Amer's office. Now as war minister, he supervised all dismissals and promotions within the military and thus functioned as the most powerful man in the military, after Amer. His main mission in life was to maintain Amer's tight grip over the military through the promotion of men loyal to his master rather than to Nasser.[36]

Professionalism in the military suffered as a result of Badran's personnel policies. General Muhammad Fawzi, the chief of the General Staff, should have picked up the slack, but he lacked adequate background for the highest position in the military hierarchy. Nasser had pushed his appointment as a means to check Amer's power. An able administrator and educator, Fawzi had been associated for seventeen years with the Egyptian Military Academy, serving as its commandant just prior to his appointment as chief of the General Staff in 1964. Instruction at the school focused on small-unit tactics at the company level, not particularly relevant for someone who would assume command of three services and to prepare them for war. Furthermore, Fawzi was never allowed to develop in his position, for Amer and Badran denied him much latitude in decision making, because of his known loyalty to Nasser.[37] In reality, the armed forces proved a ship without a strong rudder to steer a course toward high standards of professionalism and preparedness.

Without a competent, firm hand at the pinnacle of the military hierarchy, the armed forces fell prey to interservice rivalry and factionalism. General Muhammad Sidqi Mahmud and Admiral Suleyman Izzat had been in charge of the air force and navy respectively since 1953. Entrenched in power for fourteen years, both men practiced a service parochialism that undermined unity of command. The land forces, for their part, fell under the Ground Forces Command, which had been created in 1964. Its commander, General Abd al-Mohsen Kamil Murtagui, further undercut the authority of the chief of the General Staff. Fawzi had watched the size of the Ground Forces Command's staff grow until it equaled and then surpassed that of his own.[38] With Nasser exercising weak control over Amer, and Amer essentially a political animal, Egypt went to war in 1967 with little unity of command or purpose at the national level, a clear recipe for disaster.

Most troublesome was the situation of the air force. Its commander, Sidqi Mahmud, had seen his air force destroyed on the ground by the British and the French in the 1956 war. History would repeat itself in 1967, this time at the hands of the Israeli air force. Comprising over twenty thousand personnel and approximately four hundred combat and transport planes, the Egyptian air force had ten major and some fifteen minor bases. Its inventory of combat aircraft, virtually all Soviet made, contained 120 MiG-21s; eighty MiG-19s; twenty Su-7s; a hundred MiG-17s and MiG-15s; thirty Tu-16 medium bombers; and forty Il-28 light bombers. Sidqi Mahmud was also responsible for air defense, which consisted of some twenty-seven SAM (surface-to-air missile) battalions.

In preparing to face the Israeli air force, Sidqi Mahmud underestimated the capabilities of his adversary and failed to make adequate preparations for a surprise attack.[39] Egypt's air intelligence miscalculated that the maximum range of the Israeli aircraft was limited to Suez Canal zone. This assessment left a good percentage of Egypt's airfields outside of the effective reach of Israeli fighter-bombers, in effect removing the possibility of enemy pilots using the longer route from the Mediterranean Sea as a avenue of attack. Thus when Nasser asked Sidqi Mahmud on 2 June for a damage assessment in the event of an Israeli first strike, the Egyptian air force commander based his response on an erroneous assessment of a worst case scenario of only 15 to 20 percent losses. In fact, the Egyptians would lose a staggering 85 percent of their aircraft in the first three hours of the war, most of these losses occurring while the planes were still parked on the tarmac.

In addition to its gross intelligence failure, the Egyptian air force failed to prepare its airfields adequately for a surprise attack. A number of fields contained only one runway, and virtually all aircraft lacked concrete hangars as havens from Israeli bombs. This fatal blunder left Egyptian planes exposed to Israeli air strikes.

Egyptian involvement in Yemen further debilitated the armed forces. At the height of military operations in 1965, the Egyptian expeditionary force numbered some seventy to eighty thousand troops engaged in a counterinsurgency war. Morale in the EAF suffered with each passing year. To help finance the war, Amer cut training exercises for units in the Sinai. Furthermore, little of the Yemen combat experience was directly transferable to the Sinai theater, where the Israelis were preparing to wage a fast-paced war with a superiority in airpower and armor. In North Yemen, Egyptians forces generally conducted battalion-size operations with the benefit of air support. The terrain was one of high, mountainous regions, unlike the generally flat desert of the Sinai. The

Yemeni tribes relied on primitive weapons, mainly rifles, and generally fought in ambushes; the challenge for an Egyptian field commander was to prevent the escape of tribal units once they felt the tide of battle turn against them.[40] Thus, in the Six Day War, while Israel fought on three fronts against Arab armies, Egypt waged two wars, one far away, near the southwestern tip of the Arabian Peninsula.

In summary, the EAF entered the May crisis with serious internal problems. A personal rivalry between Nasser and Amer adversely affected coordination between the political and military spheres of government. Furthermore, the military had become so politicized an institution that loyalty took precedence over merit in personnel actions. The quality of both senior and junior leadership suffered as a direct result of this debilitating policy. Moreover, the war in Yemen drained scarce resources, adversely affecting the EAF's training and preparedness. Finally, and just as importantly, all these problems were compounded by the blunders made by Egypt's General Command during the crisis itself.

EGYPT'S SELF-INFLICTED WOUNDS

Before the May crisis, one reinforced Egyptian infantry division guarded the entire Sinai. By the eve of war, the Sinai garrison had increased to four infantry divisions, the 4th Armored Division, a special mobile task force of somewhat less than division strength, four independent infantry brigades, four independent armored brigades, and a paratroop brigade.[41] The bulk of this army of over one hundred thousand men and nine hundred tanks was poised close to the border, within easy striking distance of Israel's heartland. Despite the impressive numbers, the Egyptian force suffered from confusion and disorientation down to division and brigade level as a direct result of decisions made in the three weeks prior to the outbreak of hostilities.

In 1966, the Egyptian military had developed a new defensive plan for the Sinai called *Qahir* (the victor). A clearly defined chain of command was supposed to control combat forces in the Sinai. At the top of the hierarchy stood President Nasser, the supreme commander, who gave political direction to military strategy and operational plans. Then came General Command in Cairo, a joint command of all three services, under Field Marshal Amer. This headquarters directed all the ground troops in the Sinai through a field army commander, Lieutenant General Salah al-Din Mohsen, who in turn commanded the division and independent brigade commanders.

Plan *Qahir* called for the regular army to deploy across the depth of the Sinai and along the major routes of advance.[42] A security zone close to the border—manned by reconnaissance, paratroop, or border patrol battalions—would provide early warning of an Israeli attack. Behind this zone stood tactical and operational areas. The first tactical region centered on the fortified points of al-Arish, Abu Ageila, Qusaymah, and al-Tamad. An infantry division, supported by two additional infantry brigades and an armored regiment, manned this forward area. To the rear of these forces stood a second tactical echelon, consisting of an infantry division located in the region to the west of Abu Ageila and Qusaymah. The operational reserve occupied three positions: an armored brigade on the central route, two infantry brigades and a divisional command at Bir al-Hasana, and finally an armor regiment north of Nakhl. All these forces reported to the field army commander at his forward headquarters in the center of the Sinai, near Bir al-Tamada. To the rear of these tactical and operational forces stood the strategic reserves, directly under General Command. An armored division deployed around Bir al-Tamada, while a brigade of paratroopers guarded the three passes of Khatimiya, Giddi, and Mitla (see Map 1).

General Command developed a simple and straightforward concept of defense. Egyptian troops in the two tactical areas were to hold their positions and seriously attrit invading Israeli forces. The Egyptians envisioned a possible Israeli breakthrough into central Sinai where the Egyptian forces were sufficiently deployed to establish a killing zone. After the battles in the tactical and operational areas, the 4th Armored Division would counterattack to deliver the decisive blow to defeat the Israelis in the Sinai. No serious plans were in place for a major counter-offensive into Israel. Control of the central route, the best road in the peninsula, at the forward position of Abu Ageila constituted a linchpin to the Egyptian defensive strategy.

Egypt's well-prepared peacetime plans underwent significant modifications in direct response to the unfolding May crisis. The resultant military changes caused confusion and debilitated combat power. On the national level, Nasser ordered the Egyptian army into the Sinai as a deterrent force to an anticipated Israeli attack against Syria; adopting a purely defensive posture, as defined in Plan *Qahir*, would have left the Egyptians as bystanders should Israel attack Syria. The EAF had to be prepared to launch limited military operations into Israel in support of the Syrians, should the IDF attack the Syrian Armed Forces (SAF). This previously unforeseen scenario caused Plan *Qahir* to become obsolete rather quickly.

In his operational directive of 14 May, Fawzi provided general guidance to the armed forces. Soviet and Syrian sources had warned the UAR of an Israeli intent to attack Syria. Egypt had to honor its defensive pact with Syria, and therefore Fawzi ordered EAF to prepare for possible offensive operations should Israel attempt to occupy Syria or defeat its military. The wording of the directive suggested that Egypt would not go to war over a border incident. All armed forces were placed on the highest state of alert effective at noon that day. Fawzi also ordered a general mobilization, sending all officers in training courses and military schools to field units and commands. Ground and air units were to complete their deployments before 17 May. All three services would prepare both offensive and defensive plans. Meanwhile, the air force would commence reconnaissance flights over Israel.[43]

But on 15 May, for reasons that remain unclear, General Command surprised its senior officers with the sudden creation of a front command and the appointment of General Abd al-Mohsen Kamil Murtagui to head it.[44] As before,

STUMBLING INTO WAR 17

the chain of command went from Nasser to General Command under Amer. But in the new arrangement, the front command, under Murtagui, stood between General Command and the field army under Mohsen.

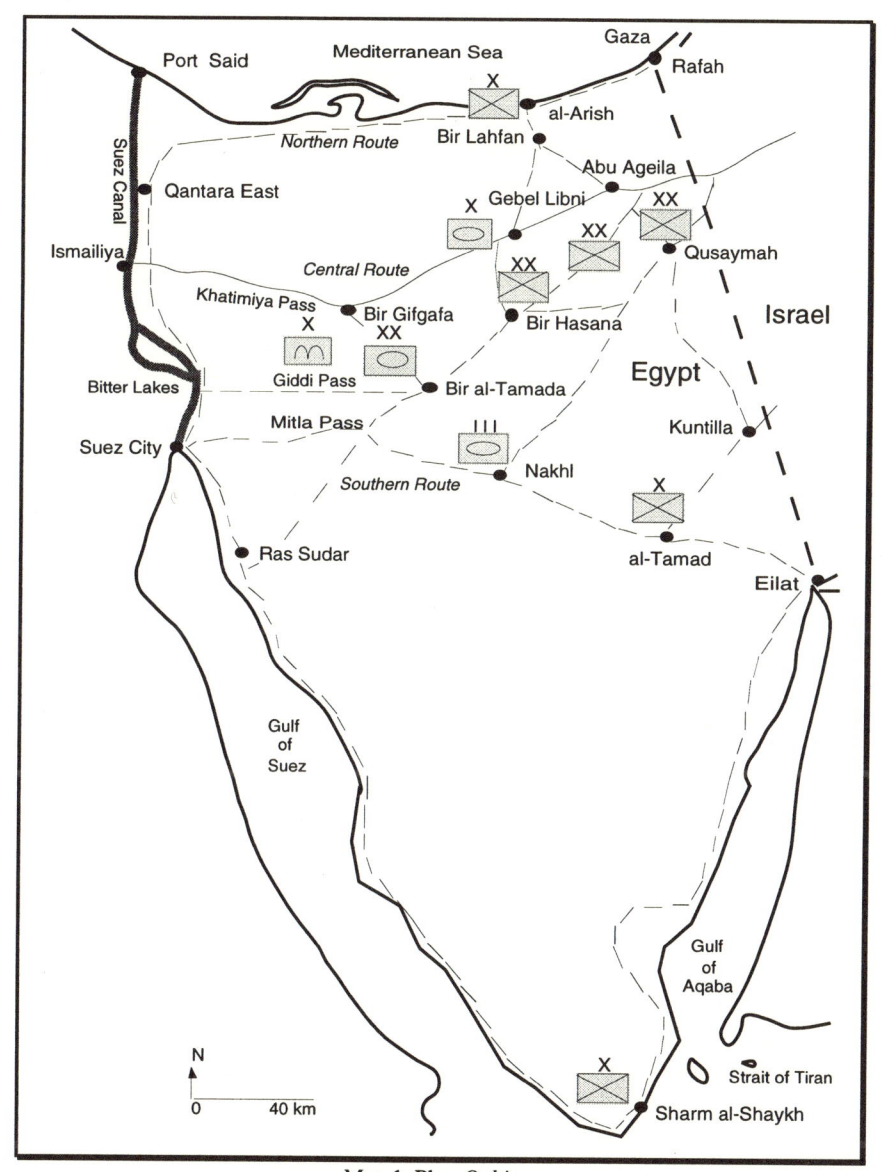

Map 1. Plan *Qahir*.

Murtagui, the new front commander, would be plagued by a number of problems. He had been chief of both the Ground Forces Command and the Egyptian expeditionary force in Yemen and consequently lacked intimate knowledge of the operational plan for the Sinai, which had been in large part crafted by Mohsen's staff. Furthermore, as a front commander in the Sinai, Murtagui should have commanded all land, air, and naval forces in theater, but Amer kept that authority for himself. This arrangement left Murtagui with control over only land forces until Amer arrived in the Sinai. In the interim, Murtagui could make only decisions that conformed closely to Cairo's directives, and Amer frequently bypassed him by communicating directly with the field army command. Murtagui thus possessed little authority for taking the initiative—although in appearance he possessed a major command with just such a mandate. Finally, Murtagui arrived at his command post in the Sinai (near Bir al-Tamada) only on 29 May—a week before the war, and with only twenty General Staff officers. The Egyptian army would have performed better without this command, which only compounded the military's other serious problems.

The Egyptian command and control system experienced further upheaval when Amer replaced virtually all the division commanders, their chiefs of staff, and a number of brigade commanders in the week or two after the creation of the front command. One informed Egyptian source counted twelve new division and brigade commanders. As a direct result of these last-minute changes, some commanders reached their units only one or two days before the outbreak of hostilities.[45] These personnel changes on the eve of war resulted in confusion ranging from senior commands down to brigades, and even lower.

Further aggravating the Egyptian army's internal situation, General Command made major changes in its war plans for the Sinai, compounding the disorientation caused by the structural and personnel shifts.[46] The first significant alteration came with the initial dispatch of forces to the Sinai. Nasser had suddenly become especially concerned about any appearance of having abandoned the Palestinians in the Gaza Strip. On 14 May, he ordered the Egyptian army to move units forward to the Rafah area to threaten any Israeli force attacking on Gaza. Moreover, the 4th Infantry Brigade, originally designated for Sharm al-Shaykh according to Plan *Qahir*, moved to reinforce the forward defenses in the Sinai. Nasser's decision to establish a blockade at the Strait of Tiran elicited further changes to the war plan. The paratroop brigade, originally earmarked to guard the passes in western Sinai, now deployed to Sharm al-Shaykh help prevent any ships under Israeli flags from passing through the Strait of Tiran.

While the armed forces deployed into defensive positions, Amer ordered the preparation of joint offensive plans involving all three services. The air force would launch a first strike against military targets, while naval units assaulted Eilat. The ground forces would attack Israel along two main axes. Operation *Fajr* (Dawn) entailed the 6th Infantry Division, reinforced with an armored brigade and independent infantry brigade, attacking from Kuntilla into the southern Negev to the port of Eilat. General Command also toyed with employing the 7th Infantry Division, the 14th Armored Brigade, and Shazli Armored Task Force to attack from the Rafah area into the northern Negev and to protect Gaza and possibly capture or destroy the Dimona nuclear reactor. Amer scheduled the offensive for 28 May, but Nasser on 25 May canceled this plan.

By the end of May, when all the dust settled from troop movements in the desert, the Egyptian army in the Sinai had deployed with a different set of priorities than those envisioned in its original plan (see Map 2). *Qahir* had emphasized the central route as the most likely place for the Israeli main effort, with primary defensive positions at al-Arish, Abu Ageila, Qusaymah, and al-Tamad. The new forward defensive area now centered on Rafah, Abu Ageila, Qusaymah, and Kuntilla, a change that had required a major deployment of Egyptian forces forward from al-Arish to Rafah and from al-Tamad to Kuntilla. Al-Arish, Gebel Libni, Bir al-Hasana, and al-Tamad now turned into the second line of defense.

These changes left little of the original *Qahir* plan. Now a much larger percentage of the Egyptian army was positioned close to the border with Israel and along its length as well. This deployment left the Egyptians strategically vulnerable should the Israelis achieve a major breakthrough and advance rapidly into the Egyptian operational depth. The Israeli army set the stage for exactly this development by helping to unbalance further Egypt's armed forces before the onset of hostilities on 5 June.

To effect their plan, the Israelis conducted an elaborate deception plan meant to focus Egyptian attention on the southern Sinai route while the IDF concentrated on the northern and central routes. All three Israeli services participated in the endeavor to fool Egyptian military intelligence into believing that the IDF would make its main effort in the south. General headquarters in Tel Aviv, for example, increased its communications with Eilat. The Israeli navy, for its part, transferred four boats over land to Eilat during the day, then during the night pulled them ten or fifteen kilometers out of the city, only to repeat the process again the next day in broad daylight. The Israeli air force flew additional missions in the south under loose security so as to catch the attention of the Egyptians. On the ground, the Israeli army placed the 8th Mechanized Infantry Brigade opposite Kuntilla, reinforcing this small force with many wooden tanks and other fake vehicles. Brigadier General Avraham Yoffe, who had assembled his division-sized task force in the southern area, moved northwest only at the last minute.[47]

Egyptian military intelligence completely fell for this ruse. On 26 May, the head of intelligence concluded that the IDF was concentrating its main effort between Qusaymah and Kuntilla, an assessment that continued for a week.[48] On 28 May, Amer, against the advice of several senior officers at General Command, directed the EAF to deploy more troops to the area of Kuntilla, al-Tamad, and Nakhl. On 29 May, for example, the Shazli Armored Task Force, created a week earlier, moved from its initial deployment east of Rafah in northeastern Sinai to the southern part of the border with Israel. In the meantime, Amer designated the area of Gebel Kharim and al-Matalla as the new killing zone for the destruction of Israeli armor, directing the 4th Armored Division to focus its attention there.[49]

20   THE ALBATROSS OF DECISIVE VICTORY

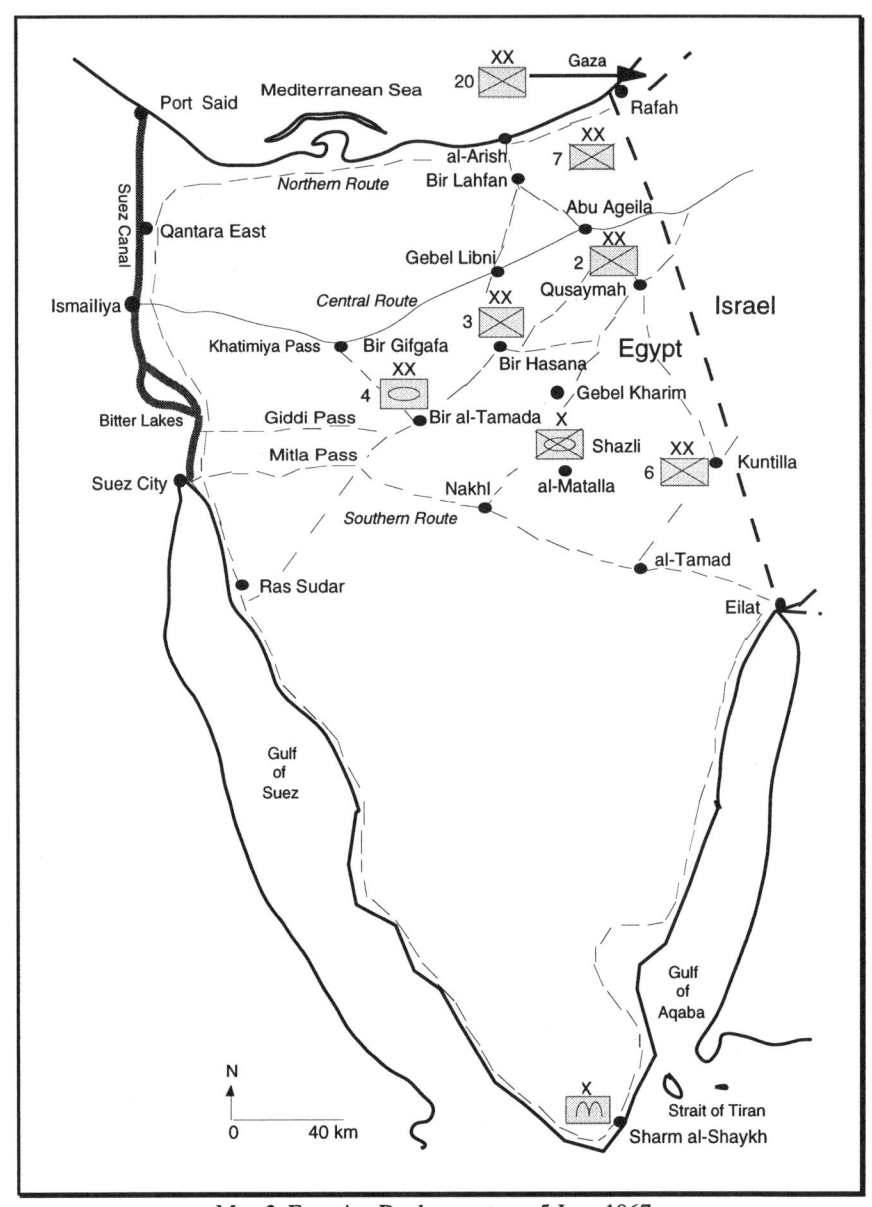

Map 2. Egyptian Deployments on 5 June 1967.

Oddly enough, Egyptian intelligence exposed the Israeli trickery. On 2 June, just three days prior to the Israeli attack, the Egyptians managed to conduct a successful reconnaissance overflight fifteen kilometers into the Negev. They discovered, much to their surprise, that the Israelis had actually not concentrated their forces in the south but were instead poised to strike in the north and center. Despite this evidence to the contrary, Amer remained fixated on his concept of operations and, as a result, made no changes.[50] But the new information had its impact on Egypt's senior commanders. As tersely stated by the Egyptian front commander Murtagui after the war, the Israeli deception plan had created "an atmosphere of confusion in the General Command."[51] Acting upon the photo evidence would have required too much change; so preparations continued on the basis of a strategic fallacy.

Through their deception plan, the Israelis succeeded in inducing the Egyptians to deplete substantially their forces in the northeastern region, where the Israeli army planned its main attack. The fact that Egypt had positioned one armored and four infantry divisions in the Sinai, reinforced with a brigade-size mechanized force, meant little. With many more Egyptian troops forward than envisioned in Plan *Qahir*—and these concentrated in the south—the Israeli army now could exploit its strategic advantage with an operational maneuver that excluded a good part of the Egyptian army from the main combat.

Another major problem area confronted Egypt's General Command. In addition to counterproductive changes in command and control, senior tactical commanders, war plans, and troop deployments, the EAF was ill prepared tactically for combat. By the eve of the war, the Egyptian army had committed some 130,000 men to the Sinai and the Suez Canal area, of which eighty thousand were reservists, including over a thousand officers. Many reservists, however, were poorly trained and inadequately equipped, because of Egyptian budget cuts to meet the immediate and pressing requirements of fighting in Yemen. One senior Egyptian official described the deplorable state of many reservists that he observed in Qantara East on 22 May.

I was surprised at the railroad station by the disorganized state of the reserves which served to weaken each man's capabilities. It was assumed that he was on the verge of battle. [Yet] everyone was in his civilian clothes with most of them in their peasant dress. They all came carrying their weapons, but not in a military manner. They had gathered from their villages in haste and without any administrative order. They received only their weapons while in civilian clothes. They were loaded on to the train like animals without any arrangements for food, drink, or comfort. These men were driven to purchase their food from peddlers at the railroad station in complete confusion.[52]

This situation left the former officer in poignant doubt: "Is this the state of our forces that will face off against the soldiers of our enemy Israel? In contrast, is our enemy Israel mobilizing its youth in this inhumane manner?" This large influx of poorly trained and poorly equipped soldiers, coupled with the creation of new units under new commanders, undermined the army's integrity, weakening its unit cohesion on the battlefield.

Finally, even the weapons and equipment had taken their toll from prewar stress. Among the nine hundred tanks deployed in the Sinai were some 450 Soviet T-54 and T-55s (100-mm gun), thirty British Centurions, ninety American Shermans, 350 Soviet T-34s (85-mm gun), sixty Soviet Stalin IIIs (122-mm gun); and twenty French AMX-13s. Moreover, over 150 SU-100 antitank weapons and nine hundred field guns, howitzers, and mortars faced the Israeli army. The T-34s and Stalin IIIs (of World War II vintage) were placed in reserve units and infantry divisions, whereas the more modern T-54s and T-55s went to the 4th Armored Division and the independent tank brigades.[53]

Mere numbers of weapon systems, however, fail to reveal the actual combat firepower of the Egyptian army. According to some estimates, at least 20 percent of the tanks were inoperable, owing to poor maintenance and the aimless redispositions just prior to the war. Undoubtedly, a similar rate of degradation occurred for artillery and armored personnel carriers.[54] Moreover, the T-34 and Stalin III tanks were obsolete, though no more so than the Israeli Sherman and AMX-13; the Egyptians wisely employed many of them only as pillboxes to function as artillery support to infantry. Even these qualifications left anywhere from four to five hundred tanks capable of employment in a counterattack role, but these tanks were dispersed over a large area in central Sinai.

On the eve of war, the Egyptian senior command, in part responding to Nasser's specific directives, had degraded its own combat power. The cumulative effect weakened the Egyptian army in the vital areas of: leadership, by replacing too many division and brigade commanders; the chain of command, by creating a weak front command; unity of purpose, by frequently changing plans, troop deployments, and strategy; integrity of force, by relying on a disproportionate number of ill-trained reservists; and operability of equipment, by redeploying units over long distances. All this self-destructive activity created an operational vulnerability in the Egyptian command system from Cairo down to below brigade level. Though large in size, the EAF was in fact brittle and hollow.

The military's internal problems were compounded by confusing and vague signals from Nasser himself. The Egyptian leader failed to provide a clear and consistent picture of the political purpose behind his diplomatic maneuvering and bellicose statements. Nasser had embraced the offensive on the diplomatic front, provoking Israel and inciting the passions of the Arab masses. Yet he left his armed forces on the defensive, forced to accept a first strike from Israel. Consequently, Egyptian field commanders were uncertain of the intent of the next-higher headquarters. Any major surprise or setback inflicted by the Israelis at the onset of a campaign could easily unnerve Egyptian commanders to the point that General Command might lose control of the battlefield. The Egyptians would lack time in the midst of battle to rectify their errors. In a nutshell, the Egyptians were ill prepared for what awaited them. Unbeknownst to Egyptian military intelligence, the IDF had drawn constructive lessons from its experience in the 1956 war and had prepared well over the previous few years to execute a classic campaign of quick and decisive victory.

ISRAELI MILITARY CULTURE

Israel developed its own unique military culture in rapid fashion. Living in a state created at Arab expense in 1948, Israeli Jews saw their country under siege from hostile neighbors: most Arabs rejected Israel's existence and many seemed determined to destroy the Jewish state. The Arab-Israeli conflict thus took on an apocalyptic nature, a life and death struggle for Jewish existence.

The Israeli siege mentality was reinforced by two tragic events in Jewish history: the Holocaust, in which six million Jews were murdered during World War II, and the defense at Masada, where some 960 Jewish fighters—including women, children, and the elderly—perished on a mountaintop in a last stand against a Roman army in 72 A.D. The Holocaust syndrome, of the world against the Jews, and the Masada complex, Israel's back to the sea, formed a foundation of Israeli military culture. Jews had created the state of Israel to ensure the survival of the Jewish people: "never again" would the Jewish people allow Holocaust to occur or Masada to fall. Perceived and real Arab hostility toward Israel's existence reinforced the need for a superior military.

Israel's national security depended upon the twin pillars of wise diplomacy and military might. On the diplomatic front, Israel, a small country, needed a strong Western ally. France assumed this role until the Six Day War; afterwards, the United States would fill those shoes. To outflank neighboring Arab states, Israel forged close ties with the non-Arab governments of Iran, Turkey, and Ethiopia. Israeli foreign policy also encouraged divisions in Arab countries, such as by support for the Kurds in Iraq and the Christian Arabs in Lebanon. Finally, Israeli officials developed a special relationship with King Hussein of Jordan, who favored reaching some accommodation with Israel.

Despite the critical importance of diplomacy, military might remained central to Israel's survival strategy. The people regarded the IDF as the last barrier against the Arab hordes. Vastly outnumbered by the surrounding Arabs, Israeli Jews saw their nation's existence as a struggle of "the few against the many," an important concept in military culture. To field an army of adequate size, the country had to depend on a nation-in-arms for defense, and virtually every Israeli Jew understood this strategic imperative. Popular culture thus embraced the concept of *ein breira*, or "no alternative" to military service and sacrifice in battle when called upon in defense of home and country. A unique umbilical cord developed between the people and the armed forces whereby every citizen was viewed as a soldier on eleven months' leave.

Israel suffered from a weak geostrategic position in the Middle East. The country lacked depth (fifteen kilometers at its narrowest width) and contained long and porous borders (some 613 kilometers in length; see Map 3). Defense of the country thus dictated an offensive doctrine designed to take the war into Arab territory as quickly as possible. With only 2,600,000 people in the country, as opposed to over twenty million in the UAR alone, Israel could not sustain a war for more than three to four weeks without serious economic repercussions. Military victory thus had to occur rapidly, which required the Israeli army to fight at a faster tempo than Arab armies.

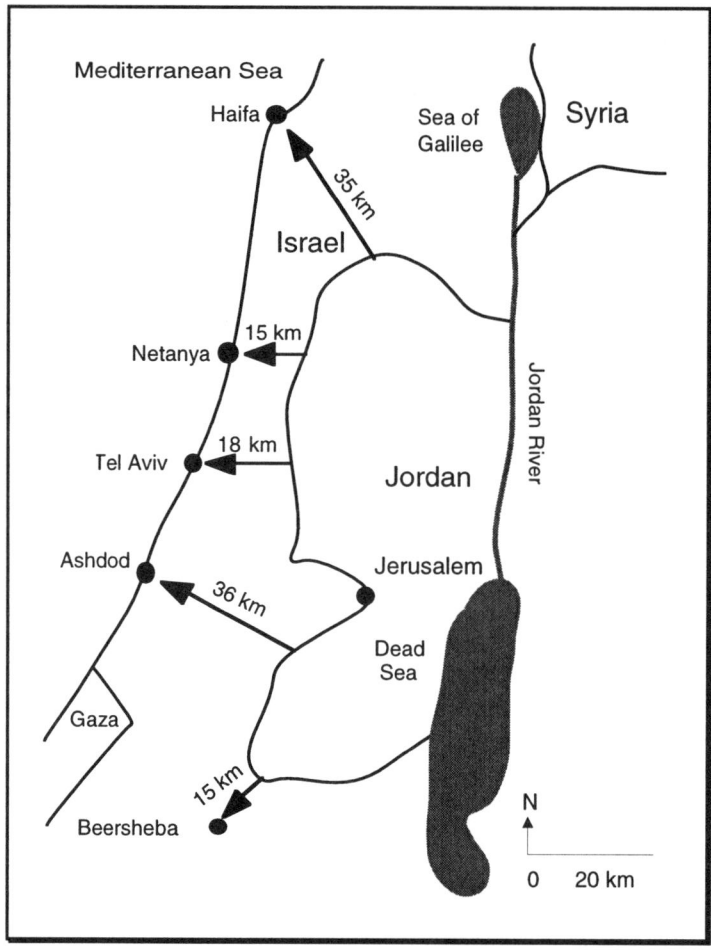

Map 3. Israel's Strategic Depth.

To achieve quick success on the battlefield, Israeli military doctrine fostered initiative down to small-unit commanders, so that they possessed the flexibility and freedom to capitalize upon any tactical advantages. In this regard, war plans, rather than setting rigid guidelines, served as the bases for change. The pioneer spirit that had created the state of Israel initially helped nurture a culture of independent thinking and action among officers and soldiers, many of whom served in the underground during the British Mandate in Palestine or in other armies during World War II. Speed, the offense, and improvization were to be the vibrant hallmarks of the Israeli military ethos.

After the 1956 war, the IDF made great strides in preparing for the next conflict. Most impressive was the progress registered by the Israeli air force in the interwar period. Israel's General Staff embraced the importance of air superiority for the conduct of effective maneuver warfare on land and assigned a priority to modernization of the air fleet. Moreover, in the early sixties, air force commanders began preparing carefully and systematically for a preemptive strike as the best means of neutralizing an opponent's air force. In fact, Israel's destruction of the air force of Egypt, Jordan, and Syria on the ground in lightning fashion would set the standard for such campaigns.

In sharp contrast to Egypt's almost exclusive reliance on Soviet planes, Israeli pilots flew mainly French aircraft. Israel's inventory of planes contained 257 combat aircraft: seventy-two Mirage Mark IIICs, twenty Super Mystères, forty Mystère Mark IVAs, forty Ouragan fighter-bombers, twenty-five Vantour II light bombers, and sixty Fouga Magister trainers converted to a ground-support role. Consisting of some eight thousand regulars, the Israeli air force could expand to twenty thousand upon mobilization. Although outnumbered by Egypt alone, without the inclusion of the other Arab states, Israel enjoyed some key advantages. Israeli pilots were better trained and had much more flying time than their Egyptian/Arab counterparts. In addition, Brigadier General Mordechai Hod, the air force commander, possessed more trained pilots than planes, whereas Sidqi Mahmud had more planes than trained pilots.

By the mid-sixties, Israel's air force doctrine revolved around the operational concept of a preemptive air strike to destroy the Arab air forces on the ground. To execute such a campaign in successive waves spanning several hours required years of training, planning, and intelligence data. Between 1962 and 1965, the Israeli air force worked diligently on developing such an operational plan, called *Moked* (Focus).[55] Intelligence formed a cornerstone of the plan. A separate file, for example, was maintained and updated periodically on each Egyptian airfield. On the day of the preemptive strike, Israeli pilots could, among other items, distinguish dummy from real planes on the tarmac. Training exercises conducted against mock-up fields in the Negev sharpened pilot skills and produced technical solutions to problems that otherwise would have been unforeseen.

Destruction of concrete runways demanded special bombs. Consequently, Israel's military industry had developed an explosive specifically designed to blow craters in runways. This "dibber" bomb contained a retro-rocket to slow the bomb's forward motion, a booster rocket to drive it deep into concrete at a perpendicular angle for greatest effect, and a time-delay fuse to produce a crater five meters wide and 1.6 meters deep. Pilots were trained to drop the bomb at a low altitude; a parachute opened to slow the bomb's descent and thus ensure that it penetrated deep into the runway. Such an attack, if properly delivered, would leave the Egyptian pilots unable either to take-off or land. After the successful conclusion of tests in 1966, the Israeli air force had ample time in which to acquire approximately 250 such bombs by June 1967.

Achieving the best results in the shortest time possible depended on massing air assets and maximizing the number of sorties from each aircraft. For the preemptive strike, Hod planned to commit 185 first-line aircraft, leaving only twelve fighters to protect Israel. Though this step involved some risk, Israeli commanders accurately predicted that Syria would not pose a serious air threat within the first three hours of the war. To increase the number of sorties flown by each plane, the air force trained its ground crews to maintain a short turnaround time. During the three-hour air campaign against Egyptian airfields, Israeli maintenance crews rearmed and refueled planes in a record seven and a half minutes. This incredible time meant that the air force could attack with many more sorties than expected by the Egyptians. Planes striking the Suez Canal area, for example, would hit their target a second time within an hour.

Finally, the Israelis, through careful intelligence gathering and assessment, discovered an Egyptian vulnerability that determined zero-hour for launching the air attack. In the few weeks prior to war, the Egyptian air force had fallen into what proved a fatal routine. Each morning, Egyptian pilots in MiG-21s would take off on patrol at first light, fly approximately an hour, and then return to base for breakfast by 7:00 A.M. Israeli time. An Israeli air strike at 7:45 would catch many Egyptian pilots away from their aircraft. Moreover, weather conditions would prove ideal, for the Israelis would not confront morning mist. The Egyptian air force thus inadvertently presented Hod with a most advantageous time for a first strike.[56]

Israel's ground forces were designed and trained to wage a fast-paced land campaign. Instead of the infantry-dominated army of 1956, however, military planners now envisioned a rapidly advancing army led by large tank formations that employed mobility, maneuver, shock, and surprise.[57] Doctrine called for an armored fist, whenever possible, to break into the enemy's rear, causing his army to collapse through the disruption of command systems and lines of communication. Tanks, which had once provided fire support for infantry, now became the decisive arm in a major land campaign, supported by the air force, paratroopers, and infantry.

Further changes occurred in force structure and tank types. Whereas the 1956 Sinai campaign saw only one fully equipped armored brigade, with two more in the final stages of formation, in 1967 the Armor Corps fielded some 1,300 tanks in ten armored brigades, five of them deployed against Egypt alone. In addition to the four hundred American Super Shermans and the 150 French AMX-13s, Israel's armor inventory now included 250 British Centurions and two hundred American Patton M-48s. Arguably the best tank in the 1967 war, the Israeli versions of the Centurion Mark 5 and 6 were perhaps unequaled in a tank-killing role. These Centurions possessed a stabilized 105-mm gun able to kill armored targets at 1,800 meters in sharp contrast to the Soviet T-54/55, with its maximum reach of a thousand meters. Israeli tankers thus possessed a marked advantage in range when fighting on the Sinai's generally flat terrain. Furthermore, the Israeli tanks carried sixty-four rounds where the Egyptian tanks could store only forty-two rounds.

The increased size of Israeli forces, and the need for a short war, forced the IDF to improve its command system. In 1967, as in 1956, the Israeli army would fight with the brigade as the primary tactical formation. But the size of the regular army had increased from forty-five thousand in 1956 to seventy thousand in 1967. Moreover, the total mobilized-strength potential for ground forces had grown during this same period from 190,000 to 250,000, organized in some ten infantry, ten armor, two mechanized infantry, and four paratroop brigades. Such a growth in manpower required a better-functioning *ugdah*, a division-size task force of two or more brigades, as a link between the front command and brigades. Consequently, in the early 1960s the General Staff regularized *ugdah*-level exercises, which helped prepare senior field officers for command of large units in a major-campaign scenario.[58] During this same period, the Egyptians failed to conduct brigade or division-sized exercises, and all exercises focused on the defense.[59]

Finally, the IDF gained a significant advantage in the intelligence field. By the mid-1960s, the Egyptian intelligence community had focused most of its assets on Yemen and internal security, leaving the EAF with inadequate or wrong tactical and strategic intelligence on Israel.[60] In sharp contrast, the Israeli intelligence community flourished during this period, registering several major coups. Eli Cohen, Israel's most famous known spy to date, succeeded in penetrating into the highest echelons of Syria's elite, gaining detailed data on Syrian defenses on the Golan Heights. In 1966, Mossad managed to convince an Iraqi pilot to defect to Israel with his MiG-21. This daring theft provided the IDF with valuable information on the capabilities of a frontline Soviet plane.

The Israelis were also successful against Egypt in the field of human intelligence. Israeli agents enlisted a Captain "X," who apparently served as a specialist in radio communications in an important headquarters. This Egyptian officer provided Israel with detailed information on troop strengths, movements, and battle plans before the war and during its first three days until he was inadvertently killed near Mitla Pass by an Israeli fighter plane.[61] By being able to obtain such disarming intelligence, Brigadier General Aharon Yariv, the head of Military Intelligence from 1964 to 1972, reduced the level of uncertainty about the enemy's capabilities and intentions, thereby allowing senior Israeli commanders to approach war with greater confidence. In brief, the IDF was well prepared for war in comparison to its Egyptian foe.

ISRAELI WAR PLANS

As on the Egyptian side, Israeli campaign plans underwent significant changes in the three weeks before the war. The Israeli General Staff had to be responsive to the troop movements of the Egyptian army and to the evolving diplomatic crisis. By the eve of hostilities, however, the Israelis had drawn up a final war plan designed to achieve a decisive victory over the EAF.

Prior to the May crisis, Israel's General Staff, aware of the broad outlines of Plan *Qahir*, had developed two basic plans, both predicated on the destruction of the Egyptian air force by a surprise attack. One plan called for the mere capture of the Gaza Strip. The other, *Kilshon*, was broader in scope. Three Israeli *ugdot* (the plural of *ugdah*) would conduct a major offensive to occupy northeastern Sinai. An armored *ugdah* would move between Qusaymah and Kuntilla along unpaved roads and over trackless stretches to hit the Bir al-Hasana area and then attack the Abu Ageila area from the rear. A second *ugdah* would assault Abu Ageila along the central route. Meanwhile, a third *ugdah* would attack Rafah and al-Arish on the northern route (see Map 4).[62]

These two plans contained some flaws. The first plan demanded the IDF to engage in urban warfare in the densely populated Gaza Strip, a prospect costly in human lives. In *Kilshon*, on the other hand, the first *ugdah* required a long time to complete its arduous trek from the south to the rear of Abu Ageila. Moreover, that *ugdah* would expose its left flank to attack by the Egyptian 4th Armored Division. Both plans focused on capturing terrain, either Gaza or northeastern Sinai, rather than on decisively defeating the Egyptian army. The goal was thus a limited military victory, followed by diplomatic negotiations. This would change with the May crisis.

As the crisis unfolded, Major General Yitzhak Rabin, the chief of the General Staff and the top military commander, experienced the strains of high office. As discussed earlier, Prime Minister Levi Eshkol, who also held the post of defense minister, was a man of compromise, so indecisive that the Israeli public began to lose confidence in his ability to steer the nation. He persisted in seeking a diplomatic solution to the crisis, while a number of senior officers, led by Ezer Weizman, former air force commander and now chief of operations for the IDF, and Aharon Yariv, the head of Military Intelligence, pushed for a military solution.

Rabin, caught between the two groups, failed to provide firm leadership to the IDF. At one point he even sought the private counsel of Ben-Gurion in retirement. Then, on 23 May, after a week of intense pressure, Rabin suffered a collapse from exhaustion, which he candidly described years later.

Late that evening, after a day of tension and meeting after meeting in smoke-filled conference rooms, I returned home in a state of mental and physical exhaustion. Ever since then I have repeatedly asked myself, what happened to me that evening? How did I get into such a state? Now, twelve years later, I still lack a definitive answer. There can be no doubt that I was suffering from a combination of tension, exhaustion, and the enormous amount of cigarette smoke I had inhaled in recent days. . . . I had hardly slept, and I was smoking like a steam engine. But it was more than nicotine that brought me down. The heavy sense of guilt that had been dogging me of late became unbearably strong on May 23. . . . [P]erhaps I had failed in my duty as the prime minister's chief military advisor. Maybe that was why Israel now found herself in such difficult straits.[63]

A doctor prescribed a sedative for Rabin, who returned to work on 25 May, or two days later. In the meantime, a major change had occurred in the war plans.

During Rabin's absence, Weizman developed a new plan for dealing with Nasser's closure of the Strait of Tiran. The Israeli army would concentrate on the northern route, and driving all the way down the coastal road to the Suez

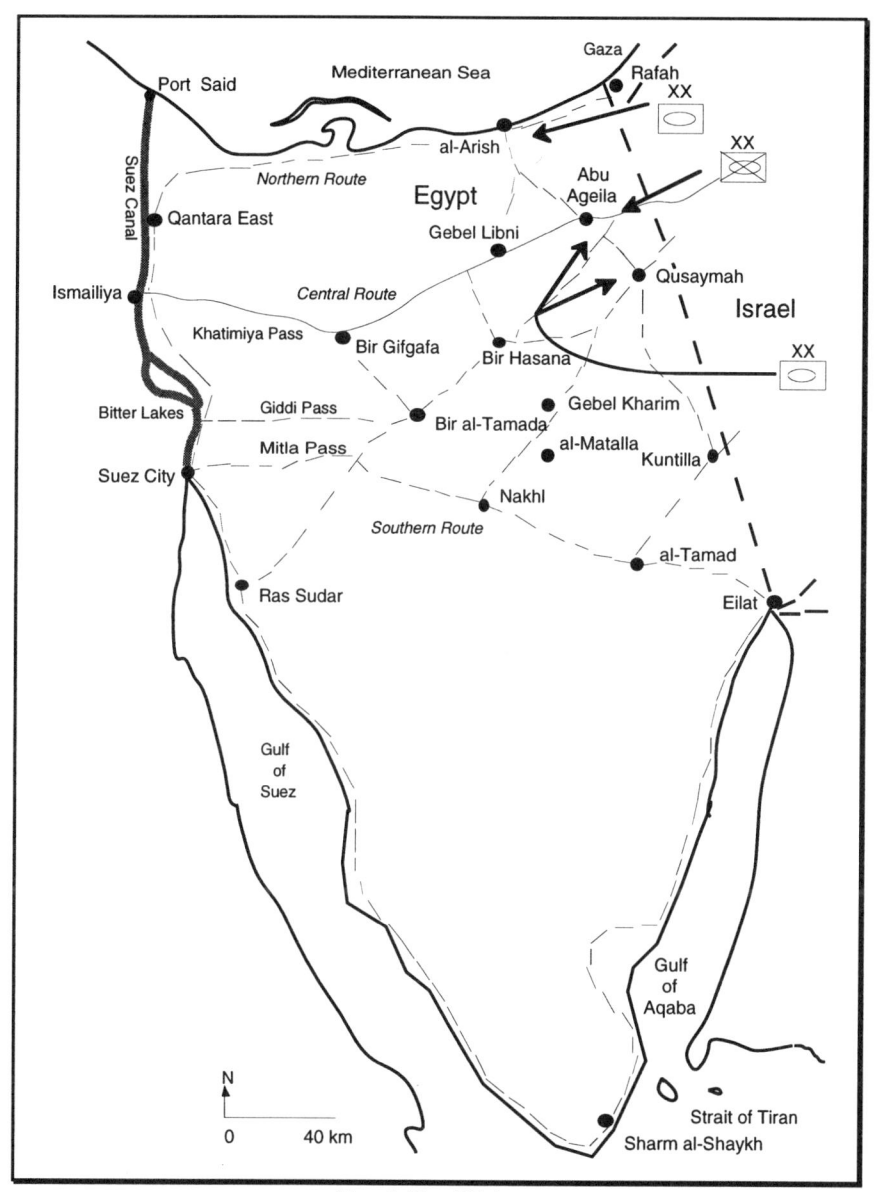

Map 4. Plan *Kilshon*.

Canal. Then the Israelis could threaten to blockade the man-made waterway, as a bargaining chip to get the Gulf of Aqaba opened to Israeli ships bound for Eilat.[64] This new plan still focused on terrain, designed to achieve a limited victory to be followed by diplomacy.

When Rabin returned to his job he discovered the new plan, but by this time his attention seems to have shifted away from operational to political matters.

To tell the truth, though, at that point I did not attach much importance to a precise definition of the size and extent of our offensive. My attention was focused on the question of when the cabinet would decide that political options have been exhausted, the IDF was to launch its attack. I assumed that the dimensions of our offensive would be dictated by the outcome of the air-force strike against the enemy's airfields. If we gained absolute air superiority and succeeded in the first phases of our plan, we could extend ourselves beyond the confines of northern Sinai and destroy the Egyptian army throughout the peninsula.[65]

Such vague thinking would continue until Dayan's arrival.

On 1 June, Eshkol appointed Moshe Dayan as defense minister, a decision that brought much relief to a concerned nation. With a black patch over the eye he had lost in a special operation before the 1948 war, Dayan had come to symbolize the new Jewish warrior. As chief of the General Staff from 1953 to 1958 he had led the IDF to victory against Egypt in 1956, with the help of France and Britain. Now, at his first news conference, the new defense minister exuded supreme confidence. He talked of giving diplomacy a bit more time, language actually intended to lull the Arabs into believing war would not occur in the near future. In fact, on 2 June, Dayan met with the General Staff and agreed on a new operational plan for war; Eshkol gave his tentative approval the next day. The cabinet gave its official blessing on 4 June. War would break out on 5 June.

Israel's new war strategy called for the Northern and Central Commands—together comprising two armored, one mechanized, and six infantry brigades—to maintain defensive postures against Syrian and Jordanian fronts, while the remainder of the IDF would attack Egypt in accordance with Plan *Nahshonim*.[66] Nahshon had led the tribe of Judah through the Red Sea in the Hebrew Exodus from ancient Egypt. Dayan opposed seizing territory for later negotiations; instead, he wanted the IDF to concentrate on defeating the EAF. "The aim of our action should be to destroy the Egyptian forces concentrated in central Sinai. We should have no geographical aim whatsoever."[67] Dayan cautioned against seizing the Suez Canal, because this might create an international crisis, and in the first phase of the campaign he wanted to avoid attacking the Gaza Strip, with its 250,000 inhabitants. Gaza might fall of its own accord once the IDF decisively defeated the EAF in the Sinai.

In changing the military strategy, Dayan was rejecting the limited operational aims of previous war plans. He specifically told the General Staff that Israel had to avoid a repetition of 1956, when Nasser, though defeated militarily, had gained a political victory. Only a crushing military defeat, Dayan believed, would prevent Nasser from producing a propaganda victory after the armed conflict. It was for this reason that Dayan changed the operational objective to destroying the Egyptian army. According to Dayan, such a decisive Israeli military triumph would not just defeat Nasser, but it would also humiliate and emasculate him as an Arab leader.[68] In this change in military objectives, operational planning was clearly driving policy. Instead of a limited military victory followed by negotiations for a return to the status quo, Israel was now seeking a decisive victory in which a vanquished Egypt would be forced to make concessions from a position of abject defeat.

Plan *Nahshonim*, code name *Sadin Adom* (Red Sheet), was worked out in detail for the first phase of the campaign; subsequent phases were left general in scope. According to an official IDF statement, the operational directive stipulated that after the breakthrough, or first phase, "the forces are to establish a line—*not east* of the line al-Arish–Gebel Libni, i.e., short of the Canal, and to be in a stage of preparedness for moving toward the Suez Canal and Sharm al-Shaykh."[69] Southern Command would attack with three *ugdot* in a three-phase campaign. First, the Israelis would penetrate the forward line of defenses at al-Arish and Abu Ageila; second, they would destroy the next line of defenses at Gebel Libni and defeat all counterattacks by Egyptian armor; and third, they would destroy the remnants of Egypt's army. A reinforced mechanized brigade would feint an attack against Kuntilla, to draw Egyptian attention away from the main effort. Sharm al-Shaykh would receive appropriate attention, depending on battlefield developments (see Map 5).

Responsibility for the Sinai campaign fell on the shoulders of Brigadier General Yeshayahu Gavish, the theater commander. Gavish, a graduate of L'Ecole de Guerre in Paris and former chief of the Training Department (1962–1965), planned to strike in the north at Rafah with an armored *ugdah* of over three hundred tanks under the command of Brigadier General Israel Tal, who also commanded the Armor Corps. After taking Rafah, Tal was to seize al-Arish in conjunction with an amphibious operation conducted by a paratroop brigade under the command of Colonel Mordechai Gur. Tal was then to send a force along the northern route to the Suez Canal and a much larger force south toward Bir Gifgafa via the central route at Gebel Libni.

Brigadier General Ariel Sharon, who also headed the Training Division, commanded a specially configured combined-arms *ugdah* with 150 tanks. His mission was to take the key Egyptian defensive fortification of Abu Ageila. Brigadier General Avraham Yoffe commanded an armored *ugdah* consisting of two armored brigades, with over two hundred tanks. Yoffe, with one armored brigade, was to move between Tal and Sharon toward Bir Lahfan, to prevent Egyptian reinforcements from reaching al-Arish from Gebel Libni. The second would use the central route, once Sharon secured Abu Ageila, to link up with Yoffe at Gebel Libni. With his two tank brigades, and Tal's assistance, Yoffe was to defeat the Egyptian 3d Infantry and 4th Armored Divisions in central Sinai. Rounding out the Israeli forces in the Sinai theater were a mechanized infantry brigade facing Kuntilla, an infantry brigade opposite Gaza, and an infantry battalion guarding Eilat. The mechanized infantry brigade, as mentioned earlier, was to feint an attack toward Kuntilla to draw Egypt's attention away from the northeastern sector of the Sinai.

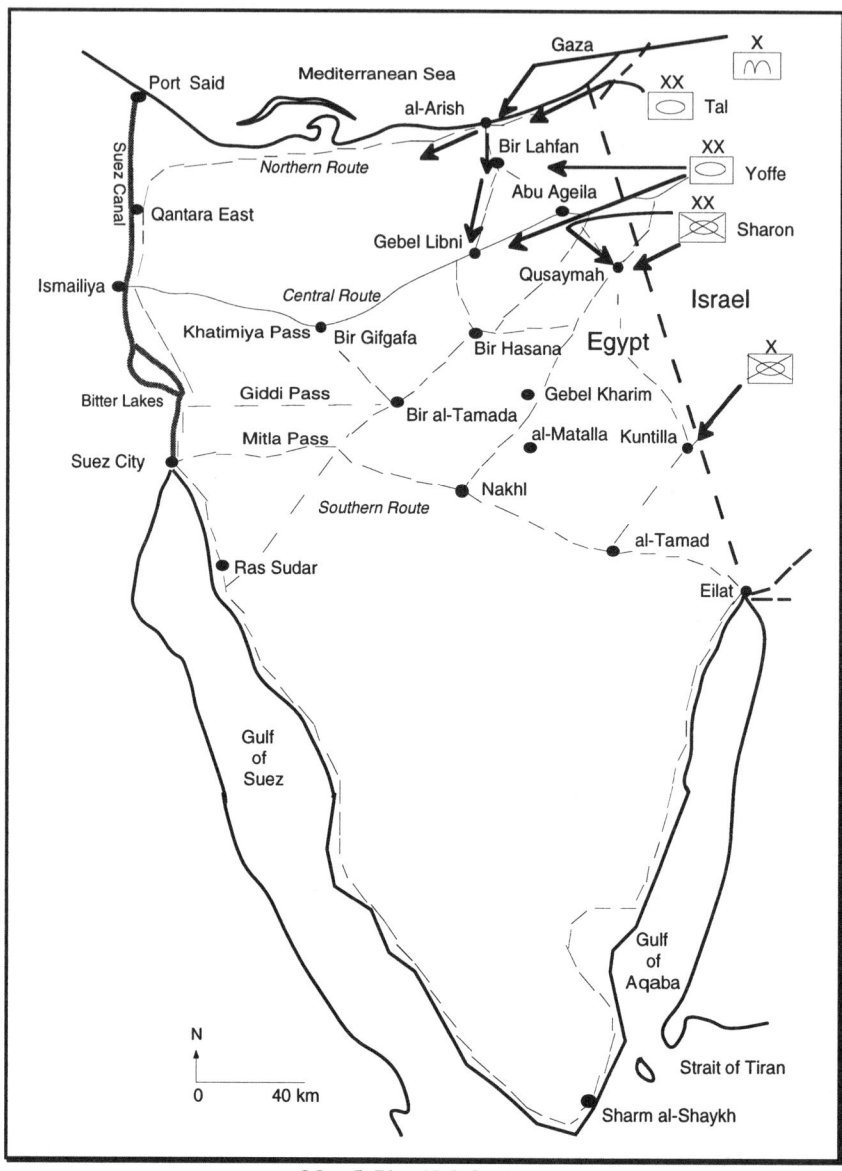

Map 5. Plan *Nahshonim*.

Plan *Nahshonim* reflected a compromise by the Israelis between a concentration on the forward-area battle and anticipation of defeating the entire Egyptian army in follow-on operations. To win quickly, mass was required on the critical axes of advance. Possessing some eighty to ninety thousand troops and 750 to eight hundred tanks, the IDF concentrated its three *ugdot*, with 650 to seven hundred tanks on a fifty-kilometer frontage in a border of 210 kilometers in length. Israeli military strategy called first for the destruction of the frontline defenses at Rafah, al-Arish, and Abu Ageila. Success in this phase would depend on each *ugdah* synchronizing its brigades—using the combined arms of infantry, armor, artillery, and engineers—to seize forward defenses. Then the Israeli General Staff hoped to roll over the Egyptian forces at Gebel Libni in order to fight a major tank battle against the 4th Armored Division. In this phase of the campaign, the Israelis would improvise, relying heavily on five armored brigades to defeat the Egyptian army.

According to Gavish, the scheme of maneuver was based on a thrust deep into central Sinai but with none of the three *ugdot* overextending itself by racing far ahead of the other two. There was some caution in this reasoning. Too rapid an advance by one *ugdah* would leave that *ugdah's* flanks or rear vulnerable to Egyptian counterthrusts.[70] Once the forward Egyptian defenses fell into Israeli hands, Plan *Nahshonim* called for synchronizing the movement of three *ugdot* from north to southwest like an expanding torrent rather than a single, rapid thrust in order to confront the Egyptian 4th Armored Division as quickly as possible. In the prewar planning adjustments made by each side, the Israelis thus set the stage for their victory, whereas the Egyptians helped create conditions for their defeat.

In the several weeks before war, Israel's military leadership played a major role in defining political objectives. While Israel's political leadership grappled for a diplomatic solution, Israeli senior commanders developed war plans in isolation from political direction. As noted later by then Major General (retired) Yitzhak Hofi in a lecture to the National Defense College Israel on 4 July 1981, "None of the military discussions or operational plans were preceded by political objectives. . . .The objective was to restore the status quo ante: removal of the Egyptian army from Sinai, reopening of the Straits, and rehabilitation of our deterrent."[71] Dayan, by changing the operational objective to destroying the EAF, raised the political stakes in the conflict; in the end, though, he would fall short of his goal of destroying Nasser.

CONCLUSION

Both Israel and Egypt stumbled into war. Neither Eshkol nor Nasser entered the month of May 1967 seeking a general conflict. But once the threat of an Israeli attack on Syria appeared on the northern front, Nasser jumped at the opportunity to restore his sagging popularity in Egypt and the Arab world. The militarization of the Sinai and the removal of UN soldiers seemed appropriate responses, the first as a viable deterrent to prevent any Israeli attack on Syria and the second as a natural assertion of Egyptian sovereignty. Both steps won popular approval for Nasser. However, Nasser went too far when he established a blockade at the Strait of Tiran. His actions fueled tensions in the region, forcing other Arab states to demonstrate their own support.

Nasser created his own problems within Egypt as well. He conducted a provocative diplomacy, but he refused to countenance the EAF attacking first.

The resultant tension between an offensive political strategy and a defensive military strategy created confusion in the armed forces. Most of the blame for the Egyptian army's internal problems, however, falls on the shoulders of its military leadership. Amer had helped transform the armed forces into a politicized institution; he also was responsible for several bad decisions in the critical three weeks prior to the outbreak of hostilities. Changes in commanders and force structure, the unexpected creation of a front command, the discarding of a good defensive plan for the Sinai, and the concomitant troop redeployments, all created havoc in the Egyptian army.

On the other side of the ledger, the last two weeks prior to war worked to Israel's advantage. During the waiting period, the IDF focused its energies on constructive training, with none of the confusion generated within the EAF. Israeli field commanders tailored their forces specifically for breakthrough and exploitation phases, taking into account terrain and Egyptian defenses. This focused activity augured well for success.

Although Israeli doctrine and military culture encouraged audacity, initiative, and improvization in its senior and junior commanders, the IDF's initial war plans were low-risk endeavors, calling for limited territorial objectives. But the Israeli cabinet failed to provide the IDF with clear political guidance. This passivity gave the IDF great latitude in formulating military objectives, which broadened in scope with the evolution of crisis. By the eve of war, Dayan, the new defense minister, had raised the operational stakes by seeking the utter defeat of the Egyptian army; he did, however, prohibit the capture of the Suez Canal. Fortunately for Dayan's war strategy, the Israeli cabinet gave its approval for a preemptive strike just when the IDF was most prepared to execute its new plan.

Despite the differences in the road to war for each country, there were some notable similarities. Both the Egyptian and Israeli armies changed war plans, troop deployments, and military objectives in response to the evolving prewar crisis. In neither case did clear political aims drive military objectives. Nasser left his army confused, whereas the IDF expanded military objectives virtually without firm political guidance from Eshkol. Both political leaders were pushed toward war by public passion, Eshkol more so than Nasser. Now war, with its primordial violence, awaited both governments, armed forces, and peoples.

NOTES

1. Raymond Aron, *Peace and War: A Theory of International Relations* (New York: Doubleday, 1966): 150–151.

2. Malcom Kerr, *The Arab Cold War: Gamal 'Abd al-Nasir and His Rivals* (Oxford: Oxford University Press, 1978): 126.

3. Muhammad Hassanayn Haykal, *The Cairo Documents* (New York: Doubleday, 1973): 238–239.

4. John W. Finney, "Egyptians Agree to Economic Reforms," *New York Times*, 14 May 1967: 10.

5. Michael Bar-Zohar, *Embassies in Crisis: Diplomats and Demagogues behind the Six-Day War* (Englewood Cliffs, NJ: Prentice-Hall, 1970): 60.

6. Daniel Dishon (ed.), *Middle East Record, 1967* (Jerusalem: Keter Publishing House, 1971): 499–500; "Three in Syria Sentenced to Life for an Article Attacking Religion," *New York Times*, 12 May 1967: 14.

7. Hanoch Bartov, *Dado: 48 Years and 20 Days* (Tel Aviv: Ma'ariv, 1981): 91–92. Elazar was the commanding general of Northern Command at the time.

8. Janice Gross Stein and Raymond Tanter, *Rational Decision-Making: Israel's Security Choices, 1967* (Columbus: Ohio State University Press, 1976): 137–138. The authors cite an interview of Brigadier General Aharon Yariv, then chief of the Intelligence Branch, in *Yediot Aharanot*, 9 August 1967.

9. Michael Brecher with Benjamin Geist, *Decisions in Crisis: Israel, 1967 and 1973* (Berkeley: University of California Press, 1980): 36. For an Israeli view that both Eshkol and Dayan were set on instigating a limited war with Syria "all along," see Martin van Creveld, *The Sword and the Olive: A Critical History of the Israeli Defense Force* (New York: Public Press, 1998): 175.

10. James Fernon, "Israelis Ponder Blow at Syria," *New York Times*, 13 May 1967: 1 and "Israel to Mark 19th Birthday in a Mood of Sober Optimism," *New York Times*, 14 May 1967: 18.

11. Anwar Sadat, *In Search of Identity* (New York: Harper and Row, 1977): 171–172. For a detailed discussion of this Soviet warning, see Richard B. Parker (ed.), *Politics of Miscalculation in the Middle East* (Bloomington: Indiana University Press, 1993): 3–35 and Richard B. Parker, *The Six-Day War: A Retrospective* (Gainesville: University Press of Florida, 1996): 42, 71–72.

12. Muhammad Abd al-Ghani al-Gamasi, *Mudhakirat al-Gamasi: Harb Oktobir 1973* (Paris: al-Munshurat al-Sharqiyya, 1990): 37.

13. Van Creveld, *The Sword and the Olive*: 172–177.

14. Muhammad Hassanayn Haykal, *1967: al-Infijar* (Cairo: Markaz al-Ahram, 1990): 445–451; Muhammad Fawzi, *Harb al-Thalath Sanawat 1967–1970* (Beirut: Dar al-Wahda, 1983): 69–70; Abd al-Mohsen Kamil Murtagui, *al-Fariq Murtagui Rawiya al-Haqaiq* (Cairo: Dar al-Watan al-Arabi, 1976): 53; and Gamasi, *Mudhakirat*: 37–38.

15. Fawzi, *Harb al-Thalath Sanawat*: 71–72. For confirmation of the general lack of concern in Syria at this time, see Khalil Mustafa, *Suqut al-Jawlan* (Cairo: Dar al-Itisam, 1980): 214–217. Major Mustafa was a Syrian military intelligence officer for Golan before the war.

16. The quote comes from Stein and Tanter, *Rational Decision-Making*, 276.

17. A detailed treatment of the Egyptian request for the removal of United Nations troops appears in a book written by the Indian major general in charge of those forces during this crisis. See Indar Jit Rikye, *The Sinai Blunder: Withdrawal of the United Nations Emergency Force Leading to the Six-Day War of June 1967* (London: Frank Cass, 1980). See also Ramses Nassif, *U Thant in New York 1961–1971: A Portrait of the Third UN Secretary-General* (New York: St. Martin's Press, 1988): 72–76.

18. Brecher, *Decisions in Crisis*: 107–111; Stein and Tanter, *Rational Decision-Making*: 139–147; and Uzi Narkiss, *The Liberation of Jerusalem: The Battle of 1967* (London: Valentine Mitchell, 1983). Then a major general, Narkiss was in charge of Israel's Central Command (facing Jordan) in the 1967 war.

36   THE ALBATROSS OF DECISIVE VICTORY

19. Haykal, *1967: al-Infijar*: 514–519; Gamasi, *Mudhakirat*: 46; and Sadat, *In Search of Identity*: 172–173. Some Egyptian sources claim that Nasser thought the likelihood of war had now increased to 100%.

20. Haykal, *1967: al-Infijar*: 625, with a photocopy of the report on p. 1024; Amin Huwaydi, *al-Furus al-Daia: al-Qararat al-Hasima fi Harbi al-Istinzaf wa Oktobir* (Beirut: Shirka al-Matbuat lil-Tawzi wa al-Nashr, 1991): 74, 551–581.

21. Lyndon Baines Johnson, *The Vantage Point: Perspectives of the Presidency 1963–1969* (New York: Holt, Rinehart & Wilson, 1971): 293; Abba Eban, *An Autobiography* (New York: Random House, 1977): 340–363; and Donald Neff, *Warriors for Jerusalem: The Six Days That Changed the Middle East* (New York: Linden Press, 1984): 146.

22. Eban, *An Autobiography*: 367; Yitzhak Rabin, *The Rabin Memoirs* (Boston: Little, Brown, 1979): 90–91; and Brecher, *Decisions in Crisis*: 142–144.

23. Eban, *An Autobiography*: 368–373; Brecher, *Decisions in Crisis*: 145–147.

24. Samir A. Mutawi, *Jordan in the 1967 War* (Cambridge: Cambridge University Press, 1987): 85–162.

25. Moshe Dayan, *Moshe Dayan: The Story of My Life* (New York: William Morrow, 1976): 335–337; and Eban, *An Autobiography*: 390–392.

26. This thesis is persuasively argued by William B. Quandt, "Lyndon Johnson and the June 1967 War: What Color Was the Light?" *Middle East Journal* 46 (Spring 1992): 198–228.

27. Moshe Dayan, *Moshe Dayan*: 341–347; Eban, *An Autobiography*: 394–402; and Brecher, *Decisions in Crisis*: 163–168. For Amit's own words on this matter given at a conference, see Parker, *Six-Day War*: 124–125, 136–141, 144–145.

28. Avner Cohen, "Cairo, Dimona, and the June 1967 War," *Middle East Journal* 50 (Spring 1996): 190–210.

29. Eban, *An Autobiography*: 384.

30. For treatment of this meeting see Haykal, *1967: al-Infijar*: 815–817; Fawzi, *Harb al-Thalath Sanawat*: 124–126; Murtagui, *al-Fariq Murtagui Rawiya*: 109; Gamasi, *Mudhakirat*: 57, 72–73; Sadat, *In Search of Identity*: 173–174.

31. Fawzi, *Harb al-Thalath Sanawat*: 258.

32. Ibid.: 33–40; Salah al-Din Hadidi, *Shahid ala Harb 1967* (Cairo: Dar al-Shuruq, 1974): 13–17; Gamasi, *Mudhakirat*: 75; and Amin Huwaydi, *Maa Abd al-Nasir* (Cairo: Dar al-Mustaqbal, 1985): 143–154.

33. The term comes from Roger Owen, "The Role of the Army in Middle Eastern Politics—A Critique of Existing Analyses," *Review of Middle Eastern Studies* 3 (1978): 71.

34. Gamasi, *Mudhakirat*: 75.

35. Kirk J. Beattie, *Egypt during the Nasser Years: Ideology, Politics, and Civil Society* (Boulder, CO: Westview, 1994): 195–196.

36. On Badran's network of influence, see al-Hadidi, *Shahid ala Harb 1967*: 25–30; Fawzi, *Harb al-Thalath Sanawat*: 36–43; and Sadat, *In Search of Identity*: 165.

37. Fawzi, *Harb al-Thalath Sanawat*: 54; Hadidi, *Shahid ala Harb 1967*: 67; and Murtagui, *al-Fariq Murtagui*: 27.

38. Hadidi, *Shahid ala Harb 1967*: 19–24; and Fawzi, *Harb al-Thalath Sanawat*: 55.

39. Fawzi, *Harb al-Thalath Sanawat*: 125, 137–138; Amin Huwaydi, *Adwa ala Ashab Naksa wa ala Harb al-Istiznaf* (Beirut: Dar al-Taliah, 1975): 80–86, 94–96; Ga-

masi, *Mudhakirat*: 91–96; and Hasan al-Badri, *al-Taawun al-Askari al-Arabi al-Mushtarak: Madihu, Hadirhu, Mustaqbalhu* (Riyad: Dar al-Mariyya, 1982): 85–86.

40. Fawzi, *Harb al-Thalath Sanawat*: 23–29; Salah al-Din al-Hadidi, *Shahid ala Harb al-Yaman* (Cairo: Maktaba Madbula, 1984); and Ali Abd al-Rahman Rahmy, *The Egyptian Policy in the Arab World: Intervention in Yemen 1962–1967* (Washington, DC: University Press of America, 1983).

41. Fawzi, *Harb al-Thalath Sanawat*: 87, 105–6.

42. The only detailed discussion of Plan *Qahir* is by the then Egyptian chief of the General Staff. See Fawzi, *Harb al-Thalath Sanawat*: 99–102.

43. For a copy of this order, see Haykal, *1967: al-Infijar*: 456–457.

44. Ibid.: 458–459; Hadidi, *Shahid ala Harb 1967*: 113, 141–142, 158–160; Murtagui, *al-Fariq Murtagui*: 58–60, 62; Fawzi, *Harb al-Thalath Sanawat*: 92, 103, 115; Gamasi, *Mudhakirat*: 76–78; and Huwaydi, *Adwa*: 38–40, 60–62. For a more detailed treatment of the Egyptian problems of command and control in the 1967 war, see George W. Gawrych, "The Egyptian High Command in the 1973 War," *Armed Forces and Society* 13 (Summer 1987): 535–546.

45. Fawzi, *Harb al-Thalath Sanawat*: 92; Murtagui, *al-Fariq Murtagui*: 114; and *Official Egyptian Military Sources* [henceforth *OEMS*]. This latter source is a series of briefings provided the author at his request. The figures come from Huwaydi, *al-Furus*: 78.

46. All the significant changes in war plans made by the Egyptian army from 15 May to 4 June are discussed in detail in Fawzi, *Harb al-Thalath Sanawat*: 102–115; Murtagui, *al-Fariq Murtagui*: 64–116; al-Hadidi, *Shahid ala Harb 1967*: 160–168; and Gamasi, *Mudhakirat*: 69-75.

47. Ze'ev Schiff, *A History of the Israeli Army: 1874 to the Present* (New York: Macmillian, 1985): 133; B. H. Liddell Hart, "Strategy of a War," *Encounter* 30 (February 1968): 18; Edgar O'Ballance, *The Third Arab-Israeli War* (Hamden, CT: Archon Books, 1972): 102; Randolph S. Churchill and Winston S. Churchill, *The Six Day War* (Boston: Houghton Mifflin, 1967): 74, 104; D. Elhannon Orren, Department of Military History, IDF, letter correspondence with author, 28 March 1991; and Amnon Reshef, interview with author, 30 June 1994, Tel Aviv, Israel. Reshef was the operations officer for the 8th Brigade.

48. Fawzi, *Harb al-Thalath Sanawat*: 120–122; and Murtagui, *al-Fariq Murtagui*: 85, 89.

49. Fawzi, *Harb al-Thalath Sanawat*: 105–106, 110–112; and Murtagui, *al-Fariq Murtagui*: 90, 94–95.

50. Fawzi, *Harb al-Thalath Sanawat:* 122–123; and Murtagui, *al-Fariq Murtagui*: 112–113.

51. Ibid.: 124.

52. Abd al-Fattah Abu Fadl, *Kuntu Naiban li-Rais al-Mukhabarat* (Cairo: Dar al-Hurriya, 1986): 279.

53. Hasan Mustafa, *Harb Haziran 1967*, I (Beirut: al-Mu'assasa lil-Dirsat wa al-Nashr, 1973): 278–280.

54. Mahmud Azmi, *al-Quwwat al-Mudarraa al-Israiliyya Abr Arbaa Hurub* (Beirut: Munazzama al-Tahrir al-Filatiniyya, 1975): 198–199; and O'Ballance, *The Third Arab-Israeli War*: 100.

55. Material on the Israeli air force comes from various sources: Edward N. Luttwak and Dan Horowitz, *The Israeli Army* (New York: Harper and Row, 1975): 192–202;

Stanley M. Ulanoff and David Eshel, *The Fighting Israeli Air Force* (New York: Arco, 1985): 53–64; Abraham Rabinovich, "First Strike," *The Jerusalem Post International Edition*, 13 June 1992: 10–11; Ehud Yonay, *No Margin for Error: The Making of the Israeli Air Force* (New York: Pantheon Books, 1993): 202–213; and Churchill and Churchill, *Six Day War:* 82–84.

56. Rabin, *The Rabin Memoirs*: 98–99 citing the description provided to him by Hod himself.

57. On developments in the Israeli Armor Corps during this period, see Luttwak and Horowitz, *The Israeli Army*: 186–192; David Eshel, *Chariots of the Desert: The Story of the Israeli Armed Corps* (London: Brassey's, 1989): 51–57; Gunther E. Rothenberg, *The Anatomy of the Israeli Army: The Israel Defence Force, 1948–1978* (New York: Hippocrene Books, 1979): 120–124; and van Creveld, *The Sword and the Olive*: 157–161.

58. Gideon Avidor, "From Brigade to Division," *Military Review* 58 (October 1978): 64–71; Yoram Movshovitz and Dan Petreanu, "The Artillery Corps—1948 to Present," *IDF Journal* 4 (Fall 1987): 18; and conversations with Israeli colonels attending the US Army Command and General Staff College.

59. Fawzi, *Harb al-Thalath Sanawat*: 60–62.

60. Ibid.: 42, 118–123

61. Samuel M. Katz, *Soldier Spies: Israeli Military Intelligence* (Novato, CA: Presidio, 1992): 153–201.

62. Details of the plan come from Colonel Benny Michelsohn, Chief, Department of Military History, IDF, letter correspondence to author, no date. For a general discussion, see Rabin, *The Rabin Memoirs*: 72; and Brecher, *Decisions in Crisis*: 160.

63. Rabin, *The Rabin Memoirs*: 81–82.

64. Ibid.: 84; Moshe Dayan, *Moshe Dayan*: 326; and Brecher, *Decisions in Crisis*: 160.

65. Rabin, *The Rabin Memoirs*: 86.

66. For discussion of military strategy and operational plans, see Ibid.: 97–98; Moshe Dayan, *Moshe Dayan*: 339–341, 347, 359–362; Ezer Weizman, *On Eagles' Wings* (New York: Macmillan, 1976): 212–216, 220; Michelsohn, letter; and Brecher, *Decisions in Crisis*: 160–161.

67. Moshe Dayan, *Moshe Dayan*: 339.

68. For Dayan's strategic thinking, Israel Tal, interview with the author, 3 July 1994, Tel Aviv, Israel. On Dayan widening the military objectives, Moshe Dayan, *Moshe Dayan*: 339–341, 347, 359–362; Avraham Adan, interview with the author, 30 June 1994, Tel Aviv, Israel; and Rabin, *The Rabin Memoirs*: 72, 84–86, 97–98.

69. As quoted in Brecher, *Decisions in Crisis*: 161.

70. Yeshayahu Gavish, "The Southern Front in the 1967 War," *Safra Sayfa* 4 (1981): 49 (in Hebrew). Special thanks to Professor Yehuda Wallach for drawing my attention to this source, and to Colonel Issak Aberkohen of the IDF for translating it.

71. Emanuel Wald, *The Wald Report: The Decline of Israeli National Security Since 1967* (Boulder, CO: Westview Press, 1992): 80–81.

2

ISRAEL'S BLITZKRIEG

> To sum it up: of all possible aims in war, the destruction of the enemy's armed forces always appears as the highest.
> —Carl von Clausewitz[1]

> [The 1967 war] is indeed lightning war of the kind whose effects we experienced everywhere in 1940, but this time [it was] compressed within a limited time frame never before realized.
> —André Beaufre[2]

Israel's military victory over the Arabs in the 1967 war recalled the German Blitzkriegs of the Second World War. In a mere six days, the Israeli army defeated the coalition of Egyptian, Jordanian, and Syrian armies; Israel reaped territorial benefits commensurate with the IDF's exemplary military performance. A combination of Egyptian mistakes and Israeli audacity during the campaign, coupled with the prewar developments discussed in the previous chapter, resulted in a military triumph worthy of a special place in the annals of modern warfare. The lightning speed of Israeli advances on the ground stemmed more from the dynamic of the battlefield than political direction from the cabinet.

ELIMINATING THE EGYPTIAN AIR THREAT

On 5 June 1967, the Israeli air force launched its campaign according to schedule.[3] Every morning over the last few weeks, Israeli war planes had been following a normal flying routine, beginning around 7:00 A.M. Israeli (8:00 Egyptian) time. Now, instead of returning home the Israeli aircraft continued due west over the Mediterranean Sea. To avoid Egyptian radar in their journey to the UAR, the fighter-bombers dipped down low to between thirty and five hundred feet over the water. Then the Israeli pilots turned south, hitting their assigned airfields at 7:45 Israeli (8:45 Egyptian) time (see Map 6).

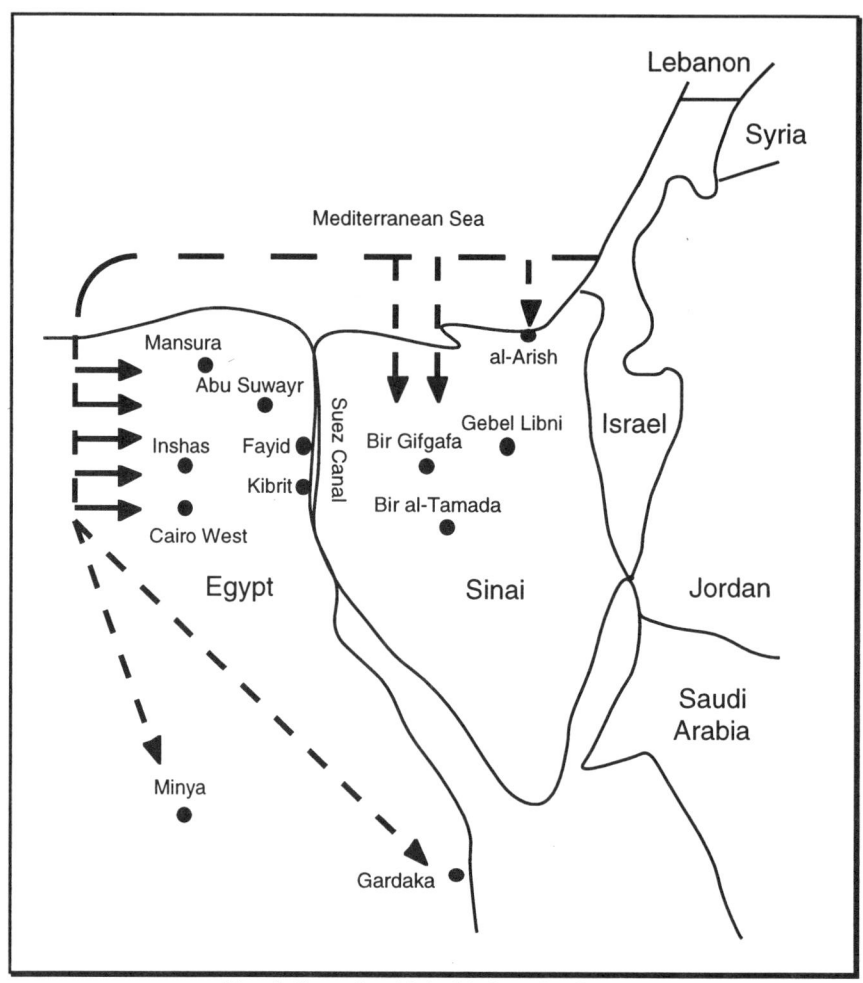

Map 6. Operation *Moked* (selected strikes).

The Israelis took a calculated risk by committing virtually their entire combat force to the attack on Egypt. Brigadier General Mordechai Hod, the air force commander, allotted 184 aircraft to strike Egypt, leaving, as noted, only twelve Super-Mystère fighters to guard Israeli skies, four in the air and eight on the ground. Priority of targets was follows: (1) damage runways, in order to prevent any take off by Egyptian pilots; (2) destroy planes on the ground, MiG-21s first, other combat aircraft second, and transports last; (3) hit radar installations, missile batteries, and maintenance centers; and (4) provide ground support.

Each assault formation comprised four aircraft. The scheme of attack went as follows: twenty-three or so minutes en route, ten minutes on target, twenty or so to return to base, and eight for refueling and rearming, with a ten-minute rest for the pilot. The time schedule per sortie naturally varied depending on the location of the Egyptian airfields. Each pilot had enough time for one bombing of the runway, followed by three or four strafing runs on the Egyptian planes on the tarmac. As one group began its return home, a second would strike within minutes. With 184 planes attacking in groups of four with ten minutes on target, each Egyptian airfield could expect little reprieve from bombing during the first hour. The seven-to-ten-minute turnaround time on the ground for each Israeli fighter-bomber set a new standard for modern warfare.

In the first wave, lasting an hour, the Israelis attacked ten airfields, destroying close to two hundred aircraft on the ground and eight in aerial combat. After a ten minute rest period, the second wave began at around 9:34 A.M. Israeli time. This time, Israeli pilots struck fourteen air bases, destroying a little over a hundred Egyptian aircraft. All total, the Israelis hit twenty-four airfields and twenty-three radar installations in some 544 sorties. At the end of the day, Amer learned that his air force possessed only forty-seven planes, thirty-five of these operational, mainly MiG-21s and MiG-17s.[4] Israeli air losses stood at only nineteen planes, most downed by Egyptian antiaircraft fire. The Israeli air force had literally strafed to death the Egyptian air force in a virtually "missileless" operation, with destruction caused almost exclusively by the fire of 30-mm cannons.

An unwise Egyptian decision played right into Israeli hands.[5] On 3 June, Amer informed his front commander, Murtagui, of his intent to inspect troops in the Sinai on 5 June. As a result of this decision, Egyptian field commanders in the Sinai, rather than focusing their attention on fighting Israel, were forced to spend part of their time and energy on 4 June preparing for the arrival of their commander in chief at Bir al-Tamada, scheduled for between 8:00 and 9:00 A.M. Egyptian time. The Israeli air force launched its campaign during Amer's flight to central Sinai! Current research suggests that the Israelis benefited more from a stroke of luck rather ingenious planning designed to take advantage of prior knowledge of Amer's decision.

The first Israeli air strikes thus caught Egypt's key military leaders away from their commands. Amer, the air force commander, and the director of operations were all flying to Bir al-Tamada when the Israeli air force launched its offensive. The Egyptian command aircraft tried to return to Cairo as quickly as possible. Unable to land for over an hour because of Israel's air attacks, Amer finally arrived at general headquarters at 9:30 Israeli (10:30 Egyptian) time, having suffered the humiliation of using a taxi to get from the airport to his command post. Thus, for the first two critical hours of the war, General Command in Cairo functioned without its most senior officers.

A similar situation took place in the Sinai theater. There, the Israeli air strikes found all the senior Egyptian tactical commanders—including the front commander, the field army commander, the air force commander of the Sinai theater, and all the division commanders—at Bir al-Tamada awaiting Amer's plane. Some division commanders, without helicopters and suddenly victimized by Israeli domination of the sky, failed to reach their units until that evening. Bringing all these commanders together for an inspection proved unwise indeed, especially given Nasser's warning of 2 June that Israel would attack by the 5th.

Thus, on the morning of 5 June, the Israeli air force had struck a decisive blow against the Egyptian army. Surprise and shock reigned throughout General Command, compounded by the disorientation of field commanders caught away from their headquarters. Gradually, the effects of the successful Israeli strikes permeated throughout the Egyptian army as well, as aptly described by then Brigadier General Muhammad Abd al-Ghani al-Gamasi, the director of operations for the front command: "When confronted with the painful effect of the air strike, General Command and the Air Force Command experienced a mental paralysis. A violent shock on the forces occurred when we learned the true results of the air strike of the previous day. The bitterness hit people when we heard military broadcasts from Radio Cairo on the great number of downed enemy planes that differed with the reality of Israeli planes traversing the Sinai with complete freedom."[6] All the confident, defiant, and bellicose statements uttered for public consumption by Egypt's political and military leadership before the war were proven hollow by the onslaught of Israeli air power.

Gaining air superiority in those first few hours greatly enhanced Israeli chances for a quick victory on the ground. Egyptian land forces in the Sinai now found themselves without air cover, which permitted Israeli pilots to strike ground targets at will. From the first air strikes of the war, the Israelis never lost the strategic initiative, although the Sinai land campaign had its tense moments. Unfortunately for Egypt, neither Jordan nor Syria launched major attacks on Israel to deflect Israeli attention away from the southern front. After destroying Egypt's air fleet, Israeli pilots attacked five Syrian, two Jordanian, and one Iraqi airfield. The results were once again quite impressive: Arab losses were some sixty out of 127 Syrian combat planes; virtually all of Jordan's small air force; and ten Iraqi aircraft. The entire cost of the Six Day War to the Israeli air force was high: forty-six of 196 first-line combat planes and twenty-six out of 210 fighter and bomber pilots, which translated to 25 and 12 percent respectively.[7] However, the decisive nature of the results soothed the national pain felt in Israel after the war.

RAFAH, THE ISRAELI MAIN EFFORT

Rafah was the site of the IDF's main effort in the Sinai campaign. Here Israel pitted its strongest armored *ugdah* against Egypt's weakest infantry division. Unfortunately for the Egyptians, the major changes in plans and deployments made by General Command before the war had most adversely affected this part of the Sinai defense system. The EAF had thus inadvertently created serious vulnerabilities for itself. The Israeli army would exploit these mistakes with a rapid breakthrough at Rafah, followed by the quick capture of al-Arish in the morning of the war's second day, setting the stage for the IDF's lightning advance into central Sinai.

Rafah, in the northeast corner of the Sinai, forms one of the main gateways into the peninsula. The small town sits astride the southern edge of the Gaza Strip. To the south, two main roads, one north-south and the other east-west, and a railway line converge in an open area called the Rafah Gap. The gap, some fifteen kilometers in width, is surrounded by stretches of impassable soft sand and low hills covered with shrubs and trees. Dry river beds, called wadis, crisscross the open plain. Although containing terrain suitable for concealment, the Rafah Gap also offers opportunity for maneuver by tanks.

In this corner of the Sinai, the northern route is the only asphalt road connecting the Gaza Strip with the Suez Canal. As this all-weather road heads west from the Israeli border, sand dunes gradually constrict the open terrain until it reaches the Giradi Pass, some thirty kilometers from Israel. Here the gap narrows to a width of twenty meters. The road winds through the Giradi Pass, approximately ten kilometers in length, until it exits into open terrain once again. Only five kilometers separate the defile's western entrance from the town of al-Arish, with its airbase to the south of the city. Al-Arish, the largest and most important town in the Sinai with a population of forty thousand in 1967, functioned as the administrative and logistical center for the Egyptian army in the peninsula.

Plan *Qahir* called for the EAF in the area to base its main line of defense on the Giradi Pass.[8] As far back as 1957, Egyptian military engineers had begun constructing concrete trenches and bunkers, machine-gun nests, and antitank gun and tank positions at both ends of the pass and within it. Since 1966, the Egyptian 11th Infantry Brigade, a regular unit, had been training to defend al-Arish in accordance with Plan *Qahir*. All this long preparation, however, proved for naught. As noted during the May crisis Nasser suddenly wanted to avoid the appearance of having abandoned four hundred thousand Palestinians living in the Gaza Strip, for the first defensive positions stood at the Giradi Pass, far from the border. This arrangement also isolated the 20th Palestinian Infantry Division, a second-rate unit composed of Palestinian soldiers and Egyptian officers, in its defense of the Gaza Strip. Consequently, Nasser made a political decision that the Egyptian army would support Gaza with a forward deployment near the border with Israel.

On 14 May, General Command complied with Nasser's wish by ordering the 11th Brigade forward to the Rafah Gap. Moreover, the General Staff also began to lay plans for a limited offensive into the northern Negev from al-Arish in the event Israel attacked Syria. To beef up forces for this new mission, Amer created a brigade-sized, mechanized task force under the command of Major General Saad al-Din Shazli and positioned it at Shaykh Zuwayd, east of Giradi Pass. By 22 May, Egyptian forces in the Rafah and al-Arish region had grown to include the newly created 7th Infantry Division, the 14th Armored Brigade, and the Shazli Task Force. Command of the division fell to Major General Abd al-Aziz Suleyman, who left his post as commandant of the Infantry School, bringing with him officers from there to serve on the divisional staff.[9] Suleyman faced a very difficult task in preparing his new command for war in three weeks.

As discussed in Chapter 1, toward the end of May General Command fell prey to the Israeli deception that the main attack would be in southern Sinai. On 29 May, in order to meet this perceived threat, Amer ordered Shazli Task Force to the southern region and the 14th Armored Brigade to central Sinai. These redeployments left only the 7th Infantry Division in the north. Furthermore, to implement Nasser's directive of defending forward, General Command had already transferred the 11th Infantry Brigade to the Rafah Gap; the 121st Infantry Brigade, a unit composed of reservists, occupied its old positions. This decision placed the division's best trained brigade in terrain more difficult to defend, while in the second echelon a poorly trained reserve brigade guarded terrain best-suited for blocking any Israeli advance on the northern route.

Thus, on the eve of war, Egyptian dispositions emphasized forward deployment at Rafah, with al-Arish constituting the second line of defense. Astride the border with Israel, the 16th Infantry Brigade guarded the northern route and the area north of the road; the 11th Infantry Brigade watched the region to the south of the highway, where the Egyptians expected the Israeli main effort. One tank company guarded the boundary between the two infantry brigades, while a second company of tanks protected the southern flank of the 11th Infantry Brigade. An artillery brigade of over forty field guns, two companies of Soviet T-34 tanks, and the 7th Division's headquarters were located in the area of Shaykh Zuwayd. To the rear, the 121st Infantry Brigade guarded the Giradi Pass. The main area of responsibility for the 7th Infantry Division encompassed a fifteen- to-twenty-kilometer frontage, with a depth of fifty kilometers (see Map 7).

To attack the recently formed Egyptian 7th Infantry Division, the Israeli General Staff committed the army's best armored *ugdah*.[10] Under the command of Brigadier General Tal, this division included the crack 7th Armored Brigade, 60th Armored Brigade (reserve), a paratroop brigade, and self-propelled divisional artillery. Tal also received a complement of Fouga Magister jet trainers for tactical air support. The Israelis possessed a marked advantage in both quantity and quality of tanks. Over three hundred Israeli tanks faced an Egyptian division with only sixty-six tanks and some twenty SU-100 tank destroyers. Moreover, the Israelis relied heavily on the more modern British Centurions and American Patton M-48s, whereas the Egyptians only possessed thirty-three T-34s and thirty-three Stalin IIIs, both of World War II Soviet vintage and virtually obsolete.

The Tal *ugdah* would begin the land campaign at a half-hour after the first strikes of the air campaign. Its primary mission was to take Rafah and al-Arish. To assist in the capture of the latter, Israeli plans called for a combined sea-air-ground operation, to which the Gur Paratroop Brigade was committed from Southern Command's reserve. If all went well with his first battles, Tal would then head for Gebel Libni to help defeat the Egyptian second line of defenses in central Sinai, while a smaller force raced for the Suez Canal along the northern route. Finally, a part of the *ugdah* would assist in the capture of the Gaza Strip.

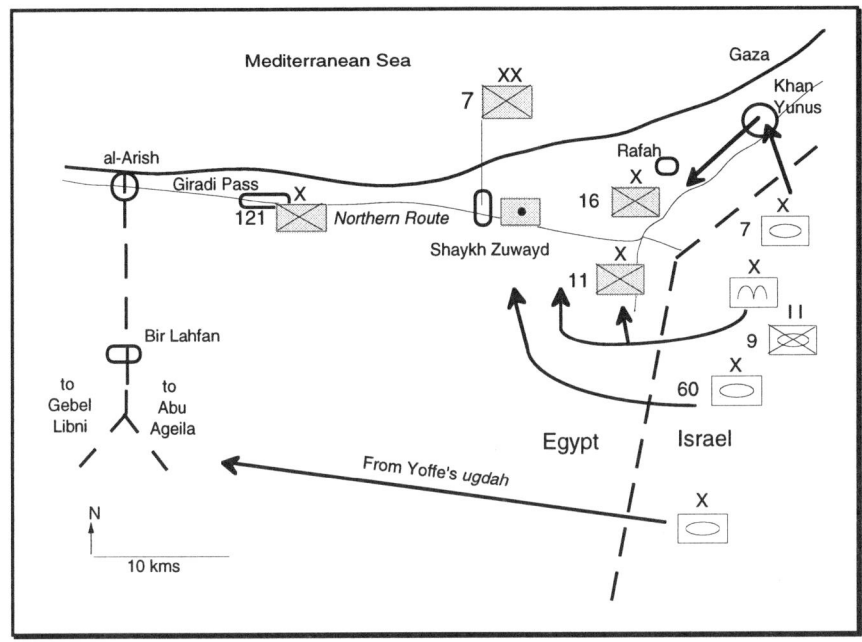

Map 7. Battle for Rafah.

Desirous of avoiding a costly frontal assault, Tal decided to conduct his main attack through the Rafah Gap by way of Khan Yunis, in the Gaza Strip. This route gave the Israelis tactical advantages. The Egyptians had failed to anticipate an attack from this direction; the Egyptian 16th Infantry Brigade had neglected to lay a dense minefield on its northern flank.[11] After a breakthrough, Tal hoped he would make a quick penetration to silence Egyptian artillery. The Israelis regarded the Egyptian field guns as a most serious threat to their operation, as Tal underscored to one of his tank battalion commanders: "Uri, you have to realize it, this artillery can kill us."[12]

To seize the Rafah Gap, Tal planned a pincer move by two brigades. While the 7th Armored Brigade, under Colonel Shmuel Gonen, attacked north to south through Khan Yunis as the *ugdah's* main effort, a paratroop brigade under Colonel Rafael Eitan, composed of two paratroop battalions and reinforced by a Patton battalion, would ride on half-tracks as mechanized infantry and hit the southern flank of the Egyptian 11th Infantry Brigade. In an emergency, Tal could employ the 60th Armored Brigade (reserve), under the command of Colonel Menachem Aviram. This reserve brigade comprised a reconnaissance squadron, a tank battalion of fifty-two Super Sherman 51s mounting the 105-mm gun, a light tank battalion of thirty-four French AMX-13s, and a mechanized infantry battalion on half-tracks. Aviram was to avoid completely the Egyptian forward defenses, by moving through the sand dunes along a track south of the northern route. Should Gonen or Eitan need help, however, Aviram could veer north and hit an Egyptian position from the south. In fact, Tal expected the 60th Brigade to provide such assistance to seize the Giradi Pass in a night operation.[13] The plan, as designed by Tal and his staff, was excellent in that it placed the main effort on the weakest flank in the Egyptian defenses.

THE BATTLE FOR RAFAH

Tal commenced his attack on the schedule with the main effort conducted by the 7th Armored Brigade. This elite armor brigade contained a reconnaissance squadron (including some twenty tanks), the 82d Armored Battalion with fifty-eight Modified Centurions, and the 79th Armored Battalion with sixty-six Patton M-48A2s. To meet any unexpected crises, Tal detached the brigade's 9th Mechanized Infantry Battalion as the *ugdah's* reserve.

Gonen expected to smash through Khan Yunis with only one tank battalion. Unexpected Egyptian resistance, however, forced him to employ both his battalions to accomplish the breakthrough. What transpired next occurred like lightning. Within four hours of beginning his attack, Gonen managed to penetrate the Egyptian left flank, pass through the Rafah Gap, and seize Shaykh Zuwayd. The speed of this advance surprised the Egyptians and kept them off balance for the remainder of the day. In the brief fight at Shaykh Zuwayd, the Egyptian division commander and his chief of staff were killed.[14] The 7th Infantry Division quickly lost its cohesion, leaving only isolated units to offer uncoordinated resistance. But even then, Tal experienced difficulty generating momentum.

Buoyed by his amazing success, Gonen gathered his forces at Shaykh Zuwayd for a dash to the Giradi Pass. The Pattons would lead the attack, with the Centurions providing flank protection to the south. Suddenly, Gonen received an order from Tal to send back part of his brigade to help Eitan's paratroopers, who were fighting the better-trained Egyptian 11th Infantry Brigade south of the northern route. Surprised by this order, Gonen, who felt compelled to maintain his momentum, requested permission to continue his advance to Giradi with part of the 7th Brigade. Tal gave his immediate consent. The time was 2:32 P.M. Israeli (3:32 Egyptian). Gonen ordered the Centurion battalion to proceed westward to the Giradi Pass, with the stipulation that it avoid any serious battle, while he took the 79th (Patton) battalion back to the Rafah Gap.[15] This decision proved wise, for it allowed the Israelis to maintain their momentum westward, taking tactical advantage of the capture of Shaykh Zuwayd.

Employing cavalry-charge tactics, the Centurions surprised the 121st Infantry Brigade at Giradi and rushed through the pass before stunned Egyptians were able to react. But the Egyptians quickly recovered their wits and sealed the eastern entrance to the defile, unbeknownst to the advancing Israelis. The Centurion battalion stopped at the outskirts of al-Arish in late afternoon, critically short of fuel and ammunition, and thus vulnerable to any serious Egyptian counterattack. Fortunately for the Israelis, the Egyptians failed to mount such an attack, for the main Egyptian forces were east of the Giradi Pass. Taking advantage of this situation, the Israelis took up defensive positions and awaited reinforcements and supplies in relative calm.

Meanwhile, Eitan's paratroopers had run into serious trouble shortly after they crossed the border. Rather than attack in mass, Eitan unwisely "piecemealed" his force into company sized elements, which became isolated from each other once inside the Egyptian 11th Brigade's defensive perimeter. Fortunately for Eitan, the Egyptians never counterattacked with sufficient force to defeat his paratroopers in detail. But Eitan did encounter sufficient Egyptian resistance to appeal to Tal for assistance. The Israeli 60th Armored Brigade, for its part, experienced tremendous difficulty navigating through the sand and was thus unable to assist the beleaguered paratroopers. So Tal turned to the 7th Brigade to save the paratroopers, at the same time releasing the 9th Mechanized Infantry Battalion from his reserve.

While en route to the Rafah Gap, however, Gonen learned that his help was no longer needed; Eitan had managed to secure the northern route, with the assistance of the 9th Battalion. Gonen now scrambled back to rejoin the Centurion battalion, by this time some several kilometers east of al-Arish. At the eastern entrance to the Giradi Pass, however, unexpected Egyptian fire stopped the Israelis dead in their tracks. Major Ehud Elad, the battalion commander, was among the Israeli fatalities. Regrouping, the Patton battalion managed to punch through, but before Gonen could move his command group, the Egyptians blocked the pass a second time. Now Gonen was cut off from both his tank battalions. Lacking additional combat forces, he immediately appealed to Tal for the 9th Battalion.

In response, Tal first turned to the 60th Armored Brigade, ordering Aviram to send his AMX-13 battalion and mechanized infantry battalion to attack Giradi from the south. Aviram, stuck in the sand and short of fuel, tried to send his infantry forward on foot, but proved unable to respond. Therefore, the 9th Mechanized Infantry Battalion, on clearing the Rafah Gap of Egyptian troops, disengaged and went to Gonen's assistance. Wishing to avoid a repeat of events at Giradi Pass, Tal ordered the battalion not proceed to al-Arish with Gonen but to stay and secure the pass. Around midnight, the Israeli mechanized infantry reached the defile, dismounted, and assaulted the pass with fire support from a tank company. Under the light of illumination flares, the dismounted infantry fought on foot in the trenches for four hours before finally opening the entrance for the third time in less than twelve hours. In the midst of the confusion, Gonen drove boldly through the defile with his command group and some supplies, reuniting with his two tank battalions in the early hours of 6 June.

Thus in less than twenty-four hours the Tal *ugdah* had routed the Egyptian 7th Infantry Division. Israeli sources set their own losses at seventy dead and thirty-four tanks destroyed.[16] In the early afternoon of 5 June, around the time of Shaykh Zuwayd's capture, Dayan and Rabin, confident of success, canceled the amphibious and airdrop landings at al-Arish scheduled for the morning of 6 June and instead sent the Gur Paratroop Brigade to Jerusalem to fight the Jordanians. Israel was well on its way to a blitzkrieg-type victory. Moreover, much of the

Israeli success in the battle for Rafah was owed to the work of one brigade, the 7th, and this force had its critical moments. Gonen had barely averted disaster at Giradi Pass, demonstrating the importance of combined arms in breakthrough operations as well as in exploitation phases of combat. In the meantime, the other two Israeli brigades had had their own problems. The 60th Armored Brigade saw no combat on 5 June, expending energy and fuel just to negotiate the sand. The Eitan paratroop brigade, for its part, had failed to concentrate and therefore nearly lost several isolated forces. Only the dogged heroism of junior officers kept the paratroopers more or less on track. Despite these problems, no one could argue with success at this point in the campaign.

ABU AGEILA, KEY TO THE SINAI

Abu Ageila constituted the main fortification in the Egyptian defensive system in the eastern Sinai.[17] Egyptian defenses were at their best here. Abu Ageila had strategic importance because of its location on the central route close to the Israeli-Egyptian border. The Israeli army had to capture this position, which guarded the best logistical route for sustaining any major campaign in central Sinai. To prevent its capture by the IDF, Egypt's General Command made the area a key link in a defensive system in the eastern Sinai, which also included a north-south road network.

Egyptian defenses in the Abu Ageila area appeared quite formidable. The 2d Infantry Division, the only division stationed in the Sinai before the May crisis, deployed the 10th Infantry Brigade in Qusaymah and the 12th Infantry Brigade in Abu Ageila. Twenty-two kilometers separated Abu Ageila from Qusaymah. The primary mission of the Egyptian 12th Infantry Brigade was to stop an invading force—or at least inflict serious damage on it—until reinforcements arrived or the field army commander launched a major counterattack. To control this vital artery in the Sinai, the Egyptians reinforced the 12th Infantry Brigade with the 6th Tank Regiment, consisting of approximately sixty-six T-34 tanks and twenty-two SU-100 self-propelled tank destroyers.

The Egyptians had anchored their defenses in Abu Ageila area on Umm Qatef, a ridge that conveniently cut across the central route. Sand dunes to the north and hills to the south made flanking Umm Qatef quite difficult. Furthermore, flat terrain to the east of Umm Qatef provided Egyptian defenders with a five-kilometer field of observation toward the border. A minefield 250 meters in width, along with barbed wire and antitank obstacles, stood in front of Umm Qatef. Given this blend of natural terrain and man-made obstacles, tactical surprise from the eastern direction was virtually impossible. To defend Umm Qatef, two infantry battalions, each reinforced with a platoon of three T-34 tanks, were deployed in two trench lines.

Several kilometers to the rear of Umm Qatef, at the base of Gebel Dalfa, the Egyptian brigade commander had dispersed two battalions of artillery with an elaborate system of trenches connecting the guns. Near the artillery positions the Egyptians had stationed an armored battalion, whose mission was to counterattack against any breakthrough into the defensive perimeter or to reinforce the forward positions at Umm Qatef. Farther west, in the Ruafa Dam area, a second echelon composed of a third infantry battalion and two additional artillery battalions formed a second line of defense. Moreover, an outer ring of observation posts provided early warning of attack. The 2d Reconnaissance Battalion, minus a company, guarded Umm Tarafa. A tank regiment, less one armored battalion, protected the brigade's logistical center at Awlad Ali, with its water well. To prevent any enemy passage along Batur Track, the Egyptians positioned a reinforced infantry battalion on the hill area known as Position 181 (see Map 8).

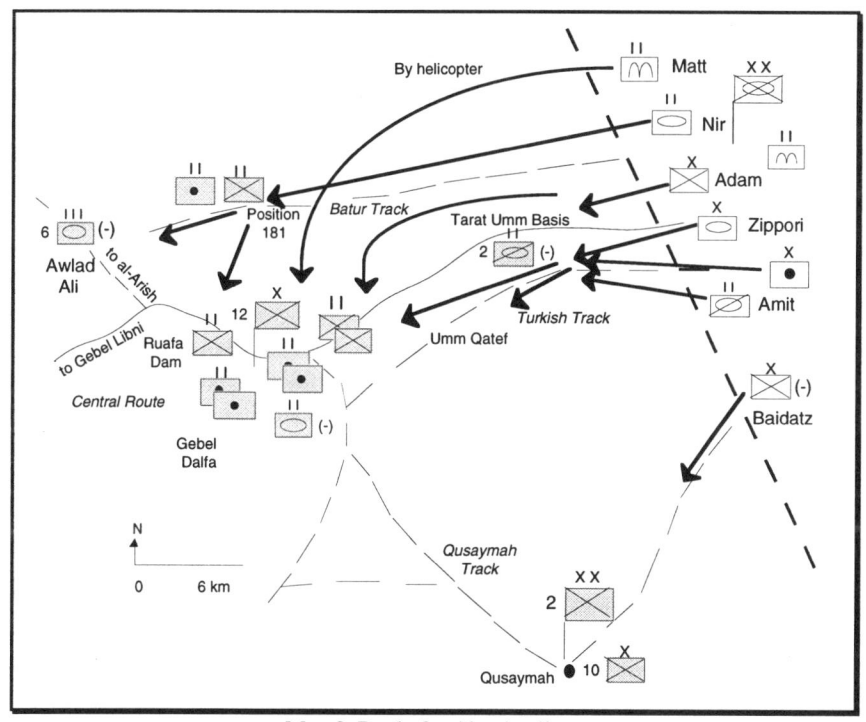

Map 8. Battle for Abu Ageila.

Though the defenses at Abu Ageila looked strong, the Egyptians unwittingly created several problems for themselves. In the week or two before the war, Amer appointed a new commander for the 2d Infantry Division. Major General Said Naguib had been stationed in Yemen until his reassignment to the Sinai at the end of May. Accustomed to fighting guerrillas in mountainous terrain, Naguib now had to adjust to a new division deployed in completely different terrain against an opponent adept at armored warfare. This unwise step created command problems for the Egyptian force. Furthermore, the 12th Infantry Brigade, like the 16th Infantry Brigade at Rafah, failed to mine its northern flank, believing the sand dunes presented the Israelis with an insurmountable barrier. Taking advantage of this error, the Israelis decided to make the northern flank the main axis for attacking Abu Ageila, much as Tal did at Rafah.

The capture of Abu Ageila fell upon the shoulders of Brigadier General Ariel Sharon, a maverick general, perhaps Israel's most controversial. Sharon prepared an elaborate plan based on a highly centralized command that he intended to decentralize in the midst of the main battle. The Israeli commander hoped to unnerve the Egyptian defenders by an encirclement operation followed by a synchronized night assault at several critical points in the Abu Ageila defenses. To accomplish these bold maneuvers, the Israeli General Staff had provided Sharon with what was a combined-arms *ugdah* by Israeli standards of the time: an infantry brigade, a reduced infantry brigade, a brigade of paratroopers, an armored brigade, an independent tank battalion, a reconnaissance force, six artillery battalions, and an engineering battalion. Sharon's *ugdah* numbered around nineteen thousand men, a force slightly larger than the Egyptian 2d Infantry Division's approximately sixteen thousand troops.

To enhance his numerical advantage over the Egyptians, Sharon took steps to draw Naguib's attention away from Abu Ageila and toward Qusaymah. He assigned a deception operation to Colonel Uri Baidatz, who received command of a reduced infantry brigade comprising two infantry battalions and a tank company. Baidatz was to feign an attack against Qusaymah. (The Egyptians were to swallow the bait; Naguib would remain focused on this sector while the Israeli main effort went against Abu Ageila.) In case the Egyptians did not fall for this wile, however, Sharon took the precaution of planning to block the Qusaymah Track, just south of Umm Qatef, by way of a path that ran south of the Turkish Track. A specially tailored force under Major Arie Amit, consisting of an AMX-13 tank company, a motorized infantry company, a engineer platoon, and a mortar battery, was to accomplish this task.

To isolate the battle at Abu Ageila, Sharon decided to send an armored force to the rear of Ruafa Dam, via the Batur Track, with two important missions: first to block any Egyptian reinforcements coming from either Gebel Libni or al-Arish, and second to assault Ruafa Dam and Umm Qatef from the west. For this dangerous mission, Lieutenant Colonel Natke Nir received a battalion-sized armored task force containing forty-five Centurion Mark 5 tanks. For his operation into the rear of Abu Ageila, Nir was to answer directly to Sharon.[18]

A combination of infantry and armor would provide the breakthrough punch at Umm Qatef. After traveling some twelve kilometers on foot from Tarat Umm Basis, an infantry brigade under Colonel Yekutiel Adam would attack the Egyptian trenches at Umm Qatef from the north. Meanwhile, the Zippori Armored Brigade, configured with two battalions of Super Sherman tanks and two battalions of mechanized infantry, would provide direct fire support to the infantry brigade in a night assault. As the Israeli infantry cleared the Egyptian trench lines, the *ugdah's* battalion of combat engineers would move in from the east to clear the minefields in front of the trenches for the passage of Zippori's tanks.

Sharon, a master paratrooper noted for intricate plans, assigned the critical mission of silencing the Egyptian artillery to the paratroop brigade led by Lieutenant Colonel Danny Matt. Helicopters would land a paratroop battalion on the northern flank of Abu Ageila. The paratroopers would proceed on foot to assault the artillery positions, while the remainder of the *ugdah* carried out its synchronized attacks on Abu Ageila from the east and west.

The Israelis had the advantage in manpower and weapons. Sharon's plan gave the Israelis a marked superiority in numbers of troops at Abu Ageila—the bulk of an Israeli *ugdah* against a reinforced Egyptian infantry brigade. In armor, the Israelis possessed a clear advantage: against sixty-six obsolete T-34s the Israelis committed over 150 tanks. The Egyptian T-34 tanks were outclassed by the longer-range guns of Centurions and Super Shermans.

Any advantages that Sharon held at the outset of hostilities could change significantly, however, depending on the Egyptian reaction. To defeat the Sharon *ugdah* the Egyptians had to commit a sizable force from the 3d Infantry Division at Gebel Libni, and in a timely manner. But as we shall see, the Egyptian command failed in this course of action.

THE CAPTURE OF ABU AGEILA

By midnight, Sharon was ready to assault Abu Ageila. Nir, Matt, Adam, and Zippori had moved their forces into position for the attack. Nir, after a heavy fight at Position 181, reached the rear of Ruafa Dam with only a tank company of seven or eight tanks, a company of mechanized infantry, and his 120-mm mortar company. Here he divided his small force, leaving one part to watch for any Egyptian reinforcements coming from the direction of al-Arish or Gebel Libni while he attacked Abu Ageila.[19] Now he awaited word from Sharon so that he could attack in coordination with Matt, Adam, and Zippori.

The Egyptians, by their own later admission, seriously erred in not anticipating an Israeli attack from the north against their artillery positions at Gebel Dalfa's base. No minefields or any extensive array of barbed wire had been placed on this northern flank to slow down an attack by Israeli special forces. Furthermore, Egyptian artillery positions within the main complex, although designed to withstand counterbattery fire and aerial bombing, were not equipped to handle an attack on foot.[20] This Egyptian omission was particularly significant since artillery formed the core of the defensive concept for Abu Ageila.

Matt divided his paratroop battalion into three companies, with each platoon targeted against an Egyptian gun emplacement. The paratroopers, armed with submachine guns, grenades, and knives, began their attack a half-hour before midnight, fanning out to silence the artillery battalions behind Umm Qatef. Darkness slowed their progress, and some paratroopers experienced difficulty finding their way. Also, despite their initial advantage in surprise, the Israelis encountered some stiff resistance from the Egyptians, who recovered from their initial shock and committed infantry units to hand-to-hand combat. In over three hours of intense fighting, the Israeli paratroopers had taken seventeen casualties, too many to continue their mission. Sharon signaled Matt to withdraw his forces so as to avoid "friendly fire" from the Israeli tanks that had just broken through at both Umm Qatef and Ruafa Dam.

Though failing to destroy all the artillery batteries, the Israeli paratroopers had dealt a crippling blow to the Egyptian defensive system. By the Israelis having effectively disrupted Egyptian artillery fire, the Egyptians lost the combined arms nature of their defenses, a fact that helped the Israeli infantry and armor brigades in their assaults on Umm Qatef. Moreover, by assaulting positions in the center of the enemy's main perimeter, the Israeli paratroopers had helped demoralize Egyptian troops in the forward trenches, by blurring the distinction between the front and rear battles. When the Israelis attacked a convoy of six or seven trucks bringing supplies and troops to Umm Qatef from the direction of Ruafa Dam, the ominous explosions could be seen for miles around. Egyptian defenders at Umm Qatef suddenly became acutely aware that there was trouble in their rear. This realization adversely affected the fighting performance of some frontline soldiers, who now felt dangerously exposed to a knife or bullet in the back. Also, a number of Egyptians fell to friendly fire in the confusion.[21] Thus, the Israeli paratrooper battalion helped bring about the collapse of Abu Ageila by attacking the Egyptians at a critical and vulnerable point, thereby unbalancing their defenses.

A second major tactical surprise awaited the Egyptian defenders at Abu Ageila. Because the Egyptian brigade commander believed that the sand dunes in the north presented an insurmountable barrier to attackers, he had failed to mine his northern flank at Umm Qatef. Sharon thus achieved two major tactical surprises by attacking from the north: the first against the artillery at Gebel Dalfa and the second against the forward infantry at Umm Qatef.

Responsibility for seizing Umm Qatef fell to the Israeli infantry brigade commanded by Colonel Yekutiel Adam. Sharon developed a complicated plan that required close cooperation and timely communication. Before the infantry assault, Israeli artillery was to mark the northernmost part of the enemy trenches for the infantry. A tank company was to provide direct fire support for each infantry battalion. Each Israeli battalion would carry fifty colored flashlights respectively—red, green, or blue—to mark its forward progress. The idea was to shoot just ahead of the advancing infantry to help clear the way. As the infantry occupied an area, the engineer battalion would begin clearing the minefield for penetration by the armor. To ensure proper coordination and avoid casualties to his advancing infantry from friendly fire, Adam was to take control of the six battalions of divisional artillery when their mission changed from general to direct fire support.

Adam's infantry brigade caught the Egyptians completely by surprise, and the Israelis experienced little difficulty getting into the two lines of trenches. But the Egyptians recovered quickly and put up a desperate fight, to the point of hand-to-hand combat with bayonets and knives. In the melee the Israelis captured the Egyptian colonel in charge of Umm Qatef, in a bunker located in the second trench line.

By 2:30 A.M., Israeli engineers had managed to clear a small path for the passage of the tank battalion. At first only four tanks punched through Umm Qatef. Eventually, just before dawn on 6 June, the remainder of the tank battalion began entering the main perimeter. While the battle for Umm Qatef raged, Nir launched his attack from the west on the headquarters of the Egyptian 12th Infantry Brigade. Nir's attack must have surprised the Egyptians at the command post and deflected its attention away from Umm Qatef to the situation directly threatening its own bunker. The Egyptian brigade commander thus faced personal danger just as his troops were entering the most critical stage of the battle.

After seizing the dam area, Nir organized his forces for the push eastward to link up with the Israeli tank force approaching from Umm Qatef. Nir's force had breached the central route and was moving cautiously in an easterly direction. At the same time, Lieutenant Colonel Sasson headed westward from Umm Qatef with his tank battalion from Zippori's armored brigade. At this point in the battle, Sharon transferred command of Nir's battalion to Zippori, who promptly ordered Sasson's tanks to stop firing. When Nir continued to receive fire, Zippori knew his men were not firing at each other; he radioed to Sasson to continue his attack against what was clearly an Egyptian force.

The Egyptians reacted belatedly to this initial penetration by Israeli tanks from the east. Rather than launch his entire force in a counterattack during the first Israeli breakthrough at Umm Qatef, the Egyptian commander of 288th Tank Battalion (minus a tank company) remained relatively idle. When Sasson entered the defensive perimeter with his battalion, the Egyptian commander ordered his crews to prepare a stopping line in the Soviet manner.[22] Accordingly, the crews used the T-34s as antitank weapons, and for two hours that night Israeli and Egyptian tanks engaged in close combat. Eventually, the Egyptian tankers found themselves surrounded by Israeli tanks, and they gave up resistance.

By dawn on 6 June the Egyptian defense had crumbled, with only a few pockets of resistance still remaining for Israeli infantry to subdue. Abu Ageila had fallen within twenty-four hours. Israel's victory had cost at least thirty-two men killed in action and nineteen tanks destroyed. Egyptian losses stood at forty tanks and an unknown number of men killed and wounded. Sharon had clearly demonstrated resourcefulness, daring, and imagination. The battle for Abu Ageila is an excellent study of a combined-arms assault against a fortified position.

In comparing the operations of Tal and Sharon, one is struck by the flexibility exhibited by the Israeli army. Each *ugdah* was task organized for its particular mission and its specific tactical challenges. Tal received a heavy armored division to conduct a daytime assault led by armor with infantry in support; his need for speed required decentralization of command from the onset of the operation. Sharon, on the other hand, was given a combined-arms division and drafted a set-piece battle plan to attack a heavily fortified defensive position. He opted for a night attack led by infantry and paratroopers, and supported by tanks and a heavy dose of artillery. Tight control characterized his complex operation, with decentralization being allowed only for particular tactical events. In planning and execution, the two Israeli *ugdah* commanders reflected their different military backgrounds. Tal was considered "Mr. Armor" in the Israeli army, whereas Sharon had gained the distinction of being the father of the paratroopers.

For their part, the Egyptians made similar mistakes in the two battles at Rafah Gap and at Abu Ageila. In each instance Egyptian tactical commanders failed to mine the northern flank, expecting the terrain to act as an impassable barrier. In both cases the omissions proved fatal. Once attacked from an unexpected direction, Egyptian defenders in both battles suffered debilitating surprise and responded in a dilatory fashion, missing opportunities to defeat or seriously damage Israeli forces. At Abu Ageila in particular, the Egyptians had little excuse for their quick defeat. Egyptian defenses were at their best here, having been in place with no major changes for a number of years. Furthermore, the Israelis attacked at night, when command of the air was not a factor in the ground battle.

If the Egyptians had made a concerted effort to defeat Nir by dispatching a major force from the 3d Infantry Division at Gebel Libni, the Sharon *ugdah* would have faced serious problems. But the Israeli campaign plan did make provision for this development on the battlefield: Gavish, the front commander, could employ the Yoffe *ugdah* should problems develop with Sharon's *ugdah*. Gavish did take this step at a critical point in the battle for Abu Ageila.

A SILENT INFILTRATION

In some regards, Brigadier General Avraham Yoffe's armored *ugdah* formed the linchpin in Operation *Nahshonim*. This tank-heavy division linked the forward tactical battles at Rafah and Abu Ageila with an operational thrust into central Sinai, a movement designed to produce an opportunity to defeat the Egyptian army in a single, unrelenting, continuous campaign waged over several days.[23] Yoffe, a reservist infantry officer, received command of two reserve armored brigades, both comprising modified Centurions. His force totaled approximately 220 tanks and 110 half-tracks, reinforced with a handful of artillery pieces. Israel's General Staff specifically configured this *ugdah* to conduct tank warfare over open terrain in the central Sinai.

Nahshonim assigned two important missions to Yoffe. The first required him to establish a blocking position just south of Bir Lahfan, at the fork in the north-south road from al-Arish, from which it travels either southeast to Abu Ageila or southwest to Gebel Libni. Israel's General Staff rightly anticipated that Egypt's General Command would attempt to reinforce al-Arish with forces from its second defensive line near Gebel Libni. To prevent this reinforcement, Yoffe assigned one armored brigade to traverse a dirt track halfway between the northern and central routes used by Tal and Sharon, respectively. After the completion of this first mission, Yoffe would proceed with Tal toward Gebel Libni to defeat the Egyptian army in central Sinai. For this task Yoffe would employ both his tank brigades. One would come from Bir Lahfan; the second would pass through Abu Ageila on the central route.

The employment of the Yoffe *ugdah* in this way gave Gavish, the theater commander, operational flexibility. At Bir Lahfan, the IDF would isolate the battlefield for Tal at al-Arish. Should either Tal or Sharon require assistance, Gavish could dispatch the armored brigade at Bir Lahfan to attack al-Arish or Abu Ageila from the rear. Alternatively, Yoffe's second armored brigade could strike Umm Qatef from the east along the central route in a breakthrough operation, should Sharon require such aid.

In conjunction with the opening moves by Tal in the north and Sharon in the south, Yoffe began his silent infiltration between the Egyptian 7th and 2d Infantry Divisions with an armored brigade under the command of Colonel Iska Shadmi. Only a few Egyptian troops were on this dirt track. Pockets of soft sand and sand dunes constituted the most serious obstacles confronting Shadmi. In late afternoon, after covering fifty to sixty kilometers in eight hours, the lead Israeli tank units reached the road intersection, which stood a kilometer and a half south of Bir Lahfan. By nightfall, advance elements of the Shadmi Armored Brigade had begun establishing blocking positions. Rather quickly, the Israeli brigade became involved in the battle for the Sinai.

As discussed earlier, Nir's armored task force encountered problems getting to the rear of the Egyptian position at Abu Ageila. Consequently, Gavish decided to send a part of Yoffe's force at Bir Lahfan to help Nir attack Ruafa Dam. Colonel Avraham Adan, Yoffe's chief of staff, received the assignment to move out immediately with a tank battalion for Abu Ageila, leaving Shadmi with only one tank battalion of over fifty tanks at Bir Lahfan. Within an hour, Adan was called back while still en route to Ruafa Dam, because his help was no longer needed; Nir had broken through the Egyptian rear on his own.[24] The sudden dispatch of Adan to Abu Ageila underscores the operational flexibility gained by Southern Command in moving the Shadmi Armored Brigade to Bir Lahfan.

Unfortunately for the Egyptians, General Command failed to exploit the opportunity briefly presented at Bir Lahfan. Sometime in the late afternoon or early evening, Major General Uthman Nassar of the Egyptian 3d Infantry Division at Bir al-Hasana was ordered to take an infantry brigade to the relief of al-Arish; the Independent 14th Armored Brigade, located on the central route west of Gebel Libni, was to support him. In the middle of the night, while driving toward al-Arish, the Egyptian general unexpectedly encountered the Israeli tank battalion at Bir Lahfan. Ordered by superiors to attack the enemy with part of his force and lead the remainder around the Israeli positions to al-Arish, Nassar procrastinated throughout the night, preferring instead to engage in a long range gunnery duel rather than attempt to bypass the Israelis.

Initially, the Egyptians outnumbered the Israelis at Bir Lahfan in tanks, artillery, and infantry, as Adan had already departed for Ruafa Dam. Even when Adan returned to strengthen Shadmi's position, the Egyptians still possessed the advantage in men and equipment—until daybreak, when the Israeli air force joined the battle. Toward noon on 6 June, Lieutenant General Salah al-Din Mohsen, the field army commander, ordered Nassar to withdraw from Bir Lahfan to form a defensive line around Bir al-Hasana. Nassar, however, failed to accomplish his mission and instead found excuses to abandon his command for Ismailiya during the general withdrawal. After the war, a military court would convict Nassar for incompetence and cowardice.[25]

As later admitted by General Abd al-Mohsen Kamil Murtagui, the front commander, the Egyptian senior leadership seriously erred in discounting any possibility of the Israelis moving a large armored force to Bir Lahfan.[26] With this silent infiltration over terrain deemed impassable by the Egyptians, the Israelis not only isolated the forward battles for al-Arish and Abu Ageila but positioned themselves for a multiaxis thrust into central Sinai for a decisive defeat of the Egyptian army. Now the remaining EAF would face two major Israeli armor forces descending from two different directions: one from Bir Lahfan, the other from Abu Ageila.

Israel's successful operational deception compounded Egypt's tactical problems. As discussed earlier, the Israeli General Staff convinced Amer that the main attack would take place between Qusaymah and Kuntilla. Two Israeli brigades were assigned the deception mission. Baidatz's infantry brigade diverted the attention of Major General Said Naguib, commander of the 2d Infantry Division, away from Abu Ageila by feinting an attack toward Qusaymah. Colonel Albert Mandler, in command of the 8th Mechanized Infantry Brigade (comprising a reconnaissance company, two mechanized infantry battalions, one armored battalion, and an artillery battalion), conducted probes against Egyptian defenses at Kuntilla.[27] A week before the war, Amer had fallen for the ruse that the IDF would launch its main attack in this region of the Sinai; he kept the 6th Infantry Division and Shazli Task Force close to the border.

The outbreak of war failed to disabuse Amer of his fixation on the area between Qusaymah and Kuntilla. Throughout 5 June, Amer still expected the Israeli main effort there. As a result, he kept a good part of his army ready for this expected onslaught, even ordering the 2d Armored Brigade of the 4th Armored Division, his general reserve, to move forward in anticipation of a major counterattack against the oncoming Israelis.[28] Amer should have focused his attention and reserve forces on the northern and central routes.

A LOSS OF EGYPTIAN WILL

By late morning on 6 June, the strategic situation in the Sinai was quickly becoming desperate for the Egyptians. Word had reached Cairo of the fate of Rafah, al-Arish, and Abu Ageila. The rapid collapse of these fortified positions on the northern and central routes surprised, shocked, and demoralized senior officers. Amer apparently fell into a state of panic and despair. Having realized his fatal error in concluding that the Israeli main effort would be in the south, the

Egyptian commander now proved incapable of providing wise counsel to his field commanders.

While tactical events were going badly for his army, Nasser turned to diplomacy. He appealed to the Soviets for immediate shipment of military hardware to compensate for the huge losses suffered on the first day of the war. The Soviet response came within hours, but it was less than satisfactory; it would take at least a week before any equipment could reach Egypt.[29] With Washington unwilling to pressure the United Nations to pass a resolution for an immediate cease-fire and a return to the boundaries of 4 June, Nasser was left to resolve the military crisis without the aid of diplomacy. This situation, in turn, gave the IDF a freer hand on the battlefield.

Egypt's General Command proved incapable of preventing the Israelis from exploiting their operational and tactical advantages. At 11:30 A.M. Egyptian time, with the loss of al-Arish and Abu Ageila already evident, Amer now ordered the formation of a second line of defense: the 3d Infantry Division at Bir al-Hasana; the 14th Armored Brigade on the central route near Gebel Libni; the 2d Armored Brigade at Bir Tamada; Shazli Task Force and the 6th Infantry Division between al-Matalla and al-Tamad. The 4th Armored Division would assume control of the passes.[30] But the IDF was determined to maintain its momentum and prevent the Egyptian Army from regrouping.

Tal, while securing al-Arish in the early morning of 6 June, decided on his next moves.[31] An AMX-13 tank company established a blocking position eight kilometers west of al-Arish to prevent any Egyptian counterattack from that direction. But Tal had to make some adjustments to the original plan, which had assigned the seizure of the airfield nine kilometers south of al-Arish to either the Eitan Paratroop or the Aviram Armored Brigade. Unexpected developments on the battlefield prevented the execution of this plan.

In the final planning of *Nahshonim*, Dayan had counseled against attacking the Gaza Strip in the opening phase of the campaign, wanting to avoid fighting in densely populated urban areas. He believed that Gaza would fall without a serious fight after the capture of Rafah and al-Arish. Gavish, however, was determined to prevent any shelling of Israeli settlements by Palestinian forces and attacked the Gaza Strip on the first day of the war.[32] To help overcome the Palestinian resistance in urban areas, Southern Command detailed Eitan's paratroopers after their battle at Rafah Gap, to help capture the Gaza Strip. In addition to the loss of the paratroop brigade, the Aviram Armored Brigade continued to experience trouble negotiating through the sand dunes and thus was unable to attack the Egyptian airfield on schedule. Consequently, Tal again turned to Gonen and the 7th Armored Brigade to lead the *ugdah's* attack.

Gonen commenced his advance at 6:00 A.M. Israeli time, seizing al-Arish's airfield by 7:30. Bir Lahfan now stood as the next Egyptian obstacle. This radar station was guarded by an infantry company and several antiair batteries; the Shadmi Armored Brigade had established its blocking position several kilometers south of Bir Lahfan. Gonen first resorted to a long-range firefight between his Centurions and the Egyptian defenders. When the initial exchange went favorably for the Israelis, Tal acceded to Gonen's request to employ the Patton battalion for the assault on Bir Lahfan. After breaking through this lightly held Egyptian position, Tal assigned the securing of Bir Lahfan to the mechanized infantry from the Aviram Armored Brigade. By late morning, the 7th Armored Brigade was once again moving, this time with the goal of a linkup with the Shadmi Armored Brigade from Yoffe's *ugdah.*

At midday on 6 June, Tal plotted his next move after the capture of al-Arish airfield. A special task force under Colonel Israel Granit—consisting of a reconnaissance company of eighteen recoilless guns on jeeps, an AMX-13 company of eight tanks, and half a dozen self-propelled guns—would take the northern route toward Qantara East on the Suez Canal. Tal kept control of the 7th Armored Brigade's 9th Mechanized Infantry Battalion, using it to secure the Giradi Pass and al-Arish. With the Gonen and the Aviram Armored Brigades, Tal expected to head for Ismailiya, using the central route.

Meanwhile, the Shadmi Armored Brigade from the Yoffe *ugdah* attempted to reach the central route from Bir Lahfan. At 11:30 Egyptian time, Nassar, in command of the task force assigned to reinforce al-Arish, began pulling back to Bir al-Hasana with his infantry brigade. Meanwhile, General Command ordered the Independent 14 Armored Brigade, under Brigadier General Abd al-Munim Wassel, to form a defensive line at Gebel Libni, with its small airfield and army depot. His three tank battalions deployed to prevent the Israelis from reaching the central route from Bir Lahfan.

Forward elements from Shadmi's brigade were the first to arrive in the area. In the late morning, the opposing brigades commenced a long-range artillery duel, followed by tank fire at a range of 1,200 meters. Wassel deployed a tank battalion to face east on the central route, when word reached him of the fall of Abu Ageila and the advance of an Israeli armor force from that direction. Meanwhile, the Israeli air force pounded Egyptian positions until darkness. Throughout 6 June, undeterred by the aerial bombings, the 14th Armored Brigade, under the dogged command of Wassel, managed to keep the Israelis from advancing. Then at 1:00 A.M. Egyptian time on 7 June, Wassel received word to withdraw, which he accomplished with the first dawn.[33]

The situation looked increasingly desperate from Amer's perspective back in Cairo. At 4:30 P.M. Egyptian time on 6 June, Murtagui, the front commander, reported that he had come under attack by the Israeli air force and requested permission to move his command center to a safer location at the Giddi Pass. Amer gave his approval and informed other commands of this decision while Murtagui organized a move under the cover of darkness.[34] Bad news continued to reach Cairo throughout the day. Amer continued to micromanage his field army, constantly on the phone talking with officers down the chain of command, giving little latitude to his staff and field commanders.[35] Eventually, he broke under the pressure.

Sometime in the early evening on 6 June, Amer decided to order a general withdraw from the Sinai to the west bank of the Suez Canal. No doubt he broached this subject with Nasser, who must have agreed in principle to this momentous step. At 8:00 P.M. on 6 June, Amer began ordering his tactical units to conduct their pullback from the Sinai during a single night. The 6th Infantry Division, the 4th Armored Division, and the Shazli Task Force had not yet seen any major ground combat when Amer sounded the retreat and could have attempted an orderly withdrawal. But Amer failed to delineate any phases in the withdrawal; nor did he inform his front commander General Murtagui, who learned of this decision by chance from the chief of military police in the early hours of the morning on 7 June.[36] The EAF never recovered from Amer's grievous blunder.

Apparently, a number of Egyptian field commanders tried to salvage what they could out of a grave situation, but with no major effect. For example, the field army commander ordered the 4th Armored Division to secure control of the passes for the passage of retreating troops until noontime of the next day, 7 June. But the division had already reached the Suez Canal, and elements were crossing to the western bank.[37] Amer's catastrophic decision had eliminated any chance for the Egyptians to manage the battlefield. Confusion spread throughout field commands as many units now simply raced to the Suez Canal, in some cases outpaced only by their commanders. One Egyptian writer referred to these officers as "chocolate soldiers"—they looked good on the outside but melted under the heat of fire.[38]

In the early hours of the morning of 7 June, Amer reversed himself; he now devoted his energies to preventing the Israelis from reaching the Suez Canal. It had become painfully clear to both Nasser and Amer that there was no prospect of a diplomatic solution in the face of the advancing Israeli juggernaut. Instructions went out to the 4th Armored Division to stop its retreat and return to guard the passes, but it was too late. General Command's efforts now focused on stopping the Israelis west of the passes. On 7 June, General Muhammad Fawzi, the chief of the General Staff, journeyed to Ismailiya, where he met with the front commander, the field army commander, the chief of staff for the front command, and the air force commander for the Sinai. Within a short time, Fawzi discerned a "lack of will or desire for battle" in all these senior field commanders.[39] Unlike Fawzi, who had followed the war from the safety of Cairo, these senior officers possessed a direct experience of the rout taking place in the Sinai.

Though hopelessness and defeatism permeated the senior field commanders, Nasser still persisted in his hope of making the Israelis pay in blood for every step of their journey to the Suez Canal. Late on 7 June, the Egyptian president refused a UN offer of a cease-fire in place. Such defiance, though admirable under certain conditions, now only provided the IDF with additional time in which to conquer the entire Sinai. The only question was how effective the Israeli army would be in exploiting the Egyptian collapse.

THE ROUT

Through various intelligence sources, Israel's General Staff learned of Amer's general-withdrawal order and of the chaos spreading through the Egyptian army in the Sinai.[40] Events on other fronts allowed the IDF to press its gains in the Sinai to the maximum. Israeli pilots had destroyed much of the Jordanian and Syrian air forces on the first day of the war. On the northern front, Syria had refused to launch a major operation in support of Egypt, instead conducting harassing raids and low-level artillery exchanges. Since the first day of the war, the IDF had been conducting offensive operations against the Jordanians. By the end of the second day, the Israelis had made deep inroads into the West Bank; the Jordanian army was on the verge of collapse by the approach of the third day. All indications from the other two fronts, plus intelligence on the Egyptians, boded well for a major pursuit of the retreating Egyptian army in the Sinai.

Late on 6 June, Moshe Dayan, who feared a cease-fire imposed by the two superpowers, urged the capture of Sharm al-Shaykh, at the southern tip of the Sinai, without securing a land route. He had learned that Egyptian forces were in the process of evacuating the position. Having turned the closure of the Gulf of Aqaba into a reason for war, Dayan felt it only fitting to capture this strategic point before an imposed cease-fire. Late on 6 June, the General Staff scrambled to find enough paratroopers for a heliborne operation to occupy Sharm al-Shaykh. In the early afternoon of 7 June, approximately 150 Israeli paratroopers embarked for Sharm al-Shaykh, expecting to receive fire support from the Israeli navy. But Israel's naval craft were already at the scene; seeing no life at Sharm al-Shaykh, the navy commander landed a small force of sailors, who found the coastal positions completely abandoned. Consequently, the Israeli paratroop force landed at the airstrip without opposition in the early afternoon, and by evening the paratroopers were well on their way along the western coast of Sinai toward Ras Sudar.[41]

Meanwhile, Gavish formulated a bold plan for his three *ugdah* commanders—Tal, Yoffe, and Sharon—with the objective of destroying the retreating Egyptian army before it escaped the Sinai. Late on 6 June, after some discussion and exchanges of views with Tal and Yoffe, Gavish decided to take advantage of the EAF's collapse; he ordered Israeli units to outpace the retreating Egyptians to the passes and seal them. Tal was to take the central route, while Yoffe headed for the Giddi and Mitla Passes. In conjunction with the movement of these two *ugdot*, the Israeli air force was to conduct deep interdiction strikes at the passes. Sharon, for his part, would head in a different direction, southeast of Abu Ageila, to capture Qusaymah.[42] Only the insertion of Israeli paratroopers at the Giddi and Mitla Passes—timed to coincide with the arrival of Israeli tanks units—would have made for a more classic rout of an army in full retreat. But Dayan had already dispatched the only available paratroop brigade for the struggle to capture the city of Jerusalem, and the added risk seemed unnecessary.

Southern Command's audacity led to amazing success (see Map 9). Commencing in the morning on 7 June, the three Israeli *ugdot* fanned out like an expanding water torrent.[43] The Shadmi Armored Brigade received the mission of breaking through Bir al-Hasana. The Egyptian 3d Infantry Division offered little resistance, as most its units were already in high gear toward the Suez Canal. From Bir al-Hasana Yoffe expected Shadmi to dash for Mitla, while the Sela

ISRAEL'S BLITZKRIEG   61

Armored Brigade raced for Giddi. Israeli units now mixed with Egyptian forces as both drove desperately toward the passes leading out of central Sinai. Some Israeli junior commanders wanted to slow down, out of concern for dwindling supplies of fuel and ammunition, but there were always some Israelis who urged the units to continue onward.

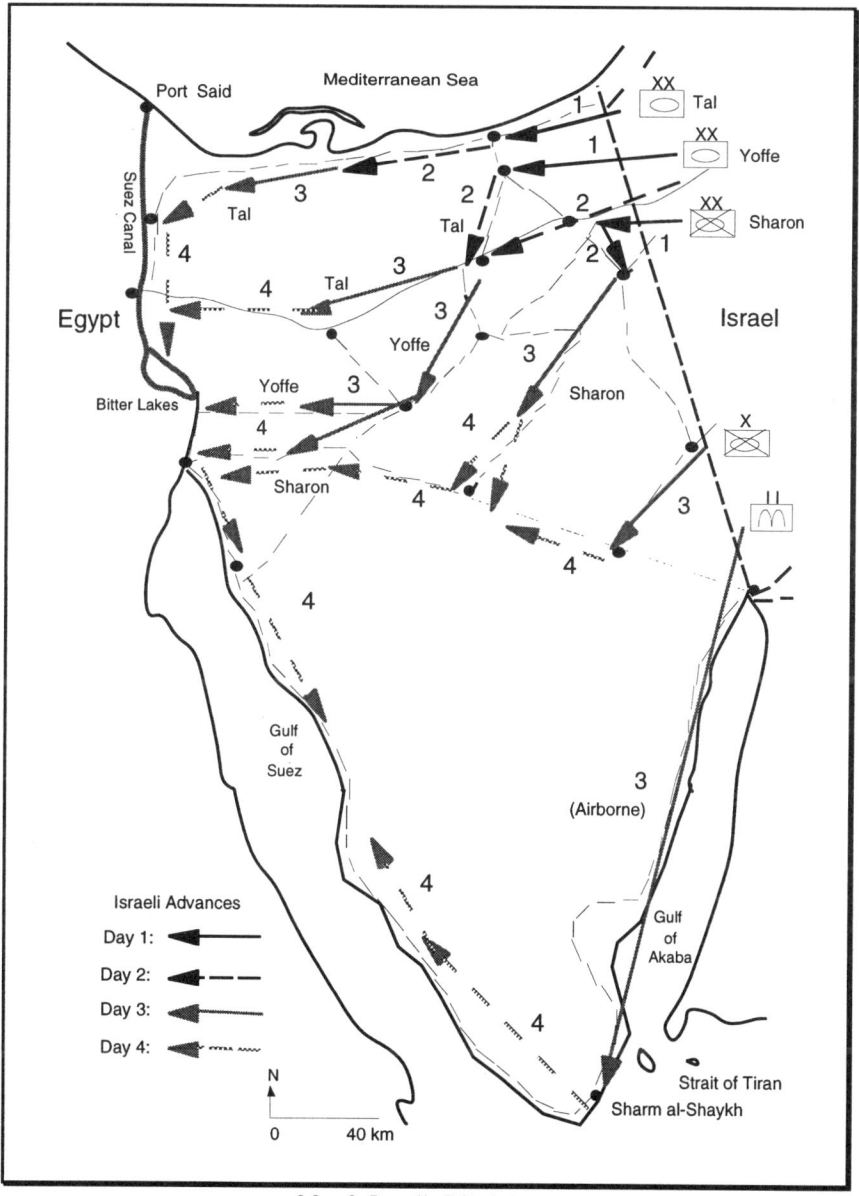

Map 9. Israel's Blitzkrieg.

With little Egyptian desire to stop and fight, Israeli units were able to advance unimpeded across large stretches of desert. In the early evening of 7 June, an Israeli force of only nine tanks (four out of fuel and being pulled by the others), two mechanized infantry platoons, and three half-tracks with 120-mm mortars reached the Mitla Pass. Fortunately for these Israelis, no Egyptian force guarded the pass. Establishing and maintaining a blocking position at the eastern entrance proved fairly easy. Retreating Egyptian units, instead of stopping to destroy this small Israeli force, sought either to break through or bypass it completely. Some Egyptians managed to get through, in many cases abandoning their vehicles in the process. Additional fuel and self-propelled artillery units joined the small Israeli force at Mitla, and fighting continued intermittently throughout the night. But in the early morning hours of 8 June, the Israeli air force entered the battle with continuous bombing missions, inflicting much damage on the road leading into the pass. Eventually, more reinforcements from the Sela Armored Brigade arrived to save this small force from extinction. It took the Israelis the good part of the remainder of 8 June to negotiate the twenty-eight-kilometer-long Mitla Pass.

Meanwhile, on 7 June, to the north of Mitla, another Israeli force, fourteen Centurions from the Sela Armored Brigade that had passed through Abu Ageila, had sealed the Giddi Pass. As before, the Egyptians erred grievously in not securing this pass for their retreating troops. In compliance with Amer's withdrawal order of 6 June, Colonel Kamal Hasan Ali, who had guarded the Giddi's eastern entrance for over twelve hours, had already withdrawn the Egyptian 2d Armored Brigade. General Command ordered him back into the pass on 8 June, but by then the Israelis had reached the western entrance. Retracing its path, Hasan Ali's lead battalion drew fire and pulled back, the brigade commander suffering a wound in the stomach during this final phase of the war.[44]

Sharon, for his part in the campaign, used the morning of 6 June to secure Abu Ageila. The remainder of day saw his *ugdah* take a much-needed rest, while Sharon awaited orders. These finally arrived late in the evening: take Qusaymah the following morning and then head for Nakhl to entrap any retreating elements of the Egyptian 6th Infantry Division.[45] But before embarking on his new missions, Sharon lost control of the Adam Infantry Brigade. Southern Command needed infantry to remove pockets of Egyptian resistance in the northeastern corner of the Sinai; it dispatched Adam to al-Arish. Arriving there by bus, Adam began a systematic sweep of the city for snipers, losing several officers in the operation. Part of the infantry brigade moved to Giradi and Shaykh Zuwayd to conduct the same mission in those places.

On the morning of 7 June, Sharon began executing his orders. The Baidatz Infantry Brigade was to advance on Qusaymah from the east, while Sharon gathered together all available armor to attack the Egyptian rear along the route from Umm Qatef. Expecting a battle, the Israelis discovered, much to their surprise, that the Egyptian 10th Infantry Brigade, along with the headquarters of the 2d Infantry Division, had already departed, leaving equipment buried in the sand. In fact, Naguib, the Egyptian division commander, had crossed to the west bank of the Suez Canal in the early hours of that morning.[46] The Egyptian general had forsaken the battle for Abu Ageila and Qusaymah in less than thirty-six hours.

In rapid fashion, Sharon departed Qusaymah for Nakhl with the Zippori Armored and the Baidatz Infantry Brigades. At one point his men came under fire from elements of the Sela Armored Brigade, which mistook the Israeli *ugdah* for an Egyptian unit. They received a few casualties from this friendly fire, but the Israelis managed to avert a major disaster. Because the Shazli Task Force had vacated the Gebel Kharim and Matalla area in the general withdrawal order, Sharon was able to reach north of Nakhl by midnight. A major surprise awaited Sharon in the morning on 8 June: the Egyptians had even withdrawn their force from Nakhl. Sharon quickly established east of the road juncture a killing zone for the Egyptian 6th Infantry Division in retreat from Kuntilla. The Israeli trap proved quite successful, destroying some 150 vehicles, some of them thanks to the intervention of the Israeli air force. After regrouping his *ugdah*, Sharon turned for Mitla, reaching this strategic pass on 9 June.

On the central route, Tal encountered serious Egyptian resistance in his westward advance to the Suez Canal.[47] Both his armored brigades moved in tandem toward Rod Bir Salim where Tal decided to give Gonen a rest. The Aviram Armored Brigade would now form the spearhead in the capture of Bir Gifgafa. Here in the midafternoon Aviram's AMX-13s ran into trouble against the superior, Soviet-made T-55s. The French-made AMX-13 tanks had to maneuver to hit the T-55s on a flank, for direct shots on the front bounced off. The situation became quite threatening for the Israelis. Fortunately for Aviram, a tank company of Shermans and one of Centurions managed to extricate the AMX-13 battalion.

Again Tal turned to the Gonen Armored Brigade to lead the *ugdah's* advance, this time through the Khatimiya Pass, while the Aviram Armored Brigade secured the Bir Gifgafa area. Beyond the western entrance to the pass, the Israelis ran into an Egyptian ambush prepared by elements of the 3d Armored Brigade, from the 4th Armored Division. To outsmart the Egyptians, the Israelis sent one tank force down the center route while a second outflanked them from the north, in the process knocking out Egyptian tanks from the rear. Despite the victory, Tal later noted for the press that it had taken his brigade six hours to advance just seven kilometers.[48]

On the northern route, Granit Force encountered its own set of problems, beginning at Romana, some sixty kilometers east of Qantara, on the Suez Canal.[49] In this sector of the Sinai, the character of the war changed somewhat. Throughout 8 June, a handful of the Egyptian combat planes now contested the skies and even provided ground support, conducting as many as thirty-two sorties, according to Arab accounts. This air support strengthened Egyptian resolve on the ground and required Israeli pilots to engage in dogfights to maintain control of the skies. As noted by Tal of this phase of the campaign, "Our Air Force intervened and helped turn the scales in our favor."[50] Moreover, on the ground, Egyptians put up a stiff defense with a combination of *sa'iqa* (commandos),

64   THE ALBATROSS OF DECISIVE VICTORY

paratroopers, infantry, T-55 tanks, and artillery. Finally, even the Egyptian navy got involved briefly, when naval boats near Port Said fired several missiles at Israeli positions.

Near Romana, Granit Task Force engaged in a two-hour battle before it could resume its advance. About eighteen kilometers from Qantara East, another Egyptian blocking position stopped Granit Force for several hours. This time Granit had to rely on timely assistance from Eitan's paratroopers, who had completed their fight in Gaza and returned to Tal's command. Eitan, who brought with him a paratroop battalion on half-tracks and a tank company of Pattons, took command of Granit Force. After an hour of fighting he suffered a head wound and was evacuated back to Israel. Lieutenant Colonel Pihotka, Eitan's second in command, would later praise some Egyptian efforts as "deeds of unusual bravery and enterprise."[51] But after several hours of intense ground fighting and numerous strikes by Israeli aircraft, the Egyptians withdrew around midday. They managed to conduct one more defense at al-Mutallat, some six to eight kilometers from Qantara, before abandoning all resistance in the Qantara area. In the morning of 9 June, Granit Force and the paratroopers linked up with Gonen's armor force near Ismailiya.

Strategically, events had gotten out of control for Israel. Originally, Dayan had wanted to keep the land campaign limited to the Mitla, Giddi, and Khatimiya Passes, out of the conviction that control of the Suez Canal would bring unwanted international complications, even possible Soviet intervention. On 6 June, the Israeli cabinet accepted this territorial limitation, reaffirming its decision midmorning on 7 June. Later in the evening, before the Security Council went into session to adopt a cease-fire resolution, Dayan dismissed his earlier political concerns and permitted Israeli forces to continue to the Suez Canal.[52] By then, a number of Israeli units had already advanced through the passes. Weizman, the chief of operations, noted later how military events outpaced political decisions: "The war was a rapid one.... Several of the most important political and military accomplishments were created by field commanders."[53]

Nasser, meanwhile, seemed determined to delay the inevitable. Having once refused a cease-fire, he finally realized on 8 June that reverses on the battlefield west of the passes had ensured the Israeli capture of the entire Sinai; shortly before midnight, therefore, he agreed to a cessation of hostilities. By this time, Israeli units were at the Suez Canal. The Sinai campaign was essentially over in four days, although Gavish officially informed Dayan of the conclusion of the Sinai campaign at 5:15 A.M. on June 9th.

This good news for Israel had its effect on the course of the entire war. Until this point, Dayan had resisted all pressure, both civilian and military, to order a full-scale attack to capture the Golan Heights. As late as 10:00 A.M. on 8 June, the Israeli cabinet had agreed to postpone any decision on this matter. Now, Dayan changed his mind. At 7:00 in the morning, he ordered Brigadier General David Elazar, in charge of Northern Command, to commence military operations against Syria. Eshkol was miffed when he was informed of Dayan's action; Rabin learned of the decision from Elazar; and the Israeli cabinet gave its approval at its session that commenced at 9:30 that morning.[54] Within two days, the IDF had added the Golan to its conquests.

On the international front, both superpowers had assumed a low-key role. The United States eschewed chastising the Israelis for starting the war and graciously forgave Israel when Israeli pilots mistakenly attacked the American spy ship U.S.S. Liberty on 8 June, some fourteen nautical miles north of al-Arish. Thirty-four Americans lost their lives, and 171 suffered wounds in what still remains a tragic incident, one shrouded in mystery and controversy. To help avert a confrontation with the USSR, President Johnson resorted to the "hot line" several times in order to maintain dialogue with Soviet leaders in the Kremlin. The Soviets, for their part, offered moral support to the Arabs but refused to get involved militarily to save them. Soviet military supplies would begin arriving only after the cessation of hostilities. Responsibility for the results on the battlefield thus fell squarely on the shoulders of the combatants themselves.

Egyptian losses were staggering. Some ten thousand Egyptian officers and soldiers were killed in action. The Egyptian army lost 80 percent of its equipment, including over seven hundred tanks out of nine hundred.[55] The Israeli air force destroyed over 330 Egyptian combat planes, to forty-six of its own, on three fronts. Egypt lost 85% of its combat aircraft, including 100% of its bomber fleet. Against Egypt's huge losses, Israel lost only 338 killed and 132 tanks destroyed.[56] This great disparity in human and material losses, coupled with the Israeli acquisition of sixty-one thousand square kilometers of the Sinai, signified a decisive military victory for Israel. For Egyptians, the war was a national humiliation and disgrace.

CONCLUSION

Israel's stunning Blitzkrieg resulted from a unique set of circumstances. Perhaps most importantly, the Egyptians cooperated in helping Israel win in lightning fashion. Egypt's political and military leaders made serious mistakes before and during the war. In the three weeks prior to hostilities, Nasser and Amer failed to coordinate their political and military decisions to ensure a unity of effort and purpose in war. Militarily, General Command changed war plans, its command system, senior personnel, and troop deployments in ways that seriously impaired the army's ability to fight against a powerful foe. These changes spread such confusion throughout the EAF that by the eve of the conflict, senior Egyptian field commanders seemed more concerned about events in Cairo than those in Tel Aviv. Tactically, division commanders at both Rafah and Abu Ageila failed to take appropriate measures to secure their northern flanks.

More major mistakes were made during the conflict itself. Despite Israeli successes on the ground within the first twenty-four hours of the war, Egypt's General Command still had other options than a general withdrawal with no phase lines. Amer could have attempted a phased withdrawal from the Sinai over two or three nights under the cover of darkness; or he could have ordered a hasty defense at the Romana, Khatimiya, Giddi, and Mitla. Either course of action, if successful for even a couple of days, might have invited superpower intervention to force an Israeli halt to military operations, a distinct possibility, especially since the Israeli cabinet had initially meant to stop short of the Suez Canal. Certainly the Israelis would have suffered more casualties in either scenario, and the Egyptians, for their part, would have saved some face. Despite such viable options, Amer panicked and ordered a general withdrawal to be executed in one night, a decision that brought about the complete rout of his army.

Taking advantage of the Egyptian mistakes, the IDF conducted a bold and imaginative campaign that unraveled the sinews of command in Egypt in Blitzkrieg fashion. In three hours, the Israeli air force established air superiority in a brilliantly executed first strike that left most of the Egypt's air force destroyed on the tarmac. This aerial success represented the culmination of years of planning, preparation, and training. For ground operations, Israel's military culture favored a faster tempo for waging war than that of the Egyptians. Israeli doctrine emphasized the offense, taking the war into the adversary's territory as soon as possible. Leadership training encouraged initiative and improvisation at lower levels of command, a style that exploited tactical and operational opportunities with audacity and speed.

In addition to its better preparation for war than the EAF, the IDF greatly benefited from the May crisis. The three weeks allowed the Israeli army to conduct realistic training exercises and develop force structures for the forward and deep battles. Each *ugdah* was designed specifically to conduct its particular mission. Moreover, the political crisis in Israel eventually led to the appointment of Dayan as war minister. His final touches on the war plans helped precondition a decisive victory, rather than the more limited objectives of previous plans.

Strategically, the Israelis deceived Amer into believing the main effort would be in the south. Tactically, smart planning and rigorous training for the forward battles allowed the Israelis to capture Rafah, al-Arish, and Abu Ageila so quickly that Egypt's General Command never recovered the initiative. Operationally, the silent infiltration of an armored brigade to a blocking position at Bir Lahfan completely surprised the Egyptians, prevented them from reinforcing al-Arish, and set the stage for the destruction of the Egyptian army in central Sinai. In actual combat, the dogged determination of Israeli tactical commanders translated all these advantages into a decisive victory on the battlefield. Gavish's decision to race to the passes ahead of the retreating Egyptians provided the final touch to a brilliant campaign.

Successes on the Sinai front expanded Israel's political aims in the war. On 6 June, the Israeli cabinet approved offensive operations against Jordan. The collapse of the Egyptian army, coupled with the conquest of the West Bank from Jordan, encouraged Dayan to throw caution to the wind and permit the capture of the Suez Canal as well as the assault on the Golan Heights. Serious losses in battles against the Egyptians might have prevented the opening of another front against the Syrians. But it was difficult to resist the juggernaut of military success. Both decisions increased Israel's territorial gains. Egypt lost the entire Sinai, including the east bank of the Suez Canal, whereas Syria suffered the humiliation of losing the Golan Heights. Both developments helped shape the character of the next Arab-Israeli war.

NOTES

1. Carl von Clausewitz, *On War*, edited and translated by Michael Howard and Peter Paret (Princeton, NJ: Princeton University Press, 1984): 99.

2. André Beaufre, "Une Guerre Classique Moderne: La Guerre Israëlo-Arabe," *Strategie* (July–August 1967): 19.

3. Yitzhak Rabin, *The Rabin Memoirs* (Boston: Little, Brown, 1979): 101–102; Edward N. Luttwak and Daniel Horowitz, *The Israeli Army, 1948–1973* (New York: University of America Press, 1983): 225–231; Ehud Yonay, *No Margin for Error: The Making of the Air Force* (New York: Pantheon Books, 1993): 228–258; and Eliezer Cohen, *Israel's Best Defense* (New York: Orion Books, 1993): 191–253.

4. Abd al-Latif al-Baghdadi, *Mudhakirat Abd al-Latif al-Baghdadi*, II (Cairo: al-Maktab al-Misri al-Hadith, 1977): 285.

5. Muhammad Fawzi, *Harb al-Thalath Sanawat 1967–1970* (Beirut: Dar al-Wahda, 1983): 128, 134–135; Salah al-Din al-Hadidi, *Shahid ala Harb 1967* (Cairo: Dar al-Shuruq, 1974): 184–188; Muhammad Abd al-Ghani al-Gamasi, *Mudhakirat al-Gamasi: Harb Oktobir 1973* (Paris: al-Munshurat al-Sharqiyya, 1990): 80, 84; and Amin Huwaydi, *Adwa ala Ashab Naksa wa ala Harb al-Istiznaf* (Beirut: Dar al-Taliah, 1975): 62–63.

6. Gamasi, *Mudhakirat*: 89.

7. Emanuel Wald, *The Wald Report: The Decline of Israeli National Security Since 1967* (Boulder, CO: Westview Press, 1992): 254, n. 8; Cohen, *Israel's Best Defense*: 252; and Yonay, *No Margin for Error*: 265.

8. On prewar developments in this area, see Fawzi, *Harb al-Thalath Sanawat*: 90–91, 102–108; and Mahmud Azmi, *al-Quwwat al-Mudarra'a al-Israiliyya abr Arbaa Hurub* (Beirut: Munazzama al-Tahrir al-Filatiniyya, 1975): 290–292.

9. Trevor Dupuy, *Elusive Victory: The Arab-Israeli Wars, 1947–1974* (1978, reprint Fairfax, VA: Hero Books, 1984): 239.

10. Material for the following narrative of the battles for Rafah and al-Arish comes from numerous sources, including ibid.: 248–255; Shabtai Teveth, *The Tanks of Tammuz* (New York: Viking Press, 1968): 121–205; Hasan Mustafa, *Harb Haziran 1967*, I (Beirut: al-Mu'assasa lil-Dirsat wa al-Nashr, 1973): 122–162; Samuel Seguev, *La Guerre de Six Jours* (Paris: Calmann-Levy, 1967): 129–142; Luttwak and Horowitz, *The Israeli Army*: 236–244; and David Eshel, *Chariots of Fire: The Story of the Israeli Armor Corps* (London: Brassey's, 1989): 60–72.

11. Azmi, *al-Quwwat al-Mudarraa al-Israiliyya:* 217.

12. Israel Defense Forces, *Commanders of the Six Day War and Their Battle Reports* (Tel Aviv: Ramdor, 1967): 70.

13. Teveth, *Tanks of Tammuz:* 189.

14. Mustafa, *Harb Haziran 1967*, I: 143; Fawzi, *Harb al-Thalath Sanawat*: 160; and Muhammad Hasanayn Haykal, *1967: al-Infijar* (Cairo: Markaz al-Ahram, 1990): 1089.

15. Teveth, *Tanks of Tammuz:* 167.

16. Edgar O'Ballance, *The Third Arab-Israeli War* (Hamden: Archon, 1972): 117.

17. For a detailed analysis of the battle of Abu Ageila, see George W. Gawrych, *Key to the Sinai: The Battles for Abu Ageila in the 1956 and 1967 Arab-Israeli Wars* (Fort Leavenworth: Combat Studies Institute, 1990): 80–122, and "The Egyptian Military Defeat of 1967," *Journal of Contemporary History* 26 (1991): 277–305.

18. Natke Nir, phone conversation with author, 5 October 1987.

19. Ibid.

20. *Official Egyptian Military Sources* [henceforth cited as *OEMS*].

21. Ibid.

22. Ibid.

23. This important part of the Israeli campaign plan and execution has received only scant attention in the military literature. Avraham Adan, interview with author, 30 June 1994, Tel Aviv; Teveth, *Tanks of Tammuz:* 207–213; Mordekhay Barkai (ed.), *Written in Battle: The Six-Day War as Told by the Fighters Themselves* (Tel Aviv: Le'Dory, 1964): 108–111; Dupuy, *Elusive Victory*: 263–264; O'Ballance, *The Third Arab-Israeli War:* 101; Luttwak and Horowitz, *The Israeli Army:* 238; Gunther E. Rothenberg, *The Anatomy of the Israel Army* (New York: Hippocrene Books, 1979): 138; and David Dayan, *Strike First!* 59. For Yoffe's own statements to the press after the war see, Israel Defense Forces, *Commanders of the Six Day War and Their Battle Reports* (Tel Aviv: Ramdor, 1967): 59–60.

24. Adan, interview; Teveth, *Tanks of Tammuz:* 208–212; O'Ballance, *The Third Arab-Israeli War:* 135; and Meir Pa'il, *The IDF Campaign against Abu Ageila in Three Wars* (Tel Aviv: IDF, n.d.): map 6.

25. Mustafa, *Harb Haziran 1967*, I: 203–209; Dupuy, *Elusive Victory:* 240; Fawzi, *Harb al-Thalath Sanawat*: 145, 147. For an Israeli version of the battle, see Teveth, *Tanks of Tammuz:* 207–213.

26. Abd al-Mohsen Kamil Murtagui, *al-Fariq Murtagui Rawiya al-Haqa'iq* (Cairo: Dar al-Watan al-Arabi, 1976): 148–149.

27. Amnon Reshef, interview with author, 30 June 1994, Tel Aviv. Reshef was the brigade's operations chief.

28. Murtagui, *al-Fariq Murtagui*: 153; and Kamal Hasan Ali, *Mudarrabun wa Mufawwadun* (Cairo: al-Ahram, 1986): 36. Kamal Hasan Ali commanded the 2d Armored Brigade during the war.

29. Haykal, *1967: al-Infijar*: 729–731.

30. Fawzi, *Harb al-Thalath Sanawat*: 147–148; Murtagui, *al-Fariq Murtagui*: 159–161; and Ali, *Mudarrabun*: 36.

31. Teveth, *Tanks of Tammuz*: 215–218; Dupuy, *Elusive Victory*: 253–255, 263–264; and O'Ballance, *The Third Arab-Israeli War*: 136–139.

32. Moshe Dayan, *Moshe Dayan: The Story of My Life* (New York: William and Morrow, 1976): 364.

33. Abd al-Munim Wassel, "Ma'raka Gebel Libni 'Anqadat al-Quwwat al-Misriyya," *Oktobir* 34 (19 June 1977): 30–31; Mustafa, *Harb Haziran 1967*, I: 207, 214–219; and Seguev, *La Guerre de Six Jours*: 163–164.

34. Murtagui, *al-Fariq Murtagui*: 162–163; and Gamasi, *Mudhakirat al-Gamasi*: 78, 103.

35. Baghdadi, *Mudhakirat*, II: 284, 286.

36. Fawzi, *Harb al-Thalath Sanawat*: 150–159; Murtagui, *al-Fariq Murtagui*: 163, 183–188; Gamasi, *Mudhakirat*: 103; and Huwaydi, *'Adwa 'ala Asbab Naksa 1967*: 69.

37. Fawzi, *Harb al-Thalath Sanawat*: 153; and Ali, *Mudarrabun*: 37.

38. Muhammad Hasanayn Haykal, *Road to Ramadan* (New York: Quadrangle, 1975): 179.

39. Fawzi, *Harb al-Thalath Sanawat*: 157; and Murtagui, *al-Fariq Murtagui*: 178–180. Murtagui talks of a meeting on 8 June.

40. Katz, *Soldier Spies*: 190–191.

41. Moshe Dayan, *Moshe Dayan*: 362; Rabin, *The Rabin Memoirs*: 107–108; Ezer Weizman, *On Eagles' Wings* (New York: Macmillan, 1976): 247–251; Mustafa, *Harb Haziran 1967*, I: 257–258; and O'Ballance, *The Third-Arab-Israeli War*: 151–152.

42. Teveth, *Tanks of Tammuz*: 222–225; Herzog, *Arab-Israeli Wars*: 160–161; Luttwak and Horowitz, *The Israeli Army*: 249–250; and Dupuy, *Elusive Victory*: 270–271. Sharon implies that he never participated in that meeting: Ariel Sharon, *Warrior: The Autobiography of Ariel Sharon* (New York: Simon and Shuster, 1989): 202.

43. Teveth, *Tanks of Tammuz*: 228–231; Mustafa, *Harb Haziran 1967*, I: 226–228, 239–241; Seguev, *La Guerre de Six Jours*: 164–167; David Dayan, *Strike First!* 99–101; O'Ballance, *The Third Arab-Israeli War*: 146–149, 160–162; Eshel, *Chariots of the Desert*: 75–77; and Dupuy, *Elusive Victory*: 272–274.

44. Ali, *Mudarrabun*: 38–39.

45. For material of the saga of Sharon's *ugdah* on 7 and 8 June, see Yaël Dayan, *Israel Journal: June 1967* (New York: McGraw-Hill, 1967): 70–90; O'Ballance, *The Third Arab-Israeli War*: 149–151, 161–163; Mustafa, *Harb Haziran 1967*, I: 228–239; Sharon, *Warrior*: 194–201; IDF, *Commanders of the Six Day War*: 82–83; and Dupuy, *Elusive Victory*: 275–277.

46. Murtagui, *al-Fariq Murtagui*: 169.

47. Teveth, *Tanks of Tammuz*: 231–248; Mustafa, *Harb Haziran 1967*, I: 241–249; Eshel, *Chariots of the Desert*: 76–77; Seguev, *La Guerre de Six Jours*: 168–171; and Fawzi, *Harb al-Thalath Sanawat*: 150.

48. Daniel Dishon (ed), *Middle East Record 1967* (Jerusalem: Keter Publishing House, 1971): 221. For identification of the Egyptian unit, see Fawzi, *Harb al-Thalath Sanawat*: 150.

49. Mustafa, *Harb Haziran 1967*, I: 249–253; O'Ballance, *The Third Arab-Israeli War*: 156–157; and Teveth, *Tanks of Tammuz*: 248.

50. Dishon, *Middle East Record 1967*: 221.

51. IDF, *Commanders of the Six Day War*: 95.

52. Michael Brecher, *Decisions in Crisis: Israel, 1967 and 1973* (Berkeley: University of California Press, 1980): 253, 259–261, 269–270, 273–275; Moshe Dayan, *Moshe Dayan*: 363; Sharon, *Warrior*: 229; and Yaacov Bar-Siman Tov, "The Bar Lev Line Revisited," *Journal of Strategic Studies* 11 (June 1988): 150.

53. Ezer Weizman, *Battle for Peace* (New York: Bantam Books, 1981): 55.

54. Moshe Dayan, *Moshe Dayan*: 330; Rabin, *The Rabin Memoirs*: 114–116; Hanoch Bartov, *Dado: 48 Years and 20 Days* (Tel Aviv: Ma'ariv, 1981): 100–109; and Brecher, *Decisions in Crisis*: 254, 280.

55. Fawzi, *Harb al-Thalath Sanawat*: 161; and Mustafa, *Harb Haziran 1967*, I: 261.

56. Paper by Colonel Benny Michelsohn, Chief, Military History Department, Israel Defense Forces; and Dupuy, *Elusive Victory*: 333.

3

THE EGYPTIAN PHOENIX

That the quality of the military order and the effectiveness of the army are influenced by the political regime and the national psychology cannot be doubted.
—Raymond Aron[1]

And the tragedy was not that they had lost the war but that they had lost it without heroism.
—Halim Barakat[2]

The Six Day War brought to Egypt the bitter pill of humiliating defeat and to Israel the sweet fragrance of decisive victory. A puny David had emasculated the giant Goliath before the eyes of the entire world. In Egypt, the devastating defeat shook the very foundations of the state and society. Eighty percent of the Egyptian army's equipment remained behind in the Sinai, and thousands of soldiers, rather than returning to their units, struggled back to their villages after crossing the Suez Canal. Only a handful of viable combat formations stood between the waterway and Cairo. The sheer magnitude of the Israeli triumph suggested that Israel had gained a generation's respite before the Arabs could ever seriously contemplate challenging the IDF in a major war. This assessment proved wrong. Israel's decisive victory on the battlefield failed to produce any appreciable movement toward peace between Arabs and Israelis. In fact, Arab determination to defy Israel hardened rather than softened after the Six Day War.

Egypt led in this regard. Egyptian national pride refused to accept any postwar settlement on Israel's terms. The Egyptians had lost the entire Sinai to Israel, but the heart of Egypt and its population still lay beyond the reach of Israeli ground troops. Defiance and reconstruction could thus exist at a relatively safe distance from the new border along the Suez Canal. Nasser, despite suffering a devastating military defeat, proved the consummate survivalist, demonstrating an uncanny ability to maintain his political power. Moreover, he helped direct a major overhaul of the EAF designed to enhance professionalism and combat effectiveness, thus laying, in no small measure, the foundation for the next Arab-Israeli war. Without the political and military reforms implemented by Nasser in the three years after the Six Day War, his successor would have been at greater disadvantage when embarking on war in October 1973.

RISING FROM THE ASHES

On 8 June, as the full extent of the Egyptian defeat dawned on him, President Gamal Abd al-Nasser faced the dilemma of how to confront the Israeli victory. He decided to shoulder blame for the military debacle and resign his office. Given the magnitude of the defeat, this momentous step should have spelled the end of his political career. Yet, such proved not to be the case. Overnight, Nasser turned into a national hero, and he returned to power. The last three years of his life were spent rebuilding the very armed forces he had helped destroy by prematurely leading them into a war against Israel.

On 9 June at 7:30 P.M., Nasser addressed the Egyptian nation. In a highly emotional speech, he portrayed himself as less the guilty party and more the innocent victim. Yet, there was no skirting the magnitude of the defeat: "We cannot hide from ourselves the fact that we have met with a grave setback (*naksa*) in the last few days." But the effort had begun nobly, in support of Syria. If Egypt had not offered military assistance to the Syrians, Israel would have eventually threatened Egyptian national security. "Who starts with Syria will finish with Egypt."

Despite some candor in his speech, Nasser did explain away a good part of the defeat by foreign intrigues and the participation of American and British aircraft. According to his calculations, the UAR and the other Arab states had confronted an air force three times the Israeli air force's normal strength. In the end, however, he had to accept blame for the defeat: "I tell you truthfully that I am ready to assume the entire responsibility." Tendering his resignation to the entire nation, Nasser promised to carry on the struggle as a private citizen.[3]

The speech resulted in instant political rehabilitation. It roused the Egyptian nation: not only the words but the manner of delivery. During the address, Nasser, once a pillar of confidence, appeared a broken man. Tears filled his eyes, and the once magnetic voice at times palpably shook. The embodiment of charismatic authority among Arabs now stood humbled before the Egyptian nation and the entire world. But who could fill his giant shoes? The Egyptian people refused to envision anyone else being able to steer the country out of its predicament; nor would they allow Israel the luxury of forcing a political change in Egypt through war. The speech unexpectedly ignited the nation's passions. The very people who had supported Nasser on the path to war now called upon him to manage the aftermath of defeat.

Bowing to the national will, Nasser returned to the presidency on 10 June, the day after his resignation, promising to eliminate the effects of the 1967 war. Acting as if he were the beneficiary of a popular referendum, Nasser seized the moment and moved quickly to address a major problem in that conflict: that he had lost clear authority over the armed forces. As discussed in an earlier chapter, effective control over the military prior had passed to Amer. Amer, although Nasser's close friend, had transformed the institution into his own personal fiefdom, encouraging the growth of cliques (*shilla*) or power centers (*markazat al-quwwat*) that depended on him for patronage. This personalized system of leadership spawned a promotion policy that favored loyalty over merit, with professionalism of the officer corps suffering as a direct result.[4] If Egypt ever hoped to wage a war against Israel effectively, with a unity of effort and purpose, Nasser needed to reassert presidential control over the military and depoliticize its officer corps.

Popular acclaim for Nasser's return allowed for a purge of the top military brass. On 10 June, armed with a mandate from the people, Nasser accepted the resignations of both Amer and Badran (the minister of war) and then removed virtually all the four-star generals, including the commanders of the air force, the navy, and the ground forces. A number of major generals and other senior officers also lost their jobs over the next several months. To consolidate his control over the armed forces, Nasser promoted a number of trusted men to the most senior positions in the high command. General Muhammad Fawzi, the chief of the General Staff, replaced Amer as the commander in chief of the armed forces; Lieutenant General Abd al-Munim Riyad, commander of the Jordanian front in the 1967 war, assumed Fawzi's position.

Firing Amer proved unpopular among many senior and junior officers, especially those who owed their careers to the former field marshal. These officers resented Nasser turning Amer and the armed forces into scapegoats for his own mistakes. Clearly, ultimate responsibility for the 1967 defeat rested upon the shoulders of Nasser himself. After all, he had mortgaged Egypt's future by a number of high-risk steps that had directly led to the outbreak of hostilities.

Feeling wronged by the political leadership, Badran began planning with a number of active and retired officers to bring back Amer, who apparently gave at least his tacit approval to the coup plotting. Before the conspirators could act, however, the regime struck; on 25 August 1967, it arrested some fifty senior officers and civilians and placed Amer under strict house arrest. By this action Nasser consolidated his control over the military, paving the way for substantive reform of the armed forces. Amer conveniently died on 14 September, a suicide according to the official reports, though many doubted the veracity of the government's version and suspected foul play.

While gradually establishing clear authority over the armed forces, Nasser also took steps to strengthen his control over the state apparatus. A reorganization of the government in 1964 had created a two-tiered structure. Below the president stood a varying number of vice presidents, each holding responsibility over a certain sphere of public affairs; under them was the cabinet. In this arrangement, Nasser and the vice presidents formulated policy, while the cabinet mainly executed their decisions. On 19 June 1967, Nasser redesigned the cabinet system, taking on the post of prime minister as well. He also eliminated the host of vice presidents so that the president worked directly with the cabinet, thereby removing an unnecessary layer of government. Nasser also strengthened his control over the Arab Socialist Union, the official political party, by assuming the position of general secretary in June 1967. These political reforms, designed to strengthen Nasser's power over the state, complemented those in the military sphere.

With more effective presidential control over the armed forces and the state, Nasser could devote his attention to rebuilding the Egyptian army. Virtually every morning for the next three years, Nasser met with Fawzi to inform himself of military development; he held periodic meetings with officers on the front and regularly attended military maneuvers.[5] Such presidential involvement enhanced Egypt's ability to conduct a war against Israel with a unity of purpose and effort. Upon Nasser's death, Anwar Sadat was thus able to inherit a strong and focused presidency, thereby easing his own journey to the 1973 war.

ARMY AND THE JULY REVOLUTION

Although Nasser had received national absolution for his errors in the Six Day War, the magnitude of the 1967 defeat changed Egypt. Shock waves and tremors reverberated throughout the state and society, cruelly intruding into the lives of virtually all Egyptians. Few Egyptians could ignore the adverse effects of the military catastrophe. As many as ten thousand Egyptian soldiers lay dead in the Sinai, with countless others having suffered wounds or war shock. In addition to the staggering human losses from the Six Day War, Egypt now faced an entirely new strategic situation. Israeli forces controlled the east bank of the Suez Canal, preventing Egypt from deriving badly needed transit revenues from the waterway. Furthermore, only a few Egyptian units and 120 kilometers separated Cairo from Israeli ground forces. Finally, the Israeli air force could fly over Egyptian skies at will; Egypt lacked sufficient numbers of war planes to challenge Israeli pilots for air supremacy. For all practical purposes, Egypt stood defenseless before Israel's military might.

The magnitude of the defeat forced a redefinition of the military's role as established in the 1952 revolution. Nasser had relied on the army to be his primary engine of change for transforming Egypt. The armed forces had thus functioned as more than a military institution, designed to defend the country from foreign aggression; they had also served as an instrument for controlling non-military institutions of society. In the process, the military turned into more a political than a professional army, concerned with helping to transform society in accordance with the evolving ideology and policies of the 1952 revolution. The EAF was now required to devote its full attention to reconstruction if there was to be any hope of redressing its serious internal problems. Consequently, shortly after the June war, Nasser met with his new commander in chief, General Fawzi, and "changed the mission of the armed forces from ensuring the regime and the Revolution to another mission, the liberation (*tahrir*) of the [occupied] land and the elimination of the vestiges of the aggression."[6] This directive was designed to depoliticize the military by reorienting its attention away from domestic concerns and toward confronting the Israeli threat to Egypt's national security.

To help focus the military's energies on national defense, Fawzi discarded many noncombat activities that had been conducted for the sake of the 1952 revolution. For example, the military transferred responsibility for customs and the war against narcotics to the interior ministry; inspection of fish and poultry to the supply ministry; and the tilling of fifty thousand *feddans* of farmland to the agricultural ministry. Management of Cairo's transportation system returned to the municipal government.[7] Hoping to obviate military involvement in internal security and riot control, the government established the Central Security Force (CSF), a paramilitary force designed to support the police in the maintenance of public order. Under the control of the interior minister, the CSF numbered a hundred thousand by Nasser's death, increasing to over three hundred thousand under Sadat.

The elimination of noncombat functions strengthened the distinction between the military and civilian worlds in Egyptian society, freeing the armed forces to focus their attention and energies on preparing for the liberation of the Sinai from Israel. A clear threat and mission allowed the army to orient itself toward solving tactical and operational problems. In this, the Soviets played an important role.

Clearly, no major reconstruction would have been possible without massive Soviet military and economic assistance. Even before the conclusion of the Six Day War, the Kremlin had committed the USSR to support its Arab allies, Egypt and Syria, as a counter to US assistance to Israel. Upon Nasser's resignation speech on 9 June, the Soviets almost immediately wired Cairo urging a change of mind and promising the dispatch of a high-level delegation as soon as possible. According to the Egyptian president's personal secretary who had been in that position since 1959, this Soviet communiqué had a very positive effect on Nasser, for it implied a commitment to help Egypt rebuild after its devastating defeat.[8] The Cold War rivalry between the two superpowers certainly dictated such Soviet support, precisely because the United States backed Israel.

The USSR commenced its military resupply of Egypt on 9 June, the day Nasser offered his resignation to the nation. By air and sea, the Soviets sent supplies to Egypt. Over fifty thousand tons of weapons and equipment, including twenty-five MiG-21s and ninety-three MiG-17s, rapidly reached Egypt. This Herculean effort involved some 550 air flights and fifteen ships racing to resupply Egypt. Such concrete support strengthened Nasser's will not to accept the effects of the defeat as permanent.

On 16 June 1967, in the midst of this transport activity, a military delegation arrived in Egypt to assess the needs of the EAF. Then on 21 June, President Nikolai Podgorni and Marshal Matei Zukharov, the Soviet chief of the General

Staff, came to Cairo. Direct talks with Nasser about Soviet support took place over two days, 22 and 23 June. The Soviet president promised to supply Egypt with an additional forty MiG-21s, six MiG-21 trainers, thirty-eight Sukhoi fighter-bombers, and one hundred tanks. Furthermore, he agreed to send between a thousand and 1,200 Soviet military advisors and experts to help in the reconstruction of the Egyptian army.[9]

Soviet military advisors had first appeared in Egypt shortly after the 1956 war. By 1967, there had been approximately four hundred military advisors in the UAR. Their main functions centered on training, the integration of Soviet military equipment, and providing advice upon request. Now after the 1967 conflict, the Soviet advisory role expanded to include all facets of military readiness. These expanding demands required an increase in numbers; by July 1970 there were over seven thousand Soviet experts and advisors in Egypt.[10]

Soviet military advisors initially focused their attention on working with Egyptians at General Command and other senior commands. Eventually, Soviet officers were assisting battalions in the army and squadrons in the air force. They participated as judges in training maneuvers, helped in the formulation of planning exercises, and provided useful intelligence about Israel. For a brief period, Soviets even manned air defense systems and flew combat missions to protect Egyptian air space from the Israeli air force. Some twenty Russians were killed in combat between 1967 and 1970. Fawzi would aptly describe the Egyptian-Soviet relationship on the eve of Nasser's death on 28 September 1970: "At the end of the Three Years War [1967–1970], the Soviet Union was in one trench with us."[11] Egypt could not have rehabilitated its armed forces without this Soviet assistance, and Nasser, though defeated militarily, gained personal resolve to defy Israel precisely because of it.

GENERAL COMMAND

The departure of Amer and his supporters gave Nasser increased control over the military so that he could embark on a major overhaul of the armed forces. Now, Nasser needed to establish a unified General Command, one headed by professional senior officers. Numerous steps were taken to reach this goal, with mixed results. Overall, however, anything would seem an improvement over the previous situation.

A relatively easy reform was simply to promote trustworthy, apolitical, professional officers into senior positions. General Muhammad Fawzi assumed the top position in the military, that of commander in chief of the armed forces. Fawzi, more a professional than a political soldier, led the demoralized EAF with an iron hand in order to rebuild an institution stripped of its prestige, pride, and sense of mission. As noted by Muhammad Hasanayn Haykal, Nasser's close confidant:

General Muhammad Fawzi . . . was not an imaginative man, but he had a deserved reputation of a strict disciplinarian—too strict, perhaps, for he rode roughshod over all human considerations. Nasser called him "the cruel disciplinarian," but his qualities were what was needed to pull together an army demoralized by incompetence and favoritism during the time of Field Marshal Amer. His successors reaped the harvest of what Fawzi sowed.[12]

Fawzi rightly deserves a prominent place in Egyptian military history for his contributions to the reconstruction of the armed forces after their devastating defeat in 1967.

Nasser wisely selected as the chief of the General Staff an officer whose personality balanced well with that of Fawzi. Lieutenant General Abd al-Munim Riyad, who had commanded the Jordanian front in the Six Day War, brought sophistication and the human touch to the senior command. Haykal described the sharp contrast between the two men, unabashedly employing the most positive terms.

General Riyad was the opposite of General Fawzi: humorous and sociable—he was bachelor and something of a *bon viveur*—he won the respect and affection of his subordinates in a matter of minutes. . . . Nasser believed Riyad understood modern warfare: he had trained in air defense and became a missile expert and an instructor in radar and antiaircraft gunnery. . . . He was one of the rare Arab generals to understand the importance of mobility. He had a breadth of vision—he would come to my house and relax over a couple of whiskies and his talk would range far beyond the usual military preoccupations.[13]

There was much practical wisdom in selecting as the two top officers in the military men who complemented each other in both temperament and intellect. Together Fawzi and Riyad sought to reconstruct the armed forces on the basis of professionalism. Considerations of merit now weighed in promotions much more heavily than those of loyalty.

To ameliorate the debilitating problem of interservice rivalry and autonomy, Fawzi reformed General Command with the goal of establishing a unity of command (*tawhid al-qiyadah*) based on the principle of centralization (*markaziyat*). He not only wanted tight control over the army, but he also worked the military institution to be of one mind. According to his thinking, "unity of thought among individuals in the armed forces is the basis of their unity of effort."[14] This was not a new command doctrine for the EAF, but Fawzi was more effective in implementing because of the primary focus on military matters. In this regard, his firm hand shattered the bifurcation of authority between Amer and Badran and significantly limited the independence of the three service chiefs.

On 20 January 1968, Nasser issued Law Number 4 significantly reorganizing the national command authority. Fawzi, who had provided major input, identified the main goal of the legislation as the creation of a "unity of command" that involved "unity of thought and execution."[15] In particular, the law delineated the powers and responsibilities of the president, the minister of war, and the chief of the General Staff.[16]

As president of the republic, Nasser naturally awarded himself wide powers in his capacity as supreme commander of the armed forces. Approval of the size and organization of the armed forces, as well as war plans and military operations, rested with him. He now approved all promotions from the rank of colonel up and controlled appointments down to division and brigade levels. Before, Nasser had affected promotions only to the grades of general and lieutenant general. To assist the president in formulating defense policy, the law created the National Defense Council, which met for the first time in 1969. Among its permanent members were the president, the director of General Intelligence, and the ministers of war, foreign affairs, and interior.

The next aspect of the reform of the high command addressed the problem of unity of command within the armed forces. In the 1967 war, Amer, who held the position of deputy supreme commander, had served as the commander in chief in charge of training and operations, whereas Badran, as the minister of war, had handled administrative and personnel matters. The reorganization now combined the positions of minister of war and commander in chief of the armed forces, in the process abolishing the position of deputy supreme commander and removing the division of authority that existed in the 1967 war. Command over the armed forces in war and peace now clearly rested with the war minister; a political appointee and a member of the cabinet, he reported directly to the president. To assist the war minister in his duties, Law Number 4 created the Supreme Council for the Armed Forces, comprising the most senior officers, including the chief of the General Staff, the service chiefs, and the chief of military intelligence.

Next in the chain of command under the war minister stood the chief of the General Staff. In the 1967 war, this individual had reported to two individuals: the deputy supreme commander and the war minister. Now the chief of the General Staff reported to only one person, the war minister. In his capacity of deputy (*naib*) commander in chief, the chief of the General Staff had the authority to issue operational directives in the name of the war minister. The most important decisions, however, required the signatures of both the war minister and the chief of the General Staff—to avoid a repetition of Amer's order to withdraw the armed forces from the Sinai in one night.

Another significant change made after the war concerned the abolishment of the Ground Forces Command. Established in 1964, this command, the largest in the armed forces, only aggravated the interservice rivalry that existed before the 1967 war and weakened the authority of the chief of the General Staff.[17] By abolishing this command, the reform strengthened the position of the chief of the General Staff, who now functioned as the commander of the land forces.

The above reforms were intended to centralize administrative and operational command in the war minister. Unlike in Israel, Egypt's minister of war was an army officer (with a couple brief exceptions since 1945) who commanded the armed forces in wartime. Post-1967 reforms awarded him great powers and responsibilities. As a political appointee, he served in the cabinet and provided political and strategic direction to military planning and operations. As the most senior ranking officer, he exercised operational control over the conduct of military operations.[18] After the Six Day War, Nasser, and Sadat after him, expected the war minister to function as a technician, focusing on operational matters, rather than as an independent thinker, with a firm grasp of military strategy. Both Nasser and Sadat felt comfortable with such a commander over the armed forces.

HEROIC LEADERSHIP IN COMBAT

The devastating defeat in 1967 reflected adversely on the entire Egyptian officer corps, creating a crisis in leadership. Stories circulated throughout Egypt of officers abandoning their units during the war to flee to safety. The actions of a minority stained the reputation and standing of the entire institution, generating ill feeling, even anger, toward the once-proud officer corps. As noted by Amin Huwaydi, who became war minister shortly after the Six Day War, "Senior commanders were afraid of visiting units, dreading the reaction of noncommissioned officers toward them."[19] To compete effectively with the IDF, the EAF needed competent leaders who could rebuild trust between themselves and their troops.

The reputation of the Israeli officer corps sharply contrasted with that of its Egyptian counterpart. In the 1967 conflict, Israeli officers had led from the front, using the "follow me" principle, whereas Egyptian officers had gained an image of leading from the rear, giving the safe command "charge." Military reforms in Egypt had to address the critical issue of leadership in combat if the EAF was to improve on its performance against the IDF.

In fact, Egypt possessed professional officers with the necessary knowledge, expertise, and experience to wage war against Israel. A number of Egyptians, for instance, had studied in the United States and Great Britain before the mid-fifties and had received further education in the USSR at the Frunze Military Academy and at other foreign military schools. Others only knew the Soviet system. Unfortunately, Amer, who suffered from personal insecurity, felt threatened by competent, Soviet-trained officers and kept a number of them away from field commands, thus wasting an important asset.[20] Now Fawzi faced the momentous task of creating a system that facilitated the identification and promotion of the competent, professional officers. Professional competence would have to replace personal loyalty as the primary consideration for advancement and assignment.

To raise the technical proficiency of the officer corps, Fawzi lured back competent officers who had left the service, some out of frustration over the political character of the military institution. A number of these individuals eventually rose to command large units in the 1973 war.[21] In addition, the personnel department weeded out many incompetent or questionable officers; by the first anniversary of the 1967 war, over a thousand officers had lost their jobs as a result of dismissal or forced retirement. The Nasser regime especially targeted Badran's 1948 graduating class from the military academy; many of its members were imprisoned, lost their jobs, or fell under suspicion.[22] This house cleaning removed many incompetent, political officers in all three services and at all levels. The overall effect was positive, enhancing professionalism.

In attempting to develop effective field-grade officers, Fawzi underscored the importance of strict discipline and task-oriented efficiency rather than broader, theoretical education. There was little time for studying military theory or gaining general knowledge. Units had to be trained and maintained at high levels of morale and combat preparedness. Promotion boards were expected to stress technical competence. Military slogans challenged officers to assume exemplary roles: "The commander is the spine of the military unit" and "There are no bad units here, only bad commanders."[23]

The main mission of the officer corps changed accordingly. Rather than being guardians of the political order, officers were now expected to be dedicated warriors, no longer populist revolutionaries but technocrats. In 1974, Ali Amin, a popular writer in Egypt, described the ideal of "the new Egyptian officer":

- The officer who did not reach his first rank because of seniority or because of his year group from the military academy.
- But he reached [his rank] not shackled by his degree from the staff college or by having studied at a military college or at Bruno Academy in Czechoslovakia or at Frunze Academy in the Soviet Union.
- He does not skip ranks. . . . But he plants his fingernails in the rock until he reaches the summit of the pyramid.[24]

The quote describes a promotion policy based on merit and competence. Only a critical assessment of the 1973 war can show how far the EAF progressed in achieving this goal.

To help instill confidence in troops toward their commanders, Fawzi demanded his officers lead by example. Here, the Israelis provided a compelling model of heroism, with their "follow me" ethos. Israeli doctrine called for commanders up to and including the brigade to lead from the front. The Egyptians attempted to adopt this type of leadership. In training exercises and clashes with Israeli forces during the Three Years War (1967–70), General Command expected its field commanders to locate themselves close to their forward troops so as to observe the combat directly and thus make appropriate decisions.

This concern for command by example becomes starkly evident in the Egyptian plan for crossing the Suez Canal in the 1973 war. Egyptian planners designated specific timetables for when commanders were expected to move with their units to the east bank after the first wave commenced at 2:20 P.M. All infantry battalion commanders were to cross at 2:35, or fifteen minutes into the operation, brigade commanders with their artillery chiefs at 3:05, and division commanders at 3:50.[25] As noted by one field commander after the war, the crossing operation witnessed a remarkable scene: the Egyptian army attacked

Israeli defenses with brigade and division commanders moving on foot with frontline troops to forward positions.[26]

This Egyptian doctrine of leading from the front resulted in the loss of many senior commanders in the 1973 war. Brigadier General Ahmad Hamdi, chief engineer for Third Army, fell while personally directing the repair of a bridge damaged by Israeli air strikes. Brigadier General Ahmad Ubud al-Zammar, commander of the 23d Mechanized Infantry Division, lost his life on 18 October while opposing the Israeli countercrossing to the west bank of the Suez Canal. By the fourth day of the war, the 16th Infantry Division had suffered the loss of two brigade commanders: Brigadier General Adil Yusri (112th Infantry Brigade) lost a leg at his forward command post, and Brigadier General Shafiq Mitri Sedrak (3d Mechanized Infantry Brigade) was killed in combat. The Egyptian Armor Corps, for its part, recorded a loss of half its battalion commanders and four of ten brigade commanders.[27]

In fact, Egypt offered up the most senior officer to die in any of the Arab-Israeli wars. On 9 March 1969, Lieutenant General Abd al-Munim Riyad, the chief of the General Staff, set an example of heroic senior leadership for the entire armed forces by knowingly placing himself in a combat environment. Shortly after returning from a trip to Baghdad, Riyad embarked on a surprise visit to an infantry battalion engaged in a firing duel with Israelis across the Suez Canal. Though the field army commander suggested stopping at the artillery base, Riyad insisted on meeting with frontline troops located in trenches, only a little more than a 150 meters from the actual Israeli positions. An Israeli artillery shell killed him and wounded the commander of the Second Army, Major General Adli Hasan Sayyid. Riyad's death dealt a major blow to the Egyptian military, for he had emerged as one of the key military reformers after the 1967 war. Upwards of a million Egyptians took part in his funeral procession, an event that turned into a national display of grief and desire for revenge, and an outcry for a war of liberation. Yet his death served as an example of heroic and courageous leadership, and 9 March became "The Day of the Martyrs" (*yawm al-shuhada*) for the entire armed forces.[28]

Even the presidential family offered up one of its own members. Within minutes of the 1973 war's commencement, Captain Atif Sadat, Anwar Sadat's twenty-six-year-old half-brother, lost his life while flying his Mirage aircraft into the Sinai. To avoid distracting the supreme commander, Anwar Sadat's wife waited until the eighth day of the war before breaking the news to him.[29] Such examples of personal courage among commanding officers no doubt inspired soldiers to perform likewise in battle.

COMBAT TROOPS

On 11 June 1967, one day after returning to the presidency, Nasser met with his senior military commanders to assess the damage suffered by the armed forces. Initial reports estimated some three thousand Egyptian soldiers as killed up to the general withdrawal order. The subsequent flight from the Sinai had added another sixteen thousand officers and soldiers to the list of missing. Time would reveal whether most of these had been killed, wounded, or made prisoners of war; eventually, the toll of Egyptian "martyrs" would reach ten thousand men. After the experience of such a military debacle, many soldiers refused to rejoin their units and instead returned home. Equipment losses were staggering as well: approximately nine hundred artillery pieces, seven hundred tanks, and eight thousand vehicles left in the Sinai.[30] Restoring order and discipline within the armed forces became a top priority.

The Egyptian rebuilding program called for the rapid creation of four divisions, anchored on a forward defensive line along the western bank of the Suez Canal. General Command turned to Yemen for additional troops. On the eve of the 1967 war, Egypt had had between twenty and thirty thousand troops in Yemen, including six infantry brigades, one armor brigade minus its command, and an artillery brigade. All these troops had equipment and weapons, and together they could form two understrengthed infantry divisions. But before withdrawing these units, Nasser had to reach an agreement with King Faysal of Saudi Arabia about Yemen. A deal was cut at an Arab summit conference convened in Khartoum at the end of August. In the meantime, the soldiers who had managed to escape the Sinai were formed into brigades, eventually constituting two divisions.[31]

By the time of Nasser's death on 28 September 1970, however, the ground forces had become larger and more mechanized and armored. In numbers alone, the Egyptians had doubled the size of their combat force to approximately two hundred thousand men, a process bringing with it increased mechanization. A comparison of forces demonstrates the EAF's evolution from an artillery-infantry to a combined-arms army. In the 1967 war, the army deployed five infantry divisions, one paratroop brigade, two mechanized infantry brigades, four independent armored brigades, and one armored division. Three years later, the EAF fielded a much more mechanized force: three mechanized infantry divisions, three independent armored brigades, and two tank divisions, as well as five infantry divisions, one reconnaissance brigade, two paratroop brigades, forty-four commando battalions, and two air assault brigades. Air defense, now a separate service and no longer a part of the air force, boasted eight divisions.[32] Egypt would go to war on 6 October 1973 with essentially this order of battle.

All these organizational reforms meant nothing if the Egyptian soldier failed to fight better. To improve combat performance of its troops, General Command instituted rigorous training programs designed to develop a "new Egyptian soldier." The end product was to be "a trained and prepared soldier" (*gundi al-muhalat*), one technically proficient to engage in combat with more advanced weapons. Better-quality recruits were desperately needed in the EAF. Consequently, a new conscription policy went into effect in order to enhance the technical competence of the armed forces. Prior to the 1967 war, university graduates had easily obtained exemptions from military service. Officers generally came from well-to-do, middle-class backgrounds; conscripts were mainly *fellah* (peasants) and urban poor, both groups with minimal education. This recruitment policy created a wide socio-educational gap between officers and soldiers, and the EAF labored under a much lower technical competence level than that of its Israeli counterpart.

To improve its combat performance against the Israelis, the Egyptian military turned to its better-educated part of society. Shortly after the Six Day War, the government began conscripting graduates from universities and other higher institutes. Over 110,000 such graduates would see service in the armed forces during the 1973 war.[33] Many of these recruits entered the more technical services and branches—air force, air defense, navy, armor, and signal. A better educated army allowed General Command to integrate more advanced military equipment into the force structure. The Egyptians could rightfully claim that with the 1973 war they had entered the age of electronic warfare.

This progress in technical proficiency can best be observed in the area of air defense. In the Six Day War, the commander of the air force also commanded all the air defenders. Based on the poor performance of both, General Command created a fourth service in 1968, the air defense forces, devoted solely to manning the various missiles and antiair artillery guns for defending Egypt and Egyptian troops from strikes by the Israeli air force. In 1969, this service became operational, under the command of Major General Muhammad Ali Fahmi, relieving the Egyptian air force from this responsibility. By October 1973, Fahmi commanded some eighty thousand personnel devoted to handling an integrated air defense system consisting of the SAM-2, SAM-3, SAM-6, SAM-7, and ZSU-23-4. Soviets had manned the more sophisticated equipment until Sadat expelled all Soviet military personnel in July 1972. Virtually every foreign expert now expected a serious degradation in Egypt's air defense capabilities as a result of the exodus of Soviet expertise. But the Egyptians proved the pundits wrong. Egyptian air defenders operated their weapons effectively, causing serious losses to the Israeli air force during the first few days of the 1973 war.

Finally, the EAF as a whole was to perform remarkably better in the 1973 war precisely because it was much better trained for war. In the 1967, General Command had cut training exercises in large measure to meet the needs of fighting in Yemen. Savings had had to be made somewhere to help finance this costly war. By the end of 1967, Egypt had withdrawn all its forces from the Arabian peninsula, and consequently General Command devoted more resources to raising the combat skills of its soldiers. Ground forces engaged in regular and more realistic training, employing live fire during both day and night exercises. Air force pilots saw a threefold increase in flying hours. More realism and rigor increased the confidence and competence of Egyptian soldiers. By 1973, with better training and increased discipline, the EAF could expect to improve on its combat performance against the IDF.

NATIONAL WILL

While the political and the military leadership tried to decipher the reasons for the devastating defeat, Egyptian society underwent a similar soul searching and self-analysis in order to make sense of the Six Day War. Personal grief, coupled with the national dimensions of the tragedy, fostered a quest for meaning and solace. People felt anger and betrayal upon learning how badly Egypt had been defeated by Israel. A new wave of Islamism, patriotism, and nationalism swept Egypt, on which the Nasser regime tried to capitalize for the reconstruction of morale within the demoralized armed forces.

Many Egyptians, by nature conservative and traditional in their philosophical approach to life and politics, naturally turned to the Islamic religion for answers, especially since the defeat had revealed major cracks in Nasser's brand of socialism and pan-Arabism. Israel's military triumph aroused an outpouring of religious sentiment in Egypt. Where religion had been a more or less dormant or a private matter, it now become more public, encroaching on government policy with greater influence. Jordan's loss of east Jerusalem, the third holiest city in Islam after Mecca and Medina, with its al-Aqsa Mosque and the Dome of the Rock, proved most galling to Muslim sensitivities. The Arab defeat now carried a serious religious fallout, unlike in 1956.

One popular religious explanation for Egypt's humiliating defeat saw the national tragedy as God's punishment of Muslims for having placed their faith in alien ideologies and for embracing the forces of materialism. A few went even farther in their analysis: Israel had won decisively on the battlefield precisely because the Jews had remained faithful to the religious ideals of Judaism. By their military triumph, the Jewish people had clearly demonstrated the immense power of religious conviction over secular values.

In the wake of defeat, Islam offered new hope, authenticity, and identity. Egypt, as other Muslim countries in the Middle East, experienced a turning to Islam for solace, strength, and courage in the face of adversity and humiliation. The resultant Islamic revival became pervasive in Egyptian society, forcing the regime to incorporate, to a much greater extent than before, Islamic discourse. For the EAF, this meant a more systematic, yet cautious, blending of religious ideals with military professionalism, a combination that helped produce a highly motivated army, much to the surprise of both Israeli and Western analysts.

Islam has always been a factor in Egyptian politics and war, albeit with varying orientations and degrees of intensity. After the military coup of 23 July 1952, the Nasser regime accepted the cultural importance and moral force of Islam in society, but politically Nasser emphasized the secular concepts of Arab nationalism and socialism. "Freedom, Socialism, and Unity" became the main staples of his state ideology. To prevent religious opposition to his 1952 revolution, the Nasser regime closed down *shari'ah* (religious) courts, reformed the curriculum at al-Azhar, transforming it into more a secular university, and had his security forces keep a close watch on Islamic groups like the Muslim Brotherhood.

As the 1967 defeat sent tremors throughout Egyptian society, many Egyptians embraced Islam as the best possible answer to the moral malaise of the state and society. Attendance at mosques, for example, increased significantly. The Nasser regime was now forced to sanction as well as harness this newfound religiosity as an important ingredient of national will. The aftermath of defeat thus saw a greater reliance on Islamic themes for rebuilding the morale of the armed forces. In a speech to troops in March 1968, for example, Nasser called upon Egyptian soldiers to deepen their faith as they trained for war: "We all believe in God and fate. This belief must lie deep in the soldier's heart. I want every soldier to believe in religion, principles, and values. Moral guidance must promote these concepts, and belief in God must be the basis of the soldier's enlightenment."[34]

General Command began to place greater emphasis on Islam to develop pride, confidence, élan, and sense of mission within the armed forces. In 1968, Major General Muhammad Gamal al-Din Mahfouz, in charge of moral direction (*al-tawjih al-manawi*) in the armed forces, later tersely summarized the new Islamic emphasis: "*Al-Jihad* was to be the fighting ideology of the army with 'victory or martyrdom' as the slogan and '*Allahu Akbar*' as the battle cry."[35] In light of this religious indoctrination, Egyptian soldiers went to war in 1973 with the call "to martyrdom for the sake of the honor of the motherland" (*bil-istishhad fi sabil karama al-watan*) as an integral part of their motivation.[36] The effects of this policy naturally varied with individual soldiers, units, and commanders, but by 1973 a greater Islamic ambiance was definitely present in the EAF.

In fact, Islamic faith was to prove an important motivating factor throughout the 1973 war. After the conflict, many Egyptians sincerely believed that the new Islamic revivalism explained, in part, their improved battlefield performance against Israel. Israelis would certainly be surprised by the new fighting mettle of Egyptian units. In explaining this Israeli intelligence failure, General Ahmad Ismail Ali, Egypt's war minister and commander in chief in the 1973 conflict, underscored that the Israelis had seriously erred in dismissing from their calculations the power of the Islamic faith—as manifest, for example, in the words *Allahu Akbar* (God is great!) uttered by Egyptian soldiers when crossing the Suez Canal.[37]

Brigadier General Adil Yusri, who commanded the 112th Infantry Brigade of the 16th Infantry Division, echoed his war minister's belief: "The religious renaissance (*nahda*). . . . had a clear impact on the inner life of the soldier and his readiness for combat."[38] While ascribing importance to the Islamic factor, however, Yusri carefully avoided extravagance in his praise of Islam. His memoirs have only scattered references to Islam; the vast bulk of the book deals with military matters. For most professional officers, Islam helped provide additional esprit d'corps for combat, but battlefield performance still rested in large measure on such military factors as proper training, appropriate equipment, and exemplary leadership.

Still, in addition to its positive effects within the armed forces, Islamic faith strengthened the national will of the society as a whole to support the war effort. Egyptians rallied behind the government in the armed struggle against Israel. When the IDF tried to capture Suez City before a UN sponsored ceasefire to end the 1973 war, for example, both the local religious leaders and the townspeople gathered at the Mosque of the Martyrs and helped the army organize a defense. In the end, after heavy fighting from street to street, the Egyptians were able to thwart Israeli attempts to capture the town. Religious conviction proved a vital ingredient in the will of a professional army and its society.[39]

Despite embracing the use of Islam in the areas of morale and motivation, the Nasser regime guarded against any tendency to let religious fervor get out of control. Such a development, if unchecked, would open the door to Muslim extremism or fanaticism. Consequently, security forces kept close vigilance on the activities of Islamic groups like the Muslim Brotherhood to ensure the religious awakening did not turn against the government or in support of the creation of an Islamic state. Maintaining a proper grip on national passions and emotions, especially in the religious realm, proved a delicate and difficult undertaking indeed.

While developing Islamic themes for the reconstruction of the armed forces, the Nasser regime still laid great stress on Egyptian patriotism and Arab nationalism. Moral instruction emphasized both "[Egyptian] patriotic and [Arab] national consciousness" (*al-way al-watani al-qawmi*).[40] In Egypt, military culture thus blended Egyptian patriotism (*wataniyya*), Arab nationalism (*qawmiyya*), and Islamic ideology (*diniyya*) in a dynamic, mutually supportive relationship.

State ideology emphasized the themes of patriotism and nationalism over Islamism, and for at least two main reasons. First, approximately 10 percent of the Egyptian population belongs to the Coptic Church. Too strong a Muslim orientation in policy would cause anxiety in this Christian community; all Egyptians were needed to rally around the flag. Second, though part of the Arab world by virtue of language, culture, and history, Egyptians also possess a distinct sense of their own history and identity as Egyptians, an identity wedded to ancient Egypt and the birth of human civilization. Compared to other Arabs living elsewhere, the Egyptian people possesses a very strong sense of national identity. In this sense, Egypt stands as the clearest example of a nation-state in the Arab world.

Therefore, the EAF had developed in the twentieth century more along the lines of a national rather than a strictly Muslim army. Compulsory national service included the conscription of Coptic Christians into the combat arms. With the passage of time, Copts rose up through the ranks of the officer corps into positions of responsibility. This national policy continued after the Six Day War. At the commencement of the 1973 war, for example, Brigadier General Fuad Aziz Ghali, a Coptic Christian, commanded the 18th Infantry Division in the crossing operation. Before the end of the year, Sadat appointed him commander of the Second Field Army with the rank of major general, no mean accomplishment for a member of a minority in any country.[41]

The incorporation of Christians into the armed forces nurtured a fairly moderate interpretation by the government of the Islamic religion. For example, religious authorities extended the notion of holy war and martyrdom to non-Muslims as well. On 12 October 1973, Shaykh al-Azhar Abd al-Halim Mahmud, the highest religious dignitary in Egypt, declared in the midst of the conflict: "*al-Jihad* is an obligation for all, without distinction between Muslims and Christians. It is the duty of all who live under the sky of Egypt, the motherland (*watan*) of all. . . . Being martyred for the sake of the motherland gives access to Paradise. This is confirmed by divine laws that have been revealed to the People of the Book."[42]

In the 1973 war, the Egyptians were to field a much better army than they did in 1967. It had conducted war preparations for over six years. Although focusing its energies on planning, training, and leadership, General Command gave serious attention to grooming its officers and soldiers to go to war with a strong sense of mission. There was a commitment to a sacred cause, to regaining the Sinai on the noble principles of Egyptian patriotism, Arab nationalism, and Islamic faith. In October 1973, Egypt went to war with its armed forces motivated by national purpose and espirit d'corps rather than by the ideological zeal that seems to have characterized the military in 1967.

A CHANGE IN MIND-SET

Nasser's public acceptance of personal responsibility on 9 June 1967 for the military defeat in the Six Day War opened a Pandora's box of unforeseen long-range effects. Although a one-party system under a charismatic leader, Egypt was far from being a totalitarian state with people living in constant fear of the secret police. Unlike Syria after the 1967 war, or Iraq after Desert Storm, Egypt eventually underwent a public examination and debate of its military defeat. Rather than reproach Western colonialism, as had been the official penchant in the past, Egyptians tended to look inwardly and blame themselves, in the spirit of Nasser's example. Public examination of failure produced a healthy dose of realism in the political and military life.

Egyptian society possesses a vibrancy that increases during times of crisis. Egyptians have a deserved reputation for humor, and this national trait turned on the military. Wounded pride and a sense of betrayal spawned a myriad of jokes deriding the officer corps. Ridicule of Egyptian officers proved especially painful for the military profession, accustomed to being held in high esteem by the people, as aptly described by Jehan Sadat.

Not only was Egypt's army the largest of any in the Arab countries, but it was the most respected by far. To be accepted as an officer in the military had always been the dream of many Egyptian youths, for such a position afforded a status in our country that they could not achieve any other way. So honored were our military officers that their very presence in uniform brought special attention from people in the streets, in cafes, in shops. Everyone respected our officers.[43]

The military disaster changed all that for a brief period of time. The joking reached such proportions that eventually Nasser publically pleaded with the Egyptian people to cease and desist in their counterproductive humor of the military. He reminded his listeners that one day these same individuals would carry weapons into battle for their country.[44] The jokes, though they gradually subsided, were a way of demanding from the country's leaders some degree of accountability and reform.

Within two weeks after Amer's apparent suicide on 14 September 1967, the government announced the convening of military tribunals to investigate officers for incompetence during the war and for plotting against the revolution. Although conducted behind closed doors, the courts eventually revealed gross military incompetence and lack of professionalism in the armed forces. On 30 October 1967, a military court convened to investigate the air force's conduct before and during the war. Placed on trial were now retired General Muhammad Sidqi Mahmud, the commander of the air force and air defense; General Gamal Afifi, his chief of staff and deputy commander; Major General Abd al-Hamid Daghdidi, the commanding general of the Eastern Military District (Sinai); and Major General Ismail Labib, the chief of the antiair defenses. Other military courts probed into the conduct of army officers during the land campaign and into the coup plotting associated with Amer.

In February 1968, the military tribunal finally announced its long-awaited decision. Sidqi received fifteen years for dereliction of duty, and Labib ten for the same offense, whereas Daghdidi and Afifi were found innocent of all charges. Major General Sidqi al-Ghul, commander of the 4th Armored Division, was dismissed from the army and sentenced to fifteen years' imprisonment for failing in his duties.[45] His sentence was announced on the same day as the verdict for the air force commanders.

The sentences imposed on the senior air force commanders seemed lenient, given the tragedy of the air force having been destroyed on the ground in three hours. The passions of the Egyptian people became aroused once again, sparking demonstrations throughout Egypt, although on a minuscule scale compared to those of 9 and 10 June in 1967. Nevertheless, the demonstrators represented important sectors of the economy and society. First, factory workers at three military plants in Hilwan took to the streets on 21 February to protest the light sentences. Agitation quickly spread to the universities, as students clashed with police in the cities of Cairo, Alexandria, and Asyut. Some demonstrators challenged the regime outright, with chants of "Not Sidqi and not al-Ghul; Abd al-Nasser is responsible." Intellectuals rallied to the side of the workers and students. Although the leaders generally avoided direct criticism of Nasser or the revolution, the possibility of a worker-student-intellectual alliance posed a serious dilemma for the Nasser regime.

Some senior advisors counseled Nasser that any compromise with the demonstrators would be interpreted as a sign of weakness and encourage similar events in the future. But Nasser, keenly aware of the populist nature of his regime and of the imperative of building national support, willingly sacrificed a few commanders to public pressure. So on 25 February, less than a week after the government's announcement of the verdicts, the regime buckled under to the demonstrators; Fawzi ordered a retrial of the four air force defendants. Government negotiations with the demonstrators eventually returned calm to the streets of Egypt. In June, a new military court opened its proceedings, and on 29 August 1968 the judges handed out stiffer sentences. Sidqi Mahmud received life with hard labor and Labib fifteen years; both Afifi and Daghdidi were again absolved of any dereliction of duty.

Another set of trials involved fifty-five alleged coup plotters who had sought to return Amer to head the armed forces. Among those former officials convicted were Shems al-Din Badran, the minister of war; Salah Nasr, the head of General Intelligence; and Major General Uthman Nassar, commander of the 3d Infantry Division. Nassar was also court-martialed for cowardice in the face of the enemy.

Although a relative calm returned to the country with the announcement of a retrial of the air force commanders, Nasser had suffered a temporary setback for his regime. The demonstrations underscored the nation's impatience with the regime's progress in addressing the country's numerous problems, including the recovery of the Sinai. Officials became more sensitized to the public's mood. According to a senior official in the government during this period, Nasser followed three issues very closely during the last years of his reign: the rebuilding of the armed forces, the food situation in Egypt, and public opinion, especially in Egypt and the Arab world.[46]

The Nasser regime, unlike in Syria, was not tight-lipped about its military problems. Much information was released after the military tribunals. The press, although under tight censorship, shed light on the professional incompetence and political intrigue that had been rampant in the EAF on the eve of the 1967 war. Certainly public discussion had its limits; condemnation of Amer and his clique tended to receive a favorable hearing, whereas Nasser and the 1952 revolution stood above serious criticism. Despite such limitations, Muhammad Hassanayn Haykal, the editor of the semi-official newspaper *al-Ahram*, took the lead in candid discussions. Egyptians learned of their regime's mistakes as well as Israeli strengths. Such candor encouraged a more realistic approach to problem solving.

Egypt's soul-searching became public forum. The press openly discussed the country's strengths and weaknesses. Unlike in the past, when revolutionary rhetoric had castigated Western colonialism as the main culprit for the country's major ills, Egyptians now began to take a more realistic look at themselves and their adversary. This more sober attitude naturally affected the military as well. Some newspaper articles or public statements were quite candid and damning in their criticisms. In a lead article in *al-Ahram* on 28 June 1968, for example, Haykal noted that "The enemy knew too much about us, and we knew too little about him."[47]

Egyptian analyses of the 1967 war highlighted three different areas. The first was Egypt's own military problems in 1967. The list of mistakes and weaknesses included the lack of a clear strategy, the absence of Arab unity, indecision and inflexibility in the high command, poor leadership in battle, and the relatively low level of technical competency among the soldiers. Second, Egyptians explored nonmilitary factors, questioning possible flaws in Arab character and society. Here writers identified Arab tendencies toward fatalism, emotionalism, lack of realism, and self-deception, all character traits that tended to debilitate the Egyptian ability to wage war effectively against Israel. Third, Egyptians admitted—courageously, and with some pain—that the Israelis deserved recognition for their own accomplishments. In this regard, the IDF received high marks for technical training, scientific knowledge, war planning, military intelligence, military deception, and combat leadership.[48] This discussion was healthy and necessary for an army and society attempting to rise from the ashes of defeat.

After the 1973 war, a number of former senior officers were to publish books analyzing the reasons for the 1967 defeat. Their explanations included political and military disunity, interservice rivalry and a lack of unity of command within the armed forces, emphasis on loyalty over merit in promotions, wrong assessments by the intelligence community, the deleterious effects of involvement in Yemen, and poor training and technical competence of conscripts.[49] These very themes had also appeared in the press.

Only research in the Egyptian military archives can determine how much critical analysis took place within the armed forces. The memoirs of former commanders, however, do suggest that serious critical analysis did in fact take place within the armed forces after the shock of defeat. Nasser himself realized the imperative of obtaining unbiased information about the armed forces if there was to be any hope of a sound rebuilding of the military. He personally directed the army's chief historian, then Major General Hasan al-Badri, to gather all relevant documents, study the reasons for the military defeat, and report his findings directly to him. In his report, al-Badri blamed much of the General Command for the defeat.[50] Other internal studies were conducted within the military. Major General Hasan Mutawai, for example, chaired a special study group that researched the disaster of the Egyptian air force. This detailed study analyzed the mistakes made by the Egyptians in the air force and air defense since the 1956 war.[51] Generals Murtagui (front commander) and Mohsen (field army commander) also filed their own versions of the war for the record.

In addition to some critical self-evaluation, the Egyptian leadership needed accurate and realistic assessments of their adversary, under the old adage: "Know thy enemy." Progress did take place in this area. Prior to the 1967 war, the Egyptian intelligence community had grossly underestimated the capabilities of the IDF, both in the air and on the ground, and had misread Israeli intentions. These failures had been a recipe for defeat. Part of this problem stemmed from Egyptian military intelligence having devoted much of its assets to internal security and to the conflict in Yemen. Now the Nasser regime redirected the energies of intelligence community toward collecting and evaluating data on the IDF.

To help military intelligence in performing its mission, the ministry of interior took over full responsibility for internal security. General Intelligence, for its part, conducted more studies of Israeli politics, economics, and society. To help the military in its studies, a number of officers were enrolled in classes to gain proficiency in the Hebrew language.[52] Senior Egyptian commanders felt that this reorientation for the intelligence branch brought concrete dividends. In 1973, General Command benefited from solid and useful information on the Israeli army, including its defensive plans, capabilities, and troop dispositions.[53] Even Israelis were to admit Egyptian accomplishments in the fields of strategic and tactical military intelligence.[54]

All these developments represented more than the efficient collection of empirical data about the IDF. Egyptians also experienced a change of mind-set or reasoning (*taghyir aqliyya*). More critical assessments of self and adversary entered the thought patterns of the country's political and military leaders. Realism, based on better information, now drove decisions more than did the idealism, based on wishful thinking, of the past. That some progress occurred is evident in the much-improved performance of the EAF in the 1973 war.

Though increased critical thinking was an admirable achievement for Egypt, institutional and human impediments kept the change of mind-set from being widespread. It was impossible for more than a small number of Egyptians, as on the Israeli side as well, to transcend, in a short time, the stereotypes that had formed over a generation. Moreover, there were institutional barriers on serious discourse in Egypt.

Politically, Egypt was still run by a single political party, which placed bounds on critical thought and free speech. Militarily, reforms stressed centralization of command, unity of effort and purpose, tough discipline, and technical competence, not intellectual inquiry integrating military theory and practice. Moreover, Egyptian commanders placed a premium on internal security and counterintelligence, to prevent penetration by the Mossad. Such emphases resulted in the compartmentalization of military functions and thought, which in turn limited the exchange of ideas among departments, branches, and services. Despite these limitations, however, the devastating defeat of 1967 did force a modicum of realism and critical thought among Egypt's more astute political and military leaders.

CONCLUSION

The defeat in 1967 created a major "earthquake" in Egypt, shattering the official image of the revolution. The country's numerous problems now saw the light of day. To save the revolution and salvage his reputation, Nasser embraced the need for change. Internal reforms encompassed the political economy and the armed forces. Nonmilitary change occurred within a modicum of political and economic liberalization, rather than a harsher police state. For the armed forces, however, reform meant firmer control by Nasser and increased centralization by the war minister.

Nasser directed a major overhaul of the EAF with the goal of transforming a revolutionary army into a modern, professional, apolitical military. Among the easier reforms to implement were firing or retiring political officers, eliminating nonmilitary roles, creating a unity of command within the armed forces, conscripting graduates of universities and higher institutes, enforcing strict if not harsh discipline, and conducting rigorous and realistic training exercises. More difficult changes involved a promotion policy favoring competence over loyalty, an expectation that commanders would lead their troops in combat by example, and a new mind-set based on a more realistic and objective analysis of self and the enemy. Performance in war would prove the litmus test.

Egypt's reconstruction took place within the larger context of regional and world politics. While reforming itself within, the Nasser regime had to formulate policies and strategies for dealing with Israel, the Arab world, and the two superpowers. Nasser lacked the luxury of a time of peace. A three-year border war followed on the heels of the Six Day War. This armed conflict offered a testing ground for Egypt's military reforms. Meanwhile, Nasser was forced to confront, once again, Israel's political strategy and military might. The outcome of this conflict helped set the stage for the 1973 war.

NOTES

1. Raymond Aron, *Peace and War: A Theory of International Relations* (New York: Doubleday, 1966): 65.

2. Halim Barakat, *Days of Dust*, translated by Trevor Le Gassick (Wilmette, IL: Medina University Press International, 1974): 179. This quote is spoken by a character in the novel. The author is Lebanese.

3. For excerpts from the speech, see *The Israel-Arab Reader: A Documentary History of the Middle East Conflict*, edited by Walter Laqueur and Barry Rubin (New York: Facts on File, 1985): 189–194; Dan Hofstadter, *Egypt and Nasser, III: 1967–1972* (New York: Facts on File, 1973): 39–42; and Walter Laqueur, *The Road to War: The Origins and Aftermath of the Arab-Israeli Conflict 1967/8* (Baltimore: Penguin Books, 1968): 399–404.

4. Salah al-Din al-Hadidi, *Shahid ala Harb 1967* (Cairo: Dar al-Shuruq, 1974): 13–17; Muhammad Fawzi, *Harb al-Thalath Sanawat 1967–1970* (Beirut: Dar al-Wahdah): 33–40; and Amin Huwaydi, *Maa Abd al-Nasir* (Cairo: Dar al-Mustaqbal, 1985): 143–154.

5. Muhammad Abd al-Ghani al-Gamasi, *Mudhakirat al-Gamasi: Harb Oktobir 1973* (Paris: al-Munshurat al-Sharqiyya, 1990): 115; and Muhammad Fawzi, *Istratijiyyah al-Musaliha: al-Giza al-Sani min Mudhakirat al-Fariq Awwal Muhammad Fawzi* (Cairo: Dar al-Mustaqbal, 1986): 55.

6. Fawzi, *Harb al-Thalath Sanawat*: 190.

7. Ibid.: 238; and al-Gamasi, *Mudhakirat*: 141–142.

8. Abd al-Magid Farid, *Nasser: The Final Years* (Reading: Ithaca Press, 1994): 1.

9. Ibid.: 3–17; Fawzi, *Harb al-Thalath Sanawat*: 347–348; and Mahmud Riyad, *Mudhakirat Mahmud Riyad 1948–1978*, I: *al-Bahth an al-Salam wa al-Sira al-Sharq al-Ust* (Beirut: al-Muessah al-Arabiyya lil-Dirasat wa al-Nashr, 1987): 84–93.

10. Ibid.: 264.

11. Fawzi, *Harb al-Thalath Sanawat*: 345.

12. Muhammad Hassanayn Haykal, *The Road to Ramadan* (New York: Quadrangle, 1975): 48–49.

13. Ibid.: 49. For a similar assesment of the two men and their contributions, see al-Gamasi, *Mudhakirat*: 139.

14. Fawzi, *Harb al-Thalath Sanawat*: 263.

15. Ibid.: 229.

16. Ibid.: 239–246; al-Gamasi, *Mudhakirat*: 140; "Supreme Command of the Armed Forces Reorganizes," *Egyptian Gazette*, 27 January 1968: 3; and Daniel Dishon (ed), *Middle East Record*, IV: *1968* (Jerusalem: Israel Universities Press, 1972): 815–816.

17. On the history of this command, see al-Hadidi, *Shahid ala Harb 1967*: 21–24.

18. For a critical assessment of these reforms, see Amin Huwaydi, *al-Furus al-Daia: al-Qararat al-Hasima fi Harbi al-Istinzaf wa Oktobir* (Beirut: Shirka al-Matbuat Lil-Tawzi'wa al-Nashr, 1991): 90–92.

19. Huwaydi, *al-Furus*: 94.

20. Anouar Abdel-Malek, *Egypt: Military Society* (New York: Random House, 1968): xxxii.

21. al-Gamasi, *Mudhakirat*: 20.

22. Huwaydi, *al-Furus*: 84; and Abd al-Munim Khalil, *Hurub Misr al-Muasirah fi Awraq Maydani: 1939–1945, 1956, 1962–1967, 1968–1970, 1973* (Cairo: Dar al-Mustaqbal al-Arabi, 1990): 103.

23. Fawzi, *Harb al-Thalath Sanawat*: 262.

24. Adil Yusri, *Rihla al-Shaq al-Mualaqa: min Ras al-Ush ila Ras al-Qubra* (Cairo: dar al-Muarif bi-Misr, 1974): 4–5.

25. Hasan al-Badri, Taha al-Magdub, and Muhammad Zia al-Din Zohdi, *The Ramadan War, 1973* (New York: Hippocrene Books, 1978): 66; and Husayn al-Tantawi, *Butulat Harb Ramadan* (Cairo: Dar al-Sha'ab: 1975): 44. The authors of the first publication were at the time senior officers in the Egyptian military, whereas the second source represents a popular account of the war with official sanction–an introduction written by the then interior minister.

26. Yusri, *Rihla al-Saq al-Muallaqa*: 62.

27. Kamal Hasan Ali, *Mudarrabun wa Mufawwadun* (Cairo: al-Ahram, 1986): 51.

28. al-Gamasi, *Mudhakirat*: 164; Gamal Hamad, *Min ina ila al-Golan* (Cairo: al-Zuhra lil-Ilam al-Arabi, 1988): 66; and Mahmud Murad, *Muharib lil-Kull al-Usur: Dirasa Tarihiyya an al-Insan al-Misri al-Mugatil* (Cairo: al-Haia al-Misriyya al-Umm lil-Kuttab, 1972): 218–226.

29. Jehan Sadat, *A Woman of Egypt* (New York: Pocket Books, 1987): 293–294.

30. Muhammad Hassanayn Haykal, *1967: al-Infijar* (Cairo: Markaz al-Ahram, 1990): 865–871.

31. Ibid.: 872; and Fawzi, *Harb al-Thalath Sanawat*: 88, 226–227.

32. Fawzi, *Harb al-Thalath Sanawat*: 230–231.

33. Egyptian military literature stresses the importance of this change in policy. As examples, see Fawzi, *Harb al-Thalath Sanawat*: 62, 247–248; Haykal, *Road to Ramadan*: 43; Tantawi, *Butulat Harb Ramadan*: 46–48; and Salah al-Din al-Hadidi, *Harb Oktobir fi al-Mizan al-'Askari* (Cairo: al-Nashr Maktabah Madbuli, 1974): 24–25.

34. Dishon, *Middle East Record*, IV: *1968*: 817.

35. Quoted by G. P. Armstrong, "Egypt" in *Fighting Armies: Antagonists in the Middle East*, edited by Richard A. Gabriel (Westport, CT: Greenwood Press, 1983): 161; and Muhammad Jamal al-Din Mahfouz, "The Military Theory of Islam, III," *King Khalid Military Academy Quarterly* 11 (Autumn/Winter 1994): 9.

36. Musa Sabri, *Wathaiq al-Harb Oktober* (Cairo: al-Maktab al-Misri, 1974): 428.

37. Sabri, *Wathaiq al-Harb Oktober*: 396.

38. Yusri, *Rihla al-Saq al-Muallaqa*: 67.

39. For a popular account of the battle for Suez City by an eyewitness, see Ahmad Ismail Subh, *Ubur al-Mihna* (Cairo: al-Haia al-Misriyya al-Umma lil-Kitab, 1976): 119 ff. Major General Hasan al-Badawi wrote the foreword to the book.

40. Fawzi, *Harb al-Thalath Sanawat*: 232–233.

41. The Egyptian case parallels that of other, but not all, Arab countries. In Syria during the 1973 war, the chief of the General Staff, Major General Yusuf Shakkur, and the deputy director of operations were both Christians.

42. Cited in Rudoplh Peters, *Islam and Colonialism: The Doctrine of Jihad in Modern History* (The Hague: Mouton, 1979): 134. People of the Book refers to Muslims, Christians, and Jews, i.e., the three monotheistic religions possessing revealed scripture.

43. Jehan Sadat, *A Woman of Egypt*: 114.

44. Riyad, *Mudhakirat* I: 81–82; and discussions with several Egyptians who lived in Egypt during this period.

45. "Court Martial Sentences 7 out of 8 Officers," *Egyptian Gazette*, 21 February 1968: 1.

46. Sayyid Mari, *Awraq Siyasiyah* (Cairo: al-Maktab al-Misri al-Hadith, 1979), II: 546.

47. Muhammad Hassanayn Haykal, "Kana al-adw yurafa aktar mimma yanbaga," *al-Ahram*, 28 June 1968: 3. Translated in "Enemy Knew Too Much and We Too Little Says Heikal," *Egyptian Gazette*, 29 June 1968: 2.

48. David Dishon (ed.), *Middle East Record III, 1967* (Jerusalem Ketor Publishing, 1971): 250–251. See, for example, *Egyptian Gazette*, 1 February 1968, 2 March 1968, 27 March 1968, 22 June 1968, providing English translations of articles published in *al-Ahram*.

49. Military writers whom I have found most critical are Generals Fawzi, Murtagui, and Hadidi. Later contributors include Gamasi and Hamad. See biography at the end of this book for their works.

50. Haykal, *1967: al-Infijar*: 878, 888–889, 921. A Saudi officer who knows al-Badri personally confirmed the outlines of Haykal's account for me.

51. Text published in Haykal, *1967: al-Infijar*: 1040–1080.

52. Chaim Herzog, *The War of Atonement, October 1973* (Boston: Little, Brown, 1975): 14.

53. al-Gamasi, *Mudhakirat*: 76, 142.

54. Discussions with Israeli officers attending the US Army Command and General Staff College, 1984–1997.

4

A THREE-YEAR BORDER WAR

> ...even the ultimate outcome of a war is not always to be regarded as final. The defeated state often considers the outcome merely as a transitory evil, for which a remedy may still be found in political conditions at some later date.
> —Carl von Clausewitz[1]

> What has been captured by force cannot be regained except by force.
> —Gamal Abd al-Nasser, 1967

Though the Israeli army had won decisively on the battlefield, pulverizing the Egyptian, Jordanian, and Syrian armies, Nasser was determined to reverse the Six Day War's outcome as quickly as possible. No Arab leader was willing to venture into direct negotiations with Israel from a position of weakness. In a way, Israel's military victory had been too decisive, leaving Arabs too humiliated to contemplate even indirect talks with the Israelis. Israeli statesmen, for their part, wanted to avoid undercutting their military gains by appearing too conciliatory, especially over the fundamental issues of Jerusalem's status and Arab recognition of Israel's right to exist in the Middle East. Intransigent attitudes on both sides suggested that more conflict was necessary to break the "iron curtain" between Arabs and Israelis.

Superpower intervention might have helped break the diplomatic deadlock, but neither the United States nor the USSR wanted to stake its prestige on pushing for a political settlement. After the 1956 Arab-Israeli war, President Dwight D. Eisenhower had willingly applied American pressure to force Israel to withdraw from Sinai and the Gaza Strip. But in 1967, the Johnson administration, faced with the growing quagmire of the Vietnam War, was unwilling to devote time and energy to the Arab-Israeli conflict. For its part, the Kremlin, frustrated by Arab incompetence in the 1967 war, wanted to avoid pressuring Washington to use its leverage on Israel for the benefit of the Arabs. With no effective foreign pressure for major Israeli concessions, postwar conditions favored the status quo, unless the Arabs resorted to the military option to force progress on the diplomatic front.

Of the three defeated Arab states, Egypt alone resorted to direct and sustained armed resistance, albeit cautiously. Other fronts gradually saw more irregular warfare: Arab guerrillas infiltrating into Israel in order to inflict casualties and damage property. The Egyptian-Israeli front, on the other hand, witnessed conventional warfare, a steady staple of clashes between regular forces. The first "major" incident along the Suez Canal erupted within a month after the conclusion of the 1967 war. By the summer of 1970, the conflict had escalated to the point of direct confrontation between Soviet and Israeli aircraft. In the end, Israeli and the Egyptian experiences during this three-year border war helped shape each country's attitudes and strategies for the 1973 conflagration.

TRIUMPHANT ISRAEL

Israeli Jews experienced great relief and euphoria upon their decisive military victory over the Arabs. Not only had Israel defeated three Arab states, but the size of land under Israeli control had increased threefold with the addition of 26,476 square miles. The conquest of the Sinai (23,622 square miles), the West Bank (2,270 square miles), and Golan Heights (444 square miles) brought Israel strategic depth and more defensible borders. Military control of the Gaza Strip (140 square miles) offered the welcome prospect of the elimination of Palestinian guerrilla raids from this troublesome base. These territorial acquisitions strengthened the country's geostrategic situation and made the Israelis feel more confident about their national security.

In its lightning campaign waged on three fronts, the IDF had lost 983 killed, 4,517 wounded, and fifteen missing, a relatively small figure when compared to the ten thousand dead Egyptians. Jordan, for reluctantly joining the Arab cause, had lost 80 percent of its armor and suffered seven hundred killed and six thousand wounded and missing.[2] Syrian figures were comparable to those of the Jordanians. For the Israelis, the magnitude of the victory made the human losses bearable; there was no criticism of the war's conduct from the Israeli public. And Israel's future looked very promising. Most Israelis expected that the IDF's demonstrated military prowess in the Six Day War would serve as an effective deterrent against a conventional threat by any Arab army for the foreseeable future.

Israeli self-confidence, understandably soaring after the Six Day War, was buoyed by international acclaim. Western writers were especially lavish in their praise of the IDF. Retired French general André Beaufre compared Israel's victory to Germany's crushing defeat of France in 1940: "[The 1967 war] is indeed lightning war of the kind whose effects we experienced everywhere in 1940, but this time [it was] compressed within a limited time frame never before realized."[3] Writing for the Institute of Strategic Studies in England, Michael Howard, who would later gain worldwide fame as a historian, likened the Six Day War to the daring campaigns of the great Napoleon: "The Third Arab-Israeli War is likely to be studied in staff colleges for many years to come. Like the campaigns of the younger Napoleon, the performance of the Israeli Defence Force provided a text-book illustration for all the classical Principles of War: speed, surprise, concentration, security, information, the offensive, above all training and morale."[4] Such analyses underscored the mystique that the Israeli military machine now had in the West, sentiments that continued unabated right up to the 1973 war.

Israelis rightly deserved to take great pride in their military accomplishment. But there was always the danger of going too far. One popular Israeli writer would recall after the 1973 war, with the benefit of hindsight, how Israeli society had tended to gravitate toward overconfidence and arrogance in the aftermath of the 1967 conflict: "We basked in the world's admiration and in our own. Writers and poets extolled the magnificent Israeli soldier whose heroism was equaled by his moral and humane values. Generals stated that our wonderful army could have crossed the Suez Canal and conquered all of North Africa, stopping only at the shore of the Atlantic (to refuel)."[5] The IDF thus placed itself on a pedestal of invincibility; so did Israeli society.

This self-indulgence in the military triumph was in one sense therapeutic for the Jewish people, both within Israel and in the Diaspora. World War II had brought the terrible tragedy of the Holocaust, in which six million Jews had been led to death chambers like sheep to slaughterhouses. Israeli Jews especially needed to demonstrate their self-defense capabilities to the world, and to themselves, so that they could say with confidence to the Gentiles, "Never again." The Six Day War, with the capture of the Old City of Jerusalem, with its Wailing Wall, felt like an expiation for the sin of passivity in the face of Adolf Hitler's Nazi Germany.

While possessing great confidence and pride in their own armed forces, most Israelis conversely regarded Arab armies as militarily inept, and Arab governments as politically corrupt. As later noted by a senior Israeli general, "The Six Day War had generated a popular conception in Israel that the Arabs were not capable of fighting a modern war, that Israel's social, technological, and industrial superiority was so great that they had no hope of closing the gap."[6] Such an attitude risked serious Israeli underestimation of the Arabs, to the point of creating a dangerous vulnerability in the IDF.

Israel's strategic posture in the Middle East was transformed by the country's new relationship with the United States. Until 1967, France had been Israel's main arms supplier. In the Six Day War, the Israeli air force defeated its Arab counterparts with French-made planes. But shortly before the outbreak of the 1967 war, President Charles de Gaulle began putting distance between France and Israel in favor of courtship with the Arab world, and in 1968 Paris imposed an arms embargo on the Jewish state. With the rather sudden French retreat, the United States moved to fill the vacuum. In 1968, the first shipment of sixty modern A-4 Skyhawk fighter-bombers arrived in Israel. In the 1973 war, the IDF would fight mainly with American-made weapons systems. This growing American military aid added to the self-confidence of both the Israeli nation and its armed forces.

Bolstered by the imports of sophisticated military hardware from the United States, Israel experienced a remarkable growth in its own arms industry. By 1973, Israel, although a small country of just over three million inhabitants, could boast the production of the Nesher attack plane, mobile medium artillery and long-range guns, the Shafrir air-to-air missile, air-to-ground missiles, the Saar and Reshef missile boats, the Gabriel surface-to-surface naval missile, sophisticated electronic devices, and most types of ammunition and fire-control systems (all with the help of Western finance and technology). These military accomplishments ushered the IDF into the age of electronic warfare and enhanced Israeli society's confidence in the deterrent capabilities of its military.

Nonmilitary indicators supported Israel's new status as *the* regional superpower. Demographically, 31,071 Jews settled in the Holy Land in 1968, a 70 percent increase in immigration over the previous year. This trend continued for the next several years, especially after 1972, when the USSR permitted its Jews to emigrate to Israel. In addition to drawing new settlers, Israel became a more attractive country for tourism, which grew dramatically from 328,000 visitors in 1967 to 625,000 in 1970, bringing with them much-needed foreign exchange. Economically, the integration of captured Arab territories brought new markets, cheap labor, and valuable natural resources. The Abu Rudeis wells in the Sinai, for example, provided Israel with over half its oil needs. Control of the Golan Heights permitted the Israeli government to channel more water from the Jordan River into Lake Galilee, thereby reclaiming twelve thousand acres in the Huleh Valley as new farmland. Meanwhile, a postwar economic boom reduced unemployment to below 3 percent in 1970, transforming the pre-1967 recession into a consumption boom: the 1 percent growth of the economy in 1967 climbed to 13 percent in 1968, dropping to a still respectable 9 percent in 1970. The number of private automobiles doubled between 1967 and 1973, a clear indication of the country's new-found prosperity.

Politically, Israel appeared firmly wedded to the dual forces of continuity and stability. The ruling Labor Party, in power since the founding of the state in 1948, maintained its hold on the reins of government through the 1973 war. After Levi Eshkol's death on 26 February 1969, Golda Meir took over as prime minister, maintaining the old guard's control of the party. Though some Israelis encouraged the government to seek reconciliation with the Arabs, the peace issue never developed into an urgent national debate. The status quo was generally desirable, from a domestic standpoint.

Militarily, no Arab state, or combination of states, appeared capable of challenging the seemingly invincible Israeli army. The sheer magnitude of the Israeli victory suggested that the Arabs would need a generation before they could embark on a major war. Israel thus appeared secure behind the impregnable fortress erected by its armed forces. Each passing month further enshrined the status quo, thereby validating a greater Israel, now containing a large but tranquil Arab population.

This new strategic situation boded ill for the Arabs. Despite all the indicators to the contrary, however, the Egyptians refused to countenance defeat and instead became a military thorn in the Israeli side for the next three years.

DEFIANT EGYPT

Although soundly defeated in the Six Day War, the Egyptian people refused to allow the Israelis the luxury of dictating the terms of peace; nor would the Egyptians accept the permanent loss of the Sinai to Israel. Regaining the peninsula became a vital issue of national pride and regime legitimacy. In this regard, Nasser identified as his main goal "the elimination of the effects of the aggression," that is, the return of all captured Arab lands. To accomplish this political objective demanded a powerful army and wise diplomacy. Nasser seemed to believe that Israel would respond more to armed force than diplomatic pressures, but the defeat in 1967 initially left him without a credible military option. The next three years would find Nasser juggling between diplomacy and armed action in an attempt to prepare his armed forces for a major war.

Before resigning on 9 June, Nasser made an important foreign policy decision whose ramifications would still be felt during the 1973 war. Egypt's relationship with the United States had been strained just before the crisis of May 1967. Now Nasser, perhaps convinced of American collusion with Israel, or just needing a scapegoat, severed diplomatic relations with the United States. However, unlike Syria and Iraq who threw out all American diplomats, Egypt kept a channel open to the Washington by allowing the US to maintain a small "interests section" in Cairo. Donald Bergus, a veteran of the Middle East, arrived in July to head it, but Nasser purposely snubbed him for six months before finally agreeing to a meeting. Nor did Cairo hurry in sending its own senior diplomat to Washington. Harvard-educated Ashraf Ghorbal waited until January 1968 before appearing to head the Egyptian interests section.

Cutting formal diplomatic ties with the United States naturally created bitter feelings back in Washington. President Johnson, who had little liking for or understanding of the Egyptian leader, felt no compulsion to pressure Israel to withdraw from Arab territories seized in the Six Day War. By alienating the United States, Nasser sacrificed the ability to play one superpower against another, and he now fell deeper into the Soviet camp. Nasser apparently understood the fallout from taking this drastic step, but he willingly abandoned direct negotiations with the United States in the hope that the Soviets would be more effective in exerting leverage on Washington.[7] This strategy failed to produce any concrete results.

Fortunately for Nasser, Leonid Brezhnev stood behind Egypt and Syria. There was little choice in the matter. The Kremlin viewed both Arab countries as in some degree client states, and therefore their defeat reflected poorly on the USSR as well. Moscow thus could not countenance an Israel victory leading to increased Western influence in the Middle East, a region bordering on the USSR and possessing rich oil reserves. Even before the conclusion of the Six Day War, the Soviets began sending supplies to both Egypt and Syria, but the Kremlin scoffed at the idea of providing offensive weapons with which to attack Israeli cities.[8]

Less than three weeks after the conclusion of the Six Day War, hostilities suddenly erupted along the Suez Canal, pitting Egypt against Israel in what turned out to be a three-year armed conflict. The first incident occurred fifteen kilometers south of Port Fuad at Ras al-Ush, a narrow causeway on the east bank separating the Suez Canal from the marshy ground farther east. There, after a several-hour engagement, an Egyptian force of some one hundred commandos (*sa'iqa*) and infantry, armed with antitank weapons and supported by artillery from the western bank, destroyed two or three of ten Israeli tanks, killed the company commander, and wounded thirteen soldiers. The Nasser regime quickly capitalized on this clash, depicting it as a moral victory, the first since the 1967 war. Since then, Ras al-Ush has come to symbolize the birth of the new Egyptian army, the turning point in the reconstruction of the armed forces from a political to a professional body.[9]

The first major engagement after the Six Day War occurred on 14 July 1967. The Israelis decided to test the cease-fire by lowering small boats into the Suez Canal, near Qantara and Port Tawfiq. The Egyptians immediately opened fire on these vessels. A firefight involving tanks, artillery, and mortars resulted. Rather quickly, the Israeli and Egyptian air forces engaged in several aerial battles. Israeli sources claimed the downing of five MiGs and one Su-7, while losing one Mirage. An Egyptian military spokesman countered with a claim of five Israeli planes shot down. Intervention by the UN brought a cease-fire after some forty-eight hours of battle, in which Israel had suffered fifteen soldiers killed and sixty-two wounded.[10] On 16 July, after arranging a cease-fire, the UN deployed a small team of forty observers to monitor both sides of the Suez Canal.

With the Suez Canal witnessing sporadic firefights, Nasser felt pressure to move on the diplomatic front in the Arab world. Arab disunity in the Six Day War had helped produce disaster on the battlefield. In addition to individual contacts with Arab leaders, Nasser attended the pan-Arab summit held in Khartoum (Sudan) from 29 August to 1 September 1967; there several important decisions were reached. Nasser and King Faysal of Saudi Arabia, the heads of the two rival camps in the Arab world, decided to reconcile their differences. Faysal led the way by offering financial support for Egypt, Jordan, and Syria. Saudi Arabia pledged fifty million, Kuwait fifty-five million, and Libya thirty million pounds sterling to help the three confrontationist states rebuild their shattered armies and economies. Nasser and Faysal also reached an agreement over the Yemeni civil war. Riyadh promised to cut its financial and military support to the royalist forces. In return, Nasser agreed to withdraw his expeditionary force from the Arabian peninsula. Finally, all the participants accepted the defiant formulation known as the "the three noes": "No truce with Israel, no recognition of Israel, no negotiations with it."

Despite these agreements, the Arab states were still far from any united action or strategy against Israel, even after a major defeat in war. For the next three years, Egypt would thus bear the brunt of the fight against Israel.

A MAJOR ESCALATION

Nasser returned to Egypt from the Khartoum summit strengthened in his resolve to defy Israel, but Egypt still lacked the military means to challenge the IDF in a major confrontation. Consequently, minor exchanges of small arms and artillery fire characterized the new border war between the two states. One side opened fire; the other responded in kind. Some incidents seemed unintentional, others premeditated, to test the adversary's resolve. It was only a question of time before a major incident would change the character of the armed conflict.

That incident took place at sea. On 21 October 1967, two Soviet-made Komar missile boats of the Egyptian navy fired Styx surface-to-surface missiles and sank the Israeli flagship, the destroyer *Eilat*, northeast of Port Said in the Mediterranean Sea. This engagement represented the first instance of such missiles sinking a warship, thereby ushering in a new age in naval warfare. The Israelis claimed that the destroyer, commissioned by Britain in 1944 and obtained by Israel in 1956, had been more than twelve nautical miles from the Egyptian coast; the Egyptian version had the Israeli vessel defiantly within Egypt's territorial waters. Israel lost forty-seven killed and ninety wounded out of 199 crew members. Moreover, the *Eilat* represented one-third of the Israel's entire destroyer fleet, and its loss was a major blow to the small service.[11]

As Egyptians basked in their naval achievement, the Eshkol government decided on a major retaliation to punish Egypt and preclude any illusions in Cairo of newfound military power. On 25 October, the Israeli air force bombed the oil refineries in Suez City, destroying 80 percent of Egypt's oil production. A red glow could be seen for thirty miles in the surrounding desert. This Israeli air attack dealt a heavy blow to the Egyptian economy. Initial estimates placed the damage to the two refineries at $161.7 million, with oil losses figured at $2.3 million. As one Egyptian officer noted, "It is easy to replace planes and tanks, but you cannot build a refinery in a few days."[12]

Israel's air strikes had two major effects in Egypt. First, the intensity of fighting along the Suez Canal dropped down for nearly a full year essentially to minor incidents. Second, the Nasser regime hastened its evacuation of the civilian population from the Suez Canal area, creating between five hundred thousand and a million refugees in the process. The large exodus left ghost towns in its wake. Before the 1967 war, for example, Suez City had numbered 260,000 inhabitants, a figure that fell to sixty thousand by September 1968; plans to relocate another twenty-five thousand people were to leave only those who provided essential services for this important port on the Red Sea. Ismailiya, on the other hand, had had a population of 173,000 before the conflict, dropping to five thousand by September 1968. The depopulation of the Suez Canal area helped limit the number of civilian casualties in the armed struggle after the Six Day War.

Israel's devastating attack on Egypt's oil refineries spurred the UN into action. On 22 November 1967, after much debate, the Security Council passed its famous Resolution 242. The one-page document called for the "withdrawal of Israeli armed forces from territories occupied in the recent conflict" and the "termination of all claims or states of belligerency and respect for and acknowledgment of the sovereignty, territorial integrity and political independence of every state in the area." It affirmed the need for freedom of navigation through international waters, for a just settlement of the refugee problem, and for "guaranteeing the territorial inviolability and political independence of every state in the area." Resolution 242 requested the Secretary-General to select "a special representative" to help achieve a peaceful settlement. U Thant complied with the appointment of Gunnar Jarring, a Swedish diplomatic. Neither Cairo nor Jerusalem accepted the resolution.

UN Resolution 242 became a very important document in the Arab-Israeli conflict, a simple yet sound framework for resolving the dispute. Israel would have to return the lands seized in the 1967 war, in return for Arab states recognizing its right to exist in the Middle East. In short, the UN Security Council advocated a land-for-peace formula. Moreover, the document acknowledged any meaningful and lasting solution to the Arab-Israeli conflict demanded addressing the Palestinian refugee problem. Finally, the drafters of the resolution recognized that any agreement between Israelis and Arabs would require outside mediation. When the UN failed to provide the necessary leadership, the United States embraced that role—but only after the catalyst of the 1973 war.

In the midst of the armed clashes and diplomatic activity, the EAF worked feverishly to regain its combat power. In the first six months after the Six Day War, its priority was constructing a defensive system along the Suez Canal. Initially, a meager force of only five infantry and two armor brigades, supported by five commando (*sa'iqa*) battalions, guarded a front that spanned 170 kilometers in length and sixty kilometers in depth.[13] By the middle of 1968, however, the EAF's position had improved considerably, at least on paper. All combat forces had been withdrawn from Yemen; the arrival of these forces, together with an aggressive recruitment policy, allowed General Command to create divisions and reorganize the ground forces into two field armies deployed along the Suez Canal. The ground forces, numbering approximately one hundred thousand men, possessed five hundred T-54/55 tanks and 150 SU-100 antitank vehicles. Some fifty-nine thousand antitank and 12,500 antipersonnel mines were in place along the entire length of the Suez Canal. The air force counted some one hundred MiG-21s, sixty MiG-17s, and twenty Su-7 fighter-bombers.[14] The EAF was now in much better shape to pose at least a limited challenge the IDF.

A NEW ISRAELI STRATEGY

The Six Day War provided Israel with strategic depth and a more defensible border. The former was especially true for the Sinai. Determined to exact a high price for the region's return, Israel's cabinet charged its armed forces with defending the entire Sinai until the Egyptians entered into direct negotiations. For the IDF, this mission meant foiling any Egyptian attempt to establish a bridgehead across the Suez Canal. Each passing year exacted a higher price for Israel's occupation of the Sinai.

For the first year after the Six Day War, the EAF was too weak to pose any serious challenge to the IDF. Consequently, the Israeli army maintained only simple, minimal defenses in the Sinai. Taking advantage of the natural water barrier, Major General Yeshayahu Gavish, the head of Southern Command, opted to establish a military presence along the Suez Canal's length as a deterrent to any Egyptian offensive operations. He ordered the construction of small, earthen fortifications to protect company or platoon-sized positions. Made largely of piles of sandbags, these positions were vulnerable to modern ordnance. Minefields between the fortifications stood as an obstacle to any Egyptian infiltrations by small units. Israeli infantry units deployed in forward positions, with armor held in the rear as a mobile reserve. This defensive scheme worked well for over a year until Nasser escalated the low-level border war along the Suez Canal.

After over a year of rebuilding his armed forces, Nasser felt confident enough to challenge Israel's occupation of the Sinai with a new ferocity. On 8 September 1968, and then again on 26 October, Egyptian field guns launched heavy barrages all along the entire front, each lasting the greater part of a day. The artillery shells exposed the vulnerability of Israel's fortifications at the water's edge, leaving twenty-five Israeli soldiers killed and fifty-two wounded. These numbers shocked Israel's army and society. Many of the Israeli casualties resulted from the collapse of the earthen bunkers under heavy fire. On 29 October, Moshe Dayan, the defense minister, informed the Knesset (parliament) that Israel had suffered 101 killed and three hundred wounded on the southern front since the 1967 war.[15] But the losses in the last month and a half proved most troublesome, for Egypt could easily deliver more massive artillery fire on the essentially defenseless Israeli positions. The Israeli General Staff had to reassess its concept of defense for the Sinai—but first the situation called for an appropriate military response.

In retaliation for the second Egyptian artillery barrage, the Israeli General Staff decided on an audacious commando raid deep into the heart of the Nile Valley. Three targets were selected around Nag Hamadi, a town in upper Egypt some 430 kilometers south of Cairo and 250 kilometers north of Aswan. On the night of 31 October/1 November 1968, French Sud 321 helicopters transported a paratroop force led by Colonel Danny Matt, of Abu Ageila fame, over three hundred kilometers of Egyptian airspace. Once on the ground, the Israeli paratroopers fanned out with lightning speed and hit two bridges over the Nile as well as a major electrical transformer some ten kilometers south of Nag Hamadi, cutting electricity in the area. Then the entire force returned to its base, apparently without any loss of life.[16] By this special operation, the Eshkol government sent a clear message of Israel's willingness to expand the war into Egypt's hinterland, hoping to embarrass Nasser and deter from him initiating any more hostilities.

The Israeli General Staff fully understood that such raids were not a solution in and of themselves. They only affected the short run at best, but offered no lasting solution against a determined adversary. The Egyptians could easily resume their artillery attacks at any time; they might even launch a crossing operation to establish a small bridgehead or toehold on the east bank of the Suez Canal. Therefore, Lieutenant General Haim Bar-Lev, the chief of the General Staff, ordered the defense establishment to rethink the issue of how to defend the Sinai while minimizing the loss of Israeli life. Colonel Avraham Adan, the deputy commander of the Armor Corps, received the assignment to head a special team to study the problem. In the meantime, the senior command deployed an additional tank brigade in the Sinai, thus creating the first regular armored division of three tank brigades in the IDF's brief history. Adan took command of this *ugdah* while at the same time leading the study team.

Adan's answer affirmed the general solution already reached by Southern Command, which had conducted its own investigation into the subject.[17] Adan recommended that the Israeli army construct twenty fortified warning stations, called *meozim* (*maoz* being the Hebrew word for the strongest part of a castle) along the water course at eleven-kilometer intervals. These fortifications would serve as tripwires for a major Egyptian crossing. So they would withstand artillery fire, Israeli engineers would construct them with virtually impregnable underground bunkers. Fifteen to twenty-two soldiers would man each position. A rampart would allow for the deployment of a tank platoon at the water's edge. A second rampart, some five hundred meters back, would permit tanks to take up positions to provide covering fire. Supply stocks would allow each strong point to maintain effective resistance for at least several days.

Electronic devices and minefields between the fortifications would warn of any Egyptian infiltrations into the Sinai. A complex road network west of the passes would allow the IDF to employ a mobile defense in rapid fashion. Small armor forces would patrol between the *meozim*, using Lexicon Road, which ran along the Suez Canal. A sand embankment of several meters' height, constructed right at the water line, would shield the road from direct artillery and small-arms fire. To facilitate a rapid Israeli response to any Egyptian attack, Adan recommended the construction of two additional lateral roads. Artillery Road would stand ten to fifteen kilometers from the waterway, for the use of long-range artillery and the first echelon of tanks. The tanks could reinforce the *meozim* within thirty to sixty minutes of an Egyptian attack. Lateral Road, some thirty kilometers from the Suez Canal, would permit the Israeli army to concentrate the bulk of its armored *ugdah* for a large counterattack to destroy any major Egyptian crossing attempt.

Adan considered his concept as a judicious balance between fixed and mobile defense. Herein lay an ambiguity that would hurt the IDF in the 1973 war. Upon its completion, the Bar-Lev Line, as it became known, consisted of sand walls along the Suez Canal, underground bunkers, tank ramps, supply depots, patrol roads, artillery positions, and staging areas. In the event of a major crossing attempt by the Egyptians, Adan expected the Israeli army to fight the Egyptians "along and near the water line," rather than give ground, as normally called for in a mobile defense.[18]

Over time, however, the expectation grew that the Israeli strong points would impede any major crossing operation long enough to allow IDF reinforcements to prevent the establishment of a major bridgehead in the Sinai. In essence, the strong points would help defeat the Egyptians virtually at the water line. Yet, as constructed, the Bar-Lev Line lacked the solid defenses demanded of a fixed defensive system like the French Maginot Line of World War II fame. But from a political point of view, Adan's plan pleased the cabinet, which feared the possibility of the superpowers' imposing a cease-fire after the Egyptian army had rapidly established a lodgment on the east bank of the Suez Canal but before the Israelis could defeat it.

In late 1968, Bar-Lev, the chief of the General Staff, and Gavish both approved Adan's solution. Most Israeli senior officers embraced the concept as well. Taking advantage of the Suez Canal as a natural barrier appeared the best and most logical course of action. Construction work on the systems of small fortifications began in earnest in December 1968 and continued at a frantic pace for the next several months, finishing on 15 March 1969. Bar-Lev and Gavish, however, implemented some modifications to Adan's concept of a warning system. Ten additional fortifications, for a grand total of thirty *meozim*, were added, to create clusters of forts at the most likely crossing sites. Army engineers also installed a system of oil installations designed to set the canal's water on fire in the event of a major Egyptian crossing attempt. These modifications tended to make the Bar-Lev Line more a defensive line in nature than a mere warning system.

A number of critics—among them Major Generals Israel Tal, chief of the Armor Corps, and Ariel Sharon, chief of Training Branch—questioned the wisdom of Adan's concept. For these officers, concrete fortifications on the water line represented a positional defense, out of character for the IDF. Instead of the small forts stretched the length of the Suez Canal, Sharon pressed for a more mobile defense, based on counterattacks by armored forces. In his view, the Israeli army should deploy its armor along the first line of hills and dunes, eight to twelve kilometers from the waterway. Between the water line and the first line of dunes, small mobile patrols would keep a constant vigil. Meanwhile, at the first line of dunes, the tank force could respond within thirty minutes to any Egyptian military crossing. A second line, twenty to thirty kilometers from the Suez Canal, would provide the larger forces necessary for a major counterattack. According to both Tal and Sharon, such a mode of defense conformed more to the Israeli way of war, which stressed offense, speed, and mobility, not holding terrain in fixed fortifications.

There was no easy answer to the dilemma of preventing the Egyptians from capturing a bit of Sinai territory. Tal and Sharon had the militarily stronger argument. Mobile defense took advantage of the Israeli superiority in maneuver warfare, which in itself is usually a more effective form of fighting than position defense. However, their concept failed to remove the problem of Israeli casualties. Although the small Israeli patrols along the Suez Canal would not be easy targets for Egyptian artillery, they would still be vulnerable to ambushes by Egyptians who had infiltrated to the west bank. Moreover, there was common ground: both sides expected to defeat the Egyptian army within five to ten kilometers of the Suez Canal. Sharon was willing to let the Egyptians make a minor penetration into the Sinai before the IDF "would be able to harass them and probe for their weak points at our convenience."[19] Neither party in the discussions expected to allow the EAF to get more than several kilometers into the Sinai. Certainly no one envisaged an Egyptian occupation of the entire Suez Canal before the IDF could launch an effective counterattack.

The Bar-Lev Line, whatever the disagreement within the Israeli defense establishment about its effectiveness, was for the Egyptians a symbol of Israel's intransigence against any notion of returning the Sinai to Egypt. It clearly presented a formidable military obstacle, one that would degrade any Egyptian attempt to cross the Suez Canal and dash to the strategic passes in the Sinai. Egypt's General Command thus had to allocate effort and resources to destroying the Bar-Lev Line before contemplating subsequent operations. By its sheer existence, the IDF gained precious time to marshal regular forces and, if necessary, mobilize the reserves. Despite the Bar-Lev Line's military value to Israel, Nasser failed to employ the EAF to prevent its construction. Israeli crews worked essentially unmolested by Egyptian fire. Eventually, however, the Egyptians would have to destroy this man-made barrier if they ever hoped to employ the military option to regain the Sinai.

EGYPT'S EVOLVING STRATEGY

As the Bar-Lev Line fast became a hard reality at the beginning of 1969, Nasser confronted a difficult strategic situation. Prospects for any serious diplomatic movement were slim indeed. The United States, the USSR, and Israel were not disposed to upsetting the status quo. Egypt could ill afford to allow both the diplomatic and military fronts to remain frozen for an indefinite period.

The beginning of the new year saw a change in Israel's political leadership. Eshkol died in February 1969, and Golda Meir became the new prime minister in March. Meir had migrated with her husband to Palestine from the United States in 1921. Immersed in Labor Zionist politics, she fell under the influence of Ben-Gurion and had played an important role in the founding the state. In comparison to Eshkol, she was tougher in her attitudes toward the Arabs and less swayed by American pressure. To an admirer, she embodied, in her own unique way, the new Jew born out of the crucible of the Holocaust: "Her craggy face bore witness to the destiny of a people that had come to know too well the potentialities of man's inhumanity. Her watchful eyes made clear that she did not propose that those she led should suffer the same fate without a struggle."[20]

During her tenure, Jewish settlements quietly continued on the West Bank, the Golan Heights, the Sinai, and the Gaza Strip.

By January 1969, Nasser became more keenly aware of the need for military action to break up the diplomatic logjam. On 21 January, the Egyptian president warned of growing pressure for armed conflict: "The first priority, the absolute priority in this battle is the military front, for we must realize that the enemy will not withdraw unless we force him to withdraw through fighting. Indeed, there can be no hope of any political solution unless the enemy realizes that we are capable of forcing him to withdraw through fighting."[21] Yet the EAF was not ready to conduct a major crossing of the Suez Canal.

The air force was clearly Egypt's Achilles' heel. The Six Day War had once again impressed upon the country's political and military leadership the critical importance of air supremacy in modern warfare. Though in possession of a relatively large number of combat aircraft, Egypt's air arm suffered from an acute shortage of trained pilots. In aerial combat, Israeli pilots possessed a clear advantage, both in quality of training and in their Western-made aircraft. Therefore, Nasser refused to embark on a major war or operation until he had a sufficient number of trained pilots and capable aircraft to challenge the Israeli air force for control of the air and strike targets deep in Israel. Because the MiG-21 and the MiG-17 lacked the range to pose such a threat to Israel, the Israeli air force could conduct strategic bombing against Cairo without concern for an Egyptian reprisal in kind against Tel Aviv or Jerusalem.

Finding himself in a militarily inferior position at the beginning of 1969 but feeling pressure to do something, Nasser drifted toward a strategy of low-level attrition, one of whose main military objectives would be to inflict on the IDF as much damage as possible in weapons, equipment, and men.[22] The Egyptians were acutely aware of Israeli society's hypersensitivity toward the loss of human life. Thus, one constant goal for the Egyptian army was to "kill the Israelis wherever you find them; the individual is more important [to the enemy] than equipment in combat."[23] Egyptian officers frequently stressed this Israeli vulnerability to their Soviet advisors.[24]

At the beginning of 1969, General Command possessed the means to inflict heavy casualties on the IDF. Since the Six Day War, the EAF had developed artillery as its main weapon for challenging Israel's occupation of the Sinai.[25] Here the Egyptians possessed a qualitative edge over the Israelis, if through nothing else than sheer numbers–by the end of 1969 they had some two thousand pieces. The IDF lacked sufficient artillery to employ in an effective counterbattery role. The Egyptian army could also employ small-arms fire, as well as quick air and infantry raids across the Suez Canal against selected targets. Nasser was especially keen on intensifying commando operations on the east bank, raising the issue in a meeting of the Council of Ministers on 16 February 1969.[26] Small elite units could infiltrate into the Sinai and set ambushes or lay mines with the aim of killing or wounding Israeli soldiers. Capturing Israelis as prisoners of war would be a bonus. Special operations would also net valuable intelligence about Israeli defenses. In the long run, Nasser expected the

EAF to gain valuable combat experience through more intense clashes with the IDF.

While Nasser contemplated a new strategy, unexpected fighting broke out along the Suez Canal, forcing his hand. On 8 March 1969, Egypt responded to an incident with a massive artillery bombardment against the Bar-Lev Line all along the canal. At the end of March, Nasser announced that he would no longer honor the cease-fire along the Suez Canal.

In a series of articles published in *al-Ahram* on 27 March, 11 April, and 27 April 1969, Muhammad Hasanayn Haykal, one of Nasser's inner circle, talked of a new armed struggle to exhaust Israel and force the United States to reassess its Middle East policy. The piece appearing on 11 April was most interesting in its discussion of possible political outcomes from limited military operations.

I am not speaking of defeating the enemy in war (*al-harb*) but I am speaking about defeating the enemy in a battle (*maarka*). . . . [T]he battle I am speaking about, for example, is one in which the Arab forces might, for example, destroy two or three Israeli Army divisions, annihilate between 10,000 and 20,000 Israeli soldiers, and force the Israeli Army to retreat from positions it occupies to other positions, even if only a few kilometers back. . . . Such a limited battle would have unlimited effects on the war. . . .

1. It would destroy a myth which Israel is trying to implant in the minds—the myth that the Israeli Army is invincible. Myths have great psychological effect.
2. The Israeli Army is the backbone of Israeli society. . . . Israel has become a military stronghold and Israeli society has become the society of a besieged stronghold—a military garrison society.
3. Such a battle would reveal to the Israeli citizens a truth which would destroy the effects of the battles of June 1967. In the aftermath of these battles, Israeli society began to believe in the Israeli Army's ability to protect it. Once this belief is destroyed or shaken, once Israeli society begins to doubt its ability to protect itself, a series of reactions may set in with unpredictable consequences.
4. Furthermore, such a battle would shake the influence of the ruling military establishment. The establishment has the whip hand in directing and implementing Israeli policy on the excuse of acting as Israel's sole protector and guardian of Zionist plans.
5. Such a battle would destroy the philosophy of Israeli strategy, which affirms the possibility of "imposing peace" on the Arabs. Imposing peace is, in fact, an expression which actually means "waging war."
6. Such a battle and its consequences would cause the USA to change its policy towards the Middle East crisis in particular, and towards the Middle East after the crisis in general.[27]

Several key ideas emerged from Haykal's articles that presaged Egypt's politico-military strategy in the 1973 war. According to Haykal's analysis, a limited war could bring broad political benefits. Rather than seizing sizable territory or decisively defeating the IDF, the EAF would seek to inflict as many casualties, and to prolong the conflict, as long as possible, thereby placing great stress on Israel's society and economy. Israelis had come to expect, as a matter of course, a short war with dramatic results on the battlefield. Thwarting this expectation would prove most unsettling to Israeli citizens. Anything short of a lightning victory could be deemed a significant setback by the Israelis themselves, and, in Haykal's scenario, the pain of an intense war of attrition would have political ramifications in Israel. The United States, for its part, would have to modify its stalwart support of Israel and adopt a policy designed to preserve stability in the region by striving to bring peace to the region. To achieve this noble goal, Washington would have to apply serious pressure on Israel to return captured lands to its Arab neighbors.

Haykal's articles revealed a strategic dilemma confronting Egypt. It was difficult to see Israel or the United States changing its policies or attitudes without a major war; how big a conflict was the pressing question. Haykal thought on a grandiose scale: ten to twenty thousand Israeli dead. In 1969, Egypt lacked such combat power, but it was hard for the country's leadership to come to grips with this harsh reality. Each year after the 1967 war, however, seemed to force Nasser to scale down his expectations and timetable for the next major conflagration. As Haykal noted shortly after the 1973 war, "It was a long time before Egypt became ready to accept the idea of a limited attack aimed at opening up political possibilities."[28]

In mid-April 1969, as the border clashes increased in intensity and frequency, Nasser seemed determined to continue the armed struggle against Israel rather than seek a cease-fire, as in the past. On 15 April, Fawzi appeared before the Council of Ministers and outlined the army's new plans. He delineated five limited goals for upcoming military operations: to provoke bloody clashes along the Suez Canal with the aim of killing as many Israelis as possible; to step up reconnaissance operations for gathering intelligence on Israeli defenses in the Sinai; to create a genuine atmosphere of battle to bring combat experience to the entire army; to increase special operations behind enemy lines; and to challenge Israeli pilots with dogfights in the air.[29] Now the questions were when and how.

By the middle of 1969, the EAF had a formidable force of three hundred thousand military. The Egyptian air force, some fifteen thousand strong, comprised over 350 fighter planes, including one hundred MiG-21 jet-interceptors and ninety Su-7 fighter-bombers, whereas the Israeli air force possessed 275 combat aircraft, including forty-eight A-4 Skyhawks and sixty-five Mirage IIIs. To help protect Egypt's skies, the air defense forces would become fully operational in June 1969 as a fourth and independent service, with some three hundred SAM-2 missiles and a slew of antiaircraft guns. Egyptian ground forces stood at 180,000 men, 915 tanks, and 750 field guns. To counter these forces, Israel could field, upon full mobilization of reserves, 290,000 men, 1,800 tanks, and three hundred artillery pieces. In the vicinity of the Suez Canal, however, some fifty to seventy thousand Egyptians squared off against over eighteen thousand Israelis in the western Sinai.[30] Despite advantages in numbers, however, Nasser sought limited aims.

TACTICAL AND OPERATIONAL ESCALATION

Unprepared for a major crossing operation, Nasser was drawn into a strategy of attrition designed to make life unbearable for Israeli troops along the Suez Canal. Over five hundred incidents took place in the month of April 1969; UN observers logged over four hundred in May. On 7 July, UN Secretary-General U Thant reported eighty-six consecutive days of incidents along the Egyptian-Israeli front.[31]

At first, the IDF responded in kind, with artillery fire and commando raids deep into Egypt. In addition to a repeat attack on Nag Hamadi, Israeli elite forces downed high-tension lines between Cairo and Aswan, destroyed bridges over the Nile, and struck coastal bases on the western shore on the Gulf of Suez. But with no end in sight to the frequent and intense armed clashes, pressure mounted within Israel for the military to reevaluate its strategy for deterring the Egyptian army from offensive operations. For the four month period ending on 13 July 1969, the Israeli army had suffered twenty-nine killed and 120 wounded.[32] Obviously, the Bar-Lev Line had failed to prevent the loss of Israeli lives. Especially troublesome for Israel was an incident on 10 July in which an Egyptian commando battalion crossed the Suez Canal and attacked a tank depot at Port Tawfiq, killing six Israeli soldiers. For the Egyptians, this bold operation in broad daylight represented a high point in the war of attrition.[33]

Israel regarded the Port Tawfiq incident as the last straw. Clearly, artillery or special operations had proved inadequate as a deterrent. A growing number of senior Israeli commanders were expressing concern that the Egyptians might be planning a large crossing of the Suez Canal. For some time, Major General Ezer Weizman, former air force chief and now head of the Operations Branch, had been advocating either a major land operation or the unleashing of the Israeli air force. The political leadership, including Moshe Dayan, and most senior air force officers had opposed the employment of air power. These individuals feared that an air war could easily degenerate into an attrition battle; they also questioned the efficacy of bombing infantry and artillery positions. The Port Tawfiq incident, however, convinced Dayan of the existence of Egyptian preparations for a major crossing operation; the defense minister now endorsed Weizman's position and obtained the cabinet's permission to unleash the air force.[34]

To facilitate the bombing campaign, the Israeli General Staff ordered ground units to demolish an important Egyptian radar station on Green Island. This tiny fortress, built on a rock formation forty meters in length and eight meters in width, was located at the southern entrance to the Suez Canal. During the night of 19/20 July, a special, combined task force of naval commandos and paratroopers raided the installation. After a battle of an hour or so, the Israelis accomplished their mission, at a loss of at least six killed and nine wounded, to some twenty-five dead Egyptians. The destruction of this early warning station would pave the way for Israeli pilots to begin their air offensive to remove Egyptian artillery positions and SAM-2 missile sites all along the Suez Canal.[35]

At 1:30 P.M. on 20 July, the day of Green Island's neutralization, before the Egyptian army had a chance to recover, Israeli pilots commenced Operation Boxer, the largest air campaign since the Six Day War. Virtually the entire bomber-fighter force attacked all along the Suez Canal in waves for over three hours. At least two SAM-2 missile batteries were destroyed that day, along with other military positions. Israel lost one Mirage. Operation Boxer continued for a week, until 28 July. According to Israeli sources, some five hundred sorties destroyed six SAM-2 missile batteries and five radar stations, at a loss of two Israeli planes.[36]

Fortunately for Israel, the air force had received by this time enough American-made, A4-E Skyhawks, a state-of-the-art, single-seat attack aircraft designed for close air support. This plane became the mainstay of this phase of the attrition battle. Over the next two months, Israeli pilots flew over a thousand sorties. Special infantry operations and artillery bombardments complemented the air war. On the night of 27/28 August, for example, Israeli commandos, transported in Super Frelon helicopters, struck an air base near Asyut, some three hundred kilometers south of Cairo. Other canal-crossing operations targeted Egyptian positions near the water line (see Map 10).

At the beginning of September, with no end in sight to the hostilities, Bar-Lev decided to conduct a daring assault on Egyptian territory. Operation *Raviv* was designed to achieve two objectives: to draw Egyptian military forces away from the Suez Canal, by conducting a raid along the western shore of the Gulf of Suez; and to force Nasser from continuing his attrition strategy. The General Staff had created a special task force, under the command of Lieutenant Colonel "Pinko" Harel. This highly secret unit consisted of captured Egyptian vehicles, mainly T-55 tanks and BTR-50 armored personnel carriers. Operation *Raviv* involved an armored task force of six T-55 tanks and three BTR-50s manned by a special team of Arabic-speakers who were trained intensively for six weeks. To divert Egyptian attention from the main effort, a team of Israeli frogmen would sink two Egyptian torpedo boats in their home port of Ras Sadat on the night of 7 September.

At 3:37 A.M. on 9 September, Harel's small force of a hundred men arrived by boats at a point twenty kilometers south of Ras Sadat. The Israelis first attacked a military camp at Abu Darag. Meanwhile, Israeli pilots flying Super Mystères dropped bombs in support of the ground forces. By 7:17, the base, along with its radar installation, was secure in Israeli hands. Then the small Israeli force traveled forty kilometers south to Ras Zafrana and destroyed another Egyptian base, with its radar position, coastal guns, and air defenses. After traveling over nine hours in broad daylight, the task force returned to the Sinai by sea. Israelis claimed the loss of only one pilot killed and one wounded soldier.[37] An Egyptian source admitted to more than two hundred Egyptians killed.[38]

The Ras Zafrana raid caught Nasser attending a training exercise for the recently created 21st Armored Division. Shocked and angered by the news of the Israeli operation, Nasser suffered a heart attack the next day (10 September); doctors had to restrict his activities until the end of the month. Upset by what he

112 The Albatross of Decisive Victory

perceived as a lack of competence among his senior commanders, the Egyptian leader fired the chief of the General Staff, the commander of the navy, and the commander of the Red Sea District. By these firings in the senior command, Nasser tried to send a clear message to the EAF of the imperative for combat proficiency.[39]

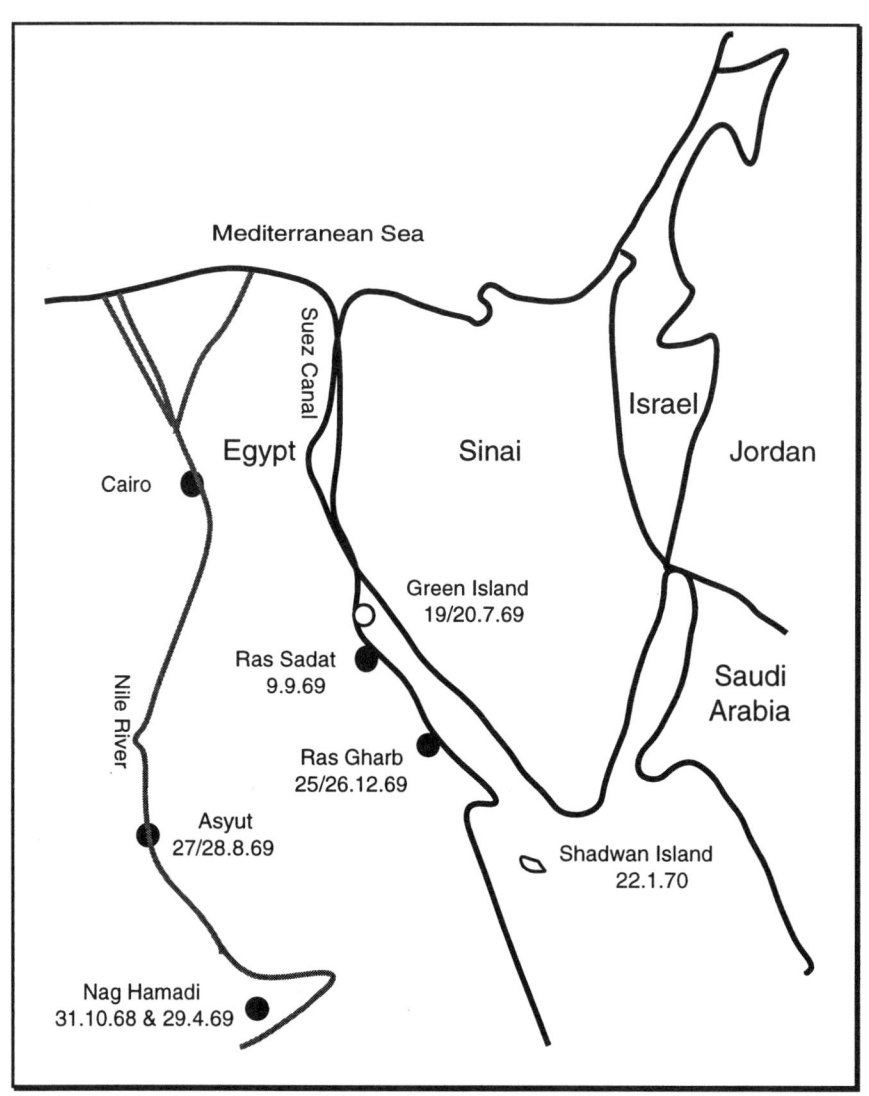

Map 10. Major IDF Raids, 1968–70.

Rather than submit to intimidation, Nasser ordered a commensurate retaliation. On 11 September, approximately seventy to one hundred MiG-17s and MiG-21s attacked the Israeli military targets stretching from Romana to Mitla Pass, at a loss of eleven Egyptian aircraft, according to Israeli sources.[40] On the ground, Egyptian commandos quietly crossed the canal and conducted ambushes on the east side. For the next three and a half months after the Ras Zafrana raid, Israel saw no appreciable decline in total casualties: forty-seven in September, fifty-six in October, thirty-nine in November, and thirty in December. Figures for Israeli soldiers killed in action increased slightly during this same period: eleven in October, twelve in November, and thirteen in December. Total Israeli losses on the Sinai from June 1967 to January 1970 stood at 244 killed and 699 wounded.[41]

The fighting maintained a steady rhythm through the month of December. By this time, Israeli fighter-bombers had virtually destroyed Egypt's air defense system along the Suez Canal. But then came a surprise. Toward the end of the year, the Egyptians installed a new radar system, the Soviet-made P-12 radar, capable of providing advance warning of low-flying aircraft. The radar was also impervious to Israel's electronic warfare devices. By chance, an Israeli reconnaissance flight discovered one such P-12 radar station at Ras Gharib, on the Gulf of Suez. Rather than destroy the site with bombs, the Israeli General Staff decided to capture the highly sophisticated Soviet radar.

The bold and audacious special operation took place on the night of 25/26 December 1969. First, the Israeli air force diverted Egyptian attention away from the Gulf of Suez by launching a heavy bombing campaign all along the Suez Canal from Qantara to Suez City on the morning on 25 December. That night, three helicopters landed a paratroop force some six kilometers from Ras Gharib. Only a small security detail of ten or so Egyptian soldiers guarded the installation. The Israeli paratroopers quickly secured the site. They rapidly dismantled the radar and loaded the equipment onto two heavy-lift helicopters for transportation back to Israel. This daring heist provided Israel and the West with invaluable information on Soviet capabilities in electronic warfare technology and allowed the Israelis to develop effective countermeasures. After the successful mission, the Israelis joked about how the Egyptians graciously served as a convenient conduit for Soviet supplies to Israel.[42] As Israelis beamed with pride, Nasser, chafing in embarrassment, ordered the court-martial of local commanders for negligence.[43]

Shocked by this new and audacious special operation conducted by the IDF, Nasser called a series of meetings of the Supreme Council of the Armed Forces to assess the military situation. The first session took place in the evening of 6 January 1970. Among those participating were the war minister, chief of the General Staff, the service chiefs, and the commanders of the field armies and military districts. Part of the meeting was taken up with discussion of the recent theft of the P-12 radar. Nasser posed a compelling question: "Why are the Israelis superior to us in planning and execution?" In Nasser's view, the EAF needed to improve in planning, training, and execution. The armed forces were clearly poor in combined-arms and joint operations involving air and ground assets. All these considerations suggested that any hope of a major crossing of the Suez Canal with one or two divisions was at least six months away.[44] While

Egyptian senior commanders were in session with Nasser, the Israelis were preparing to escalate the border war with a strategic bombing campaign.

A STRATEGIC ESCALATION

At the beginning of 1970, the Meir government decided to escalate the conflict, ordering the air force to conduct a deep strike into the Nile Valley. The decision proved a difficult one as cabinet members expressed serious concern over whether such an escalation might result in direct Soviet military involvement. Although in the past the Soviets had failed to back their verbal threats with concrete military action, to predict the future with certainty based on past behavior was fraught with danger. In the end, the cabinet gave a green light. The Israeli political leadership hoped that strategic bombing would force Nasser to call off his attacks along the Suez Canal.[45]

Fortunately for Israel, back in September 1969 the United States had begun supplying the IDF with the F-4 Phantom, a potent fighter-bomber with a speed of Mach 2.4 and a range of two thousand miles. The two-seat Phantom provided Israel with its first multipurpose plane that could conduct strategic bombing missions with heavy ordnance. Fitted with electronic counter measures, the F-4 possessed the capability to detect and divert incoming missiles. However, Israel possessed only twenty such planes. On 7 January 1970, Phantoms struck two military bases close to Cairo and one fifty kilometers from the Suez Canal. The message was starkly clear—Egypt's heartland had become the new battlefield.

Nasser felt compelled to retaliate in kind. Egyptian fighter-bombers quickly struck bases in the Sinai, causing casualties and some damage, but at a loss of two Su-7s. But this retaliation proved too meager to dissuade Israel from pursuing its bombing campaign. A severe condemnation by the United States of the bombings on 7 January might have brought a stop to the strategic bombing, but none was forthcoming. So on 13 January, less than a week after the first raid, the Israeli air force resumed its deep strikes, this time hitting military installations at Tel al-Kabir, fifty kilometers west of Ismailiya, and Khanka, twenty kilometers northeast of Cairo. Again the Nixon administration appeared unconcerned, and Yitzhak Rabin, the Israeli ambassador in Washington, reported unofficial American approval of these attacks.[46]

For Nasser, in the absence of an adequate air defense, the "war was transformed from a war of liberation into a war of survival."[47] General Command decided to move key military schools out of reach. The military academy moved from Cairo to Gebel al-Awliya, near Khartoum in the Sudan; the naval college from Alexandria to Tabruq, in Libya; and the air college from Cairo to Gamal Abd al-Nasser Airport in Libya.[48] These moves underscored Egypt's inability to defend its own airspace. Nasser could not endure such a situation for too long. With the initiative entirely in Israeli hands, the Egyptian leader decided to stand firm and make a desperate appeal to the Soviets for military assistance. On 22 January, he secretly flew to Moscow.

From 23 to 25 January, Nasser held a series of meetings with his Soviet counterparts.[49] Nasser outlined the seriousness of his situation. The lack of adequate air defense had left Egypt completely vulnerable to Israel's air force. For him, the problem was quite clear; so was the solution: Egypt needed a major upgrading of its air defense capabilities. This included the rapid delivery of SAM-3s to augment the SAM-2s currently in the country, as well as more trained pilots to fly sophisticated combat planes. Training Egyptian crews on the new missiles would take at least six months, during which time Israeli fighter-bombers would roam Egypt's skies virtually at will, which would undermine public morale and threaten the regime. The only solution militarily was for the USSR to provide its own military personnel to handle the sophisticated air defense equipment and fly the additional aircraft. If the Soviets failed to send combat units, Nasser warned, he had no alternative but to turn to the United States for political help.

Nasser was clearly blackmailing Brezhnev, but it worked. The Kremlin could ill afford to allow American influence to increase at Soviet expense in the largest and most important Arab country. The Soviet leadership had apparently anticipated Nasser's hard sell, for Brezhnev quickly agreed to meet Egyptian needs with the unprecedented step of committing Soviet combat troops to the defense of a country outside Europe. In the agreement carved out on 25 January 1970, the Kremlin promised to send a complete air defense division of thirty-two SAM-3 battalions, three air brigades of ninety improved MiG-21s, four highly sophisticated P-15 radar systems, fifty Su-9 light bombers, ten MiG-21s for training, and four high-altitude MiG-23s for reconnaissance. Soviet combat personnel would man the SAM-3 sites and fly the MiG-21s and MiG-23s, while trained Soviet technicians operated the complex radar systems. Furthermore, the Soviets agreed to host an entire Egyptian air defense brigade of 1,800 soldiers for six months of intensive training on the SAM-3 in the USSR. By this agreement, the Kremlin moved to match Israel's escalation.

While Nasser was hatching a coup in Moscow, Israel launched a special operation. On 22 January 1970, the day of Nasser's departure, Israeli naval commandos landed at 11:30 in broad daylight on Shadwan Island, thirty kilometers from Sharm al-Shaykh in the straits connecting the Red Sea with the Gulf of Suez. They gained control of the island, some sixteen kilometers in length and from three to five in width. The Israelis proceeded to dismantle the radar equipment for transport back to Israel. With Nasser and the war minister in Moscow, Vice President Anwar Sadat and the chief of the General Staff, Major General Muhammad Sadiq, were in charge. The Egyptian response proved inept. The next day found General Command still unable to produce any effective response, and the Israelis departed of their own volition at 5:30 that afternoon, having been on the island for thirty-six hours.[50]

The Egyptian press tried to present this incident in the best light possible. The propaganda machine focused on the heroic actions of a naval commander, Captain Hosni Hamad, who had lost his life attempting to reach Shadwan Island in his torpedo boat. However, his action, taken on his own initiative, failed to relieve the beleaguered Egyptians on the island. An official Egyptian spokesman admitted to eighty soldiers killed, wounded, or missing.[51] Essentially, the Egyptian garrison had been left to its own fate, as Israeli planes prevented the arrival of reinforcements. This incident embarrassed and frustrated Sadat, no doubt leaving a strong impression on a man who would assume the presidency eight months later.

After the Shadwan operation, Israel continued its strategic bombing, unaware of the secret agreement reached in Moscow between Egypt and the USSR. On 28 January, Israeli planes bombed a military camp in the suburb of Maadi, only ten kilometers from the center of Cairo. Israeli bombs inadvertently blew out windows at an American school, which at the time was filled with students and teachers. Israel's psychological warfare directed at the Egyptian population had now caught American citizens in the crossfire. Rather than apply pressure for a cessation of air strikes, the Nixon administration chose to downplay the Israeli action; the State Department issued a mild statement of concern. Washington, also unaware of the new agreement between the Egyptians and Soviets for the employment of Soviet combat troops in Egypt, considered it wise not to impede Israel's strategic bombing campaign.[52]

The Kremlin, on the other hand, chose to issue a stern warning to the White House. On 31 January 1970, President Kosygin sent a tough letter to Nixon, issuing a veiled threat to increase Soviet involvement in Egypt should Israel persist in its strategic bombing offensive: "The Soviet Union will be forced to see to it that the Arab states have the means at their disposal, with the help of which a due rebuff to the arrogant aggressor could be made."[53] Washington did not take Kosygin's warning seriously.

Buoyed by his secret agreement with the Soviets, Nasser approved a bold retaliation against Israel. On 6 February, Egyptian frogmen sank two Israeli ships in the harbor of Eilat. The Israeli air force responded within forty-eight hours, bombing two different military camps, one thirty kilometers from Cairo and the second within five kilometers of Hilwan. On 12 February, Israeli planes, striking a military camp and air force supply depot at al-Khanka, twenty kilometers northeast of Cairo, accidentally bombed the Abu Zaabel metalwork factory, killing seventy civilian workers and wounding over a hundred civilians. European newspapers gave front-page coverage to this incident, and Washington, no longer able to ignore Israeli actions, issued an official statement of disapproval.

At the end of February, Soviet military personnel began deploying the first Soviet SAM-3 battalions and MiG-21s. Top priority went to protecting the cities of Cairo and Alexandria as well as the Aswan Dam. On 19 March, the *New York Times* broke the news of the presence of Soviet combat forces. Both the Nixon and Meir governments had to reassess their policies as a result of this surprise. Desiring to avoid a direct confrontation with the USSR, and under pressure from Washington, the Israeli cabinet decided to select different targets and lower the frequency of attacks. Instead of bombing military installations around Cairo and Hilwan, where Soviet crews now manned SAM-3 sites and Russian pilots flew

MiG-21s, the Israeli air force instead hit SAM-2 batteries, radar stations, and military camps, all in the northeastern Nile Delta region.[54] Moreover, the IDF decreased the number of deep strikes, dropping from twelve in January and thirteen in February to five in March and four in April.[55]

The Meir government also sought to reach a tacit agreement about a "red line" between the opposing forces. On 29 March, Major General Benyamin Peled, the new Israeli air force commander, proposed such an arrangement by observing that there would exist only a low probability of direct confrontation between Israeli and Soviet forces if the Soviets kept their military activities away from the Suez Canal.[56] On 9 April, Dayan affirmed this new policy, telling Tel Aviv University students that while the Soviets could protect Egypt's depth, the Israelis had every right to move in the Suez Canal area, which meant within thirty to forty kilometers of the waterway.

The record of bombings was impressive for Israel's small fleet of Phantoms. From 7 January to 13 April 1970, the air force flew 3,300 sorties and dropped approximately eight thousand tons of ordnance on Egypt. A total of thirty-four strategic bombing missions were conducted during this four-month period; eight missions took place within thirty kilometers of Cairo.[57] Although military installations were being targeted, it was only a question of time before innocent children would suffer from stray bombs. That tragedy occurred on 8 April, when Israeli pilots accidentally bombed a primary school at Bahr al-Baqar, some 120 kilometers north of Cairo, killing forty-six schoolchildren. Condemnation from the international community was both swift and widespread. The Meir government called a halt to strategic bombing within a week of this incident.

With Israel's cessation of its strategic bombing campaign, the Soviets could rightly claim that their intervention had scored a victory for Egypt at no cost in Soviet lives. Nasser breathed a sigh of relief; his regime no longer faced a direct threat to its stability. Fighting could now be limited to the zone around the Suez Canal. By the beginning of April, sixty to eighty Soviet pilots and approximately four thousand missile crews guarded Egypt's major cities, air bases, and industrial factories. Egypt's strategic position continued to improve as more Soviet troops steadily poured into the country. By the end of June, these figures would double, to over a hundred pilots and eight thousand air defense personnel at thirty-four missile sites.[58] This steady Soviet buildup caused much consternation in both Washington and Jerusalem.

But even after the suspension of Israel's strategic bombing campaign, the military situation along the Suez Canal looked ominous. Israel and Egypt were locked into an escalating war of attrition. The mere presence of Soviet combat troops in Egypt's heartland seriously complicated matters, enhancing the possibility of an armed confrontation between the USSR and Israel. To avoid this, and save Israel from a potentially dangerous situation, the Nixon administration decided to intervene, to hold talks with Nasser in an attempt to bring at least a temporary respite to hostilities.

In April, Washington dispatched Assistant Secretary of State Joseph Sisco to meet with Nasser in Cairo. The Nixon administration hoped to open a serious dialogue with Nasser; a cool reception, however, awaited the American diplomat. Nasser made clear that he rejected direct talks with the United States, instead preferring to use the USSR as an intermediary in any negotiations. Sisco returned to Washington and reported of Nasser's disinclination to deal with the United States.[59]

Meanwhile, the month of April 1970 was witnessing raging battles between Egyptian and Israeli forces. The EAF had adopted a more aggressive strategy. Egyptian planes conducted numerous sorties into the Sinai, including six major strikes in an eleven-day span. One mission dropped bombs on Israeli military targets near al-Arish, in northeastern Sinai. In the meantime, Egyptian artillery fire, coupled with commando raids, added to the Israeli casualty figures. By the end of the month, Israel had suffered twenty-seven battle deaths, the highest monthly toll since the previous summer.[60] May saw continued hostilities and the increasing danger of a serious escalation.

A CEASE-FIRE

Washington remained apprehensive about the presence of Soviet combat troops in Egypt. There was the growing danger of an Israeli-Soviet confrontation that might draw the United States into the turmoil. To avoid such a possibility, the Nixon administration decided on a diplomatic initiative. In June 1970, Secretary of State William Rogers presented a proposal designed to bring a temporary halt to hostilities. He envisioned a ninety-day cease-fire, during which Egypt and Israel would conduct indirect talks through the intermediary of a Swedish diplomat, Dr. Gunnar Jarring. The American secretary of state hoped to break the diplomatic deadlock with this initiative. A pleasant surprise awaited him.

On 29 June 1970, Nasser made an emergency trip to Moscow, staying in the country until 17 July.[61] For two weeks he convalesced in a hospital. Political concerns, however, drove the trip. First, the Egyptian leader sought more military aid and better military cooperation between the two countries. His wish list included more sophisticated electronic equipment for air defense, modified SAM-3s, the new SAM-6s, and the long-range Tu-16 bombers. A top priority was to gain the capability to retaliate against Israeli cities: "A defense without the capability of reaction remains a weak defense."[62] Aware of the Soviets concern about the presence of their combat troops in Egypt, Nasser reportedly promised that he would not drag the Soviets into a major war. "It is I who wanted from the Soviets experts and pilots, and it is I who will want the Soviet Union to withdraw them when they end their mission."[63] The Soviets promised to provide more support, to the tune of four hundred million dollars by the end of the year, as well as to dispatch a SAM-6 brigade to guard the Aswan Dam.

On 16 July, the day before his scheduled return to Egypt, Nasser dropped a bombshell on his Soviet hosts: he would accept the American initiative for a cease-fire. Caught completely off guard, Brezhnev immediately expressed serious reservations over the seeming shift in Egyptian foreign policy toward the United States. To assuage the Soviet leader's anxieties, Nasser outlined his reasoning. The US proposal for a cease-fire represented nothing new in the Washington's position, and thus it would fail, leaving Egypt's relationship with the United States unchanged. Egypt's acceptance of the American initiative would disabuse critics who claimed that only Israel wanted peace. More importantly, Egypt needed a respite from the fighting. Over the last several months, Egypt had suffered four thousand killed and wounded in its attempts to construct SAM sites. A pause in the fighting would provide much needed rest and allow the Egyptian army to consolidate its forward air defenses positions. The Soviet leadership had little choice but to go along with his decision.

A major change took place in the air war during Nasser's seventeen day stay in the Soviet Union. After several months of intense work, and with the arrival of new missiles, the Soviets and Egyptians managed to establish a more sophisticated, integrated, and lethal air defense network over the west bank. The upgraded SAM-2 brought the minimum engageable altitude down to three thousand feet, whereas the newly arrived SAM-3 could be used down to three hundred feet. In addition to this greatly enhanced technical system, air defense crews began employing a new tactic, called "ripple firing." An entire battery would launch its six missiles in a short, timed sequence, making evasive action more difficult. Moreover, the batteries were numerous enough to provide overlapping coverage.[64] A more serious threat now awaited Israeli pilots who ventured over Egyptian air space.

The new air defense system brought quick results. On 30 June 1970, the day after Nasser's departure from Moscow, air defenders shot down two Phantoms, the most serious loss of combat planes in a single day since the 1967 war. Eitan Ben Eliahu, then a Phantom pilot and later a brigadier general, would recall the blow to self-confidence experienced in the Israeli air force as a result of this one incident: "For the first time, we started to get a feeling that . . . the real threat was a missile, not a plane. All along, we felt that with tenacity and flying skills we could overcome any obstacle. Our entire doctrine, our whole air culture had been based on flying virtuosity. In case of missile, it meant minimal exposure, precise diving, good timing, cutting-edge performance—all of which we knew inside out. Now for the first time, it was not enough."[65] In a press conference held on 6 July, Lieutenant General Haim Bar-Lev, the chief of the General Staff, expressed concern over the gravity of the threat posed by the denser and better integrated air defense system. The Israelis admitted to three of their planes having been shot down in the previous week.[66]

The Nixon administration considered it vital for American interests to maintain Israel's favorable military balance. To help the Israeli air force cope with this new missile threat, the United States quickly shipped to Israel electronic systems for deflecting incoming missiles. The first crates arrived on 13 July, and on 18 July the Israelis conducted their first mission with these aluminum pods. Twenty Phantoms, backed by Skyhawks, launched an offensive to destroy ten missile sites. Israeli sources claim the destruction of four sites and damage to three others, but at a loss of a plane and its crew to a missile, despite the use of the pods. Senior Israeli military commanders felt unsure about the capability of the new system, while the Israeli cabinet grew anxious over the increasing loss of combat aircraft.[67] Fortunately for the Israeli air force, a cease-fire was in the offing.

On 23 July, as promised back in Moscow, Nasser accepted the American initiative, thus putting immediate pressure on Israel to show her willingness to strive for peace. The American administration sought Israel's consent. The Israelis naturally expressed serious concern about the likelihood that the Egyptians would make use of the cease-fire to strengthen their missile positions along the Suez Canal. To entice Israel to accept, on 23 July Nixon made three promises in a historic letter to Meir. The United States would not insist that Israel agree to Arab interpretations of UN Resolution 242. Furthermore, any solution to the Palestinian refuge problem would not alter the Jewish character of the Israeli state. Finally, the American government would refrain from pressuring Israel to withdraw its troops from occupied territories until the achievement of a peace agreement to Israel's satisfaction. Yitzhak Rabin, Israel's ambassador in Washington, eagerly proclaimed this letter "a latter-day Balfour Declaration."[68]

While the Israeli cabinet debated the merits of the American proposal and generous offer, the war of attrition escalated to a direct confrontation between Israel and the USSR. On 25 July, Soviet-piloted MiG-21s challenged Israeli pilots in Egyptian airspace near the Suez Canal. The Israeli planes backed down and returned to base. For Israel to retreat from this challenge would have serious repercussions for future Israeli overflights; the senior command set a trap for the Soviets. On 30 July, Soviet pilots once again moved to intimidate Israeli pilots, only to find themselves engaged in a major dogfight. The Israelis shot down four or five of them.[69] Egyptians, who had experienced much Soviet criticism for losing so many planes in aerial combat with Israelis, drew some satisfaction from this Israeli victory. That Soviet pilots fared no better in this engagement than Egyptians had in the past suggested that Israeli air superiority stemmed more from an inferior Soviet product rather than from poor Egyptian performance. Any chance to test this theory, however, was averted on 31 July, when the Israeli cabinet opted to accept the cease-fire proposed by the US.

The cease-fire went into effect on 8 August, at 1:00 A.M. Egyptian time. As the dawn drew near, Nasser ordered his air defense commander to transfer as many missile sites to the Suez Canal area as possible. The Egyptians took advantage of the cover of darkness to do so. Working feverishly at night, especially on 7/8 August, the Egyptians claimed they transferred fourteen SAM battalions to within thirty kilometers of the Suez Canal.[70] Israel disputed the timing of these transfers, claiming they had taken place after the cessation of hostilities, a clear violation of the agreement. Egypt denied anything of the sort. Initially, the United States preferred to avoid a direct confrontation over the issue, but eventually Washington accepted Israel's version of events. Regardless of the issue of culpability, Nasser gained an important victory with the establishment of air defense coverage over the eastern bank of the Suez Canal, an achievement that enhanced the chances of success in a limited crossing operation in the near future.

Egypt and Israel, as well as the United States and the USSR, heaved a sigh of relief with the implementation of a three month cease-fire. Israel had paid a high price during the Three Year War. From 11 June 1967 to 7 August 1970, Israel had lost 750 killed and 2,750 wounded on all three fronts; of these dead, over four hundred had been killed in action fighting the EAF. But the last several months had been the worst. Major General Ariel Sharon, the Israeli commander of the southern front at the time of the cease-fire, voiced the opinion of most Israelis: "The cease-fire came as a relief to everyone concerned. We were suffering daily casualties on the Bar-Lev Line."[71] In particular, Mirage and Phantom pilots, who bore the brunt of the air war and were exhausted, voiced similar sentiments. One pilot recalled years later the joy of a respite from the conflict. "When the cease-fire was declared we thanked God. I never thought such a thing would happen, but we were at Bir Gifgafa one night, and I[sraeli] A[ir] F[orce] Operations called down and wanted us to scramble. I told them 'Dear friends, scramble from the North because we have no strength left.'"[72]

At the time, Egypt's General Command was unaware of the emerging signs of exhaustion on the Israeli side of the Suez Canal. But the EAF had its own problems. Despite some tactical gains in the air war, Egypt also needed a lull in the fighting. In the last three months of the war, Egypt had suffered 1,500 killed in combat.[73] Nasser had made this point clearly to the Soviets in Moscow.

Dawn on 8 August thus brought a welcome calm on both sides of the Suez Canal. History suggested that this tranquillity would last only a short time. Suddenly, in September 1970, during the cease-fire, a civil war unexpectedly erupted in Jordan, creating the biggest crisis in the Arab world since the Six Day War. The Jordanian government was determined to crush Palestinian guerrillas who were attempting to build a state within a state. There loomed the danger of an Israeli intervention should King Hussein appear on the brink of a defeat at the hands of the Palestinians. In an attempt to mediate the Jordanian crisis, Nasser hosted in Cairo an Arab summit that included King Hussein and Yassar Arafat among its participants. By skillful and persistent diplomacy, Nasser managed to carve out an agreement. On 28 September 1970, the day after the summit's conclusion, Nasser suddenly died of an apparent heart attack.

Job stress had taken a fatal toll. Rebuilding Egypt after its devastating military defeat in 1967 had demanded an Herculean effort, and Nasser, who seemed driven to make amends for his mistakes of 1967, had devoted his life to this formidable task. He had often spent long hours at his job, sometimes working sixteen or eighteen hours a day. To help handle the enormous stress, Nasser, a heavy smoker, had consumed upward of sixty cigarettes a day during this period.

As early as 1958, Egyptian doctors had diagnosed Nasser as suffering from diabetes. Then came arteriosclerosis of the calf in the right leg, which caused considerable pain throughout the sixties. In 1965, a team of Soviet and British medical experts had reportedly discovered Buerger's disease, iron in the liver. Matters turned for the worse after the Six Day War, when Nasser suffered several heart attacks, including a major one in 1969 that required six weeks of convalescence. Nasser had definitely suffered from poor health during the last three years of his presidency. Official medical reports attributed his death on 28 September 1970 to cardiac arrest.[74] A new Egyptian president would have to make the tough decisions about war or peace.

THE BALANCE SHEET

The Three Years War, more commonly known as the War of Attrition, forms an important link between the 1967 and the 1973 wars. The Six Day War left Israel in an awkward position, a clear military victor without a commensurate political resolution. Armed clashes erupted within a month of the war's conclusion. To limit casualties while maintaining a physical presence on the Suez Canal, the IDF built the Bar-Lev Line. This scheme gradually wedded the IDF to positional defense at the expense of the army's forte in maneuver war. Moreover, many Israelis were unsatisfied by the outcome of the Three Years War. A clear military victory had eluded the IDF, as its last month had seen high losses of Israeli planes to Soviet-made missiles. This development boded ill for the Israeli air force in the next war.

Nasser, for all his mistakes in 1967, had rebounded with remarkable resilience from an overwhelming defeat. The three-year armed struggle with Israel helped prepare the EAF for the big battle of 1973 by providing both officers and soldiers with valuable combat experience. The end of the war saw the EAF's strategic situation strengthened by the establishment of an integrated air defense umbrella over the Suez Canal and some fifteen kilometers of the east bank. But the Egyptians had not achieved this missile coverage by their own efforts. The Soviets had been compelled to man a new SAM system as well as to provide pilots to fly combat planes during the spring and summer of 1970. This direct Soviet military intervention saved Nasser from a major military and political setback.

Israelis emerged from the conflict frustrated but confident. The IDF could easily defeat the Egyptians in a major war. After all, it had taken the Soviets to bail out the Egyptians at the end of the Three Years War. Moreover, the IDF had fought with one hand tied behind its back: the air campaign had been limited in goals and means, and the ground forces had not been called upon to cross the Suez Canal to the western bank. Israelis knew that the next major war against Egypt would see the full weight of the IDF unleashed against Egypt. In such a conflict, the Israeli army should perform another Blitzkrieg. A rude awakening awaited Israel in this regard.

Perhaps the most important link between the Three Years War and the 1973 conflict concerned the relationship between war and policy for Egypt. Despite all the reforms, the EAF failed to demonstrate the ability to inflict serious damage on the IDF in a major war. A small number of astute Egyptian officials began to accept the need to wage a rather limited war designed to force serious diplomatic movement. After three years of rule, Sadat embarked on just such a course.

NOTES

1. Carl von Clausewitz, *On War*, translated by Michael Howard and Peter Paret (Princeton: Princeton University Press, 1984): 80.

2. Samir A. Mutawi, *Jordan in the 1967 War* (Cambridge: Cambridge University Press, 1987): 164.

3. André Beaufre, "Une Guerre Classique Moderne: La Guerre Israelo-Arabe," *Strategie* (July–August 1967): 19.

4. Michael Howard and Robert Hunter, *Israel and the Arab World: The Crisis of 1967* (London: The Institute for Strategic Studies, 1967): 39.

5. Michael Bar-Zohar, *Facing a Cruel Mirror: Israel's Moment of Truth* (New York: Charles Scribner's Sons, 1994): 10–11.

6. Ariel Sharon, *Warrior: The Autobiography of Ariel Sharon* (New York: Simon and Schuster, 1989): 265.

7. Muhammad Hassanayn Haykal, *The Sphinx and the Commisar: The Rise and Fall of Soviet Influence in the Middle East* (New York: Harper and Row, 1978): 190–191.

8. Mahmud Riyad, *Mudhakirat Mahmud Riyad 1948–1978*, I: *al-Bath an al-Salam wa al-Sira al-Sharq al-Ust* (Beirut: al-Muessah al-Arabiyya lil-Dirasat, 1987): 84–96; Muhammad Fawzi, *Harb al-Thalath Sanawat 1967–1970* (Beirut: Dar al-Wahda, 1983): 193–196, 346–348; and Muhammad Hassanayn Haykal, *Road to Ramadan* (New York: Quadrangle, 1975): 46–48.

9. Fawzi, *Harb al-Thalath Sanawat*: 219–220; Muhammad Abd al-Ghani al-Gamasi, *Mudhakirat al-Gamasi: Harb Oktobir 1973* (Paris: al-Munshurat al-Sharqiyya, 1990): 151; and Chaim Herzog, *The Arab-Israeli Wars: War and Peace in the Middle East from the War of Independence through Lebanon* (New York: Vintage Books, 1984): 196.

10. Terence Smith, "Fighting Flares along the Suez," *New York Times*, 15 July 1967: 1, 2 and "Israelis Repeat Downing 6 Planes in Suez Clashes," *New York Times*, 16 July 1967: 1, 2; Michael Wolfers, "UN Men Greeted by Air Attack," *The* [London] *Times*, 17 July 1967: 4; Herzog, *The Arab-Israeli Wars*: 197; and Lon Nordeen, *Fighters over Israel: The Story of the Israeli Air Force from the War of Independence to the Bekaa Valley* (New York: Orion Books, 1990): 88.

11. Fawzi, *Harb al-Thalath Sanawat*: 222–224; Herzog, *The Arab-Israeli Wars*: 197–198; and James Feron, "Egypt's Missiles Sink a Destroyer of Israel's Navy," *New York Times*, 22 October 1967: 1, 4. and "Israelis Blame Soviet Missiles in Sinking of Ship," *New York Times*, 23 October 1967: 1, 3;

12. Colin Chapman, "Egyptians Count Suez Cost," *The* [London] *Times*, 26 October 1967: 4; and Jay Walz, "Cairo Sees Reinery Loss as Grave Economic Blow," *New York Times*, 26 October 1967: 1, 12.

13. Fawzi, *Harb al-Thalath Sanawat*: 226–227.

14. Detailed information on Egyptian forces comes from Amin Huwaydi, *al-Furas al-Daia: al-Qararat al-Hasima fi Harbi al-Istinzaf wa Oktobir* (Beirut: Shirka al-Matbuat Lil-Tawzi wa al-Nashr, 1991): 108, 111–114. Huwaydi became war minister on 21 July 1967, holding this position until January 1968.

15. David Dishon (ed.), *Middle East Record,* IV: *1968* (Jerusalem: Israel Universities Press, 1972): 361.

16. Fawzi, *Harb al-Thalath Sanawat*: 227–228; Dishon, *Middle East Record,* IV: 361–363; and David A. Korn, *Stalemate: The War of Attrition and Great Power Diplomacy in the Middle East, 1967–1970* (Boulder, CO: Westview Press, 1992): 98.

17. For a general discussion of the debate over the construction of the Bar-Lev Line, see Avraham Adan, *On the Banks of the Suez* (San Francisco: Presidio Press, 1980): 42–49; Sharon, *Warrior*: 218–222, 229–230; Chaim Herzog, *The War of Atonement: October, 1973* (Boston: Little, Brown, 1975): 4–7; Edward N. Luttwak and Daniel Horowitz, *The Israeli Army* (New York: Harper and Row, 1975): 318–319; Ya'acov Bar-Siman-Tov, "The Bar-Lev Line Revisited," *Journal of Strategic Studies* 11 (June 1988): 153–156; and Korn, *Stalemate*: 99–105.

18. Adan, *On the Banks of the Suez*: 46.

19. Sharon, *Warrior*: 220.

20. Kissinger, *White House Years*: 370.

21. Quoted in Ahmed Khalidi, "The War of Attrition," *Journal of Palestinian Studies* 3 (1973): 77.

22. al-Gamasi, *Mudhakirat*: 163; Trevor Dupuy, *Elusive Victory: The Arab-Israeli Wars, 1947–1974* (1978, reprint Fairfax, VA: Hero Books, 1984): 362. For a detailed discussion of Egyptian strategic thinking by an Israeli scholar, see Ya'acov Bar-Siman-Tov, *Israeli-Egyptian War of Attrition, 1969–1970: A Case Study in Limited War* (New York: Columbia University Press, 1980): 43–59

23. Fawzi, *Harb al-Thalath Sanawat*: 279.

24. Lieutenant General Vadim Kirpichenko, paper presented at Conference on the October War, 9 October 1998, Washington, DC. Kirpichenko had been a member of the KGB stationed in Cairo during this period.

25. Fawzi, *Harb al-Thalath Sanawat*: 269–273.

26. Farid, *Nasser*: 135.

27. Muhammad Hassanayn Haykal, "al-Gaysh al-Israeli wa al-dawai sal-mulha lihazima fi maarka," *al-Ahram*, 11 April 1969: 1, 3. An English translation appears as "The Strategy of the War of Attrition," *The Israel-Arab Reader*, edited by Walter Laqueur and Barry Rubin, 4th ed. (New York: Facts on File, 1985): 423–424.

28. Haykal, *Road to Ramadan*: 168.

29. Farid, *Nasser*: 135–136.

30. William Beecher, "Attention Draws to Build-ups," *New York Times*, 12 May 1969: 19; Institute for Strategic Studies, *The Military Balance 1969–1970* (London: Institute for Strategic Studies, 1969): 35–37; and Bar-Siman-Tov, *Israeli-Egyptian War of Attrition*: 214–215, nn 10, 12.

31. Kathleen Teltsch, "Thant Tells U.N. Open War Rages Along the Suez," *New York Times*, 8 July 1969: 1.

32. Moshe Dayan, *Moshe Dayan*: 448.

33. Fawzi, *Harb al-Thalath Sanawat*: 280–281; and al-Gamasi, *Mudhakirat*: 166.

34. Ezer Weizman, *On Eagles' Wings: The Personal Story of the Leading Commander of the Israeli Air Force* (New York: Macmillan, 1976): 271–273; Moshe Dayan, *Moshe Dayan*: 448; Bar-Siman-Tov, *Israeli-Egyptian War of Attrition*: 84–86, and "The Myth of Strategic Bombing: Israeli Deep-Penetration Air Raids in the War of Attrition, 1969–1970," *Journal of Contemporary History*, 19 (1984): 550–551; and Korn, *Stalemate*: 165–168.

35. Edgar O'Ballance, *The Electronic War in the Middle East 1968–1970* (Hamden, CT: Archon, 1974): 67–68; David Eshel, *The Israeli Commando's* (Hod Hasharon: Eshel-Dramit, 1979): 51–53; Dupuy, *Elusive Victory*: 363; Herzog, *The Arab-Israeli Wars*: 210; Eliezer Cohen, *Israel's Best Defense: The First Full Story of the Israeli Air Force* (New York: Orion Books, 1993): 281; and James Feron, "Air-Land Battle Rages for Hours Along the Suez," *New York Times*, 21 July 1969: 19, 21.

36. Cohen, *Israel's Best Defense*: 281–282; and Ehud Yonay, *No Margin for Error: The Making of the Israeli Air Force* (New York: Pantheon Books, 1993): 274.

37. Adan, *On the Banks of the Suez*: 51–52; David Eshel, *Chariots of the Desert: The Story of the Israeli Armoured Corps* (London: Brassey's, 1989): 90–91; Herzog, *The Arab-Israeli Wars*: 211–212; Korn, *Stalemate*: 169–170; and Dupuy, *Elusive Victory*: 363–364.

38. Abd al-Azim Ramadan, *Tahtim al-Aliha: Qissa Harb Yunyo 1967*, II (Cairo: Maktaba Madbuli, 1986): 32.

39. Fawzi, *Harb al-Thalath Sanawat*: 282–284; al-Gamasi, *Mudhakirat*: 169–170; and Haykal, *Road to Ramadan*: 73–74.

40. Fawzi, *Harb al-Thalath Sanawat*: 299; and Herzog, *The Arab-Israeli Wars*: 212.

41. Luttwak and Horowitz, *The Israeli Army*: 321 n, 322; and Daniel Dishon (ed.), *Middle East Record*, V: *1969–1970* (Jerusalem: Israel University Press, 1973): 172.

42. Cohen, *Israel's Best Defense*: 288–293; Eshel, *Chariots of the Desert*: 90–92 and *Israeli Commando's*: 62; Luttwak and Horowitz, *The Israeli Army*: 320–321; Korn, *Stalemate*: 175–176; and Nordeen, *Fighters over Israel*: 102–103.

43. Fawzi, *Harb al-Thalath Sanawat*: 284.

44. Abd al-Munim Khalil, *Hurub Misr al-Muasirah fi Awraq Qaid Maydani: 1939–1945, 1956, 1962–1967, 1968–1970, 1973* (Cairo: Dar al-Mustaqbal al-Arabi, 1990): 116–120; Fawzi, *Harb al-Thalath Sanawat*: 288–290; and al-Gamasi, *Mudhakirat*: 171–172. Khalil provides critical details of the points raised during the meeting. Fawzi provides a brief but upbeat account, while Gamasi merely repeats the data presented in Fawzi's book.

45. Moshe Dayan, *Moshe Dayan: The Story of My Life* (New York: William Morrow, 1976): 449; Abba Eban, *Abba Eban: An Autobiography* (New York: Random House, 1977): 465; Bar-Siman-Tov, *Israeli-Egyptian War of Attrition*: 117–132, and "The Myth of Strategic Bombing": 553–555.

46. Yitzhak Rabin, *The Rabin Memoirs* (Boston: Little, Brown, 1979): 165.

47. Ramadan, *Tahtim al-Aliha*, II: 102.

48. Fawzi, *Harb al-Thalath Sanawat*: 342; al-Gamasi, *Mudhakirat*: 175; and Riyad, *Mudhakirat* I: 200.

49. Haykal, *Road to Ramadan*: 83–89; Fawzi, *Harb al-Thalath Sanawat*: 317–320, 351–352; and Huwaydi, *al-Furus*: 259.

50. Huwaydi, *al-Furus*: 196; and Herzog, *The Arab-Israeli Wars*: 214.

51. "Israel Forced to Withdraw from Shadwan," *Egyptian Gazette*, 24 January 1970: 1, 3; and "Naval Hero Capt. Hammad Given Alex. Funeral," *Egyptian Gazette*, 26 January 1970: 1, 4.

52. Korn, *Stalemate*: 180–182.

53. Kissinger, *White House Years*: 560.

54. Ramadan, *Tahtim al-Aliha*, III: 43–44; and Bar-Simon-Tov, *The Israeli-Egyptian War*: 134–135.

55. Bar-Simon-Tov, "The Myth of Strategic Bombing": 555–559.

56. Jon Glassman, *Arms for Arabs: The Soviet Union and War in the Middle East* (Baltimore: John Hopkins University Press, 1975): 78.

57. Bar-Simon-Tov, "The Myth of Strategic Bombing": 555.

58. *Strategic Survey, 1970* (London: Institute for Strategic Studies, 1971): 47.

59. Korn, *Stalemate*: 238–241

60. Raymond H. Anderson, "Egyptian Troops Cross Suez Canal," *New York Times*, 1 May 1970: 11.

61. For material on this trip and Nasser's thinking at this time, see Riyad, *Mudhakirat*, I: 247–261; Fawzi, *Harb al-Thalath al-Sanawat*: 323–324; 353–355; Haykal, *Road to Ramadan*: 93–96; and Farid, *Nasser*: 175–191.

62. Riyad, *Mudhakirat,* I: 261.

63. Ibid.: 259.

64. Discussions with Egyptian officers attending the US Army Command and General Staff College, Fort Leavenworth, Kansas.

65. Yonay, *No Margin for Error*: 286.

66. Richard Eder, "Israelis Expecting Forces to Counter Suez Missiles," *New York Times*, 9 July 1970: 1, 3; "Mrs. Meir—Israel Facing a Grave Situation," *Egyptian Gazette*, 8 July 1970: 1, 4; and O'Ballance, *Electronic War*: 124–125.

67. Korn, *Stalemate*: 231–232; Yonay, *No Margin for Error*: 291–298; and Iftihar Spector, interview with author, 7 July 1994, Tel Aviv, Israel.

68. Rabin, *Rabin Memoirs*: 178–180; Quandt, *Peace Proceess*: 90–91; Kissinger, *White House Years*: 584; and Korn, *Stalemate*: 254–255.

69. This incident has received much attention in the literature. For a detailed account, see Yonay, *No Margin for Error*: 299–302.

70. Fawzi, *Harb al-Thalath Sanawat*: 324; and Muhammad Ali Fahmi, interview with author, 22 June 1994, Cairo, Egypt.

71. Sharon, *Warrior*: 234.

72. Yonay, *No Margin for Error*: 304–305.

73. Ramadan, *Tahtim al-Aliha*, II: 135.

74. For a detailed discussion of Nasser's health problems, see P. J. Vatikiotis, *Nasser and His Generation* (New York: St. Martin's Press, 1978): 303–306.

5

"NO WAR, NO PEACE"

> If you concentrate on [a military] victory, with no thought for the after effect, you may be too exhausted to profit by the peace, while it is almost certain that the peace will be a bad one, containing the germs of another war.
> —Basil Liddell Hart[1]

> [T]he highest realization of warfare is to attack the enemy's plan; next is to attack their alliances; next to attack their army; and the lowest is to attack their fortified cities. This tactic of attacking fortified cities is adopted only when unavoidable.
> —Sun Tzu[2]

Anwar al-Sadat's emergence as Nasser's successor opened the door for a new direction in the Arab-Israeli conflict: a three-year interlude of "no peace, no war" followed the Three Years War. But the absence of violence along the Suez Canal failed to bring about significant diplomatic progress. Eventually, domestic pressures mounted upon the Egyptian leadership to employ the military option against Israel. Unable to achieve parity in combat power with the IDF, even with a Syrian alliance, Sadat faced the challenge of formulating a limited war strategy designed to gain political benefits *without* a clear military victory.

AN EGYPTIAN ENIGMA

Sadat, upon assuming the presidency, inherited a generally sound foundation upon which to advance preparations for war. The last three years of Nasser's rule had established firm presidential control over the military, to enhance unity of purpose; restructured General Command, to ensure unity of effort within the armed forces; reformed personnel policies, to create a more apolitical and professional officer corps; and implemented rigorous and realistic training programs, to raise the preparedness of combat units. In addition to these reforms, Nasser had left Egypt with an integrated air defense system over the Suez Canal. Finally, some eight thousand Soviet military personnel, many of these assigned to combat roles, stood as deterrents to Israeli air strikes deep into Egyptian territory.

Few people inside or outside Egypt gave Sadat much chance of surviving. Most regarded him as a yes-man who had worked all his political career under the Nasser's hypnotic spell and thus would serve only as a transition figure until someone more astute emerged to take the reins of government. Nothing in Sadat's background suggested that he would become one of the most prominent Middle East statesmen of the twentieth century.

Sadat came from a humble background, born in the small village of Mit Abul Kum in the Nile Delta. His father had the distinction of a secular rather than religious education, which served as an example for all his children. His mother was the daughter of a freed African slave. Sadat managed to gain entrance into the military academy, eventually rising to the rank of lieutenant colonel. He spent time in jail for his opposition to the British presence in Egypt. Although a member of the Free Officers, who seized power with the military coup of 23 July 1952, Sadat failed to build a power base for himself, instead biding his time in largely ceremonial positions, such as speaker of parliament and vice president.

But there was ample opportunity to learn about the relationship between war and policy. Nasser entrusted Sadat with a good deal of responsibility for the war in Yemen. Sadat handled the political side of the conflict, whereas Amer supervised military operations. Coordinating political and military activities to defeat the Yemeni royalists proved a frustrating experience for both men. In the Six Day War, and once again during the Three Years War, Sadat observed firsthand the problem of linking clear political purpose to attainable military objectives.

Upon assuming the presidency, Sadat needed time to consolidate power. Consequently, he extended the cease-fire with Israel, due to expire on 5 November, for three months. Meanwhile, Ali Sabri, noted for his pro-Soviet orientation, emerged as the main rival for Nasser's mantle. During the next several months, Sadat carefully built bridges to senior commanders in the armed forces, in particular gaining the support of the chief of the General Staff, Lieutenant General Muhammad Sadiq. On 2 May 1971, assured by Sadiq of the military's loyalty, Sadat removed Ali Sabri from all his official positions, including that of vice president. On 13 May, security forces arrested Sharawi Gomah, the powerful interior minister, for allegedly plotting a coup. Sadat also removed General Muhammad Fawzi, the war minister and commander in chief. Sadiq replaced Fawzi, while Major General Saad al-Din al-Shazli, commander of the Red Sea District, became the new chief of the General Staff. Ahmad Ismail Ali came out of retirement to take charge of General Intelligence, the equivalent of the Central

Intelligence Agency or Mossad. The latter two men would be the top two commanders in the 1973 war, faithfully implementing Sadat's strategy.

On the diplomatic front, Sadat sought a major shift in Egypt's foreign policy. Nasser had severed formal diplomatic relations with the United States, preferring to rely on the Soviets for leverage with Washington. Sadat, on the other hand, disliked the Soviets and wanted to establish a close working relationship with the United States as quickly as possible. Like Nasser, he understood that any significant diplomatic progress depended on American involvement. Unlike his predecessor, however, Sadat preferred dealing directly with the Americans, with as little to do with the Soviets as possible. But gaining American trust and confidence proved a bridge too far.

Nasser's funeral served as a forum for the first outreach to Washington. During the ceremonies, held over several days, Sadat twice met privately with the head of the American delegation, Eliot Richardson, the Secretary of Health, Education, and Welfare. On both occasions, the new Egyptian ruler expressed his desire to establish good relations with the United States. Richardson faithfully reported his discussions to the White House, but Washington failed to take the overture seriously, preferring to see who would emerge as Egypt's new leader.[3]

Undeterred by the Washington's indifference, Sadat continued to press his case. On 23 December 1970, he granted an interview with a correspondent from the *New York Times*.[4] Sadat outlined his conditions for reaching an accommodation with Israel: the Israelis were to return every inch of Egyptian soil captured in the Six Day War, and then Egypt would "recognize the rights of Israel as an independent state as defined by the Security Council of the United Nations." Moreover, Cairo was willing to enter into negotiations over Israeli rights of passage through the Strait of Tiran and the Gulf of Aqaba. But then Sadat revealed a set of hard-line positions to the interviewer. Israel's use of the Suez Canal depended on a comprehensive solution to the Arab-Israeli conflict, including the Palestinian refugee problem. Furthermore, any normalization of diplomatic relations would have to await coming generations, because as it was, the Egyptian people would overthrow any leader who tried to achieve this goal. Finally, Sadat singled out the United States as the main stumbling block to a Middle East settlement by virtue of its unwavering support for Israel. These statements made him seem to the American audience as another Arab hard-liner.

Before the expiration of the second ninety-day cease-fire, Sadat softened his diplomatic position. In a forty-five-minute address to the Egyptian National Assembly on 4 February 1971, the Egyptian president offered a new initiative for breaking the political deadlock. As a sign of Egypt's desire for peace, he unilaterally extended the cease-fire, but only for another thirty days. The speech also contained a major surprise: if Israel would implement a partial withdrawal of her troops from the eastern bank of the Suez Canal, Egypt would permit immediate clearance of the waterway of the sunken vessels. Within six months, the Suez Canal would reopen to international shipping. (No mention was made of Israeli ships, however.) This offer departed from Nasser's insistence that *all*

Israeli troops had to withdraw from the entire Sinai before he would open the waterway. Parliament was stunned by Sadat's statement, and no one in the audience applauded this part of the speech.[5]

In Israel, Prime Minister Golda Meir responded rather coolly to Sadat's new offer. She complained that the address had failed to mention the passage of Israeli ships through the Suez Canal. An Egyptian spokesman replied that Sadat's proposal was not the last word, only an opening position. A final settlement could include an Israeli right of passage.[6] Israel's formal reply to Sadat's initiative came in a speech by Meir to the Knesset on 9 February. In it, the prime minister reiterated the cabinet's position of no withdrawal of forces without a peace agreement. "To our great regret it was not a speech of peace. In the course of the entire speech, the President of Egypt refrained from saying that Egypt was ready to make peace with Israel."[7]

Still, Sadat persevered. On 22 February 1971, *Newsweek* published an interview in which Sadat outlined his basic thinking.[8] A fundamental change in Israel's approach to Egypt had to occur, he felt, before there could be any hope for peace. "The starting point for every Israeli attitude is that we were defeated and they can, therefore, dictate whatever they want. Our starting point is that we lost a battle—but not a war. If their starting point is erroneous, everything else is wrong." The Egyptians, being a proud people, refused to negotiate as a defeated nation, whatever had happened on the battlefield. Blaming Israel's intransigence for the impasse in the Arab-Israeli conflict, Sadat encouraged the United States to be an honest broker between the two sides. As a superpower and a friend of Israel, the United States held "the key to peace," precisely because only it possessed "the means to convince Israel of our good intentions." Furthermore, if there was to be peace based on justice, Washington had to be "neutral and objective" in its policy toward the conflict.

In the interview, Sadat expressed willingness to enter indirect negotiations. Rather than demand a comprehensive settlement among all parties, Egypt would accept partial solutions along the way. In concrete terms, he proposed, Israel would withdraw to a line behind al-Arish; Egypt would reciprocate by opening the Suez Canal to all international shipping, including Israeli. To guarantee free passage through the Strait of Tiran, the United States, Britain, France, and the USSR could maintain an international force at Sharm al-Shaykh, even though such an arrangement risked upsetting the Egyptian people. Sadat also made a bold promise concerning Israel's future status in the Middle East should Egypt regain every inch of territory lost in the 1967 war: "If Israel returns our land under the Security Council Resolution [242], [we will accept] the inviolability and political independence of every state in the area, including Israel. We pledge our solemn word." But there was a caveat: "There must be a just solution to the Palestinian problem." Israeli leaders viewed this qualifying statement as indicating Sadat was not negotiating in good faith; to them, it indicated that everything hinged on the Palestinian issue.

Sadat hoped his public statements would generate momentum on the diplomatic front. His suggestions finally sparked some movement. On 29 March, the Nixon administration offered its own version of a more limited, two-phased withdrawal. The Meir government responded on 19 April with a proposal for an end to the state of belligerence between the two countries in return for a limited withdrawal from the Suez Canal, with the stipulation that no Egyptian troops would cross to the east bank. Sadat refused to accept these two conditions. Once again, the future looked bleak for meaningful diplomatic progress in the Arab-Israeli conflict. Neither Washington nor Tel Aviv regarded Sadat as anything more than a weak, transitional leader.

EDGING TOWARD WAR

By the beginning of 1972, domestic pressure and diplomatic inertia threatened to destabilize Sadat's regime. Growing resentment of Egypt's social and economic woes stemmed, in large measure, from the country having been on a war footing since the June 1967. The lack of any diplomatic progress toward regaining the Sinai aggravated the people's frustration over internal problems. Inability to address effectively either dilemma reflected badly on Sadat's leadership. Acutely aware of this situation, Sadat began the new year with a strategic reassessment of the Arab-Israeli conflict.

On 2 January 1972, Sadat called a special meeting of senior military commanders at his residence in Giza.[9] The discussions, which lasted three hours, assessed Egypt's military situation. Most officers present counseled against war in the near future. Sadiq, the war minister, spoke for this point of view. He argued against a limited war and instead advocated waiting until the armed forces were able to liberate most, if not all, of the Sinai. According to his reasoning, it would be very difficult to keep a war limited; therefore, the EAF needed more offensive weapons in order to conduct a major campaign of land maneuver supported by a strong air force.

In a major conflagration with Israel, Sadiq pointed out that according to the army's internal estimates the EAF would suffer seventeen thousand casualties in crossing the Suez Canal; Soviet experts had calculated that Egyptian losses over the first four days of combat could reach as high as thirty-five thousand. Egypt would gain nothing politically from such a bloody conflict, even if it could hold on to some territory in the Sinai. Therefore, before embarking on any hostilities, Sadiq wanted to have a well-trained and well-equipped force of 250,000 troops, one which would be capable of defeating the Israelis in a decisive battle. Sadat dismissed Sadiq's position. Political and economic pressure did not allow the government the five to ten years required for the military to reach such a state of preparedness. Sadat wanted General Command to prepare the armed forces for a limited war as quickly as possible.

New domestic unrest now surfaced its ugly head on the Egyptian landscape. In January and February 1972, university students demonstrated in Cairo, demanding an end to the politico-military stalemate. Slogans criticized all the key players: the United States for supporting Israel; the USSR for failing to provide Egypt sufficient arms; and Sadat and Sadiq for questionable leadership. A series of clashes with security forces resulted in the government temporarily closing down the universities of Cairo and Ayn Shams. These student outbursts reflected growing anxiety in Egyptian society over the country's numerous social and economic problems. Later in the year, Canal Zone refugees and private-sector workers rioted in Cairo over working and living conditions. The Egyptian people were feeling the strain of a war economy in place since the Six Day War. In 1966, defense spending represented 11.1 percent of the gross national product. It would stand at 21.7 percent in 1972.[10]

The armed forces were also experiencing problems stemming from three years of conflict followed by continual preparation for a possible new war. To maintain a higher level of combat preparedness, the government was keeping recruits on active duty after their obligatory service. General Command especially needed university and higher institute graduates, who could provide the education and skills necessary for electronic warfare against the IDF. However, many of these individuals, drafted as early as 1967, wanted to return to civilian life and establish careers for themselves. Others, especially those from Islamic educational institutions, "introduced a leaven of student militancy into the officer and non-commissioned officer ranks."[11]

Unfortunately for Sadat, the diplomatic front was failing to provide any safety value. In the first half of 1972, the United States and the USSR were seriously experimenting with détente, and neither side wanted to jeopardize that delicate relationship by becoming involved in the volatile Arab-Israeli conflict. In this regard, Henry Kissinger, the American national security advisor and then secretary of state, was a major proponent of keeping Egypt and Syria on a back burner. By his reasoning, time served American interests:

The longer the stalemate continued the more obvious would it would become that the Soviet Union had failed to deliver what the Arabs wanted. . . . Sooner or later, if we kept our nerve, this would force a reassessment of even radical Arab policy. . . . Nobody could make peace without us. Only we, not the Soviet Union, could exert influence on Israel. Israel was too strong to succumb to Arab military pressure, and we could block all diplomatic activity until the Arabs showed *their* willingness to reciprocate Israeli concessions.[12]

In the early seventies, American policy toward the Arab-Israeli conflict thus required little effort on Washington's part, other than maintaining Israel's military edge over its Arab adversaries. The Soviets, for their part, adopted a similar hands-off policy. Superpower aloofness became starkly evident to Sadat when Nixon visited Moscow on 20 May 1972. A joint statement from the Brezhnev-Nixon summit underscored a lack of urgency in addressing the Arab-Israeli conflict. The two heads of state encouraged all parties to adopt an attitude of moderation and patience.

After almost two years of virtually no political progress, and no prospect for any after the Brezhnev-Nixon summit, Sadat, largely out of frustration, began contemplating a dramatic move: the expulsion of all Soviet advisors and combat troops from Egypt. His air defense and air force commanders assured him that their two services could easily assume the Soviet role of protecting Egypt's air space without any significant degradation in combat capabilities.[13] On 6 July 1972, armed with this assurance, Sadat informed his vice president of the decision; the Soviet ambassador received the word on 8 July. On 13 July, the prime minister, Dr. Aziz Sidqi, journeyed to Moscow to complete final preparations for the Soviet departure and to offer to purchase Soviet equipment.

The public announcement of the expulsion came on 17 July. By this time, the eight thousand Soviet military personnel in the country included eight hundred to 850 advisors at various commands and a hundred technical experts training Egyptians on sophisticated equipment. Soviet combat forces comprised four air force brigades, a division of SAM-3s, training detachments, two SAM-6 brigades, and four MiG-25 reconnaissance planes.[14]

Numerous reasons have been suggested for Sadat's dramatic move. Sadat himself blamed the Soviets for advocating maintenance of the status quo under the rubric of international détente and for procrastinating on the delivery of weapons agreed upon in previous contracts.[15] Both complaints had kernels of truth. A domestic factor, no doubt, also weighed on Sadat's historic decision. Both the Egyptian army and people had grown weary of the heavy Soviet military presence. News of the Soviet expulsion thus won approval among both the public and the military, although Sadiq and other senior officers viewed the wholesale exodus as too drastic.[16] However, a diplomatic consideration most likely played the biggest role in the decision: Sadat was keen on jarring Washington and the Kremlin from complacency about the Arab-Israeli conflict.

But no diplomatic movement followed the ouster. The Israelis jumped to the conclusion the Soviet departure delayed any possibility of a canal crossing. As noted by Ezer Weizman, "As the last Soviet advisors left Egyptian soil, Israel adopted the view that without the Russians the Egyptian army was so weakened that it would be beyond its power to cross the Suez Canal."[17] Israel thus felt no need to budge diplomatically. Washington, for its part, was overjoyed at having gained an easy victory without cutting any deals with Sadat. In any case, the Nixon administration remained too preoccupied with the war in Vietnam, détente with the Soviet Union, and relations with Communist China to give much consideration to Egypt.

The lack of serious response from that corner gradually prompted Sadat to think seriously about the military option. In this regard, a surprise awaited Sadat at a meeting of the Supreme Council of the Armed Forces on 24 October 1972.[18] Most senior commanders resisted initiating hostilities in the near future. Sadat had ordered Sadiq to be ready for war by 15 November 1972. At the council held at his home in Giza, the president learned, much to his chagrin, that Sadiq had not only failed to undertake the necessary preparations but still resisted the notion of a limited war.

Sadat opened the meeting with a long outline of all his attempts to reach a diplomatic solution. Having exhausted all political avenues, and with the superpowers locked in a duet of détente, Egypt had no choice but to initiate war. Gaining even ten centimeters of ground on the canal's east bank would spark diplomatic movement. The commanders raised serious objections, such as inadequate weapons and the prospect of high casualties. Losing patience with these familiar arguments, Sadat at one point unexpectedly exploded at two senior officers, cautioning them to keep to soldiering and leave political matters to politicians. The meeting ended in a charged atmosphere, with Sadiq attempting to apologize to Sadat for comments made by him and others. But the damage had been done.

The disagreement between Sadat and Sadiq reflected, in one sense, the traditional tensions between political and military institutions over the preparation and conduct of war. In his capacity as war minister and commander in chief, Sadiq embraced an essentially narrow view of warfare—war made sense only if one was able to defeat the enemy's armed forces or capture strategic terrain. Sadiq essentially considered a clear victory on the battlefield as the only goal worthy of a military. The quest for such a victory had become an albatross for Sadiq, preventing him from appreciating the military possibilities offered by broader policy considerations in the conduct of war.

On the other hand, Sadat, as head of state, was responsible for developing an effective strategy, one that judiciously balanced force and statecraft to achieve political ends. For him, policy mattered more than war; war was only the means of attaining political objectives. A wise head of state could win politically even without winning militarily, as Nasser had unintentionally demonstrated in the 1956 Arab-Israeli War. Capturing the entire Sinai was clearly out of the realm of possibility, and the prospects for a major seizure of land in a crossing operation were not much brighter. But Sadat could ill afford to wait several years to wage war. The public was clamoring for decisive action, while the economy was threatening to come apart at the seams. Egypt had to go to war, for limited territorial objectives, in the hope that doing so might cause a political earthquake, shattering the status quo in the Middle East so as to compel superpower involvement. Before Sadat could embark on war, he first had to remove an important obstacle: Sadiq and other senior commanders who failed to conform to his thinking.

After the heated meeting of 24 October 1972, Sadat moved with lightning speed and decisiveness. The next day, he fired the war minister, the deputy war minister, and the commanders of the navy and the Cairo military district. To ensure compliance with his directives, Sadat appointed Ahmad Ismail Ali as his new war minister. From the perspective of loyalty, the selection proved a wise choice. Within eight months, the EAF was prepared to fight a limited war according to Sadat's design.

The IDF, to its detriment, misread the significance of Sadiq's firing. Israeli military intelligence interpreted it as an attempt to appease the Soviets by removing their most vocal critic within the Egyptian military. With Sadiq out of the way, Israelis reasoned, Sadat could smooth over relations with the USSR, which had been very strained since the expulsion of all Soviet advisors in July

1972.[19] This assessment was dead wrong; Sadat removed Sadiq and replaced him with someone who would faithfully prepare the armed forces for war and as soon as possible.[20] Moreover, by this time Sadat no doubt saw in Sadiq a political rival.

Ironically, Egyptian-Soviet relations did improve, but not because of the firing. From 16–18 October 1972, an Egyptian delegation had visited Moscow in an attempt to smooth over tensions between the two countries. Though the Soviets promised to support Egypt, the major breakthrough came in March 1973, when an agreement was reached for a resumption of military aid. The Soviets promised to deliver, among other weapons, a MiG-23 squadron, a Soviet-controlled brigade of R-17E surface-to-surface missiles known to NATO as Scuds, a SAM-6 brigade, two hundred T-62 tanks, two hundred BMP armored personnel carriers, and sophisticated electronic equipment. Of this package, only the MiG-23s failed to reach Egypt before the war. The arrival of the Scuds on 18 July 1973 proved important for Egypt. The missile's reported range of 180 miles brought Israel proper within striking distance, giving the Egyptians a much-sought-after strategic weapon.[21] However, the missile was in fact rather inaccurate and thus of only psychological benefit to the Egyptians.

By October 1973, although saddled with problems and vulnerabilities, the EAF was ready for another major round in the Arab-Israeli conflict, much better led and trained for war than in 1967.

EGYPT'S ARMED FORCES

Senior military commanders had meticulously prepared their war plans and had clearly identified attainable objectives for the first phase of the crossing operation. Field-grade officers, for their part, possessed technical competence and clear understandings of their tactical missions. Finally, the troops were well trained and motivated for a major offensive against the Bar-Lev Line. Six years of steady preparation would bear fruit.

Egypt's General Command in 1973 represented a sharp contrast with that of the Six Day War. Ahmad Ismail Ali, both war minister and commander in chief, had had a checkered career in the military, but his overall competency was a marked improvement over that of Field Marshal Muhammad Abd al-Hakim Amer. Ahmad Ismail was better prepared by education and experience for high command than Amer. He had studied in England, then at Frunze Academy in the Soviet Union, and finally at the Nasser Higher Military Academy, equivalent to a war college in other armies. His assignments had included infantry company commander in the 1948 war; instructor at the staff college from 1950 to 1953; commander of an infantry battalion and then an infantry brigade; chief of staff of the front command during the Six Day War; and brief stints as front commander and field army commander after that conflict. In 1969, Ahmad Ismail had served for six months as chief of the General Staff, before Nasser fired him when an Israeli commando operation seized a highly sophisticated Soviet radar system. In May 1971, Sadat brought Ahmad Ismail back from retirement and appointed him Director of General Intelligence. On 26 October 1972, Ahmad Ismail took over the war ministry, with the rank of full general.[22] This appointment gave Ahmad Ismail Ali roughly a year to prepare for war.

Ahmad Ismail's personality fit Sadat's war strategy well. Sadat sought a loyal, cautious man who would scrupulously adhere to his supreme commander's intent.

Ismail was a classic officer, the soldier *par excellence*—an infantryman, professional, wholly above politics. He compensated for any lack of brilliance by dogged hard work; in Moscow he was the most studious of all our generals. . . . But it was, apart from any considerations of expertise, largely because of Ismail's lack of politics that the President appointed him.[23]

Sadat felt he did not need a bold, imaginative war minister for the task ahead; the great challenge of a crossing all along the Suez Canal was plain enough. After that, the main concern would be not to jeopardize any initial accomplishments through risky operations.

Directly below Ahmad Ismail in the operational chain of command stood Lieutenant General Saad al-Shazli, appointed chief of the General Staff in May 1971. Shazli had seen service as a commander of an infantry company in 1948, a paratroop battalion in 1956, a brigade in the Yemeni civil war (1965–66), and a special armored task force in 1967. His overseas assignments included an infantry course at Fort Benning in the United States, two years of study in the USSR, and service as military attaché in London from 1961 to 1963. Prior to becoming chief of the General Staff, Shazli had headed the Red Sea Military District from 1970 to 1971.[24]

In Shazli, Sadat possessed a charismatic, dedicated professional officer who inspired troops through sheer personality and work ethic.

Shazli was dashing. . . . Beneath his charm and his daring, Shazli was a calculating and meticulous officer. He was not a military genius, but he did have that precise grasp of logistics and attention to detail which is essential to the paratroop officer. Shazli's planning of the crossing, and the studies behind it which he personally supervised, were to be so brilliantly successful at least in part because Shazli concerned himself with the individual movements of virtually every boat in the operation.[25]

Indeed, Shazli imposed cooperation and coordination among the ground forces, air force, air defense, and navy, no mean accomplishment after the disunity of senior command in the Six Day War.

Despite the competence of the top two commanders, there was bad blood between Ahmad Ismail and Shazli, and it strained their relations. Shazli almost resigned when Sadat informed him of Ahmad Ismail's selection as war minister. The two officers had had a major falling out when they served together in the then Congo (later Zaire) as part of a UN peacekeeping force. Apparently, Shazli had little respect for Ahmad Ismail and considered his appointment as war minister a poor one. Sadat, however, persuaded Shazli to remain as the chief of the General Staff, even promising that there would be little interference from Ahmad Ismail.

Nonetheless, the EAF embarked on war with unity of effort and purpose. Even Shazli, who in his memoirs expressesd harsh criticism of Ahmad Ismail as a military leader, confirms mutual cooperation during the year before the war.

As it happened, in the 11 months we worked together before the war, Ismail and I differed little. We were both trying hard. Besides, there was little to differ about. Our plans had been laid. Of course we updated them constantly as information flowed in about the enemy or new units of our own became operational. But the core remained. In departmental matters, Ismail had continued to control the Defense Intelligence Department and the Officers Department; but he did allow me a free hand in the Finance Department. . . . He never attacked me in public. We got along.[26]

During the war, a clash between the two men would spark a command crisis, a subject for a later chapter. But for the moment, intense preparations for war acted as a lubricant for personality differences.

Below the war minister and the chief of the General Staff stood the director of operations, Major General Muhammad Abd al-Ghani al-Gamasi. After studying in both the United States and the USSR, Gamasi had served as the director of operations for the front command in the 1967 war, directly under Ahmad Ismail Ali, then the command's chief of staff. According to Haykal, "Intellectually, Gamasi was perhaps Egypt's best equipped general; he read a good deal and he pondered what he read. . . . Gamasi, too, was non-political—indeed, Arab politics shocked him to his bones."[27]

Thus, Ahmad Ismail, Shazli, and Gamasi, who formed the military triumvirate in the 1973 war, were all professional officers, dedicated to their mission.

The three services were headed by competent commanders as well. Major General Muhammad Ali Fahmi had commanded air defense forces since the 1968 decision to form them into a separate service. An air defender since World War II, Fahmi had gained invaluable experience commanding his service through its trials and tribulations in the Three Years War. The Egyptian air force fell under the command of Major General Hosni Mubarak, who was appointed to this position in 1972. After twice studying in the USSR, Mubarak had served as commandant of the Air Academy from 1967 to 1969 and then chief of staff from 1969 to 1972. In 1981, he would assume the presidency upon Sadat's assassination. Rear Admiral Ahmad Fuad Zekri commanded the navy. Fired along with Ahmad Ismail in 1969, Zekri had been reinstated in 1972. None of these three service chiefs had built independent fiefdoms as Muhammad Sidqi Mahmud and Suleyman Izzat had done in the air force and navy respectively in the 1967 war. Most importantly, Ahmad Ismail, Gamasi, and Zikri had been classmates at the Nasser Higher Academy in 1965 and 1966 and thus knew each other quite well.[28] The 1973 General Command was certainly more competent and united than its counterpart in 1967.

The rank structure and lines of authority of the General Command reflected the reforms implemented by Nasser and Fawzi after the Six Day War (discussed in Chapter 3). The president, in his capacity as supreme commander, commanded the armed forces through the minister of war, who also functioned as the commander in chief, with operational control over the military. There was no field marshal, a rank that in 1967 had epitomized the semiautonomous position of the military in society. The war minister was a four-star general, the only Egyptian officer of this grade. Further, only one lieutenant general stood in the operational chain of command: the chief of the General Staff. All other senior commanders, including those of the two field armies, held the rank of major general:[29]

General Ahmad Ismail Ali	CinC and war minister
Lieutenant General Saad al-Shazli	chief of the General Staff
Major General Muhammad al-Gamasi	director of operations
Major General Ibrahim Fuad Nassar	director of military intelligence
Major General Muhammad Ali Fahmi	commander, air defense
Major General Husni Mubarak	commander, air force
Rear Admiral Ahmad Fuad Zekri	commander, naval forces
Major General Saad Mamun	commander, second army
Major General Abd al-Munim Wassel	commander, third army

All these commanders had been in their positions at least eleven months when the war broke out, with Fahmi having served five years and Shazli twenty-eight months. Such length of service was adequate time to prepare for war.

Field command was also much improved over the situation of 1967. No wave of last-minute changes of division and brigade commanders rocked field units, as had taken place in 1967. Instead, Ahmad Ismail, upon becoming war minister in October 1972, instituted a policy of keeping field commanders, down to brigade level, in their commands, if possible, to provide them sufficient time to prepare themselves and their units for the crossing operation.[30] Nor were any major commands created at the last minute. Thus, the Egyptian ground forces entered the 1973 war with a continuity of leadership and clarity of purpose.

Finally, the troops themselves were much better prepared for combat than before the Six Day War. Soldiers had trained with rigor for the past year. Realistic exercises had rehearsed over and over again the crossing of the Suez Canal and the establishment of secure bridgeheads, with defenses in depth. Virtually every soldier knew his task like the back of his hand. Most importantly, Egyptian planners had used the annual training exercises, begun a little over a week before zero-hour, as final preparation and cover for war. Almost all the Egyptian army participated without knowing it was about to initiate actual war. On the day of the commencement of hostilities, the EAF was thus already deployed at its assigned positions, much as had the IDF been on 5 June 1967. Still, despite the meticulous war preparations over nearly a year, Egyptian commanders were acutely aware that they faced an adversary superior in key aspects of modern warfare.

ISRAEL'S WAR MACHINE

In comparison with the EAF, the IDF changed little between the years 1967 and 1973. The amazing victory of 1967 gave the Israeli army a feeling of invincibility on the battlefield, while the acquisition of the Sinai, the West Bank, and the Golan Heights had provided the country with strategic depth for the first time in its brief history. In the aftermath of an impressive victory, Israeli senior commanders saw little need to make substantive changes in doctrine or force structure, instead choosing to reinforce what had worked best in 1967. Specifically, the Israeli General Staff focused on its superiority in intelligence, air power, and armored warfare, neglecting others branches of the armed forces. This approach essentially meant that the IDF planned to defeat the same adversary as in the last war with similar results—a quick and decisive victory with few casualties.

One IDF pillar was certainly its intelligence branch, or Aman. The victory in 1967 had stemmed in large measure from excellent information and analysis that military intelligence had provided to the General Staff about Arab armies. On the eve of the war and throughout the campaign, senior Israeli commanders had possessed invaluable information on Arab war plans, capabilities, vulnerabilities, troop dispositions, and redeployments. Well-placed spies, technological resources, and poor Arab security had been the keys to the Israeli intelligence coup. After the 1967 war, the Israeli intelligence community appeared destined to remain first-class. But any institution can make a major blunder, precisely because humans are involved in assessments of such critical intangibles as enemy intent and morale.

Israel's senior military leadership came to expect too much from its intelligence branch. By 1973, Major General Eliyahu Zeira, the director of military intelligence, had arrogantly promised the General Staff that he could deliver a forty-eight-hour warning of an Arab attack on Israel. Consequently, all war plans depended on wake-up call two days ahead of an impending Arab attack, ample time for mobilization of the reserves and for the Israeli air force to gain mastery of the skies by eliminating the Arab air defense threat. An Arab surprise assault on the Bar-Lev Line did not seriously figure into Israeli calculations.[31]

This unrealistic dependence on another intelligence coup proved a grave mistake. After all, the Egyptians could easily degrade Israel's intelligence capabilities through operational security and deception operations. As will be discussed in the next chapter, this is precisely what the Egyptians did in 1973. In the end, Israeli military intelligence failed to deliver on its contract, offering only nine and a half hours of warning. Moreover, Zeira wrongly reported that the Arab attack would begin at 6:00 P.M.; the Egyptians and the Syrians attacked at 2:00 P.M. instead. These two errors caused confusion in the IDF during the first day or two of the war and helped prevent the Israelis from decisively engaging either the Egyptian or Syrian attack on 6 October.

In addition to an unhealthy reliance on intelligence, the IDF had drawn what would prove to be a wrong lesson from the Six Day War. The Israeli General Staff had decided to go with what had worked best in battle in the last war: the dynamic combination of plane and tank.[32] By 1973 Moshe Dayan, Israel's defense minister throughout the period between the 1967 and 1973 wars, and the Israeli General Staff had assigned more than 50 percent of its defense budget to the air force and 30 percent to the Armor Corps, all at the expense of infantry.[33] The plane and tank are critical for desert warfare, but the combat arms of infantry, artillery, and engineers also play important roles under most battle conditions. By placing so much emphasis on air power and armor, the IDF created a weakness for itself in combined-arms warfare.

A second IDF pillar was the Israeli air force, certainly a first-class service by any standard. Comprising nineteen thousand personnel, the air force saw its combat aircraft increase from 275 in 1967 to 432 by the summer of 1972. By this time, it had transitioned from being a French-equipped to an American-supplied war machine, with an inventory that included 150 A-4 Skyhawks and 140 F-4 Phantoms, as against fifty Mirages and twenty-seven Mystère IVAs. Its opponent, the Egyptian air force, some twenty-three thousand officers and men, fielded a Soviet fleet of 550 aircraft—160 MiG-21s, sixty MiG-19s, two hundred MiG-17s, 130 Su-7s, forty-eight bombers (Tu-16s and Il-28s), and eighty-two helicopters (Mi-6s and Mi-8s). To the Egyptians' disappointment, the Soviets had refused to provide the UAR with the more advanced MiG-23s and Tu-22s.

Despite Egyptian advantages in numbers, especially when combined with the Syrian air force, the Israelis were markedly ahead in avionics and air-to-air missiles, possessing the American Sidewinder and Sparrow as well as the Israeli Shafrir. In addition to a technological advantage, the Israelis maintained a clear edge in pilot expertise. Israeli pilots received approximately two hundred flight hours per year with emphasis on initiative, whereas their Egyptian counterparts garnered only seventy hours in a more centralized system based on ground direction centers. In air-to-air combat, Israeli pilots and planes outclassed their counterparts. The Egyptians clearly understood that the air force was the weak link in their armed forces; consequently, Egyptian air force doctrine called for the employment of at least two MiG-21s against each Phantom.[34]

Waging modern warfare in an open desert without a competitive air force appears suicidal. The Six Day War had confirmed beyond any doubt the critical importance of air supremacy for successful ground operations over open terrain. But the dilemma of achieving air-to-air competitiveness constituted only half of Egypt's problem. The Egyptians also wanted to conduct deep strikes with either long-range missiles or long-range bombers, both as a deterrent and as a way to retaliate in the event the Israelis turned to strategic bombing, as in the latter part of the Three Years War. In light of these two imperatives, Israeli military intelligence predicated all its strategic analyses on the assumption that Sadat would avoid launching a major war against Israel without sufficient airpower to challenge the Israeli air force and pose a threat to Israel proper. This basic assumption became known as "the Conception." During the year before the 1973 war, Zeira consistently assessed a very low probability of war. The Conception proved dead wrong, as underscored by the Agranat Commission, established after the 1973 war.[35]

The EAF could inflict heavy damage on the Israeli air force with a dense and integrated air defense system. In the six months before the war, the Soviets supplied weapons to equip eight battalions of upgraded SAM-2s and one SAM-6 brigade, the latter being the first of its kind in Egypt's possession. The EAF would thus cross the Suez Canal protected by a lethal air defense system of some eighty SAM battalions. The improved SAM-2 and the SAM-3, though together covering the area from high to low altitudes, were difficult to move. The mobile SAM-6 could go as low as 100 feet, giving the EAF essentially complete coverage of the air over the battlefield. According to doctrine, three missile battalions would overlap their coverage. Meanwhile, Egyptian infantrymen carried the SAM-7 on their shoulders to challenge low-flying planes. In addition to the surface-to-air missiles, the Egyptian air defense forces possessed some 2,500 antiaircraft guns, including the self-propelled, radar-guided ZSU-23-4. By relying on the rich array of air defense weapons, the EAF could attain effective air parity with the Israeli air force out from fifteen to twenty kilometers east of the Suez Canal.[36]

The Armor Corps constituted the IDF's third pillar. On the ground, Israelis possessed a clear advantage in armored warfare, as demonstrated in the Six Day War. Israeli tankers, with little or no infantry support, had spearheaded the IDF's lightning breakout across the Sinai desert. The IDF's success had rested on the initiative in combat of its tactical commanders while Israeli tank crews had exhibited mastery of fire and movement over their Egyptian counterparts. Thus, after the war, the IDF placed even greater emphasis on tanks in budget allocations, doctrine, organization, and tactics. A number of infantry brigades were converted to armor. By 1973, the IDF possessed sixteen armored brigades (as against ten in 1967), in addition to nine infantry, six mechanized, five paratroop, and three artillery brigades for a total force of 315,000 men. Each tank brigade supported 115 tanks. In 1973, the Israelis fielded over two thousand tanks, including one thousand British Centurions, 450 Patton M-48s, 150 Patton M-60s, three hundred Shermans, and 150 captured Soviet T-54/55s. Despite a numerical disadvantage when fighting on two fronts, Israeli armor units were more adept at maneuver warfare, based on a more flexible command system and better gunnery.

Infantry and artillery were the weak links in combined arms, as a result of the IDF's heavy emphasis on planes and tanks. Israeli mechanized infantry, under the control of the Armor Corps, suffered from poor equipment, improper integration, and limited training. Armor officers consigned mechanized infantry mainly to mopping-up operations, without adequate training in fighting on foot or in unison with tanks. Mechanized infantry was not even an organic part of tank battalions or brigades. To accompany the tank forces, the IDF possessed over five hundred M-113s, an armored personnel carrier with a high profile, not much armor, and poor firepower. There was one M-113 for every four tanks. This arrangement represented a weak infantry-to-tank ratio with which to attack well-prepared defensive positions. To deploy additional infantry into battle, the Israeli army would use half-tracks, essentially death traps when under fire.

The EAF, accordingly, could negate Israeli advantages in armored warfare by forcing the Israelis to attack well-prepared defenses. In such a battle, the Egyptians could rely on their strengths in artillery and infantry. The Israeli Artillery Corps possessed only 570 guns, the majority of them towed, against 1,280 in Egypt. To arm its infantry against Israeli tanks, Egypt's General Command had obtained some six thousand rocket-propelled grenades (RPG) and two thousand antitank guided missiles, mainly Saggers. Egyptian planners hoped to defeat armored attacks using combined-arms tactics, centered on infantry armed with antitank weapons.

But for all the possible Egyptian counters to the three IDF pillars, the EAF needed an effective political strategy from its president, a strategy in which political goals were commensurate with military capabilities. Israeli defenses in the Sinai helped define for Sadat the relationship between policy and war.

ISRAELI DEFENSES IN THE SINAI

In addition to an overall advantage in combat power, the Israelis were confident in their defensive scheme for the Sinai. The first major obstacle for the Egyptians to overcome was the Suez Canal, which Dayan once referred to as "one of the best antitank ditches in the world."[37] The waterway itself was only 180 to 220 meters in width and sixteen to twenty meters in depth. To prevent sand erosion, Israeli engineers lined the banks with concrete walls rising two or three meters above the water at low tide. At high tide, the water flowed a meter below the top of the concrete wall.

Immediately at the water's edge, the Israelis constructed vertical sand ramparts that rose at an angle of forty-five to sixty-five degrees with heights of twenty to twenty-five meters. These obstacles prevented the Egyptians from landing tanks and heavy equipment without engineering preparation (that is, demolition) on the east bank. In view of the dimensions of their sand obstacle, Israeli military planners expected the Egyptians would need at least twenty-four, if not forty-eight, hours to break through and establish a sizable bridgehead.

As a final touch to take advantage of the water obstacle, the Israelis installed an underwater pipe system that would pump flammable crude oil into the Suez Canal to create a sheet of flame. Some Israeli sources claim the system was in fact unreliable. Nevertheless, Egyptians took this threat very seriously, and on the eve of war, during the late evening of 5 October, the day before the outbreak of hostilities, teams of Egyptian frogmen blocked the underwater openings with concrete.[38]

At the tops of the sand ramparts, which ran the length of the canal, Israeli engineers had constructed over twenty strong points at seven to ten-kilometer intervals. Built several stories down into the sand, these concrete forts were designed to provide troops with shelter from thousand pound bombs as well as to offer creature comforts, such as air conditioning. Above ground, a strong point's perimeter averaged two hundred by 350 meters, surrounded by barbed wire and minefields to a depth of two hundred meters. The entire length of the Suez Canal also contained emplacements for tanks, artillery pieces, mortars, and machine guns so that Israeli soldiers could foil an Egyptian crossing at the water line.

Defense of the Sinai rested on two plans, Dovecote (*Shovach Yonim*) and Rock (*Sela*). In both plans, the Israeli General Staff expected the Bar-Lev Line to serve as a "stop line," or *kav atzira*, a defensive line to be held.[39] As noted by an Israeli colonel shortly after the Three Years War, "The line was created to provide military answers to two basic needs: first, to prevent the possibility of a major Egyptian assault on Sinai with the consequent creation of a bridgehead which could lead to all-out war; and, second, to reduce as much as possible the casualties among the defending troops."[40]

Envisioning a limited Egyptian crossing, Dovecote called for the employment of only regular forces. Responsibility for defending the Sinai mainly fell upon the regular armored division, supported by an additional tank battalion, a dozen infantry companies, and seventeen artillery batteries, for a total of over three hundred tanks, seventy artillery pieces, and more than twenty thousand troops. The mission of these regular forces was to defeat an Egyptian crossing at or near the water line.

Dovecote called for an infantry brigade, divided into small detachments of fifteen to hundred men, manning the twenty or so strong points along the Bar-Lev Line. Behind the forward line of fortifications stood a single armored brigade, 110 tanks, positioned along Artillery Road. This brigade was deployed in three tactical areas running from north of Qantara to Port Tawfiq in the south. Each area contained a tank battalion (thirty-six tanks) whose primary mission in case of an Egyptian attack was to move quickly to the water line and occupy the firing positions along the ramparts and between the fortifications. Behind this tactical line of defense, the IDF positioned two armored brigades, one to reinforce the forward armored brigade and the second to counterattack against the Egyptian main effort. One of these brigades was located at Bir Gifgafa on the central route, the other at Bir Tamada, east of the Giddi and Mitla passes.

Should the regular armored division prove inadequate, the Israeli General Staff would activate Rock, the mobilization of two reserve armored divisions with support forces. Their deployment, committing over a hundred thousand troops into battle, would signify a major war.

After the Three Years War, the IDF began to lay plans and train for a major countercrossing operation on to the west bank. In January 1972, the Sinai's armor division conducted an amphibious exercise called Operation Oz. Southern Command selected Ruafa Dam, near Abu Ageila, for the training. Here, engineers dug a facsimile of the Suez Canal, complete with walls and banks, and awaited for the winter rains to flood the area. Both Meir and Dayan attended the spectacle of Israeli troops training for what had become routine for the Egyptian army. The exercise, though expensive, provided invaluable experience for a similar operation that would be conducted during the 1973 war. The IDF obtained a roller bridge and purchased float rafts, known as Gilboas. Logistical, operational, and technical problems were identified, and attempts were made to address them. In conjunction with Operation Oz, Ariel Sharon, the commander of the southern front—which included the Sinai, Gaza, and the Negev—drew plans for three possible crossing sites: Qantara, Ismailiya, and Deversoir.[41] The Israeli army could take some comfort in being better prepared than it had been for taking the fight into enemy territory, as had been Israeli military doctrine since the state's creation.

Despite a serious attitude toward training and combat readiness, the IDF did let its guard down. Sharon, who commanded the southern front from 1970 to July 1973, made some alterations to the Sinai defenses, creating some physical cracks in the process. Opposed to the Bar-Lev Line, he reluctantly rebuilt the positions that had been damaged by Egyptian bombardment in 1970. However, under his watch a dozen strong points were closed down, and Southern Command began constructing new strongpoints, called *ta'ozim*, along the hill line near Artillery Road, some ten to fifteen kilometers to the east of the Suez Canal.[42] This new line never took shape, and its construction was at the expense of the strong points along the Suez Canal. When Sharon retired from the army in July 1973, his replacement lacked time to restore all the *meozim* to their former state.

An general attitude of arrogance and superiority spawned a morale issue in the IDF. Moshe Dayan articulated a sense of invincibility to the graduating class at the staff college on 10 August 1973, less than two months before the outbreak of war: "The balance of forces is so much in our favor that it neutralizes the Arab considerations and motives for the immediate renewal of hostilities."[43] Because of the low probability of war, the defense ministry decided to reduce, beginning in April 1974, male compulsory service by three months from the previous three years of mandatory duty.

In addition the IDF, as well as society in general, set an incredibly high standard of military performance, based on the compelling example of the Blitzkrieg in the Six Day War. Writing with the benefit of hindsight, Major General Avraham Adan, who commanded both the Armor Corps and a tank *ugdah* in the October War, expressed this unrealistic standard thus: "The common expectations from the IDF were that any future war would be short with few casualties."[44] For Israelis to win again in a decisive fashion required the Arabs to repeat their grievous mistakes, an unlikely prospect for an adversary who had been preparing for over six years. To its detriment, the Israeli army never seriously comprehended the major blunders committed by the Arabs that had allowed for such a decisive victory. Blitzkriegs are not the norm in war, and societies that expect quick and "easy" results stand to experience serious disappointment. The Egyptians went to war to teach the Israelis just such a lesson.

SADAT'S WAR STRATEGY

Sadat faced a major problem in developing a viable war strategy. The EAF was clearly in a position of military weakness, not strength, in comparison with the IDF. As supreme commander of a military weaker than its foe, Sadat understood that a quick and decisive victory on the battlefield stood outside the realm of possibility. The memory of the devastating defeat of 1967 loomed heavy in his mind; the EAF had to avoid undertakings that might lead to another disaster. Sadat had to make do with the weapons at hand, and he had to formulate political aims that General Command could translate into a war plan with attainable military objectives. Undertaking a limited war against the Israeli army, however, involved risk and courage on Sadat's part. There was the real danger, as demonstrated in 1970, of the IDF escalating the conflict beyond the capabilities of the EAF. In such a scenario, the Soviets would not be likely to bail the Egyptians out with their own combat forces, as they had in 1970. A wise politico-military strategy thus became an ever more critical element in the success or failure of a limited war.

Sadat's political goals in going to war were simple and clear. One important aim was to regain lost national pride. The Six Day War had left Egyptians a humiliated people, and by the end of 1972 Egypt had failed to rise much out of its demoralization. The stigma of defeat left Egypt in a weak position from which to negotiate. Nasser's and Sadat's failure to regain even a single centimeter of lost territory in the Sinai had only reinforced the image of diplomatic and military impotence. In his own words, Sadat needed "to wipe out the disgrace and humiliation that followed the 1967 defeat."[45] The Egyptian people readily embraced the 1973 war as "the battle for honor and dignity" (*al-maraka al-izz wa karama*).

In attacking Israel, Sadat also sought to discredit the "Israeli security theory," an Egyptian term to describe what most Egyptians considered the main obstacle to peace. According to Egyptian analysis, the Israeli security theory was founded upon the Israelis' firm belief that the IDF could deter the Arabs from attempting to regain lost territories through military action. This article of faith carried political implications for the Arab-Israeli conflict. The Israeli government, believing in the invincibility of its armed forces, would refuse to negotiate with the Arabs other than from a position of strength, from which it could dictate terms. In other words, military supremacy and political arrogance had spawned a diplomatic stalemate. To soften Israeli intransigence toward indirect negotiations, Sadat felt he needed to undermine Israeli confidence in the IDF by tarnishing its image in Israel through an Arab military action of operational and tactical significance—military victory was not essential. The political goal was to rupture the status quo with a military operation designed to spur diplomatic activity on the part of the superpowers, in particular the United States.

Sadat shed some light on his strategic thinking in an interview in *Newsweek* magazine in April 1973, six months before the war.[46] The Egyptian president drew upon the contemporary example of the Vietnam War to explain how Egypt might approach a new conflict with Israel. The Vietnamese people should have taught the United States the critical ability of national will to wear down an opponent superior in technology. "You Americans always use computers to solve geopolitical equations and they always mislead you. . . . You simply forgot to feed Vietnamese psychology into the computer." In much the same way, Sadat felt, the United States, not to mention Israel, lacked any understanding of the Egyptian psyche, how determined the Egyptian people were to regain their lost lands—whatever the odds and cost. Without American pressure on Israel, war was inevitable. "The time has come for a shock," warned Sadat. However, Sadat promised, should war breakout, dialogue would continue, even in the midst of hostilities. "Diplomacy will continue before, during, and after the battle." Here the Egyptian leader alluded to the use of war in a rational sense to achieve political benefit. Diplomacy, rather than waging war, would constitute Egypt's main effort in the next conflict.

Arnaud de Borchgrave, *Newsweek*'s senior editor who conducted the interview, provided additional insight into the Egyptian president's thinking by noting his own discussions with Sadat's aides. According to these unnamed sources, Sadat had learned an important lesson from the Vietnam War when, in 1968 and 1972, the Vietnamese Communists had suffered military defeats but still gained psychological victories. Egypt could achieve similar results. Even a defeat in battle could bring significant psychological results, followed by tangible advantages.

As far back as 1971, Sadat had begun talking to his senior commanders about a limited war designed to have political effect by seizing a small area of land. On 3 June 1971, for example, he told a large gathering of officers, "When we plan the offensive, I want us to plan within our capabilities, nothing more. Cross the canal and hold even ten centimeters of [the] Sinai. I'm exaggerating, of course[:] and that will help me greatly and alter completely the political situation both internationally and within Arab ranks."[47] Senior Soviet advisors, before their expulsion in July 1972, heard the same message of preparing to seize land on the east bank—even as little as ten centimeters would suffice.[48] Concerned about precipitating a military defeat by attempting to go beyond the capabilities of his armed forces, Sadat commended to his war minister the merits of caution so as not to lose the army, as had happened in 1967.[49]

On 1 October 1973, six days before war, Sadat provided Ahmad Ismail with a strategic directive for the war. Haykal might actually have written the document, for it echoed his articles of *al-Ahram* discussed in Chapter 4.

To challenge the Israeli Security Theory by carrying out a military action according to the capabilities of the armed forces *aimed at inflicting the heaviest losses on the enemy* and convincing him that continued occupation of our land exacts a price too high for him to pay, and that consequently his theory of security—based as it is on psychological, political, and military intimidation—is not an impregnable shield of steel which could protect him today or in the future.

A successful challenge of the Israeli Security Theory will have definite short-term and long-term consequences. In the short term, a challenge to the Israeli Security Theory could have a certain result, which would make it possible for an honorable solution for the Middle East crisis to be reached. In the long-term, a challenge to the Israeli Security Theory can produce changes which will, following on the heels of one another, lead to a basic change in the enemy's thinking, morale, and aggressive tendencies.[50]

In this strategic directive Sadat clearly wanted the EAF to focus on achieving a psychological effect upon Israel by causing as many casualties as possible—rather than on seizing strategic terrain or destroying the IDF.

Egyptian military literature on the 1973 war stresses the centrality of inflicting as many human casualties as possible.[51] Here, the EAF targeted the Israeli people. Life was precious in Israel for numerous reasons, and many killed and wounded in battle could have an adverse psychological effect on Israeli society after the war, making the continued occupation of Arab lands appear an unbearable proposition. The EAF could inflict high casualties by simply taking up defensive positions on the east bank near the Suez Canal area to await Israeli counterattacks—hence Sadat's repeated references to ten centimeters.

On the eve of war, Ahmad Ismail seems to have requested an additional directive from Sadat designed to clarify unequivocally, for the historical record, that the EAF was embarking on a war for limited objectives proportional to its capabilities.[52] On 5 October, the day before the war, Sadat complied, identifying three strategic objectives, thereby clearly affirming the limited character of the upcoming conflict:[53]

- To end the current military situation by ending the cease-fire on 6 October 1973
- To inflict on the enemy the greatest possible losses in men, weapons, and equipment
- To work for the liberation of occupied land in successive stages according to the growth and development of possibilities in the armed forces.

Moreover, Egypt would definitely commence hostilities on 6 October, with or without Syrian participation.

This strategic directive, like its predecessor, avoided mentioning the defeat of the IDF as a military objective; nor was there any mention of capturing specific territory. Clearly, Sadat risked a war without much hope, if any, of destroying, or even soundly defeating, the IDF on the battlefield. Rather, he called upon his military to begin the war, make the Israelis suffer high losses in blood and treasure, and seize as much terrain as opportunity permitted. The directive, however, failed to identify a final military objective or describe a clear end-state. By merely discrediting Israel's security theory, Egyptian pride was to be restored at the IDF's expense, and Egypt could then enter negotiations after the war from a position of strength. In the end, astute diplomacy, based on strategy of opportunism, would transform military gains into a political victory.

An analogy can be made between Israel and a bully living in a neighborhood filled with children. From the Egyptian perspective, Israel was a classic bully in the Middle East. A neighborhood bully uses his physical strength to intimidate or terrorize other kids into conforming with his wishes, for he believes no one can beat him in a fair fight. He relates with others only from a position of strength, with little if any desire for compromise. The bully's reasoning and attitude are what the Egyptians labeled, on the macro level, the Israeli security theory. But in real life, one often does not need to beat the bully to elicit a change in his attitude. A serious fight that bloodies his nose can often change a bully's attitude and behavior, even gain his respect. Rather than engage in another bloody fight—with its physical and emotional costs—the bully is willing to relate differently to the one kid who has stood up to him, even if the child lost the fight. This analogy of the neighborhood bully provides some insight into Sadat's strategic thinking and war aims.

PREWAR DIPLOMACY

In addition to challenging Israel, Sadat also targeted the two superpowers in his war strategy. A delicate balancing act between Washington and Moscow was essential if Sadat was to achieve maximum political success in any military adventure. His strategic assessment suggested that the United States was more important for reaching a political solution, the USSR for waging war.[54] In other words, only the Kremlin would provide the necessary military hardware for war against the IDF; only American pressure could nudge Israel into returning captured lands to the Arabs. A limited military success, Sadat reasoned, would shake the superpowers, in particular the United States, out of their diplomatic lethargy with respect to the Arab-Israeli conflict and force a positive attitude and policy toward Egypt. Egypt would immediately gain diplomatic maneuverability and regain its rightful place in international politics. In essence, Sadat sought to establish close diplomatic relations with Washington and then use the Americans as a lever on Israel.

In dealing with the United States, Sadat first had to set the stage for Washington becoming involved in the Arab-Israeli conflict. A secret "back channel" direct to the White House would be the most convenient and effective means of dialogue between the two countries. The United States actually initiated the idea of holding secret talks. In October 1971, then Foreign Minister Mahmud Riyad secretly met with National Security Advisor Henry Kissinger in New York at a private home.[55] As he edged toward deciding on war, Sadat moved to solidify his back channel to the White House. At the end of February 1973, his own national security advisor, Muhammad Hafez Ismail, journeyed to Washington to conduct secret discussions with his counterpart. At the time, Kissinger was disinclined to become involved in the Arab-Israeli conflict. "The strategy I favored [was] a prolonged stalemate that would move the Arabs toward moderation and the Soviets to the fringes of Middle East diplomacy."[56]

Contacts between Washington and Cairo continued for several more months. Hafez Ismail met secretly with Kissinger again in April and May, both times in Paris. The communiqués between the two national security advisors ceased at the end of July as the EAF made final preparations for war.[57] Despite the lack of any progress from these clandestine exchanges, Sadat possessed a secret channel directly to the White House, one that bypassed the U.S. State Department. Sadat planned to negotiate with the United States during the war, and he would direct Hafez Ismail to activate this direct line to the White House on the second day.

Going alone against Israel would have been foolhardy, if not suicidal; Egypt needed allies in the Arab world. Consequently, Sadat devoted a good deal of energy to developing a broad Arab coalition in support of his war effort. At the very least, Egypt needed Syria to open a second front against Israel. A Syrian assault on the Golan Heights would force Israel to divide its efforts, thus allowing the Arabs to use exterior lines to counter Israel's advantage of interior lines.

The roots of the Egyptian-Syrian military alliance actually went back to Nasser; on 9 August 1969, the two countries had formed a secret political command consisting of both presidents, war ministers, and foreign ministers. While there was cooperation and sharing of information, the two armies were still far from a firm commitment to a joint war effort when Nasser died in September 1970.[58] Nasser's death put Egyptian-Syrian cooperation into abeyance. On 13 November 1970, as Sadat focused on consolidating power within Egypt, Syria experienced a military coup. Lieutenant General Hafez al-Asad, the war minister and commander of the air force and air defense, seized control of the government from the more radical Salah Jadid. Asad needed time to consolidate his control over Syria before embarking on serious preparations for war.

On 10 January 1973, Egypt and Syria moved closer to war with the appointment of Ahmad Ismail as the general commander of both armies, with the authority limited "to coordination of the independent efforts on two operational fronts."[59] This arrangement, although bringing the two armies closer together, avoided a unified command. Instead, each army was to report to its respective head of state. A small staff headed by an Egyptian major general served as a liaison between the two fronts. In April 1973, Sadat and Asad held secret meetings in Alexandria, Egypt, and Burg al-Arab, Syria, where they agreed in principle to go to war before the end of the year.[60]

Despite such loose coordination, the Syrian Armed Forces (SAF) added significant numbers and material to the Egyptian war effort. The Syrian air force possessed more than three hundred aircraft, including 110 MiG-21s, 120 MiG-17s, and forty-five Su-7s. An integrated air defense system, similar to that in Egypt, guarded Syrian airspace. For the ground offensive, Syria committed over seventy thousand men, organized in two armored and three reinforced infantry divisions with a total of 1,500 tanks and 675 artillery pieces. With a two-front strategy, the Arabs would stretch Israel to its limit.

As they cemented their alliance, Sadat and Asad began considering Jordan's role in the next conflict. Both Egypt and Syria had severed their relations with Jordan. Now in 1973, Sadat and Asad decided to gain Jordanian cooperation in order to raise their own chances for operational and tactical success. Accordingly, Sadat, Asad, and Hussein held a summit in Cairo on 10–12 September 1973. They gained no Jordanian commitment to open a third front, but Sadat and Asad won assurances that Hussein would deploy his forces so as to prevent the IDF from using Jordanian territory to hit Syrian forces from the south. On 13 September, both Cairo and Damascus announced the restoration of full diplomatic relations with Amman.[61]

Sadat also helped gain the support of Saudi Arabia and other oil-rich Gulf states. Egypt needed petrodollars, and there was the possibility of gaining diplomatic leverage using oil as a weapon. As far back as 21 July 1972, Haykal had published an article in *al-Ahram* arguing for such use of oil, and in January 1973, Sadat raised the issue with King Faysal during a pilgrimage to Mecca.[62] In a *Washington Post* interview published on 18 April 1973, Ahmad Zaki Yamani, the Saudi petroleum minister, raised the possibility of a link between the continued flow of Mideast oil to the United States and changes in American policy toward Israel. Similar statements came from King Faysal and other Arab leaders. There were even warnings from American oil men, but none received serious consideration by the Nixon administration. Still, by September, the American media was openly discussing the potential of an oil boycott.[63] Saudi Arabia, producing eight million barrels of oil per day and expecting a cash surplus of six billion dollars by the end of the year, could stop the flow of oil without a drastic effect on the kingdom's economic development. By hinting at oil politics, Faysal was clearly working in tandem with Sadat and Asad in preparing for another armed conflict. He was, most likely, also encouraging the United States to avert an outbreak of hostilities by launching a major diplomatic initiative.

Meanwhile, Egypt and Syria enlisted Arab military support as well. In December 1972, for example, the various chiefs of the General Staff in the Arab League gathered in Cairo and reached an agreement on the kind of military assistance each country would provide once hostilities broke out. Between 27 and 30 January 1973, the Combined Arab Collective Defense Council met in the Egyptian capital, and again each Arab state pledged to offer aid.[64]

This promised military, not to mention financial, support from the Arab world proved more than symbolic. On the Egyptian front, three air squadrons arrived from Algeria, two from Libya, and one from Iraq. Algeria and Libya each provided one armored brigade, whereas Morocco and Sudan contributed one infantry brigade each. The Egyptians also deployed one Kuwaiti and one Tunisian infantry battalion. The Syrians gained the use of four Iraqi air squadrons, one Iraqi division, one Moroccan tank regiment, and a Jordanian armored brigade. Finally, a Saudi infantry brigade reinforced the Jordanian front. Most of these combat forces arrived during the conflict. A few were in place before hostilities, and some came after the second cease-fire. This support demonstrated to Israel that the Arabs were capable of forging a measure of strategic cooperation on the battlefield, however tenuous and ephemeral.

By October 1973, Sadat had prepared the strategic environment for the EAF to wage war with more favorable odds than it had once faced. A military alliance with Syria assured a two-front war against Israel. Jordanian guarantees prevented an Israeli counterattack on the Syrian southern flank. Better relations with Saudi Arabia opened the possibility of the Arabs resorting to the oil weapon. The Soviets had provided the EAF with much-needed military hardware, and Cairo possessed a secret channel to the White House, through Kissinger. The stage was thus set for another Arab-Israeli war.

EGYPT'S CAMPAIGN PLAN

Egyptian and Syrian military planners quickened the pace of their preparations during the summer of 1973. To ensure proper cooperation between the two fronts, Ahmad Ismail chaired a joint planning conference in Alexandria on 22 and 23 August 1973; it was attended by senior officers from both countries. The participants put final touches on the war plans and recommended either September 7–11 or October 5–11 as the best dates for war. They requested that the political leadership provide a fifteen-day advance warning before the date of attack.[65]

The combined Egyptian-Syrian war plan is still shrouded in mystery and controversy. After the war, the Syrians would claim that the Egyptians had deceived them. According to the Syrian version, the Syrians agreed to capture the Golan Heights in four to five days, during which time the Egyptians would cross the Suez Canal and race to the passes. The actual Egyptian intent was to establish bridgeheads, with no firm commitment to capture the passes. Shazli agrees with the Syrian position. According to him, Sadat ordered Ahmad Ismail to lie to the Syrians in order to ensure their participation in the war. The Syrians would have opposed war had the EAF only limited its objectives to the bridgeheads. Syria needed an immediate Egyptian advance to the passes to divert Israeli attention and forces away from the Golan front.[66] Most likely, both Sadat and Asad were not fully forthcoming between themselves or with their respective militaries.

To ensure a successful military operation in the Sinai, the Egyptian General Command had to formulate specific operational and tactical objectives that were within the capabilities of the EAF. In this regard, Egyptian expectations had dwindled with the passage of time. Immediately after the Six Day War, Nasser had planned to liberate the entire Sinai in a major campaign within thirty-six months. The harsh reality of the Three Years War, however, suggested that this goal lay outside the realm of possibility. No concrete offensive plan, with a supportive training program, for a major crossing of the Suez Canal existed at Nasser's death.[67] Preparing the armed forces took a full year once Sadat made the decision for war.

In 1971, General Command began more serious planning for a major crossing operation. Sadiq, who replaced Fawzi as war minister in May, wanted to seize the entire Sinai. Sadiq gave in to pressure from his subordinates and allowed planning for the seizure of the strategic passes of Mitla, Giddi, and Bir Gifgafa. By September 1971, war planners drafted Operation 41, which called for capturing the passes in one major operation.[68] After Sadiq's firing and Ahmad Ismail's appointment as war minister in October 1972, General Command developed a two-phase campaign, eventually given the code name Operation *Badr*.

The first phase committed five infantry divisions, organized in two field armies, to cross the Suez Canal dispersed across on a broad front. According to this concept, Israeli senior commanders in the Sinai would lose precious hours seeking to discover the main Egyptian effort. Operation *Badr* outlined the following missions for the crossing operation:[69]

- Cross the Suez Canal and destroy the Bar-Lev Line.
- Establish bridgeheads of ten to fifteen kilometers depth on the east bank.
- Inflict as much damage as possible in men, weapons, and equipment.
- Repel and destroy Israeli counterattacks.
- Be prepared for further missions depending on the situation.

Egyptian planners allotted four to five days for crossing the Suez Canal, capturing the Bar-Lev Line, and establishing bridgeheads twelve to fifteen kilometers in depth. Each field army would form one continuous bridgehead, with the Bitter Lakes serving as a natural boundary between the Second and Third Field Armies.

On the fourth or fifth day of the war, a decision would have to made whether to proceed with an offensive eastward to capture the three strategic passes or wait for further developments.[70] While the EAF planned for and expected an attack toward the passes, with timing as the variable, Sadat and the top political and military leadership lacked serious commitment to the second phase of Operation *Badr*. This tiny circle included Sadat, Hafiz Ismail, Ahmad Ismail, and Shazli. Sadat was willing to make bold political moves, but not military ones. Establishing bridgeheads on the east bank would suffice to break the diplomatic stalemate; anything that risked these military gains would jeopardize his bargaining position after the war.[71]

Military considerations argued for a firm commitment only to establish bridgements. The Egyptian air force lacked the capability to challenge Israeli pilots for control of the skies, and the strategic passes lay outside the Egyptian air defense umbrella, which extended only twenty kilometers into the Sinai at the outset of hostilities. The passes were between fifty and fifty-five kilometers from the Suez Canal. A drive that far appeared an unnecessary gamble, given the history of the EAF in fighting the IDF. Consequently, Operation *Badr* included the possibility of an operational pause to evaluate battlefield conditions before determining the most appropriate action.

Clearly, war plans rested on the principles of caution and flexibility. Sadat's strategic directive to the armed forces on 5 October made abundantly clear that the completion of the crossing operation would be followed by an assessment before assigning any further missions. As head of state, Sadat no doubt expected to assess both the political and military situation before making his decision. He was concerned with shattering the diplomatic deadlock through a military operation, not in capturing land per se. Expressed in the Arabic language, his concept was more a war of political movement (*al-tahrik*) than territorial liberation (*al-tahrir*). Breaking the diplomatic stalemate would force the United States to modify its commitment to Israel and to bring pressure to bear on Israel to negotiate in good faith with the Arabs. Essentially, Sadat sought psychological effects that would strengthen his diplomatic position, for which any seizure of territory in a major operation would suffice. Ahmad Ismail and Shazli clearly understood his reasoning. Other senior commanders were kept in the dark.

Most senior Egyptian commanders expected a war designed around a traditional military goal in war: the capture of decisive terrain. For them, the Sinai passes constituted just such a worthy prize. Remaining in bridgeheads ten to fifteen kilometers in depth presented numerous military problems. Over a hundred thousand men squeezed into such a small area would present a lucrative target to the IDF. Furthermore, there being no tactical depth, long-range Israeli artillery could easily prevent the opening of the Suez Canal. Capturing the passes, however, presented a major problem, for they stood outside the integrated air defense umbrella. To provide air cover to ground forces moving to the passes, the Egyptians had to transfer their air defense system to the east bank, a process requiring at least nine hours. For a move to the passes, Operation *Badr* called for the transfer of five of seven air defense brigades, including both SAM-2s and SAM-3s, to the east bank.[72] Such a transfer of immobile missiles in the midst of war, however, threatened to compromise the integrity of the system.

Despite the later controversy over the issue of final military objectives in the war, there was clarity and unity of purpose within the political and military leadership with respect to the first phase. Herein lay the strength of Operation *Badr*, and hence the greatest threat to the IDF.

EGYPT'S TACTICAL OBJECTIVES

Despite the primary military objective of establishing bridgeheads on the east bank, Sadat identified several tactical aims in the crossing operation. First of all, he wanted the swift occupation of Qantara East. It had been the second most important town in the Sinai before the 1967 war, and its capture would carry great propaganda value. To facilitate the rapid capture of Qantara East, Ahmad Ismail decided to reinforce the 18th Infantry Division, in whose zone of operations the town fell, with an armored brigade. Later, Sadat directed General Command to take Ismailiya and Suez City outside the range of Israeli artillery as quickly as possible so as to avoid the embarrassment of having these two Egyptian cities struck by Israeli ground fire. Again, the war minister solved the tactical problem by attaching a tank brigade each to the 2d and 19th Infantry Divisions. Finally, the commanders of the 16th and 7th Infantry Divisions, the last two divisions involved in the crossing operation, clamored for their own tank brigades, and Ahmad Ismail yielded to their requests. Operation *Badr* thus ended up with five infantry divisions crossing the Suez Canal on a broad front, each augmented by an armored brigade.[73]

These decisions underscored the great emphasis Sadat and Ahmad Ismail placed on the crossing operation, and also their reticence about follow-on missions. To commit five tank brigades to the crossing operation required stripping armored assets from each field army's operational reserves, the very forces that would be used in a move to the passes. In Second Army, the 23d Mechanized Division transferred its 24th Armored Brigade to 2d Infantry Division, while the 21st Armored Division attached its 14th Armored Brigade to the 16th Infantry Division. The 15th Independent Armored Brigade, with the newly received T-62 tanks, joined the 18th Infantry Division. Meanwhile, the same dynamic occurred in Third Army's sector. The 6th Mechanized Division lost its 22d Armored Brigade to the 19th Infantry Division and had to assign its 1st Mechanized Infantry Brigade to the capture of Ras Sudar, south of Port Tawfiq, as well. The 25th Independent Armored Brigade, also armed with T-62 tanks, was attached to the 19th Infantry Division. In terms of operational reserves on the west bank, the Second Army now possessed one armored and four mechanized infantry brigades, whereas the Third Army had two each. Both field armies also possessed a commando group for special operations (see Map 11).

General Command committed more resources than necessary to the crossing operation. In addition to an armored brigade of ninety-six tanks and 1,800 troops, each infantry division received one battalion of self-propelled SU-100 antitank guns and one antitank guided-weapons battalion.[74] Each infantry division's bridgehead should contain 220 tanks (124 in four tank battalions organic to the division and 96 in the attached armored brigade) and approximately twenty thousand troops, cramped into an area twelve to fifteen kilometers in depth and with a frontage of twenty kilometers. With five reinforced infantry divisions, the crossing operation comprised approximately 1,100 tanks and over one hundred thousand troops. Such a mass of weaponry for the crossing operation should compensate for any Israeli advantages in maneuver.

Armor in the operational reserve was as follows. Second Army contained 220 tanks: thirty-one in the 10th Mechanized Brigade, 161 in the 21st Armored Division (one tank and mechanized infantry brigade), and sixty-two in the two mechanized infantry brigades from the 23d Mechanized Infantry Division. Third Army's tanks were deployed with 285 in the 4th Armored Division (each armored brigade received an additional tank battalion) and sixty-two in the 6th Mechanized Infantry Division. The operational reserve had close to six hundred tanks.

Even General Command's strategic reserve failed to escape cannibalization. The 3d Mechanized Infantry Division, stationed in the Cairo area, lost its 10th Mechanized Infantry Brigade to the area on the west bank opposite Qantara East, the area vacated by the 15th Armored Brigade, which had joined the 18th Infantry Division. This decision left only one armored and one mechanized infantry brigade in the 3d Mechanized Infantry Division, for a total of 127 tanks. General headquarters also contained two independent tank brigades (192 tanks),

"NO WAR, NO PEACE" 155

a paratroop brigade, two air assault brigades, and a commando group. The strategic reserve contained approximately 320 tanks.[75]

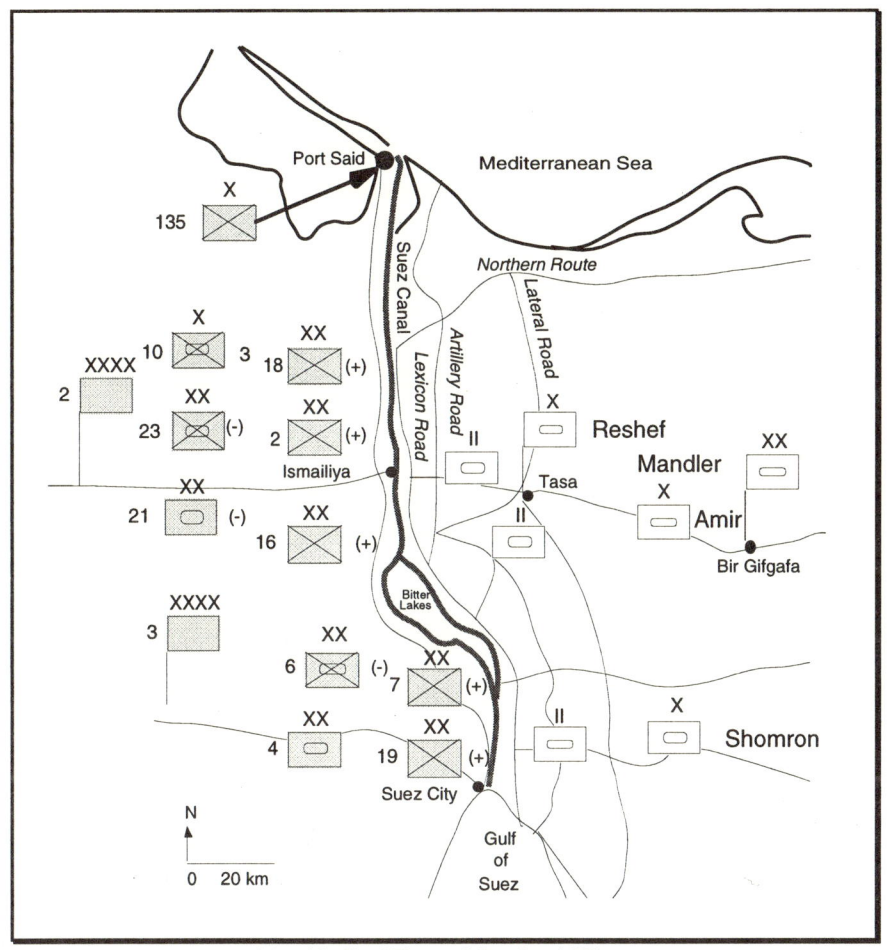

Map 11. Sinai Front, 6 October 1973.

Crossing the Suez Canal with 1,100 tanks and over a hundred thousand troops required a Herculean effort in planning, training, and execution. To facilitate the transportation of troops and equipment to the east bank, Shazli established the Crossing Command, some five hundred officers and one thousand enlisted men, armed with five hundred radios and two hundred field telephones. This command, under Shazli's watchful eye, worked directly with the chiefs of staff for the two field armies and the five divisions.[76]

To compensate for the weakness of the air force, General Command assigned the air defense forces the mission of neutralizing the Israeli air force over the battlefield. The Soviet-type integrated air defense system based on 150 SAM batteries and 2,500 antiaircraft guns. Sheer numbers and sophistication provided lethal coverage over the west and east banks of the Suez Canal. But that air parity would disappear quickly once Egyptian operations extended beyond twenty kilometers east of the waterway.

The Egyptians took advantage of the IDF's tank heavy force structure by employing a combined-arms doctrine. The centerpiece was the Egyptian infantryman armed with a Soviet antitank missile. Operation *Badr* called for infantry, supported by artillery and tanks, to defeat Israeli armor formations counterattacking during the crossing operation. Egyptian planners expected the IDF to make breakthroughs but felt proper training would ensure tactical success. As noted by then Brigadier General Adil Yusri, commander of the 112th Infantry Brigade, who crossed with his unit in the first hour of the war, the EAF had trained to turn Israeli armor penetrations into opportunities, "The enemy's tanks making a penetration are a rich meal for starved men if our defenses are in depth."[77] To the killing zones, the Egyptians had assigned 1,100 tanks, two thousand artillery pieces, five thousand RPG-7s and one thousand RPG-43s, and 1,900 antitank guided weapons.[78] These numbers proved more than adequate for establishing defensive positions in congested bridgeheads.

The Egyptian crossing of the Suez Canal would etch for itself a place in the annals of modern warfare. Limited land objectives minimized Egyptian vulnerability to Israeli air strikes and armored counterattacks while at the same time they maximized Egypt's defensive capabilities. Operation *Badr* was based on a strategic offensive coupled with a tactical defense. It called for the use of defensive weapons, in particular the SAM-2s and the SAM-3s, in support of an offensive operation. Using offensive weapons defensively proved most effective politically.

CONCLUSION

Nasser, although deserving much of the credit for preparing the EAF for next war, left it to Sadat to reverse the lack of diplomatic progress over three years of conflict. Sadat rose to the challenge, placing his own distinctive imprint on the 1973 war with at least five major contributions.

First, Sadat overcame resistance from his own General Command to a major confrontation with Israel. To have his way required firing the war minister and a number of senior officers in October 1972. Second, Sadat engineered a broad Arab coalition. At its epicenter stood the military alliance with Syria. A two-front strategy would stretch the Israeli war effort to its limits. Saudi Arabia, for its part, would lead other Arab Gulf states in employing oil as a political weapon, a weapon that shook the global economy and transformed the Arab-Israeli problem into an international issue. Third, Sadat formulated a clear war strategy with specific tactical goals, easily within the capabilities of the EAF. His limited war focused on establishing bridgeheads to a fifteen kilometer depth. Fourth, Sadat managed to persuade the Soviets to provide military equipment without which the EAF would have been at an even greater disadvantage in battle. Fifth, he laid the diplomatic groundwork by which the United States assumed the role of mediator in the Arab-Israeli conflict. Both open and secret diplomacy served this purpose.

Meanwhile, Israel had lapsed into complacency since the Three Years War. Moreover, the IDF, as well as Israeli society, expected to refight the last war. The next war would short, decisive, and with minimum casualties; and the Arab armies would repeat their incompetence in battle. By this unrealistic expectation, Israelis had set themselves up for a cruel awakening. The notion of a major Arab effort for limited military objectives was far from Israeli thinking in September 1973. In the last few weeks before the outbreak of the October War, Egypt's task was to keep Israel in such a frame of mind.

NOTES

1. Basil Liddell Hart, *Strategy* (New York, 1974): 353.

2. Sun Tzu, *The Art of War*, translated by Ralph D. Sawyer (Boulder, CO: Westview Press, 1994): 177.

3. David A. Korn, *Stalemate: The War of Attrition and Great Power Diplomacy in the Middle East, 1967–1970* (Boulder, CO: Westview Press, 1992): 271–272; and Yoram Meital, *Egypt's Struggle for Peace: Continuity and Change, 1967–1977* (Gainesville: University Press of Florida, 1997): 83–84.

4. James Reston, "Egyptian Leader Gives Conditions for Peace Accord," *New York Times*, 28 December 1970: 1, 14–15; Raphael Israeli, *The Public Diary of President Sadat, I: The Road to War (October 1970–October 1973)* (Leiden: Brill, 1978): 14–15.

5. Raymond H. Anderson, "Sadat Affirms 30-Day Truce," *New York Times*, 5 February 1971: 3.

6. Raymond H. Anderson, "Egypt is Pressing Proposal on Suez," *New York Times*, 7 February 1971: 23.

7. Peter Grose, "Israel Willing to Discuss Canal," *New York Times*, 10 February 1971: 10.

8. Arnaud de Borchgrave, "A Talk with Sadat on Peace Terms," *Newsweek*, 22 February 1971: 40–41.

9. Saad al-Shazli, *The Crossing of the Suez* (San Francisco: American Mideast Research, 1980): 127–129; Muhammad Hassanayn Haykal, *Oktobir 1973: al-Silah wa al-Siyasat* (Cairo: al-Ahram, 1993): 248–251; Abd al-Munim Khalil, *Hurub Misr al-Muasirah fi Awraq Qaid Maydani: 1939–1945, 1956, 1962–1967, 1968–1970, 1973* (Cairo: Dar al-Mustaqbal al-Arabi, 1990): 161–164; and Mahmud Riyad, *Mudhakirat Mahmud Riyad 1948–1978, I: al-Bahth an al-Salam as al-Sira al-Sharq al-Ust* (Beirut: al-Muessah al-Arabiyya lil-Dirsat wa al-Nashr, 1987): 370–371, 429.

10. Michael N. Barnett, *Confronting the Costs of War: Military Power, State, and Society in Egypt and Israel* (Princeton, NJ: Princeton University Press, 1992): 81.

11. John W. Amos, *Arab-Israeli Military/Political Relations: Arab Perceptions and the Politics of Escalation* (New York: Pergamon Press, 1979): 103; and Amos Perlmutter, *Egypt: The Praetorian State* (New Brunswick, NJ: Transaction Books, 1974): 59.

12. Henry Kissinger, *White House Years* (Boston: Little, Brown, 1979): 376–379, and *Years of Upheavl* (Boston: Little, Brown, 1982): 196, 203; and William B. Quandt, *Peace Process: American Diplomacy and the Arab-Israeli Conflict since 1967* (Washington, DC: Brookings: 1993): 65–75.

13. Muhammad Ali Fahmi, interview with author, 21 October 1996, Leavenworth, Kansas.

14. Muhammad Hassanayn Haykal, *The Road to Ramadan* (New York: Quadrangle, 1975): 170–176; Shazli, *Crossing of the Suez*: 162–167; Riyad, *Mudhakirat*, I: 403–404; Muhammad Abd al-Ghani al-Gamassi, *Mudhakirat al-Gamassi: Harb Oktobir 1973* (Paris: al-Munshurat al-Sharqiyya, 1990): 220-221; and Muhammad Fawzi, *Istratijiyyah al-Musaliha: al-Giza' al-Sani min Mudhakirat al-Fariq Awwal Muhammad Fawzi* (Cairo: Dar al-Mustaqbal, 1986): 285. Figures vary as to actual number of Soviet advisors. Sadat gives fifteen thousand and Haykal twenty-one thousand. Shazli and Gamasi claim eight thousand. See Gamal Hamad, *Min Sina ila al-Golan* (Cairo: al-Zuhra lil-Ilam al-Arabi, 1988): 254; and Ariel Vitan, "The Soviet Military Presence in Egypt 1967–1972: A New Perspective," *The Journal of Slavic Military Studies* 8 (September 1995): 547–565.

15. Anwar Sadat, *In Search of Identity* (New York: Harper and Row, 1987): 228–229.

16. Shazli, *Crossing of the Suez*, 163.

17. Ezer Weizman, *Battle for Peace* (New York: Bantam, 1981): 67.

18. Haykal, *Road to Ramadan*: 181; Sadat, *In Search of Identity*: 234–236: Shazli, *Crossing of the Suez*: 172–181; Gamasi, *Mudhakirat*: 225–227; and Musa Sabri, *Wathaiq Harb Oktobir* (Cairo: al-Maktab al-Misri, 1974): 17–18.

19. Avraham Adan, *On the Banks of the Suez* (Novato, CA: Presidio Press, 1980): 63.

20. Gamasi, *Mudhakirat*: 229.

21. Shazli, *Crossing of the Suez*, 172; Riyad, *Mudhakirat*, I: 420–421; and Hamad, *Min Sina ila al-Golan*: 497–498.

22. *al-Nasr* 405 (November 1972): 3. This newspaper is published by the Egyptian army. See also Trevor Dupuy, *Elusive Victory: The Arab-Israeli Wars, 1947–1974*:(1978, reprint, Fairfax, VA: Hero Books, 1984): 388–389.

23. Haykal, *Road to Ramadan*: 181–182.

24. Insight Team, *Insights on the Middle East War* (London: The Sunday Times, 1974): 116–117; and Perlmutter, *Egypt*: 225, n. 15.

25. Haykal, *Road to Ramadan*: 182.

26. Shazli, *Crossing of the Suez*: 187–188. For the same assessment, see Gamasi, *Mudhakirat*: 231. The relationship between the minister of war and the chief of the General Staff during the period 1967–73 deserves a separate study, especially with regard to the exact delineation of lines of authority and responsibility in both peacetime and war. Shazli does mention a squabble between himself and Minister of War Muhammad Sadiq over this issue (see Shazli, 239 ff). Muhammad Fawzi, *Harb al-Thalath Sanawat 1967–1970* (Beirut: Dar al-Wahda, 1983): 241–242, also addresses this important problem, although briefly.

27. Haykal, *Road to Ramadan*: 183.

28. Gamasi, *Mudhakirat*: 232.

29. Gamal al-Hamad, *al-Muarik al-Harbiyya ala al-Gebha al-Misriyya: Harb Oktobir 1973 al-Ashir min Ramadan* (Cairo: al-Zuhra lil-Ilam al-Arabi, 1989): 970–971.

30. Muhammad Abd al-Ghani al-Gamasi, interview with author, 25 June 1994, Cairo, Egypt.

31. Adan, *On the Banks of the Suez*: 77; Hanoch Bartov, *Dado: 48 Years and 20 Days* (Tel Aviv: Ma'ariv, 1981): 252, 262; Chaim Herzog, *The War of Atonement, October 1973* (Boston: Little, Brown, 1975): 43-51; and Iftihar Spector, interview with author,

7 July 1994, Tel Aviv, Israel. Spector, then a lieutenant colonel, commanded an F-4 squadron. For the claim of only a twenty-four-hour warning, see Eliot A. Cohen and John Gooch, *The Anatomy of Failure in War* (New York: The Free Press, 1990): 102 and n. 26.

32. For a discussion of Israeli doctrinal developments after the Six Day War, see Edward N. Luttwak and Daniel Horowitz, *The Israeli Army, 1948–1973* (Lanham, MD: University Press of America, 1983): 327–336; David Eshel, *Chariots of the Desert: The Story of the Israeli Armoured Corps* (London: Brassey's, 1989): 87–93; and Jac Weller, "Foot Soldiers in the Desert: Infantry and the October War," *Army* (August 1974): 24.

33. Moshe Dayan, *Moshe Dayan: The Story of My Life* (New York: William Morrow, 1976): 438.

34. Discussion with an Egyptian officer attending the US Army Command and General Staff College, Fort Leavenworth, Kansas.

35. "The Agranat Report: The First Partial Report," *The Jerusalem Journal of International Relations* 4 (1979): 74.

36. Muhammad Ali Fahmi, interview, 21 October 1996; author's interviews with several Egyptian air defenders attending the US Army Command and General Staff College, Fort Leavenworth, Kansas; and Anthony H. Cordesman and Abraham R. Wagner, *The Lessons of Modern War*, Volume I: *The Arab-Israeli Conflicts, 1973–1989* (Boulder, CO: Westview Press, 1990): 72–82.

37. Discussions with Israeli officers attending the US Army Command and General Staff College, Fort Leavenworth, Kansas, 1986-90.

38. Dupuy, *Elusive Victory*: 395–396.

39. The concept of "stop line" comes from Amnon Reshef, interview with author, 30 June 1994, Tel Aviv, Israel; and Aryeh Keren, interview wth author, 4 July 1994, Israel. Both men commanded armored brigades in the Sinai. For a general discussion of Israeli war plans, see Adan, *On the Banks of the Suez*: 57–58; and Bartov, *Dado*: 283–284.

40. Arnold Sherman, *In the Bunkers of the Sinai* (New York: Sabra Books, 1971): 23.

41. Adan, *On the Banks of the Suez*: 247–249; Ariel Sharon, *Warrior: The Autobiography of Ariel Sharon* (New York: Simon and Schuster, 1989): 237, 269–270; and Bartov, *Dado*: 128–129.

42. Sharon, *Warrior*: 237–238; and Adan, *On the Banks of the Suez*: 55–56.

43. Quoted in Avi Shlaim, "Failures in National Intelligence Estimates: The Case of the Yom Kippur War," *World Politics* 28 (1976): 362. An Israeli colonel attending the US Army Command and Staff College confirmed the quote; he was in that graduating class and heard Dayan speak.

44. Adan, *On the Banks of the Suez*: xii.

45. Sadat, *In Search of Identity*: 215.

46. "Anwar Sadat's Uncertain Trumpet," *Newsweek*, 9 April 1973: 43–45, 49.

47. Shazli, *Crossing of the Suez*: 106; and Khalil, *Hurub*: 261.

48. Mahmut Gareev, interviews with the author, 12 and 14 September 1995, Moscow, Russia. Gareev was a senior military advisor in Egypt during this time, and Sadat told him this.

49. Muhammad Ali Fahmi, interview with author, 22 June 1994, Cairo, Egypt.

50. As cited in Sadat, *In Search of Identity*: 327; Muhammad Hafez Ismail, *Amn Misr al-Qawmi fi Asr al-Tahaddiyat* (Cairo: Markaz al-Ahram lil-Targama wa la-Nashr, 1987): 303–304; Gamasi, *Mudhakirat*: 276–279, 444; and Haykal, *Oktobir 1973*: 311–312.

160   THE ALBATROSS OF DECISIVE VICTORY

51. Hafez Ismail, *Amn Misr al-Qawmi*: 199; and Gamasi, *Mudhakirat*: 208.
52. Shazli, *Crossing of the Suez*: 38; and Gamasi, *Mudhakirat*: 282.
53. Sadat, *In Search of Identity*: 328; Hafiz Ismail, *Amn Misr al-Qawmi*: 304; Gamasi, *Mudhakirat*: 281, 444–445; and Haykal, *Oktobir 1973*: 312–313.
54. Haykal, *Oktobir 1973*: 239.
55. Hafez Ismail, *Amn Misr al-Qawmi*: 186–188; Meital, *Egypt's Struggle for Peace*: 98–99; and Riyad, *Mudhakirat*, I: 374–377.
56. Kissinger, *Years of Upheaval*: 196.
57. Hafez Ismail, *Amn Misr al-Qawmi*: 288; and Kissinger, *Years of Upheaval*: 209–216.
58. Fawzi, *Harb al-Thalath Sanawat*: 205–211; Gamasi, *Mudhakirat*: 216–217; and Gamasi, interview, 25 June 1994. In his memoirs, Fawzi claims the two countries were much closer to war than suggested by Gamasi.
59. Hasan al-Badri, Taha al-Magdub, and Muhammad Zia al-Din Zohdi, *The Ramadan War, 1973* (New York: Hippocrene Books, 1978): 21.
60. Sadat, *In Search of Identity*: 241; and Gamasi, *Mudhakirat*: 269. Asad confirmed Sadat's account in an interview; see Patrick Seale, *Asad of Syria: The Struggle for the Middle East* (Berkeley: University of California Press, 1988): 192–193.
61. Hamad, *Min Sina ila al-Golan*: 333–334, 540–541.
62. Sayyid Mari, *Awraq Siyasiyah*, III (Cairo: al-Maktab al-Misri al-Hadith, 1979): 698–703; Hafez Ismail, *Amn Misr al-Qawmi*: 266–267, 297; and Bassam Tibi, *Conflict and War in the Middle East, 1967–1991: Regional Dynamic and the Superpowers* (New York: St. Martin's Press, 1993): 136.
63. "Saudis Tie Oil to U.S. Policy," *Washington Post*, 19 April 1973: 1, 25; "The New Politics of Mideast Oil," *Newsweek*, 10 September 1973: 34-37; and "Oil: The Miller Letter," *Newsweek*, 20 August 1973: 56-57. For a general discussion see Neff, *Warriors against Israel*: 110–114.
64. Gamasi, *Mudhakirat*: 239–246.
65. Shazli, *Crossing of the Suez*: 201–203; Gamasi, *Mudhakirat*: 269–270; and Haykal, *Road to Ramadan*: 11–14.
66. Shazli, *Crossing of the Suez*: 36–38. Asad confirms Shazli's claim that the Syrians expected the Egyptians to reach the passes in the first phase of the war. For Asad's statement, given in an interview, see Seale, *Asad of Syria*: 197.
67. Sadat, *In Search of Identity*: 235–236; Shazli, *Crossing of the Suez*: 18; Gamasi, *Mudhakirat*: 302–303; Muhammad Ali Fahmi, interview with author, 28 September 1996, Leavenworth, Kansas; and Gamasi, interview, 25 June 1994.
68. Haykal, *Road to Ramadan*: 155; Shazli, *Crossing of the Suez*: 27–30; and Hamad, *Min Sina ila al-Jolan*: 44–46.
69. Badri, *Harb Ramadan*: 34.
70. Sadat, *In Search of Identity*: 289; Gamasi, *Mudhakirat*: 211, 382–384, 387–395; Gamasi, interviews, 31 October 1993 and 25 June 1994; Fahmi, interview, 22 June 1994; and Murad Ibrahim al-Dessouki, interview with author, 28 June 1994, Cairo. In the 1973 war, Dessouki, currently chief of the military section at the al-Ahram Strategic Studies Institute, was a commander of a mechanized infantry battalion in the 19th Infantry Division.
71. Shazli, *Crossing of the Suez*: 27–39; Hafez Ismail, *Amn Misr al-Qawmi*: 305, 323–324; and Gamasi, *Mudhakirat*: 388–391.
72. Fahmi, interview, 21 October 1996.

73. Saad al-Din al-Shazli, "al-Makal allathi arsul ila majjalla *Oktobir* fi 31/3/87: Hal arid al-qada al-askariyun iqtirah al-Shazli bisahb al-alwiya al-mudarraa," *al-Gabha* 75 (1988): 9. The author received a copy of this article from Shazli, whose account was confirmed by Gamasi, interview. See also Shazli's letter published in Hamad, *al-Maarik al-Harbiyya ala al-Gabha al-Misriyya*: 910–911. On the special importance of Qantara East, see Gamasi, *Mudhakirat*: 343.

74. Shazli, *Crossing of the Suez*: 225.

75. Hamad, *al-Maarik al-Harbiyya ala al-Gebha al-Misriyya*: 102–104, 359–360; and Khalil, *Hurub*: 187.

76. Shazli, *Crossing of the Suez*: 68.

77. 'Adil Yusri, *Rihla al-Shaq al-Mualaqa: min Ras al-Ush ila Ras al-Qubra* (Cairo: Dar al-Muarif bi-Misr, 1974): 184.

78. Dupuy, *Elusive Victory*: 590-591; and Cordesman, *Lessons of Modern War*: 57, 60, 64–65. The numbers come from Abd al-Azim Ramadan, *Harb Oktobir fi Mahkama al-Tarih* (Cairo: Madbuli, 1984): 64.

6

EGYPT'S ASSAULT

War is not merely an act of policy but a true political instrument, a continuation of political intercourse, carried on with other means.
—Carl von Clausewitz[1]

In the midst of war he [Sadat] began to walk the path to peace.
—Henry Kissinger[2]

The 1973 Arab-Israeli war was a clear mismatch with respect to the opposing armies: the IDF possessed a clear superiority in air and tank forces. But as Israeli commanders would soon learn, these two important advantages in maneuver warfare were partly offset by the Arabs beginning the war with simultaneous offensives on two fronts. To take the initiative away from the EAF and the SAF would prove no easy matter, for the IDF was now battling against a determined foe prepared to wage attrition battles. Yet despite all the political and military preparations by Egypt and Syria for the opening hostilities, the October War took many unexpected turns and twists, both on the battlefield and the diplomatic front. Sadat would have to make some tough political decisions in the midst of war.

THE FINAL WALK TOWARD WAR

On 13 September 1973, an unexpected incident occurred that would cloud Israeli military intelligence's judgment for the next three weeks. A routine Israeli reconnaissance overflight of Syria and Lebanon turned into a major dogfight when Syrian fighters challenged the Israeli planes. By the end of the air combat, Israeli pilots had downed twelve Syrian MiGs while losing only one Mirage. This incident formed an important backdrop to the outbreak of war, recalling a very similar incident before the Six Day War. Now, however, Egypt avoided the saber rattling it had indulged in May 1967, in order to keep Israel's guard down.

Israeli leaders expected Syria to retaliate for the humiliation suffered in the aerial encounter. Within two weeks, the IDF noted unusual military activity on its northern border. On 26 September at 8:15 A.M., Elazar, the chief of the General Staff, convened a high-level meeting with senior officers and staff to evaluate military events unfolding in Syria. Syria's General Command had canceled leaves, activated reserve officers and soldiers, and commandered civilian vehicles. Despite these disconcerting moves, Zeira, the director of military intelligence, confidently insisted that Syria would not go to war on its own and that Egypt was too preoccupied with internal matters to contemplate military adventurism. The Asad regime might opt for a show of force or, in the worst-case scenario, try to snatch part of the Golan Heights, but, Zeira assured his fellow senior officers, there was a low probability for war.

One senior Israeli commander, however, refused to accept a rosy picture. Major General Yitzhak Hofi, the head of Northern Command and responsible for the defense of the Golan Heights, prudently demanded reinforcements. Elazar, although accepting Zeira's assessment, decided to take precautionary steps in direct response to Hofi's request. Regular troops assigned to the Golan suddenly learned of the cancellation of their anticipated leaves for Yom Kippur, a decision that left elements of the elite Golani Brigade manning the strong points of the Purple Line (the armistice line between Israel and Syria after the 1967 war). In the Sinai, however, regular units manning the Bar-Lev Line received permission to take the holiday and were replaced by reservists from the Jerusalem Infantry Brigade. To bolster defenses on the northern front, Elazar ordered the 77th Tank Battalion, stationed in the Sinai, to transfer its headquarters, two tank companies, and a heavy artillery battery to the Golan. By this action, the armor force on the Golan Heights increased from seventy-five to over a hundred tanks.[3]

Suddenly, an international terrorist incident caught Israel's attention. On 28 September, three Arab guerrillas seized five Jews on board a train traveling from Czechoslovakia through Austria. In return for the safe release of the hostages, the Austrian government offered to close Schönau Castle as a transit center for Jews leaving the Communist bloc. On 30 September, Meir departed Israel, as scheduled before the crisis, to address an European conference in Strasbourg, but now with the intent of returning home via Vienna. There, on 2 October, she met with the Austrian chancellor in the hope of changing his decision, but to no avail. Arriving in Israel late on 2 October, Meir met with her cabinet the next morning, devoting a good part of the session to Austrian-Israeli relations.

Meanwhile, the SAF continued its methodical mobilization of forces on the Golan front, heightening concerns back in the "Pit," the IDF's command center located in Tel Aviv. Each day brought new information challenging Zeira's assessment of a low probability for war. Su-7 aircraft, for instance, had relocated to forward air bases, and reports of Syrian armor units moving from northern Syria to the front reached Elazar and Zeira. By the beginning of October, virtually the entire Syrian army had deployed to positions from which it could easily assume the offensive. Northern Command thus faced three Syrian infantry divisions forward and two armored divisions in the second echelon.

While the Syrians moved into position, the Egyptians implemented a carefully orchestrated deception plan designed to prevent Israeli military intelligence from getting wind of the impending war.[4] They succeeded in lulling the Israelis into complacency; developments along the Sinai front caused far less concern for the Israeli General Staff than those in the north, even though the events occurred simultaneously and should therefore have aroused more suspicion. Past experience had, no doubt, convinced Israelis of the Arab inability to form a working coalition for war.

The Egyptians ingeniously used their annual autumn maneuvers on the west bank, announced far in advance, to mask their actual intent. Consequently, initial Egyptian military movements near the Suez Canal seemed nothing out of the ordinary. The EAF's training exercise began on 26 September, the day before Rosh Hashanah, the Jewish New Year, and was scheduled to end on 7 October, one day after what was to be the outbreak of hostilities. General Command used this training exercise to bring combat units to their staging areas near the Suez Canal, where the forty-meter sand rampart along the waterway permitted field commanders to conceal a portion of their troops. These maneuvers proved an effective cover for final war preparations.

Strict operational security formed an integral part of the Egyptian deception plan. Sadat and Asad severely limited the number of people privy to the date of the attack, in order to prevent Israeli spies from learning of the decision for war. On 22 September 1973, both heads of state ordered their respective war ministers and chiefs of the general staffs to begin hostilities on 6 October, thus providing them the fourteen days of warning that had been requested by the joint military conference held in Alexandria in August.[5] Slowly word filtered down to subordinate commands. On 1 October, Ahmad Ismail informed the two field army commanders of the actual date. Division commanders were notified on 3 October, brigade commanders on 4 October, and battalion and company commanders on 5 October. Platoon commanders learned of the war only six hours before the attack.[6] Because the EAF was already in place as a result of its training exercise, General Command could issue the attack orders quite late.

On the civilian side, only a few key individuals learned at least of the approach of war. On 30 September, Sadat called a surprise meeting of National Security Council in his Giza home for the purpose of preparing senior civilian officials for war. He began by reviewing the events that had left Egypt in a diplomatic impasse of "no peace, no war" for over three years. Neither superpower was committed to changing this unacceptable situation. "Indeed, the United States, from our point of view, has become, to use our expression, a stiff corpse. . . . and the Soviet Union temporizes and dodges in delivering on contracts of purchased weapons." Egypt had to take matters into its own hands, and only military action could break the deadlock and force political progress. In war, stress would be laid on inflicting a high level of damage on the enemy and, if appropriate, on using oil as an economic weapon. By the meeting's end, everyone in attendance clearly understood war was just around the corner. But no one departed the meeting knowing the date.[7]

A number of other steps were taken in order to prevent Israel's intelligence community from discovering the approach of war. Business on the political front, for example, continued on a routine basis. An invitation was sent to the Romanian defense minister to visit Cairo on 8 October, two days after the scheduled attack. In addition, the foreign, economic, commerce, and information ministers were all out of the country, conducting their normal business activities. These cabinet ministers were kept completely in the dark. To paint a picture of normalcy in the armed forces, Egyptian newspapers announced the holding of sailboat races that would involve the commander of the navy and other naval officers. To lull the Israelis further into complacence, the Egyptian government announced on 4 October 1973 a demobilization of twenty thousand troops and ostensibly granted leaves for men to perform the minor pilgrimage to Mecca. Moreover, stories were planted in Arab newspapers of serious problems with Soviet equipment, thereby suggesting EAF unpreparedness. As a final touch, on the very morning of the attack, Egyptian soldiers innocently fished alongside the Suez Canal, projecting an ordinary, peaceful appearance to the day. The Egyptian deception plan was thus comprehensive, covering both political and military spheres and integrating strategic, operational, and tactical movements from the president to the individual soldier—all designed to fool the Israelis until too late.

There was another important reason why Elazar failed to take adequate measures in anticipation of the Arab attack. In the eyes of the West and of Israelis as well, Israel had a first-class intelligence organization, as evidenced in the 1967 war. Military intelligence had been consistently right in its assessments that Egyptian maneuvers staged between 1971 and 1973 did not threaten war. In particular, back in May 1973, a similar situation of heightened Egyptian military activity near the Suez Canal had raised an alarm in Israel. Zeira dismissed the possibility of war, but despite his assurances, Elazar had convinced Meir to mobilize large numbers of reservists, at great cost to the treasury. The intelligence community proved right once again when the Egyptians completed their exercise without incident. Now, in September and early October, as a result of this last experience, Zeira's assessments received little cross-examination from senior commanders.[8] The IDF and Israeli society would experience a rude awakening.

THE LAST STEPS

Proper coordination between the two fronts loomed as a last major item for Arab consideration. On 3 October, Ahmad Ismail, in his capacity as general commander for the EAF and SAF, and Major General Baha al-Din Nofal, the chief of operations for both fronts, flew to Damascus to meet with senior Syrian commanders to inspect last-minute preparations and determine the time of attack. A surprise awaited them. The Syrians apparently wanted a twenty-four- to forty-eight-hour delay, and disagreement surfaced over the timing of the offensives. Syrian commanders pushed for a dawn attack, so that the sun would be in the eyes of the Israeli defenders on the Golan, but the Egyptians argued for an assault at 6:00 P.M. so the darkness could cover their canal crossing. To resolve the matter expeditiously, Ahmad Ismail appealed to Asad, who agreed to an attack on 6 October and compromised on 2:00 P.M. for the combined offensive.[9] This compromise proved fortuitous, for Israeli military intelligence later reported the combined Egyptian-Syrian attack as commencing at six o'clock in the evening, the time originally set by the EAF.

Jordan surfaced as an issue during the discussions. Asad was especially concerned that King Hussein fulfill his September agreement to ensure that no Israeli troops used Jordanian territory to outflank Syrian forces from the south. The Jordanian monarch had already deployed army units along the northern border with Israel to fulfill his promise to block any such attempt. As a result, Asad had repositioned an entire infantry division closer to the Golan for the offensive, a move that Israeli military intelligence had dismissed as a Syrian gesture of good will in its recent détente with Jordan. Now, Asad wanted to be sure Hussein would fulfill his agreement. While Ahmad Ismail returned to Cairo by plane the next day, Nofal traveled by land to Amman, where he made final arrangements with the Jordanian chief of the General Staff.[10] The new Arab coalition was thus in basic coordination for war, a major improvement from the last conflict in 1967.

The Egyptians and the Syrians almost inadvertently divulged the secret of their combined offensive. Because the conduct of the war depended on Soviet assistance, Sadat and Asad decided to give the Soviets an advance warning. On 3 October, Sadat informed the Soviet ambassador, Vladimir Vinogradov, of Egypt's intent to go to war against Israel in the near future and requested assurances of Soviet assistance.[11] He also requested that the Soviet ambassador remain in Cairo "for the time being."[12] Clearly, the Egyptian president was hinting that war would break out very soon.

On 4 October, Asad was even more forthcoming with the Soviet ambassador in Syria, Nuritdin Mukhitdinov. On much closer terms with the Soviets than Sadat was, the Syrian leader revealed both the decision for war and some of his own strategic thinking. According to Asad, the Syrians planned to capture all or part of the Golan in a few days. Syria was unable to conduct a protracted war against Israel, and therefore, Asad wanted the Soviets to be ready to propose a cease-fire during the first few days of the conflict if called upon. But the Syrian leader, like Sadat, declined to reveal the exact date of the war.[13] However, the Kremlin already knew that Egypt and Syria would attack on 6 October, probably from its own contacts.[14]

In response to these indicators of impending war, Moscow requested permission to evacuate the families of Soviet diplomats and advisors from Egypt and Syria. Sadat and Asad reluctantly granted the request, even though both men were afraid that the Soviet exodus might reveal the Arab hand to the Israelis. Word of the sudden departure of Soviet families caught the Israeli leadership completely by surprise. At 8:25 in the morning of 5 October, Elazar held a conference with senior commanders to discuss the latest developments.[15] No one could find an adequate explanation for such an unusual move. Even Zeira found his self-confidence shaken a bit as he groped for a satisfactory explanation. But the intelligence chief quickly found comfort in his firm convictions that Syria would not dare fight alone and that Egypt would not fight a major war without a capable air force.

Despite assurances from Zeira that there was little likelihood for war, Elazar now took precautionary measures on both fronts that proved critical. He canceled all military leaves, placed the armed forces on C (the highest-level) alert, and ordered the air force to assume a full-alert posture. In addition, he ordered the immediate deployment of the remainder of the 7th Armored Brigade to the Golan Heights to join its 77th Tank Battalion (which had been there since 26 September). By noon on 6 October, the Israeli force on the Golan numbered some 177 tanks and forty-four artillery pieces organized into two armored brigades (see Map 12). These additional reinforcements would save the Golan from certain Syrian capture. To replace the departed 7th Armored Brigade in the Sinai, the Armor School, under the command of Colonel Gabi Amir, received word to activate its tank brigade for immediate airlift to Bir Gifgafa in Sinai, less its tanks. The brigade would use the tanks left behind by the 7th Brigade.[16] The Amir Armored Brigade was in place when war began the next day, helping avert a disaster in the Sinai.

Despite these measures, no decision was taken to mobilize the reserves, and there was good reason for that. Elazar and other senior commanders still expected at least a day or two warning of an impending Arab attack, as had been promised by military intelligence.[17] Such an alert would provide ample time for the mobilization of the reserves and for the air force to destroy the Arab air defense systems. Nothing of the sort occurred, however; the Israeli plans were founded on a best-case scenario. Moreover, the religious factor complicated Israeli decision making. Yom Kippur (the Day of Atonement), the most solemn day in Judaism, fell on 6 October, the day of the Egyptian and Syrian offensives. To call up the reserves on the eve of this holy period without a clear warning from Zeira was not an easy decision.

Israel finally learned of the Arab intention for war: definite word reached Meir, Dayan, and Elazar around 4:30 A.M. on 6 October.[18] An "indisputable" source had indicated a joint Egyptian-Syrian attack scheduled for 6:00 P.M. that day. Israeli military intelligence had failed to deliver on its contract and now provided a wake-up call only nine and a half hours before the expected outbreak of hostilities. Zeira erred further in identifying the time of the Arab attack at six o'clock, when in fact the Egyptians and Syrians planned their assault for two o'clock. These two failings created confusion for the IDF by catching Israeli reservists in the first stages of their mobilization; moreover, regular units were still making final preparations for the onslaught now expected in the early evening. After the Six Day War, the Israelis had been rightfully confident in their intelligence community. To its detriment, however, Israel's political and military leadership had depended too much on receiving timely intelligence, and the Arabs had in fact won the first phase of the information war.

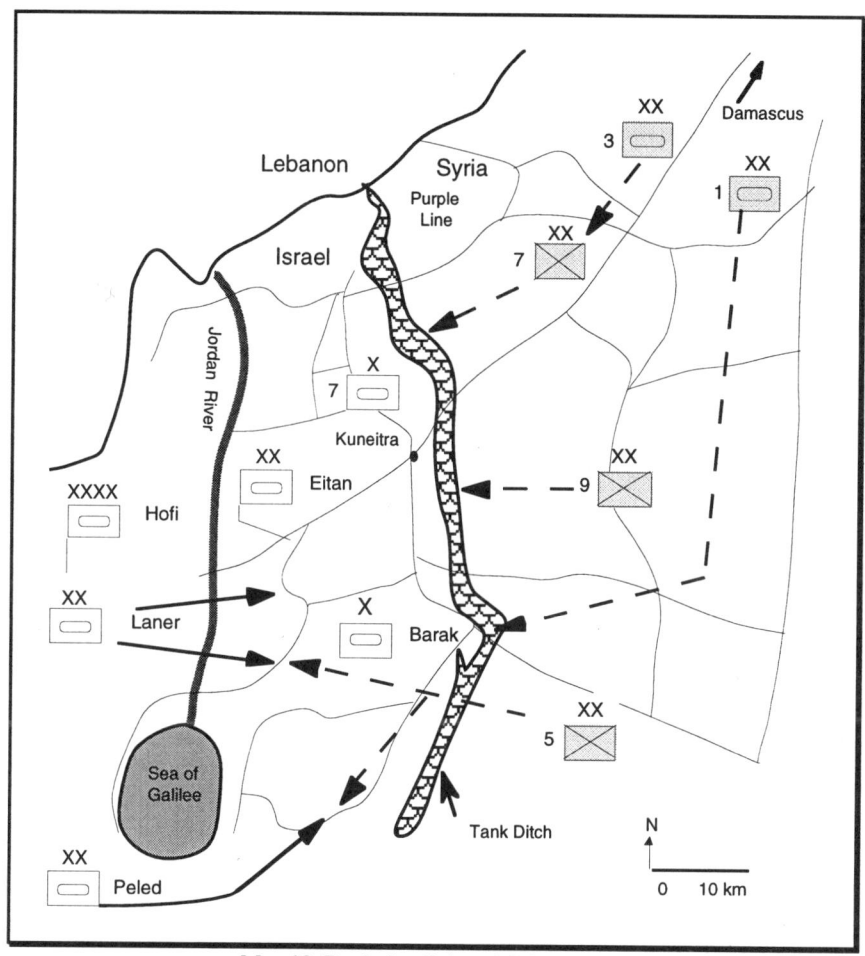

Map 12. Battle for Golan, 6-8 October.

As soon as word arrived of the impending Arab offensives, Israel's political and military leadership went into action. Elazar telephoned his air force chief, who promised to be ready for a preemptive air strike by noon. The chief of the General Staff also held a series of high-level meetings with his staff, senior commanders, and Dayan, where steps were taken to prepare the armed forces for war. But the most important decisions were for the political leadership.

At 8:05 in the morning, Elazar met with Meir and her "kitchen cabinet," a small group of most trusted officials. That meeting lasted to 9:20. Two key issues received serious attention. To produce a favorable military situation at the onset of hostilities, Elazar recommended launching a preemptive air strike against Syria, but Dayan counseled against such an action, citing potentially adverse American reaction to Israel suddenly starting a war. Meir supported her defense minister on this issue. With the strategic depth gained from the 1967 war, Israel could accept a first strike.

Israel's political leadership confronted a more complicated strategic situation in 1973 than the Eshkol government had in 1967. Before the Six Day War, the Arabs appeared very much the aggressor. They had engaged in bellicose attacks on Israel in the press; had mobilized and deployed forces near the Israeli border; and had placed their armed forces in the highest state of alert, with much fanfare. In 1973, however, Sadat and Asad avoided giving any appearance of hostile intent; an Israeli preemptive attack would have required some justification after the fact.

Failing on the first issue, Elazar pressed for the mobilization of the entire air force and four armored divisions, or over 120,000 troops. Dayan, however, favored only two armored divisions, seventy thousand men, the minimum required for defense against full-scale attacks on two fronts. Meir, on this issue, sided with Elazar and authorized a larger mobilization. Her decision helped save the Golan from certain capture by Syria.

Seven years after the Six Day War, the IDF was once again confronted with another major conflict. This time, however, the initiative lay squarely with the Arabs, as the outbreak of war found Israeli reservists scrambling to reach their mobilization centers. Because the Egyptians and Syrians had won the opening round, the intelligence struggle, they would dictate the tempo for at least the first phase of the war. As a result, numerous failings and mistakes would beleaguer the IDF and beg for accountability after the war. All this would play directly into Sadat's war strategy of unbalancing both the army and society in Israel.

ASSAULT ON THE BAR-LEV LINE

Egypt and Syria achieved a complete surprise, stunning virtually everyone in Israel. This combined Arab success allowed the crossing operation to go very much according to plan. Meanwhile, Israeli units experienced difficulty adjusting to the fact that the initiative lay with the Egyptians.

The Egyptians assaulted the Bar-Lev Line with two field armies and forces from Port Said and the Red Sea District. The Second Field Army covered the area from north of Qantara to south of Deversoir, while Third Field Army had responsibility from Bitter Lakes to south of Port Tawfiq. On the east bank of the Suez Canal, the Bitter Lakes separated the two field armies by forty kilometers. The initial phase of the war involved an attack by five infantry divisions, each reinforced by an armored brigade and additional antitank and antiair assets, on the Bar-Lev Line. Operation *Badr* called for these units to cross the Suez Canal and establish bridgeheads to a depth of twelve to fifteen kilometers over a period of four days, from 6 to 9 October. By the end of the first phase, this assault force would have some hundred thousand combat troops and 1,020 tanks on the east bank of the Suez Canal.

The responsibility for breaching the earthen embankments of the Bar-Lev Line before the IDF could react with sufficient force fell to the Engineer Corps. Upon this engineering problem depended much of the crossing operation's tempo. Clearing a path seven meters wide for the passage of tanks and other heavy vehicles through the sand embankment involved removing 1,500 cubic meters of sand. In Egypt's worst-case scenario, Israeli tank companies and battalions would counterattack within fifteen to thirty minutes, with an armored brigade arriving in several hours. Breaching operations, therefore, had to be effected quickly.

To accomplish the crossing operations, General Command assigned six missions to the Engineer Corps:

- Open seventy passages through the sand barrier
- Build ten heavy bridges for tanks and other heavy equipment
- Construct five light bridges, each with a capacity of four tons
- Erect ten pontoon bridges for infantry
- Build and operate thirty-five ferries
- Employ close to 750 rubber boats for the initial assaults.[19]

Of the six tasks, the first proved the most critical.

To expedite the breaching operation, the Egyptians discovered a simple yet ingenious native solution: a water pump. Other methods involved explosives, artillery, and bulldozers; these were too costly in time and required near ideal combat conditions. Toward the end of 1971, a young Egyptian officer suggested a small, light, gasoline-fueled pump as the answer to the crossing dilemma. His discovery provided the EAF a way to undermine Israel's prewar calculations. The Egyptian military purchased three hundred British-made pumps and found that five such pumps could blast 1,500 cubic meters of sand, with streams of high-pressured water, in three hours. In 1972, the EAF acquired 150 more-powerful German pumps. A combination of two German and three British pumps cut the time down to only two hours. This timetable was below that predicted by the Israelis.

At 2:00 P.M. on 6 October, the Egyptians and Syrians began their simultaneous air and artillery attacks. On the southern front, 250 Egyptian planes attacked their assigned targets in the Sinai: three air bases, ten Hawk missile sites, three major command posts, and electronic and jamming centers. Meanwhile, two thousand artillery pieces opened fire against all the strong points along the Bar-Lev Line, a bombardment that lasted fifty-three minutes and dropped 10,500 shells in the first minute alone—175 shells per second. The first wave of troops, eight thousand commandos and infantrymen in a thousand rubber assault rafts, began crossing the Suez Canal at 2:20. After scaling the ramparts, the Egyptians, armed with antitank missiles known as Saggers, bypassed the Israeli strong points and established ambush positions for the anticipated armored counterattacks. Subsequent waves of Egyptians brought additional infantry and combat engineers, the latter to clear the minefields around the strong points. General Command hoped to deploy a total of two thousand officers and thirty thousand troops to a depth of three to four kilometers by dusk.

Within the first hour of the war, Egyptian engineers tackled the sand barrier. Seventy groups, each one responsible for a single passage, worked from wooden boats. With hoses attached to water pumps, they began attacking the sand obstacle, and many breaches occurred within two to three hours—according to schedule. At several places, however, breaching openings in the sand barrier unexpectedly created mud—over a meter deep in some areas. The engineers had to emplace floors of wood, rails, stone, sandbags, steel plates, or metal nets for the passage of heavy vehicles. The Third Army, in particular, had difficulty in its sector, since the clay proved resistant to high-water pressure, and the engineers experienced delays in their breaching. Engineers in the Second Army completed their bridges and ferries within nine hours, whereas Third Army needed more than sixteen.

Two hours after the initial landings on the east bank, ten bridging battalions on the west bank began placing bridge sections into the water. The heavy, Soviet-made BMP folding pontoon bridge allowed the Egyptians to shorten the construction time of bridges to a few hours and to repair damaged bridges rapidly by wholesale replacement. The BMP bridge caught the Israelis (and many Western armies) by surprise. Unfortunately for the Egyptians, the EAF possessed only three such state-of-the-art structures; the remainder of their bridges were older types. Concomitant with the construction of actual bridges, other battalions constructed decoys. These dummies proved effective in diverting Israeli pilots from attacks on the real bridges. Meanwhile, engineers worked frantically to build landing sites for fifty or so ferries.

By the next day, all ten heavy bridges (two for each of the five crossing infantry divisions) were operational, although some already required repair from damage inflicted by Israeli air strikes. The bridges and ferries allowed the Egyptians to transport heavy equipment to the east bank at a pace faster than anticipated by the Israelis before the war. Ten hours into the operation, the first tanks began crossing under the cover of darkness to reinforce the bridgeheads. By the next morning (October 7), the Egyptians counted some four hundred tanks on the east bank, much to the surprise of the Israelis.

THE INITIAL ISRAELI SHOCK

The Egyptian achievements in crossing the Suez Canal caught the Israelis completely off guard. The surprise was complete and dramatic, shocking both the armed forces and the civilian society. It would take time for the Israelis to recover from the earthquake.

Israeli reactions to the surprise attack varied. At the political level, Golda Meir later described hers this way:

The shock wasn't only over the way that the war started, but also the fact that a number of our basic assumptions were proved wrong: the low probability of an attack in October, the certainty that we would get sufficient warning before any attack took place and the belief that we would be able to prevent the Egyptians from crossing the Suez Canal. The circumstance could not possibly have been worse. In the first two or three days of the war, only a thin line of brave young men stood between us and disaster.[20]

Dayan would note wryly, "The Egyptian and Syrian attack on Yom Kippur came as a surprise, though it was not unexpected."[21] Yitzhak Rabin, who was called out of retirement at 8:30 in the morning of the 6th to attend a meeting of former chiefs of the General Staff scheduled at three o'clock in the afternoon, never suspected war. At that gathering of veteran warrior chiefs, "The faces around the room remained expressionless, concealing the stupefaction we all felt."[22]

Regular officers were as hard hit by the war's outbreak as the civilians. As discussed earlier, Zeira, the intelligence chief, had expressed disbelief at the notion of an Arab attack even though he had obtained information to that effect from an indisputable source. Major General Avraham Adan, commander of the 162d Armored (Reserve) Division earmarked for the Sinai, left his morning meeting with Elazar puzzled by the prospect of war and even skeptical of its occurrence that evening. He found it "incredible" that Egypt and Syria would contemplate waging war against Israel, for the EAF and the SAF faced the prospect of "a painful defeat" owing to the IDF's marked superiority.[23] Such Israeli reactions were widespread.

Israeli society undoubtedly experienced even greater surprise and shock than the armed forces. On the eve of Yom Kippur, military service was far from any civilian's mind, for the media had not provided any inkling of gathering war clouds. As noted by Abba Eban, Israel's then foreign minister, "Historians who read the Israeli newspapers published in the first days of October will be startled to find that there was no hint of any crisis, let alone of imminent war."[24] (Censorship prevented newspapers from publishing information about the Arab buildup.) Without any preparation for the horrors of war, the mental and emotional adjustment to the battlefield would have to be quick for the civilian reservists. Dayan would recall,

Despite our self-confidence, there was disquiet in our hearts. It was not only that we were not used to a campaign where the initiative was in the hands of the enemy. The entire situation was out of keeping with our character and with the organic structure of our army, based as it is on reserves and their orderly mobilization. The transition within twenty-four hours from desk, tractor, and lathe to the battlefield is not at all easy.[25]

Israeli military intelligence's failure to provide adequate warning demanded from Israeli reservists just such a rapid transformation from civilian life to war.

Although Israeli reservists managed to reach both fronts in time to prevent a major disaster, the mobilization had its share of problems. Getting equipment quickly out of storage and to the front created numerous difficulties. Traffic jams developed along the few routes across the Sinai as reservists rushed to the front. One Israeli general who had fought in the Sinai in both the 1956 and 1967 wars later underscored that if the Egyptian air force had bombed the Israeli convoys stalled on the northern route, it could have created a logistical nightmare of the scale and magnitude that the Israelis had inflicted on the EAF in the Six Day War.[26] Israel's mobilization in 1973 was a far cry from that in 1967. The latter situation, which had been spread over two weeks, had provided reserve Israeli units with adequate time to train and prepare for war.

Most important from the point of view of military operations, the Arab surprise had negated the very foundation of Israeli war plans—prior warning of an Arab attack. Consequently, the Sinai garrison numbered only twenty thousand troops, 290 tanks, and forty-eight artillery pieces.[27] Major General Avraham Mandler commanded the 252d Armored Division, while Major General Shmuel Gonen headed Southern Command, a position he assumed in July. However, only 460 Israeli reservists from the Jerusalem Infantry Brigade, with little or no combat experience, manned the twenty strong points of the Bar-Lev Line. As noted, they had been activated to relieve regular forces who had gone on leave for Yom Kippur. Behind them stood three armored brigades: Colonel Amnon Reshef's in the forward tactical zone of the Suez Canal, with Colonel Dan Shomron's concentrated near the Giddi and Mitla Passes, and Colonel Gabi Amir's near Bir Gifgafa.

Though placed on C alert and informed of the anticipated Egyptian attack, none of the three Israeli tank brigades had deployed according to Dovecote (the defensive plan), a failure that Elazar became aware of only after the war. Gonen had ordered armor units to commence their final deployments at 4:00 P.M. in the afternoon, or two hours before the expected hour—actually two hours too late. Apparently, only Orkal, the northernmost strong point on the Suez Canal south of Port Fuad, was to be reinforced by a tank platoon, according to Dovecote.[28] A proper deployment would have no doubt resulted in many more Egyptian casualties during the crossing operation.

The Israeli air force had expected to concentrate its effort on destroying the Egyptian air defense system but instead found itself having to provide ground support to stop the Egyptians attempting to cross the Suez Canal. Israeli pilots flying to the front thus encountered the dense and integrated Egyptian air defense system. The mobile SAM-6s, new to the theater, proved especially troublesome, but it was the sheer density of fire that inflicted havoc on Israeli pilots. As described by one Skyhawk pilot, "It was like flying through hail. The skies were suddenly filled with SAMs and it required every bit of concentration to avoid being hit and still execute your mission."[29] The barrage of missiles downed a number of Israeli planes. One pilot avoided five missiles before the sixth destroyed his plane. This missile onslaught forced pilots to drop their bombs from safer distances, and they frequently missed their targets altogether.

Meanwhile, on the ground, war plans called for a positional defense of the Bar-Lev Line. In accordance with Dovecote, Reshef rushed his tank units forward to support the strong points and defeat the Egyptian effort to cross to the east bank. Because none of the Israelis expected to find swarms of Egyptian soldiers already waiting in ambush, company commanders failed to conduct reconnaissance. Consequently, Egyptian antitank teams succeeded in ambushing a number of Israeli armor units attempting to reach the water line. Those Israelis who pushed through to the Suez Canal found themselves in the midst of massive Egyptian fire, some of it from the Egyptian sand barrier constructed on the west bank.

While Israeli units confronted the tactical challenge of defeating Egyptian forces on the east bank, Southern Command faced the operational problem of determining the location of the Egyptian main effort. There was none—in direct "violation" of the principle of mass. Instead, as we have seen, Egyptian strategy had opted for a broad-front attack. As a result, Gonen lost precious hours attempting to discover something that conventional wisdom suggested should exist for any military operation of this scope—but did not.

Caught by surprise, Israel's High Command failed to withdraw its troops from the strong points, a decision that haunted the IDF for the next several days. All war planning had presumed adequate and accurate advance warning, which had failed to materialize. Despite the Egyptian surprise attack, Gonen felt no urgency to order the immediate evacuation of strong points. Rather, the troops were left to fend for themselves. Meanwhile, rear units sought to reinforce them without a clear understanding of what to do, because of the confusion of the battlefield. During the first night, for example, an Israeli tank force from the Amir Armored Brigade managed to reach the Israeli strong point at Qantara East, but Southern Command ordered the tanks to withdraw without evacuating the fort's troops. Ironically, the Israeli tanks had to fight their way back to the rear, while the garrison troops were left to their fate.[30]

Until midmorning of 7 October, Elazar's instruction to Gonen was to evacuate only those outposts not in the proximity of any major enemy thrusts, even though by the late evening of 6 October, Egyptian soldiers had in fact virtually surrounded all the strong points. Only some twenty hours into the war did Gonen finally order those troops able to evacuate their strong points to do so.[31] But by then, it was too late, and the strong points would remain a thorn in Southern Command's side. The troops inside them had become, in effect, hostages requiring rescue.

The Israeli delay in evacuating their strongpoints actually abetted the Egyptians in their strategic objective of inflicting as many casualties as possible in men, weapons, and equipment. Because Israeli military doctrine and ethos calls for Israelis not to abandon their fellow soldiers, whether alive or dead, many commanders and soldiers experienced great anxiety and desire to relieve or support the isolated troops, especially since desperate calls for help occasionally emanated from them. There was thus a tendency, as noted by then Major General Avraham Adan, among tank units to react "instinctively—just as they had learned to do during the Three Years War—by rushing to the strong points."[32] During the first several days of the war, the area around these fortifications became killing grounds, where Egyptian troops aggressively ambushed Israeli counterattacks. The majority of the high losses experienced by the IDF during the first two days of the war can be attributed to the Israelis' stubborn determination to relieve their troops at the strong points.

To enhance their troops' chances for successful crossings, Egyptian planners had provided for two types of special operations designed to strike into the operational depth of the IDF. The purpose of both was to delay the arrival of Israeli reservists and to increase the shock and confusion in the Israeli rear. The first special mission involved an amphibious operation across the Bitter Lakes, to be conducted by the 130th Amphibious Mechanized Brigade, under the command of Colonel Mahmud Shaib. Created in January 1972, this marine brigade of one thousand men was organized into two mechanized battalions, one antitank Sagger battalion, one antiair battalion, and a 120-mm mortar battalion. Each mechanized battalion contained ten PT-76 light tanks and forty amphibious armored personnel carriers. The brigade crossed the Bitter Lakes on 6 October in a half hour, without casualties. Each reinforced battalion then made a dash for the Mitla and Giddi passes to capture the western entrances to the Sinai and prevent the Israeli reserves from arriving at the Suez Canal.

The battalion heading toward the Mitla Pass ran into Israeli M-60 Patton tanks, and its light tanks proved no match for the heavier, American-made armor. The battalion sustained heavy losses and retreated in great haste. Egyptian sources claim the second battalion passed through Giddi Pass to disrupt communications east of the passes. Remnants of the 130th Brigade managed to reach Kibrit East on the Suez Canal, where the commander established a bridgehead.[33] Overall, however, this special operation proved unsuccessful.

The second special operation employed airborne commandos to conduct "suicide attacks" in the operational depth of the Sinai. These elite forces were to establish ambushes along the major roads and in the passes for the purpose of delaying the arrival of Israeli reserves; they were also intended to add to the shock and confusion experienced by the IDF. For their transportation, the Egyptian commandos relied mainly on a fleet of thirty Soviet-made Mi-8 medium-transport helicopters, each capable of ferrying approximately twenty-five soldiers. These crafts were very vulnerable to combat planes; but General Command was determined to risk its elite forces. At dusk on 6 October, thirty helicopters departed on their missions. The Egyptians repeated these dangerous operations over the next couple of days.

The report card on these air-assault special operations remains controversial. Israeli sources have tended to downplay their significance, whereas Egyptians have attributed great importance to them. In a number of cases, the Israeli air force discovered the helicopters and shot them down easily; other instances saw the accomplishment of missions—but generally at very high cost in lives. One Israeli source estimated that seventy-two Egyptian sorties, involving 1,700 commandos, were attempted and that the Israeli air force shot down twenty Egyptian helicopters and killed, wounded, or captured 1,100 commandos.[34]

Whatever the exact figures of missions and casualties, the commandos achieved some successes in the Israeli rear. In perhaps the most famous case, a battalion under the command of Major Hamdi Shalabi landed a company along the northern route between Romana and Baluza and established a blocking position at 6:00 A.M. on 7 October. This small force stopped the advance of a reserve armored brigade under the command of Colonel Natke Nir, of Abu Ageila fame, killing some thirty Israeli soldiers and destroying a dozen or so tanks, halftracks, and transports, at a loss of seventy-five Egyptians.[35] Furthermore, the Egyptian ambush delayed the arrival of Israeli reservists at the battlefield by several hours. It also sent a new message to Israeli war veterans. Adan, Nir's division commander, noted the significance of the performance of the Egyptian commandos at Romana. "This was no longer the same Egyptian army we had crushed in four days in 1967. We were now dealing with a well-trained enemy, fighting with skill and dedication."[36]

The presence of Egyptian commandos in the IDF's operational depth caused anxiety among senior Israeli commanders, who subsequently allotted forces for special security. Southern Command even assigned its elite reconnaissance companies to hunt down commando troops and protect command centers. Moreover, installations and command centers were placed on high alert, and some combat forces were diverted from the front lines for rear guard duties.[37] While at present it is difficult to reach a definitive conclusion, the Egyptian airborne commando assaults appeared to have represented more than a minor nuisance. These special operations slowed the Israelis and caused confusion, anxiety, and surprise in the rear, although at a great cost in lives of highly trained and motivated Egyptian troops. Overall, the commandos did enhance the chances of success for the crossing operation and the establishment of bridgeheads on the east bank.

AN EVALUATION OF THE CROSSING

The Egyptians could claim a major achievement by the evening of the first day, 6 October, for nightfall brought them the cover necessary for the transfer of tanks, field artillery pieces, armored vehicles, and other heavy equipment to the east bank. Detailed planning and countless training exercises ensured the rapid transportation to the east bank of five infantry divisions. To get across as fast as possible, each piece of equipment, each bridge, each unit, and each headquarters had a fixed time of departure and arrival.

Much of the crossing operation's success hinged on the ability of the Corps of Engineers to construct and maintain bridges across the Suez Canal. At first, the Israeli air force targeted bridges as an efficient means of defeating the crossing; Israeli morale rose whenever word reached the Pit or Southern Command of the destruction of a bridge. But after several days of fighting, Elazar finally realized the limited results of such missions: "We destroyed seven of their bridges, and everyone was happy. The next day the bridges were functional again. [IAF aircraft] destroyed every bridge twice.... [One plane] drops a bomb weighing a ton, one of the bridge's section is destroyed, and after an hour another piece is brought in and the bridge continues to function."[38] The fifteen thousand members of the corps of engineers played a major role in the success of the crossing operation.

Despite the surprising onset of war, Israel's senior political and military leadership remained confident of success in quick order. At ten o'clock the evening of the 6th, the Israeli cabinet met to hear Elazar's report on military operations. The chief of the General Staff was upbeat, believing in an early victory. Dayan, for his part, presented a pessimistic evaluation of the military situation and recommended a pullback to a second line some twenty kilometers from the Suez Canal. Elazar was adverse to any withdrawals unless absolutely necessary.[39] The cabinet found comfort in Elazar's confidence.

In the United States, although the war's outbreak caught it completely by surprise, virtually everyone in Washington expected an early Israeli military victory. Such a prospect played well into American interest in seeing its main ally in the Middle East defeat Soviet-sponsored regimes. In the Cold War's strategic environment, Washington would reap political gains from such an outcome. Consequently, the Nixon administration initially adopted a wait-and-see policy, confident the Israelis would win in only few days or so.[40]

With such positive expectations, American officials were at first naturally skeptical when the Israeli ambassador made an urgent request for military assistance, special items the air force needed to counter the Arab air defense systems. But within two days of the war's commencement, Nixon agreed to the dispatch of counterelectronic equipment, chaff to confuse Soviet-made radars, and eighty Sidewinders, air-to-air guided missiles designed to hit targets with pinpoint accuracy. To transport these items, El Al, the Israeli civilian airline, employed its small fleet of Boeing 707s and 747s.[41] The first shipments arrived in Israel by 9 October.

Jerusalem and Washington greatly underestimated the fighting capabilities of the Egyptian and Syrian armies, especially the former, and more time would elapse before Israel's senior commanders grasped the extent of Arab combat power. Even then, Israeli commanders generally expected a quick recovery and resolution of the conflict. Once again, their timetables would prove dead wrong. More surprises would occur in the latter part of the war, as the Egyptians and Syrians continued to demonstrate unexpected combat mettle in the face of the clearly superior Israeli military machine.

Dawn on 7 October found the Israelis facing some fifty thousand Egyptian troops and four hundred tanks on the east bank of the Suez Canal. On average, each Egyptian infantry division's bridgehead was six to eight kilometers in frontage and three to four kilometers in depth. The Egyptians had achieved this amazing feat with minimal losses: only 280 men, fifteen planes, and twenty tanks.[42] Moreover, the EAF was now entrenched in defensive positions, ready to inflict more losses in Israeli men, arms, and equipment.

To dislodge the Egyptians from their bridgeheads would require the Israelis to mount frontal attacks without adequate air support. The Egyptian air defense system had, for the most part, neutralized the Israeli air force over the battlefield. Israel could ill afford to divide its air assets between two fronts, because the situation on the Golan Heights had become particularly desperate for Northern Command, eventually forcing Elazar on the second day of the war to commit the bulk of his air force to stabilize that more threatening front.

A difficult tactical situation thus awaited the Israelis in the Sinai on the second day. The IDF had to direct its main effort against the SAF, complicating matters for Southern Command. Without air support, and lacking sufficient artillery and infantry, Israeli tankers on the southern front found themselves at a disadvantage in firepower. They had to resort to cavalry attack tactics, which would prove largely ineffective against ambushes and killing zones prepared by Egyptian troops. More heavy casualties awaited the IDF.

INITIAL DIPLOMATIC ACTIVITY

Committed to a limited war against a superior armed force, Sadat placed his main effort on the diplomatic level. In an interview with *Newsweek* before the war (discussed in the last chapter), the Egyptian leader had promised to conduct diplomacy before, during, and after the war. The outreach to the United States, including the establishment of a secret channel to Kissinger, had already taken place. Also, just prior to the commencement of hostilities, Sadat had warned the Soviet ambassador of approaching war and asked for assurances of continued support during hostilities. Now, Sadat faced the challenge of working the diplomatic front in the midst of war.

While the war's outbreak surprised the United States, the USSR had had sufficient advance warning, more than the IDF had received. Brezhnev was not pleased about the prospect of war, preferring that the Arabs seek a political solution instead. Conflict in the Middle East carried the potential of disrupting his own cordial relations with the West, and Brezhnev, a major proponent of détente, wanted an end to hostilities as quickly as possible. Moreover, Soviet assessments, like those of the Americans, expected an Arab military defeat, which boded ill for the USSR's interests in the Middle East. The Soviets did not wish to suffer the embarrassment of Israel defeating two Soviet-supplied armies for a second time; the political gains for the United States would prove intolerable for Moscow. The Soviets had to stand by their two Arab allies. Before embarking on any major diplomatic move, however, the Kremlin needed some appreciation of Sadat's strategic thinking and goals.[43]

In the early evening of 6 October, the first day of the war, the Soviet ambassador in Egypt requested an audience with Sadat. The two men met at Tahra Palace at eight o'clock. Vinogradov related how Asad had met with Mukhitdinov on 4 October and how the Syrian president had explored the possibility of an early, Soviet-sponsored proposal for a cease-fire. Moscow desired clarification of Sadat's position on such a diplomatic initiative. Sadat, taken aback by this news, rejected outright any proposal for a cease-fire.[44]

For the next three days, 7 to 9 October, Vinogradov met daily with Sadat to encourage him to seek an early cease-fire. Each time, Sadat, confident because the EAF was holding the military initiative and inflicting heavy casualties on the Israelis, held firm, determined to continuing the struggle in order to exhaust Israel.[45] Meanwhile, the Egyptian president kept urging Asad to persevere in his struggle against the Israelis. On 7 October, for example, the gist of his message to the Syrian leader went as follows: "Be careful. . . . The problem is not a problem of land. . . . The problem is that we shatter the Israeli concept of security. . . . Press on. Don't retreat from what you have gained."[46]

Despite Egypt's initial military successes, Sadat remained focused on his limited war objectives; according to plan, he opened the diplomatic front with the United States, activating the secret channel to the White House through Henry Kissinger, who had just become secretary of state. On the morning of 7 October, with the war not yet twenty hours old, Muhammad Hafiz Ismail, the national security advisor, sent a secret letter to Kissinger, the first such contact between the two men since July.

Sadat wanted to reiterate the standard Egyptian position: Egypt remained committed to peace but not one based on partial solutions. Moreover, Sadat refused to countenance Israel holding occupied lands as hostages for bargaining purposes. Israel had to withdraw from all captured territories, after which Egypt would participate in a peace conference under the auspices of the UN. Sadat also agreed to the freedom of navigation through the Strait of Tiran, even to the point of allowing international control of the waterway for a limited period as a guarantee. Most importantly, Hafez Ismail wrote, "We do not intend to deepen the engagements or widen the confrontation." By this statement, Sadat implied that he sought only a limited war, not a general conflagration enflaming the region, and that he had no intention of dragging the superpowers into the conflict.[47] His words, carefully crafted, painted the picture of a war conducted rationally for the purpose of opening a diplomatic dialogue.

Cairo's letter surprised the White House. Writing years later, Kissinger expressed admiration for Sadat's strategy: "What was significant was the fact of the message, not its content."[48] The Egyptian president was clearly seeking to draw the Americans into breaking the diplomatic deadlock. The military operation had demonstrated Egyptian resolve, whereas the letter showed restraint and moderation. Despite his claim years later to have understood the letter's significance, however, Kissinger chose to keep the Arabs at arm's length during most of the war. As he notes in his memoirs, "The time to show understanding for the Arab position was *after* the war, when the peace process started."[49] This American stance complicated matters for Sadat, who wanted to see US action during the conflict.

The revelation of Hafez Ismail's letter after the war elicited much discussion in Egypt. On the negative side, some Egyptians saw in it Sadat unwisely revealing his hand to the Israelis, giving them an opportunity to focus against Syria, knowing Sadat's goals were limited territorially. In fact, even if Kissinger immediately notified the Israelis of the communiqué's contents, it remains highly doubtful that the Israeli political leadership would have put much stock in Sadat's one sentence. All Israeli commanders understood the limited capability of the EAF, to the point of serious underestimation; concentration on the Syrian front was the only course for Israel after the first day. Nothing was compromised by Sadat's letter.

Sadat also might have wanted to underscore to the United States, through the secret channel, the limited nature of the war so that Washington would restrain Israel from resorting to nuclear weapons should Tel Aviv contemplate such a course of action. By this time, Israel possessed some twenty warheads, as both Sadat and Asad were aware. But the EAF did not pose a serious enough threat to Israel's existence to warrant the Meir government taking such a drastic step.

Asad, however, faced a more delicate situation. A rapid capture of the Golan would raise fear in Israel that the Syrians would next descend into the populated areas of the Huleh Valley. Asad accordingly showed restraint. The Syrian air force, for example, avoided striking Israeli airfields on the first day of the war. Also, in meetings with the Soviet ambassador on 7 and 8 October, Asad continually raised the issue of a Soviet proposal in the UN Security Council of an early cease-fire.[50] While Israel's use of nuclear weapons loomed in both Arab leaders' strategies, Sadat perceived less danger from it than Asad and therefore focused his diplomacy on getting the United States involved to break the longstanding diplomatic stalemate. The letter of 7 October reflected Sadat's political acumen.

THE SECOND DAY

The EAF and the SAF both maintained the initiative on the second day of the war. In the Sinai, the Egyptians gradually expanded their bridgeheads, and on the Golan Heights the IDF faced a desperate situation. Top priority for Israeli air assets had to go to the northern front, and reserve units scrambled in piecemeal fashion to engage the advancing Syrians.

By the morning of the second day, Syrian forces had virtually wiped out the Barak Armored Brigade, killing its commander. Only fifteen out of the original ninety tanks remained in the southern half of the Golan, leaving the road to the escarpment open. Israel faced a very dangerous situation indeed. Wisely, Elazar had already committed the only armored division in the strategic reserve to the Golan. At six in the morning on 7 October, Dayan bypassed Elazar in the command chain and ordered Peled, the air force commander, to commit his pilots to stop the Syrian assault. Without the air force, Dayan warned, Israel faced the distinct possibility of the Third Temple's collapse, a clear reference to the state's survival. Peled reluctantly called off most air operations against Egypt in favor of the Syrian front.[51]

Fortunately for Israel, the Syrians decided to halt their offensive at five that afternoon, thereby allowing the Israelis time to bring up enough tanks for spoiling counterattacks. Perhaps Asad wanted to avoid too rapid an advance to the escarpment, lest Israel resort to nuclear weapons. Whatever the reasons for the temporary halt, by 8 October the SAF had culminated, and the IDF began slowly pushing Syrian forces back to the prewar Purple Line. The tide was turning in Israel's favor.[52]

The commitment of the bulk of the Israeli air force to the northern front on 7 October, however, adversely affected operations in the Sinai. Without air support, Israeli tankers found themselves more vulnerable to Egyptian ground forces. This was a difficult pill for the Israeli pilots to swallow. As noted by one pilot, "Never in its history was the IAF bigger and stronger—and never more helpless in carrying out its share of the war's burden."[53] But the air force could not place all the blame upon itself. Israeli doctrine had emphasized armor too much, at the expense of artillery and mechanized infantry.

By the end of the morning on 7 October, the toll in Israeli armor in the Sinai had become especially heavy. Mandler reported that his armored *ugdah* numbered some one hundred tanks, down from 291 at the war's commencement. Especially hard hit was the Shomron Armored Brigade in the south, whose tank count had fallen from over a hundred to just twenty-five.[54] In light of such heavy losses, Gonen decided at noon to form a defensive line along Lateral Road, thirty kilometers east of the Suez Canal, and he ordered his commanders to deploy their forces accordingly. Small mobile units were to patrol along Artillery Road, ten to fifteen kilometers from the waterway, with the mission of reporting and delaying any Egyptian advance. Concurrent with this decision, Southern Command also ordered the evacuation of all strong points—an order that, as noted, was too late, for by now all were surrounded by Egyptian troops.[55]

Then at four in the afternoon, Elazar learned to his great dismay that the air force had lost thirty planes in the first twenty-seven hours of the war—a staggering figure given that the IDF was still on the defensive while engaged in fierce fighting on both fronts.[56] In addition to losses of planes and tanks, initial setbacks on the northern and southern fronts were taking a heavy emotional toll on Israeli soldiers. Sharon later recalled his observations of the troops pulling back from the Suez Canal on 7 October:

I . . . . saw something strange on their faces—not fear but bewilderment. Suddenly something was happening to them that had never happened before. These were soldiers who had been brought up on victories—not easy victories maybe, but nevertheless victories. Now they were in a state of shock. How could it be that these Egyptians were crossing the canal right in our faces? How was it that *they* were moving forward and *we* were defeated?[57]

The lethality and intensity of the fighting in the 1973 war would bring a new type of casualty to the IDF—one resulting from combat stress.

Back in the Pit, tensions also ran high. Especially affected among the senior officials was Dayan, the defense minister since June 1967. His confidence shattered on 7 October in a morning visit to the Sinai. In a meeting at 2:30 that afternoon at general headquarters in Tel Aviv, Dayan offered a doomsday prediction. The spectacle of the symbol of Israeli military prowess caving in under the pressure of war was quite unsettling. "Even first-hand accounts can scarcely convey the emotional upheaval that gripped them as they witnessed the collapse of an entire world view and with it the image of a leader who had embodied it with such charismatic power."[58] Cooler heads, however, prevailed and brought a modicum of calm to an otherwise very tense situation.

Despite a steady flow of bad news, some battlefield reports were upbeat. By noontime on 7 October, both Adan and Sharon had arrived with forward elements of their two reserve armored *ugdot*. Gonen promptly divided the front into three divisional commands: Adan with the 162d Armored *Ugdah* in the northern sector, Sharon with the 143d Armored *Ugdah* in the central sector, and Mandler with the 252d Armored *Ugdah* in the southern sector. Israeli commanders now had to rely on improvisation to meet the Egyptian challenge.

That afternoon, Elazar received an encouraging report from Peled. The air force had knocked out seven bridges and expected to finish off the remainder by nightfall. In actuality, several of the destroyed or damaged bridges were dummies, and the Egyptians were able to repair the real bridges in quick order. Unaware of these facts, and therefore buoyed by the positive report, Elazar decided to visit Southern Command in person to meet with the theater and three divisional commanders to formulate a plan for the next day.[59] He arrived at the forward command post at Gebel Umm Hashiba at 6:45 P.M. Gonen, Adan, and Mandler participated in the conference. Sharon missed the gathering entirely, arriving just after it had broken off.

To avoid the crowd and noise around them in the war room, the senior officers, tired from lack of sleep, moved for a two-hour meeting to the theater commander's personal quarters, where there was little but standing room. Gonen began the meeting by presenting a review of the war, followed by a summary of the current tactical situation.[60] By the next day, Southern Command expected to have 640 tanks, with 530 of them dispersed among three *ugdot*: Adan with two hundred, Sharon with 180, and Mandler with 150 tanks. Intelligence estimates placed the number of Egyptian tanks on the east bank at four hundred, when in fact eight hundred was closer to the mark. In light of the low estimate, Gonen recommended a frontal, two-divisional attack at night against the Egyptian bridgeheads, with Adan crossing to the west bank at Qantara East and Sharon doing likewise at Suez City. Adan, who lacked sufficient infantry and artillery, urged a more cautious approach, that of waiting until all the reserves arrived at the front before embarking on any major operation.

Elazar opted for a compromise. The Golan was clearly the more critical front at the time and thus required a major counterattack. But rather than adopt a defensive posture in the Sinai, Elazar decided on a limited, but still sizable, attack for the next morning. Adan would attack with his armored *ugdah* southward from the Qantara area, staying at least three to five kilometers east of the Suez Canal to avoid the heavy concentration of Egyptian antitank weaponry. Meanwhile, Sharon would remain at Tasa with his armored *ugdah* as a reserve, ready to move northward to assist Adan if needed. Should Adan succeed in his mission, Sharon would head south and attempt to roll up the Egyptian Third Army's bridgehead by moving in a manner similar to that of Adan. Meanwhile, Mandler would remain on the defensive, reorganizing his badly battered division, now down to a few dozen tanks, essentially the Shomron Armored Brigade and paratroopers holding the Giddi and Mitla Passes. Elazar was clear and emphatic about two items: under no circumstances would either Adan or Sharon attempt a crossing to the west bank without his approval, and no attempt would be made to approach the strong points. The conference finally broke up at 10:00 P.M.

As Elazar headed toward his helicopter, Sharon suddenly arrive. Rather than brief him personally, Elazar exchanged a few words with Sharon and then directed him to obtain his instructions from Gonen. Sharon, a maverick general noted for a predilection for bold action, disliked Elazar's cautious approach for the next day. Sharon recommended a concentrated attack by two *udgot* to defeat the EAF, an idea that had more appeal more to Gonen than Elazar's plan. Although eager to attempt a countercrossing, Gonen had his orders; all he could do was to offer general approval to Sharon's idea without specifically endorsing it. A final decision would have to await developments on the battlefield.

THE FOILED ISRAELI COUNTERATTACK

The day of 8 October 1973 would prove to be one of the darkest days in the short history of the IDF.[61] A combination of Israeli mistakes and Egyptian resilience would defeat the Israeli counterattack. At the end of the day, further shocks reached Israeli senior commanders, who now began to grasp the seriousness of their military situation in the Sinai.

After the conference at Gebel Umm Hashiba, Adan hurried back to his *ugdah*, which was deployed along the Baluza-Tasa road. The command comprised three armored brigades. Natke Nir possessed seventy-one tanks, Gabi Amir fifty M-60 tanks, and Aryeh Keren (still en route to the area) sixty-two tanks, for a grand total of 183. A mechanized infantry brigade, under the command of Brigadier General Kalman Magen, was expected to join the operation by late morning and deploy in the Qantara sector.[62] For his attack north to south, Adan planned to lead with Amir and Nir and keep Keren as his reserve (see Map 13). For fire support, the division possessed but a single battery of four self-propelled 155-mm guns along Artillery Road, but Adan expected sufficient air support. The Israeli air force, however, would have to concentrate its main effort on the Golan, where the Israelis could ill afford to give ground. Adan would not see the air cover he needed.

In war, battles never conform exactly to plans, even the best prepared ones, and the offensive of 8 October proved no exception. The Israeli plan began to unravel even before the commencement of the operation. Shortly after midnight on 8 October, Gonen suddenly changed the operational concept. Instead of focusing on clearing the area between Lexicon and Artillery Roads, the front commander wanted Adan to approach the strong points at Firdan and Ismailiya and prepare for the possibility of crossing to the west bank at Matzmed, in the Deversoir area at the northern tip of the Great Bitter Lakes.[63] Apparently, optimistic reports from the field, coupled with his own wishful thinking, had spawned the expectation of an imminent Egyptian collapse.

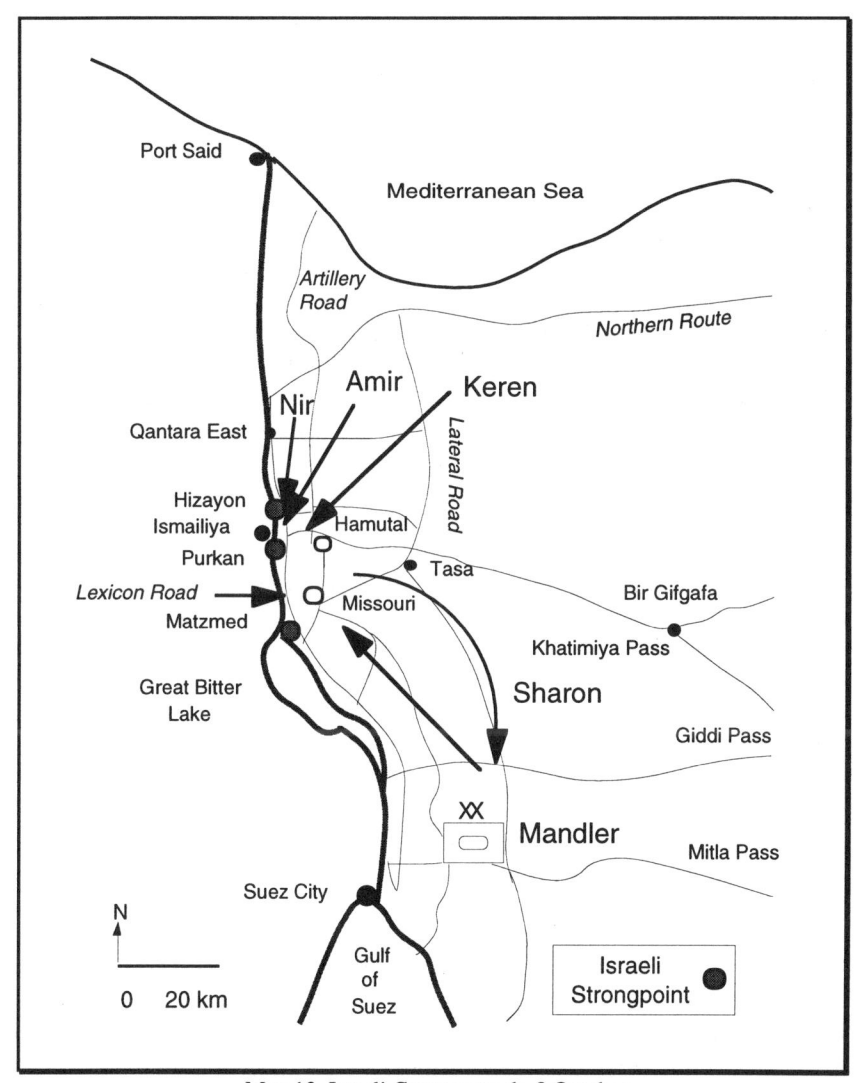

Map 13. Israeli Counterattack, 8 October.

But the change in plans, formulated without precise tactical intelligence, smacked of bravado. At the same time, the Israelis appeared to let their doctrine blindly dictate their tactical and operational objectives. As Adan later noted with the benefit of hindsight, the IDF had become a "prisoner" of its own doctrine of having to transfer any war to the enemy's territory as quickly as possible, even though the 1967 war had given Israeli army strategic depth in the Sinai.[64] The ghost of the Six Day War beckoned a quick resolution to the armed conflict.

Adan's scheme of maneuver north to south had Amir and Nir move between Lexicon and Artillery Roads, with Amir on the western avenue and Nir on his left. Keren would move his brigade east of Artillery Road. Each brigade would reach positions designed to link up with the strong points of the Bar-Lev Line: Amir opposite the Hizayon strong point at Firdan and the Purkan strong point at Ismailiya; Nir before Purkan; and Keren facing Matzmed or Deversoir. At this juncture, the brigade commanders would await orders from Adan as to the feasibility of attempting a crossing operation to the west bank, a decision Elazar had unequivocally reserved for himself.

A second major change in plans occurred at 7:53 A.M., just before the attack. In the Qantara sector, Israeli forces suddenly found themselves engaged in a heavy firefight with the Egyptian 18th Infantry Division. To help contain the Egyptians, Gonen ordered the Nir Armored Brigade to stay behind at Qantara, under the command of Magen. This decision left Adan with only Amir's two battalions of twenty-five tanks each—a far cry from the divisional attack expected by Elazar at the previous night's conference. Rather than delay or abort the counterattack, Adan followed Gonen's order, and at 8:06, Amir began moving south, even though the Keren Armored Brigade was still en route to the area. Adan ordered Amir to be prepared "to link up with the Hizayon and Purkan strongpoints, but to do so only upon a specific order." Keren would conduct offensive operations against the Egyptian 16th Infantry Division's bridgehead at Deversoir.[65]

The move south quickly went awry. Instead of advancing just east of Lexicon, Amir drove along Artillery Road, completely missing the Egyptian bridgeheads. Around nine o'clock, advance elements of Amir's brigade reached the plain between Artillery Road and the Firdan Bridge without having encountered any significant Egyptian opposition. Awaiting Amir, however, was the Egyptian 2d Infantry Division, reinforced with the 24th Armored Brigade from the 23d Mechanized Infantry Division. Two Egyptian infantry brigades formed the first echelon, and a mechanized infantry brigade the second. The 24th Armored Brigade was the divisional reserve, which Brigadier General Hasan Abu Saada, the division commander, could commit in the event of an Israeli penetration into the divisional bridgehead.[66] In the face of a reinforced Egyptian infantry division, Amir's two-battalion force lacked light reconnaissance units, 81-mm self-propelled mortars, and armored infantry. Without air cover and artillery, Amir had to rely on tanks alone to attack defended positions.

Gonen, however, was confident of victory; after all, Adan's division had managed to advance virtually unopposed from north to south. Consequently, Gonen wanted Adan to link up with the strong point at Hizayon for the purpose of crossing to the west bank, and he telephoned to Tel Aviv for permission to do so. After an hour of communications going back and forth, Elazar eventually gave the green light for a countercrossing.

At 10:40, Southern Command ordered Adan to cross to the west bank at three places and Sharon to head south toward Suez City. Adan, for his part, directed Amir to capture the crossing site, but an unexpected problem awaited his brigade commander. Lieutenant Colonel Haim Adini was ready to attack with his battalion, but Lieutenant Colonel Amir Joffe's battalion had to disengage in order to replenish its fuel and ammunition supply. Now, only a tank battalion of some twenty-five tanks would carry out the entire *ugdah*'s attack! At eleven o'clock, Adini attacked with two companies in line and a third in reserve. His assault ran into the right side of the Egyptian 2d Infantry Division. At first, success shined upon the Israelis, who broke through the first Egyptians and penetrated to within eight hundred meters of the Suez Canal. But then a torrential downpour of antitank, tank, and artillery fire descended upon Adini's meager force, destroying eighteen of twenty-five tanks within minutes and wounding Adini, along with two company and two platoon commanders. The battalion suffered some twenty killed. Making the situation worse, Adan lost communications with his brigade commander and was therefore initially unaware of the fate of the attack (see Map 14).[67]

Despite this first tactical setback, the Israelis had an opportunity to regroup and conduct a coordinated three-brigade assault toward the Firdan bridge, but this idea proved no more successful than the previous one.[68] Nir had disengaged at Qantara and, having left one battalion behind with Magen, arrived at 12:30 in the area of the Firdan bridge with two tank battalions. Nir and Amir held a brief conference to discuss an attack toward the bridge. Meanwhile, the Keren Armored Brigade moved into the area as well; Adan ordered it to support Amir and Nir by attacking in the direction of Purkan.

Once again, the tactical situation began to unravel for the Israelis. Gonen, confident of an Egyptian collapse, had already ordered Sharon to vacate Tasa for a move to Suez City. Sharon left only a reconnaissance company to hold the critical ridges of Hamadia and Kishuf, but not the hills north of them, such as Hamutal. Sharon's departure suddenly exposed Adan's southern flank, at a time when the battle with the Egyptians was going badly. The Keren Armored Brigade, by default, assumed responsibility for Adan's left side in addition to the attack on the Egyptian bridgehead.

Meanwhile, the anticipated attack by Nir and Amir faced enormous difficulties. Nir possessed some fifty tanks in two battalions, one under Lieutenant Colonel Asaf Yaguri and the other under Lieutenant Colonel Natan. Gabi Amir, for his part, was in dire need of additional forces to assault entrenched positions. He had lost virtually Adini's entire battalion and had released Joffe to replenish his battalion. Suddenly and fortuitously, Lieutenant Colonel Eliashiv Shimshi appeared with his armored (reserve) battalion of twenty-five tanks, two halftracks, and two jeeps. Shimshi had just arrived on the battlefront, trying to join the Keren Armored Brigade. Desperate for more armor, Amir quickly received Adan's permission to commandeer Shimshi's battalion to use in coordination with Nir's assault on Firdan bridge; Shimshi was to provide covering fire.

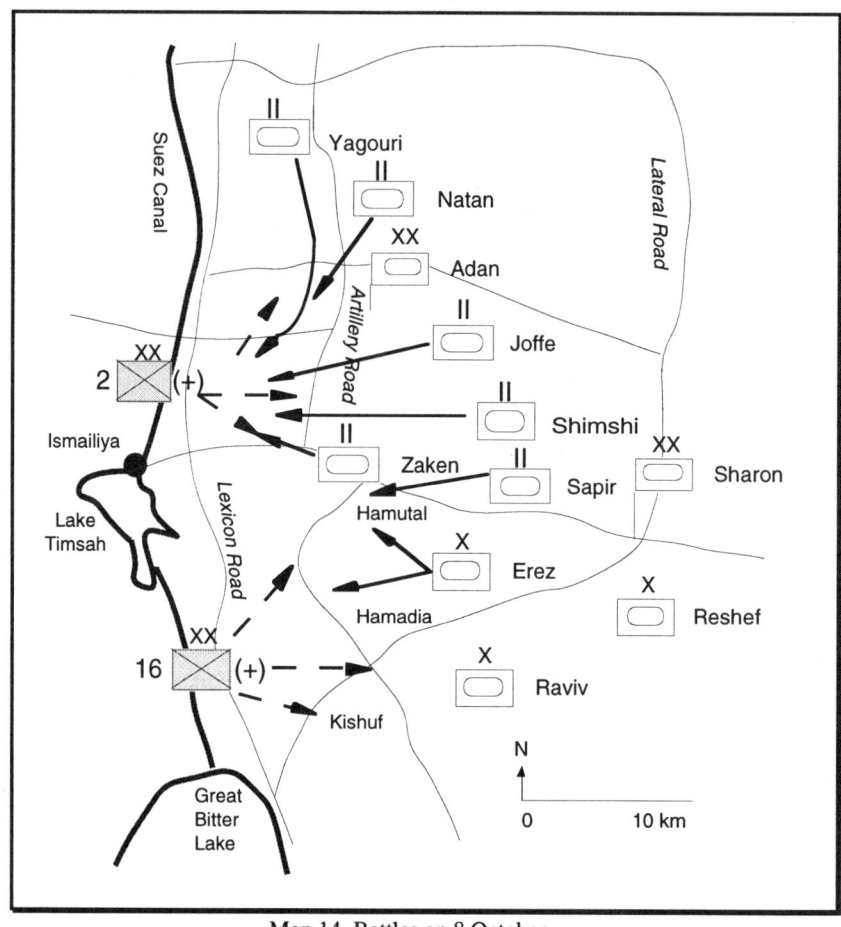

Map 14. Battles on 8 October.

At 1:30, the Israelis pressed a second attack toward Firdan bridge. Like the first attempt that morning, this combined assault lacked proper coordination in the face of overwhelming enemy forces. Natan and Yaguri began to move their battalions at the same time, the former on the right, the latter on the left. Suddenly, heavy Egyptian fire stopped Natan's tank battalion, leaving only Yaguri to proceed with twenty-five tanks. Yaguri attacked in line, cavalry style, leaving Shimshi to watch helplessly as fellow Israeli tankers charged into the jaws of disaster.

The second assault on Firdan failed miserably. Warned in advance, the Egyptians had quickly prepared for the attack. Yaguri now stumbled into a killing zone between the two forward brigades and straight into an Egyptian mechanized infantry brigade. Within minutes, an avalanche of Egyptian fire destroyed eighteen tanks and killed thirty-two Israelis. Yaguri and three other soldiers were captured. By the end of the day, Nir reported fifty-four men missing in action. Among the Egyptians killed were Colonel Fatin Diyab and Lieutenant Colonel Ibrahim Zeydan, the latter a battalion commander. That evening, the Egyptian military displayed its prize captive, Lieutenant Colonel Asaf Yaguri, to bolster public morale. (A military spokesman in Cairo identified Yaguri as a colonel and a brigade commander.) The next day, Egyptian newspapers carried exclusive stories and pictures of Israeli prisoners of war.[69] Such positive reporting was naturally intended to bolster national will during the war.

EXPANSION OF EGYPTIAN BRIDGEHEADS

Unknown to the Israelis, Operation *Badr* called for the expansion of the bridgeheads on 8 October to a depth of ten to twelve kilometers, with each field army forming one continuous bridgehead in its sector. This required a redeployment of forces. In the crossing operation, each Egyptian infantry division had placed two infantry brigades forward, with its mechanized infantry brigade in the second echelon. Behind these three brigades stood the attached armored brigade. For the widening of the bridgeheads, Operation *Badr* required the mechanized infantry brigade to push forward between the two infantry brigades, thereby creating a three-brigade front, with the attached armor brigade now forming the division's second echelon and tactical reserve.[70]

Suddenly, during the afternoon of the 8 October, the Israeli units facing the Egyptian Second and Third Armies found themselves under an artillery barrage and air strikes followed by attacks by Egyptian troops determined to expand their bridgeheads. Progress was uneven among the five Egyptian infantry divisions; not all covered the ten or twelve kilometers necessary to gain control of Artillery Road. In the Second Army sector, however, the 16th Infantry Division proved most successful occupying the important positions of Missouri, Televizia, Machshir, and Hamutal, the latter overlooking the juncture of Ismailiya and Artillery Roads. These four positions would later be obstacles to the Israeli countercrossing operation to the west bank.[71] The Israelis had unwittingly allowed this Egyptian tactical success.

By midafternoon on 8 October, Gonen had realized the gravity of Adan's predicament and at 2:45, ordered Sharon to return to Tasa. Sharon was back by twilight, having made a full circle without any combat. Now, growing doubt began to set in among senior Israeli commanders as to Gonen's ability to command the Sinai front. Gonen had pushed Adan to attempt a crossing to the west bank after enticing Elazar to grant his consent. Then he had sent Sharon prematurely south, only to recall him. Had Sharon remained in support of Adan in the Tasa area, the Egyptian 16th Infantry Division might have failed to seize its objectives.

Adan's *ugdah* had suffered heavy losses that day. Three tank battalions had been virtually wiped out in frontal assaults against fortified Egyptian positions: Adini's and Joffe's battalions in Amir's brigade and Yaguri's battalion in Nir's brigade. Three battalion commanders had been lost too: Dan Sapir killed in action, Haim Adini seriously wounded, and Asaf Yaguri taken as a prisoner of war. Adan, at times, had lost control of his own forces, unable to observe or communicate with them. In terms of combat power, the Adan *ugdah*, with the number of its operational tanks down from 183 to approximately a hundred, now amounted to a single brigade. As Adan recalled later, "There had been moments when I was no longer sure I had a division."[72]

The bad news for the Israelis did not end there. At eight in the evening, or fifty-four hours into the war, the Israeli air force reported losses of forty-four planes, a rate that would bring the air force to the dangerous "red line" in just a few days.[73] Even Northern Command filed a sobering update: although the Israelis had stopped the Syrian advance and had begun pushing back the attackers in a few places, the Syrians were expected to commit fresh armor the next day. Unfortunately for his reputation, Elazar had held his first news conference at six o'clock before he was fully aware of the actual situation on both fronts. Before the media, he bragged how the IDF would soon "break their [the Arabs'] bones," already claiming to have "begun the destruction of the Egyptian Army."[74] These overconfident words would haunt him after the war as evidence of unmitigated arrogance.

Numerous mistakes in planning and execution had caused heavy losses in men and equipment, and there had been no tactical or operational gains. On the fateful day of 8 October, the standard set by the Six Day War and the doctrine of taking the fight to the enemy's territory as soon as possible had compelled Israeli commanders to try to defeat the Egyptian army in quick order. These factors, combined with an arrogant attitude toward the Arabs, had created a perfect recipe for Israeli disaster. As Adan described this situation,

Every IDF commander was deeply imbued with the idea that we would have to cross at some point; this was an organic part of the IDF's doctrine of transferring the war to enemy territory and terminating it there quickly. . . . Virtually no one on the Israeli side doubted that the war would be decided only after we had crossed to the west bank and destroyed the main enemy force. The crossing idea was like some siren song, beckoning the commanders on, teasing them to dare and reach for the prize.[75]

The IDF, driven in some measure by overweening pride, had underestimated its thrice-defeated foe. Many Israeli officers had assumed a quick and easy victory would ensue from their cavalry-like counterattacks. The subsequent rude awakening jarred the Israeli military, as evidenced by Gonen's terse comment at day's end: "It's not the Egyptian Army of 1967."[76] This lesson would be relearned by Israeli commanders toward the end of the war.

TWO OPERATIONAL PAUSES

For the Egyptians, the eighth of October, in sharp contrast to the Israeli experience, was "the decisive day of the crossing operation."[77] The EAF had defeated a division-sized Israeli counterattack, ensuring the success of the first phase of Operation *Badr*. Euphoria spread throughout the Egyptian high command.

Pressure from various sources mounted on Sadat and Ahmad Ismail to exploit the favorable tactical situation by moving immediately to the Sinai passes. Such a move, though risky, could deal a major blow to the IDF in the Sinai at a time when the Israelis were focused on defeating the Syrians. More concerned about political ends than military means, Sadat was unyielding and refused to countenance a quick expansion of the war. He alluded to this in his letter to Kissinger on 7 October.

At 1:30 A.M. on 9 October, for example, Haykal broached the subject of the passes with Sadat, who dismissed the notion out of hand: "As I told Hafez Asad, territory isn't important; what is important is to exhaust the enemy. I don't want to make the mistake of pushing too fast just for the sake of occupying more territory. We must make the enemy bleed." Nonetheless, Sadat gave Haykal permission to call Ahmad Ismail. At three o'clock, Haykal telephoned Center Ten, the command center for the EAF, and spoke with Shazli, who declined to wake the war minister and politely stated his own opposition to the idea. Finally, at 7:15 that same morning, Haykal talked with Ahmad Ismail, who unequivocally supported Shazli's position.[78]

The issue did not die there, however. Later that morning, the fourth day of the war, a group of senior officers approached Ahmad Ismail, advocating an immediate offensive to the passes without an operational pause. These officers believed that stopping would transfer the initiative to the Israelis, who could then attack at their leisure. Dismissing their arguments, the cautious war minister underscored his desire to continue inflicting heavy damage on the Israelis. Fighting on the defensive, he felt, best achieved that objective. Going to the passes was out of the question—for the time being.[79] Here, Ahmad Ismail echoed Sadat's own words to Haykal earlier that morning.

There was, however, disagreement within the Egyptian military in the field over the wisdom of going to the passes. Nearer the battlefield, away from the safety of Center Ten, the issue was not so obvious. In a few sectors, infantry divisions had failed to reach their tactical objectives, falling short by several kilometers. As a result, both field army commanders pressed for an operational pause to consolidate their bridgeheads and reorganize their forces before contemplating an offensive to the passes.[80]

Whatever the positions of Egypt's most senior military commanders, Sadat wanted an operational pause. The president had gone to war in large measure to draw the United States into the conflict as an honest broker. Having activated his back channel to the White House on 7 October, Sadat was still determined to keep the war strictly limited, focused on inflicting heavy losses on the IDF while exploiting the diplomatic front. It was important to appear reasonable and moderate to the Americans. On 8 October, even before his discussion with Haykal, Sadat ordered Ahmad Ismail to implement an operational pause. Meanwhile, the EAF was to continue wearing down the Israelis.[81]

Vinogradov, Soviet ambassador in Cairo from 1970 to 1974, years later recalled at a public forum in the USSR how committed Sadat was to a strategy of attrition. In conversations with the Soviet diplomat, Sadat had repeatedly declared that all he sought was "ten centimeters of land east of Suez" in order to draw world attention to the Middle East problem. When on one occasion Vinogradov raised the issue of more Egyptian military support for Syria, Sadat reportedly responded: "Let it [Syria] go on the defensive and wage guerrilla warfare. Our main goal is to knock out as many enemy forces as possible."[82] As Sadat had outlined in his strategic directive of 5 October, inflicting heavy casualties on the Israelis constituted a key military objective of the war, and he remained wedded to that goal. Still, despite his political aims, Sadat would learn that he could not ignore the dynamic of the battlefield in the Sinai and on the Golan.

There was merit in the argument for making a dash for the passes. The Israelis had suffered heavy losses during the first three days of fighting, over four hundred tanks in the Sinai alone. For the Egyptian army to wait several days would allow the Israelis to defeat the Syrians and then turn their attention to the Sinai. The time thus appeared propitious for a dash to the passes.

The arguments against an offensive seemed stronger, however. Transferring the bulk of the air defense umbrella to the east bank in order to provide cover for advancing ground troops might jeopardize the system's integrity, thereby exposing the Egyptian rear to Israeli air strikes. On the other hand, to attack without the integrated air defense system on the east bank would expose Egyptian forces to Israel's flying artillery, unless Sadat and Ahmad Ismail were willing to commit the Egyptian air force. Given its track record, Egypt's air force could expect to lose an unacceptably high number of pilots and planes in combat. Furthermore, to launch the offensive demanded the transfer of tanks from the operational reserve on the west bank, which meant the attack could not be conducted before 10 or 11 October. Already on 8 October, Northern Command had stopped the Syrian offensive and had begun slowly pushing the SAF back toward Damascus. With this positive development for the Israelis, Elazar could easily transfer the bulk of the air force to the Sinai front.

Finally, an important argument for an operational pause was that Operation *Badr* had been based on caution. General Command had devoted the bulk its effort to the crossing operation at the expense of preparing for a rapid transition to a major breakout along several axes to the passes. This attitude, no doubt, explains why Ahmad Ismail, Shazli, and both field army commanders favored a stop. Caution, rather than risk, defined the Egyptian strategic mindset of senior commanders. Sadat thus seemed more right than wrong in his decision for an operational pause.

While Sadat contemplated his next moves on the diplomatic and military fronts, the Meir government decided to threaten to take a drastic step. Late on 8 October, the kitchen cabinet ordered the preparation of missiles and planes for possible delivery of several nuclear warheads. American intelligence quickly noted this development. The Soviets did also and informed Sadat. Most likely,

Meir did not intend to employ these weapons but was merely attempting to blackmail the United States into committing itself to a massive resupply with conventional weapons. The United States responded to Israel's warnings by promising to make up all Israeli material losses, but the massive American airlift commenced only some days after the Israeli threat.[83] As for a possible effect on Egypt, Sadat apparently had decided on an operational pause before word reached him of the Israeli action. Asad had more to fear in this regard, since the Golan Heights overlooked the heartland of Israel.

As Sadat was applying the brakes on his armed forces moving toward the passes, Elazar reached a similar decision for the IDF. Just after midnight on 9 October, he and Dayan met with senior commanders at Gebel Umm Hashiba to assess the military situation. Now, a degree of realism descended upon Israel's military leadership, brought about by the harsh realities of the battlefield. Elazar wanted to suspend offensive operations in the Sinai for at least twenty-four hours while the IDF focused on finishing off the Syrians. With only five hundred or so tanks left in the Sinai, Israel could ill afford major offensives on two fronts simultaneously. The chief of the General Staff instructed his subordinates to avoid battles of attrition. Reorganization and conservation were now the top priorities; the countercrossing to the west bank would take place at a later date.[84]

On the battlefields of the Sinai, there would be little rest for combat units, even though both Ahmad Ismail and Elazar had ordered operational pauses. All along the front, the Egyptians conducted probing attacks to expand their bridgeheads, and Israeli commanders often responded with counterattacks. In Sharon's sector, the fighting became especially intense.

There, the Egyptian 16th Infantry Divisions attempted on 9 October to seize some important ridges. Sharon, who opposed Elazar's decision to move to the defensive and reconstitute, decided to retaliate and ordered a number of counterattacks throughout the day in clear violation of Elazar's intent to avoid battles of attrition. In response, Munim, the commander of the Second Army, released a tank battalion from the 14th Armored Brigade to help Brigadier General Abd Rab al-Nabi Hafiz, the commander of the 16th Infantry Division, thwart Israeli attempts at penetration. Meanwhile, the Reshef, Erez, and Raviv Armored Brigades attempted in several attacks to seize the Egyptian positions at Hamutal, Televiza, and Machshir, but to no avail. Lieutenant Colonel Shaul Shalev, a battalion commander from Reshef's brigade, lost his life that day. By nightfall, Sharon had squandered some fifty tanks, a number comparable to the losses of Adan the previous day, and without any territorial gains, although Reshef did extricate the Israeli garrison from Purkan strong point.[85]

Upon learning of Sharon's brash action, Elazar became livid. But rather than remove Sharon, a controversial but gifted commander with political connections to the opposition party, Elazar opted to replace Gonen. Though a hero in the Six Day War, Gonen lacked the intellect and temperament to be a theater commander. His two subordinates, Adan and Sharon, had once been his superiors, which further complicated matters. Gonen's worst flaw, however, was that he remained preoccupied with current tactical problems. As Elazar remarked later: "I think about tomorrow. . . . That's my job. Whoever's shooting now, neither the front commander nor I can help anymore. That's a divisional commander's problem. I'm constantly telling him: Shmulik [Gonen], let's talk about what will happen tomorrow."[86] Gonen had failed to transform himself from being a tactical (division) to an operational (theater or front) commander.

Part of Gonen's problem was that the Egyptians maintained the initiative, something the Israelis found unfamiliar and unsettling. But Elazar could not ignore the critical issue of competent command, and he and Dayan decided to replace Gonen with former chief of the General Staff, Haim Bar-Lev. Although he would have his own share of problems controlling Sharon, Bar-Lev brought a firmer hand to the Sinai theater. To avoid the appearance of firing Gonen, Elazar retained him as deputy when Bar-Lev assumed front command on 10 October. The next major round in the struggle would come in four days.

CONCLUSION

By 10 October, when both the Egyptians and the Israelis settled down into their respective versions of an operational pause, the EAF clearly had the upper hand on the battlefield. A weaker adversary had dealt a serious blow to a stronger foe, sending him reeling in surprise. That accomplishment, for the time being, was sufficient for maintaining the initiative and shaping the course of events on the battlefield. The Israelis learned how important it is to start a war. All Israeli prewar plans and expectations fell by the wayside as a result of the Arabs attacking first. Most disconcerting for the Israelis was the failed counterattack of 8 October. In some ways, the Israeli defeat on that day was a greater surprise to them than the Egyptian and Syrian offensives on 6 October—for on 8 October, the full extent of Israel's unpreparedness for war became starkly evident. However, the Egyptians, by going into an operational pause on 9 October, gave the Israelis time to recover from the shock of the first four days of fighting. The remainder of the war would see increased diplomatic activity, as the fortunes on the battlefield changed dramatically.

NOTES

1. Carl von Clausewitz, *On War*, translated by Michael Howard and Peter Paret (Princeton, NJ: Princeton University Press, 1984): 87.

2. Henry Kissinger, *Years of Upheaval* (Boston: Little, Brown, 1982): 528.

3. Moshe Dayan, *Moshe Dayan: The Story of My Life* (New York: William Morrow, 1976): 467–469; Hanoch Bartov, *Dado: 48 Years and 20 Days* (Tel Aviv: Ma'ariv, 1981): 238–239; and Avigdor Kahalani, *The Heights of Courage: A Tank Leader's War on the Golan* (New York: Praeger, 1992): 3–18.

4. Numerous sources discuss deception. See Salah al-Din al-Hadidi, *Harb Oktobir fi al-Mizan al-Askari* (Cairo: Madbuli, 1974): 53–58; Adil Yusri, *Rihla al-Shaq al-Mualaqa: Min Ras al-Ush ila Ras al-Qubra* (Cairo: Dar al-Muarif bi Misr, 1974): 271–273; Muhammad Hassanayn Haykal, *The Road to Ramadan* (New York: Quadrangle,

1975): 16–17, 32; Saad al-Shazli, *The Crossing of the Suez*: (San Franscisco: American Mideast Research, 1980): 206–207; Muhammad Abd al-Ghani al-Gamasi, *Mudhakirat al-Gamasi: Harb Oktobir 1973* (Paris: al-Munshurat al-Sharqiyya, 1990): 285–288; and Hasan Mustafa, *Maarik al-Jabhah al-Misriyya fi Harb Ramadan* (Baghdad: no publisher, 1982): 209–232.

5. Shazli, *Crossing of the Suez*: 205.
6. Ibid.: 211.
7. Sayyid Mari, *Awraq Siyasiyah* III (Cairo: al-Maktab al-Msri al-Hadith, 1979): 703–721; and Muhammad Hafez Ismail, *Amn Misr al-Qawmi fi Asr al-Tahaddiyat* (Cairo: Markaz al-Ahram lil-Targama wa al-Nashr, 1987): 302–303. Both men participated in the meeting.
8. Chaim Herzog, *The War of Atonement, October 1973* (Boston: Little, Brown, 1975): 42; Trevor N. Dupuy, *Elusive Victory: The Arab-Israeli Wars, 1947–1974* (1978, reprint Fairfax, VA: Hero Books, 1984): 406; and Ehud Yonay, *No Margin for Error: The Making of the Israeli Air Force* (New York: Pantheon Books, 1993): 314.
9. Shazli, *Crossing of the Suez*: 211–212; Gamal Hamad, *Min Sina ila al-Golan* (Cairo: al-Zuhra lil-Ilam al-Arabi, 1988): 533–534; Haykal, *Road to Ramadan*: 29–31; Muhammad Hassanayn Haykal, *Oktobir 1973: al-Silah wa al-Siyasa* (Cairo: al-Ahram, 1993): 313; and Gamasi, *Mudhakirat*: 280.
10. Haykal, *Road to Ramadan*: 31; Hamad, *Min Sina ila al-Golan*: 334, 385, 541. On the Israeli intelligence assessment, see Golda Meir, *My Life* (New York: Putnam, 1975): 421–422.
11. Anwar Sadat, *In Search of Identity: An Autobiography* (New York: Harper & Row, 1977): 246.
12. Victor Israelyan, *Inside the Kremlin during the Yom Kippur War* (University Park: The Pennsylvania State University Press, 1995): 9–10.
13. Ibid.: 13–15.
14. Ibid.: 1-2; and Vadim Kirpichenko, comments at a conference on 1973 war, Washington, DC, 9 October 1998. Kirpichenko, a retired lieutenant general, served as a KGB agent in Cairo during this period. He confirms that the Soviets learned in advance of war through unnamed sources in Egypt.
15. Bartov, *Dado*: 258–260; Dayan, *Moshe Dayan*: 472; Herzog, *War of Atonement*: 50; and Michael Brecher, *Decisions in Crisis: Israel, 1967 and 1973* (Berkeley: University of California Press, 1980): 172, 192–194.
16. Gabi Amir, interview with author, 6 July 1994, Tel Aviv, Israel.
17. Bartov, *Dado*: 262.
18. On the reaction of Israel's leadership during the critical hours before the war, see "The Agranat Report: The First Partial Report," *The Jerusalem Journal of International Relations* 4 (1974): 74, 76–78; Meir, *My Life*: 425–427; Bartov, *Dado*: 273–292; Herzog, *War of Atonement*: 52–54; Dayan, *Moshe Dayan*: 459–461; and Brecher, *Decisions in Crisis*: 197–203.
19. Shazli, *Crossing of the Suez*: 52–53.
20. Meir, *My Life*: 427–428.
21. Dayan, *Moshe Dayan*: 465.
22. Yitzhak Rabin, *The Rabin Memoirs* (Boston: Little, Brown, 1979): 235.
23. Avraham Adan, *On the Banks of the Suez* (Novato, CA: Presidio Press, 1980): 4.
24. Abba Eban, *Abba Eban: An Autobiography* (New York: Random House, 1977): 496.

25. Dayan, *Moshe Dayan*: 463.

26. Adan, *On the Banks of the Suez*: 41; and discussions with Israeli veterans at the US Army Command and General Staff College.

27. These figures come from personal calculations based on various Israeli sources.

28. Adan, *On the Banks of the Suez*: 20, 81–82; Bartov, *Dado*: 293–294, 297; and Chaim Herzog, *The Arab-Israeli Wars: War and Peace in the Middle East from the War of Independence through Lebanon* (New York: Vintage Books, 1982): 245.

29. Arnold Sherman, *When God Judged and Men Died: A Battle Report of the Yom Kippur War* (New York: Bantam Books, 1973): 37.

30. Amir, interview.

31. Bartov, *Dado*: 302–304, 317–318; Herzog, *War of Atonement*: 157; Adan, *On the Banks of the Suez*: 92; and Herzog, *The Arab-Israeli Wars*: 249–250.

32. Adan, *On the Banks of the Suez*: 82; and Ariel Sharon, *Warrior: An Autobiography of Ariel Sharon* (New York: Simon and Schuster, 1989): 294–295.

33. Shazli, *Crossing of the Suez*: 51–52, 223, 225–226, 234–235; Gamal Hamad, *al-Maarik al-Harbiyya ala al-Gabha al-Misriyya* (Cairo: al-Zahra lil-Ilam al-Arabi, 1989): 156–160, 837–841; Hasan al-Badri, Taha al-Magdub, Muhammad Zia al-Din Zohdi, *The Ramadan War, 1973* (New York: Hippocrene, 1978): 67; and Herzog, *War of Atonement*: 161–162.

34. Yonay, *No Margin for Error*: 342.

35. Hamad, *al-Maarik al-Harbiyya*: 154, 794–796; Badri, *Ramadan War*: 78–79; Elazar, *Dado*: 319; Adan, *On the Banks of the Suez*: 35; Edgar O'Ballance, *No Victor, No Vanquished: The Yom Kippur War* (San Rafael, CA: Presidio Press, 1978): 89–91, 97; and Eliezer Cohen, *Israel's Best Defense: The Full Story of the Israeli Air Force* (New York: Orbis, 1993): 338–342.

36. Adan, *On the Banks of the Suez*: 95.

37. Yuval Dvir, interview with author, 4 July 1994, Israel. In the 1973 war, Dvir, then a captain, was the deputy commander of the reconnaissance battalion in the Sinai.

38. Cohen, *Israel's Best Defense*: 354.

39. Dayan, *Moshe Dayan*: 476–478; Bartov, *Dado*: 306–308; and Brecher, *Decisions in Crisis*: 203–204.

40. Kissinger, *Years of Upheaval*: 471–473; William B. Quandt, *Peace Process: American Diplomacy and the Arab-Israeli Conflict since 1967* (Washington: Brookings Institution, 1993): 152–56; and Richard Nixon, *RN: The Memoirs of Richard Nixon*, II (New York: Warner Books, 1978): 476.

41. Kissinger, *Years of Upheaval*: 477, 486; and Julian Thompson, *The Lifeblood of War: Logistics in Armed Conflict* (London: Brassey's, 1991): 230–231.

42. Shazli, *Crossing of the Suez*: 232–233; and Gamasi, *Mudhakirat*: 332, 342.

43. Israelyan, *Inside the Kremlin*: 10–11, 17–18, 30–35, 53–56.

44. Sadat, *In Search of Identity*: 253–254; Haykal, *Road to Ramadan*: 208–209; and Israelyan, *Inside the Kremlin*: 39–40.

45. Sadat, *In Search of Identity*: 254–255; and Israelyan, *Inside the Kremlin*: 43–49.

46. Mari, *Awraq Siyasiyah*, III: 726–727.

47. Hafez Ismail, *Amn Misr al-Qawmi*: 317–319; and Haykal, *Oktobir 1973*: 358–359, 792–793.

48. Kissinger, *Years of Upheaval*: 481–482.

49. Ibid.: 479, 483.

50. Israelyan, *Inside the Kremlin*: 43–48, 73.

51. Dayan, *Moshe Dayan*: 481–483; and Yonay, *No Margin for Error*: 329–331.

52. For the Golan front, see Jerry Asher and Eric Hammel, *Duel for the Golan: The 100-Hour Battle That Saved Israel* (New York: William Morrow, 1987); Charles Wakebridge, "The Syrian Side of the Hill," *Military Review* (February 1976): 20–30; relevant sections in works by Dupuy, Herzog, and O'Ballance; and Pierre Razoux, *La Guerre Israélo-Arabe d'Octobre 1973: Une Nouvelle Donne Militaire au Proche-Orient* (Paris: Economica, 1999): 92–100, 109–126.

53. Yonay, *No Margin for Error*: 337. Similar sentiments were expressed to the author in a lengthy discussion with a Israeli squadron commander in the war. Iftach Spector, interview with author, 7 July 1994, Tel Aviv, Israel.

54. Bartov, *Dado*: 314; and Herzog, *The Arab-Israeli Wars*: 248, 250.

55. Adan, *On the Banks of the Suez*: 92, 109; and Bartov, *Dado*: 318.

56. Bartov, *Dado*: 332.

57. Sharon, *Warrior*: 295.

58. Bartov, *Dado*: 324–328; and Meir, *My Life*: 428–429.

59. Martin van Creveld, *Command in War* (Cambridge, MA: Harvard University Press, 1985): 210; Bartov, *Dado*: 332; and Eliezer Cohen, *Israel's Best Defense*: 353–354.

60. For a discussion of this important meeting, see Adan. *On the Banks of the Suez*: 95–100; Bartov, *Dado*: 334–336; Sharon, *Warrior*: 298–300; Herzog, *War of Atonement*: 183–184; Creveld, *Command in War*: 211–215; and David Eshel, "Counterattack in the Sinai: 8 October 1973," *Military Review* (November 1993): 56–57.

61. For a detailed critical analysis of the day's events and their background from an Israeli perspective, see Adan, *On the Banks of the Suez*: 91–164; Bartov, *Dado*: 334–372; Sharon, *Warrior*: 301–306; van Creveld, *Command in War*. 203–231; Eshel, "Counterattack," 54–66; and Edwin L. Kennedy, "Failure of Israeli Armored Tactical Doctrine, Sinai, 6–8 October 1973," *Armor* (November–December 1990): 28–31.

62. Adan, *On the Banks of the Suez*: 118–119.

63. Ibid.: 107–113.

64. Ibid.: 218.

65. Ibid.: 119.

66. Hamad, *al-Maarik al-Harbiyya*: 195–200.

67. Adan, *On the Banks of the Suez*: 136; and van Creveld, *Command in War*. 224.

68. For material from the Israeli side on this second attack, Aryeh Keren, interview with author, 4 July 1994, Israel; Amir, interview; Elyashiv Shimshi, interview with author, 7 July 1994, Tel Aviv, Israel; Ariel Sharon, interview with author, 7 July 1994, Tel Aviv, Israel; Elyashiv Shimshi, *Storm in October* (in Hebrew) (Tel Aviv: Ma'arachot, 1986); Adan, *On the Banks of the Suez*: 137–140; Sharon, *Warrior*: 301–302; Bartov, *Dado*: 360; Herzog, *War of Atonement*: 188–190; and van Creveld, *Command in War*: 224–225. Egyptian perspective appears in Musa Sabri, *Wathaiq Harb Oktobir* (Cairo: al-Maktab al-Misri al-Hadis, 1974): 530–535; Hamad, *al-Maarik al-Harbiyya*: 198–201; and Mustafa, *Ma'arik al-Jabhah al-Misriyya*: 327–331.

69. For example, see *al-Ahram*, 10 October 1973: 1, 3.

70. Yusri, *Rihla al-Shaq al-Mualaqa*: 175; Hamad, *al-Maarik al-Harbiyya*: 203; and discussions with several Egyptian officers attending the US Army Command and General Staff College, Fort Leavenworth, Kansas, 1984–1994.

71. Hamad, *al-Maarik al-Harbiyya*: 203–209; Yusri, *Rihla al-Shaq al-Mu'alaqa*: 163–185; and Sabri, *Wathaiq Harb Oktobir*: 552–555.

72. Adan, *On the Banks of the Suez*: 152.

73. Bartov, *Dado*: 367; Terence Smith, "Fighting Is Bitter," *New York Times*, 9 October 1973: 1; and "Excerpts From Israel's News Parley," ibid.: 17.

74. Bartov, *Dado*: 365–366.

75. Adan, *On the Banks of the Suez*: 249–250.

76. Zeev Schiff, *October Earthquake: Yom Kippur 1973* (Tel Aviv: University Publishing Projects, 1974): 113.

77. Gamasi, *Mudhakirat*: 353, 358.

78. Haykal, *Road to Ramadan*: 218–220, and *Oktobir 1973*: 392–394.

79. Muhammad Abd al-Ghani al-Gamasi, interview with author, 31 October 1993, Cairo, Egypt; Muhammad Ali Fahmi, interview with author, 22 June 1994, Cairo, Egypt; Gamasi, *Mudhakirat*: 382–384; and Haykal, *Oktobir 1973*: 438.

80. Muhammad Abd al-Ghani al-Gamasi, interview with author, 25 June 1994, Cairo, Egypt; Fahmi, interview, 22 June 1994.

81. Haykal, *Oktobir*: 376-381.

82. Gareev and et al., "Comment on Yom Kippur War," *Foreign Broadcast Information Service, JPRS-UMA* (11 January 1989): 102.

83. Seymour M. Hersh, *The Samson Option: Israel's Nuclear Arsenal and American Foreign Policy* (New York: Random House, 1991): 225–231; and Shlomo Aronson with Oded Brosh, *The Politics and Strategy of Nuclear Weapons in the Middle East: Opacity, Theory, and Reality, 1960–1991, An Israeli Perspective* (New York: State University of New York Press, 1992): 139–149.

84. Batov, *Dado*: 369–372; and Adan, *On the Banks of the Suez*: 169–172.

85. For the Egyptian side see Hamad, *al-Maarik al-Harbiyya*: 222–226; Yusri, *Rihla al-Shaq al-Mualaqa*: 198; and Mustafa, *Maarik al-Jabhah al-Misriyya* 331–332. Israeli accounts include Amnon Reshef, interview with author, 30 June 1994, Tel Aviv, Israel; Bartov, *Dado*: 385–387; Adan, *On the Banks of the Suez*: 185–191; Sharon, *Warrior*: 306–309; and Herzog, *War of Atonement*: 193–195.

86. Bartov, *Dado*: 389.

7

ISRAEL'S RESURGENCE

Invincibility depends on one's self; the enemy's vulnerability on him.
—Sun Tzu[1]

In such a case, total destruction has ceased to be the point; the engagement is nothing but a trial of strength. In itself it is of no value; its significance lies in the outcome of the trial.
—Carl von Clausewitz[2]

Although by 10 October both the Egyptians and the Israelis had settled down into their separate versions of an operational pause in the Sinai, the war had developed its own internal dynamic, outside either combatant's control. Syria and Israel remained locked in a fierce battle to determine that front's fate, placing pressure on Cairo to conduct a major offensive in support of its northern ally. As the war dragged on, longer than expected by all the foreign experts, neither the United States nor the USSR could afford to maintain only minimal involvement; both superpowers gradually became more involved to ensure that the armed struggle ended in a military position favorable to their respective clients. Regionally, other Arab states had to demonstrate their solidarity with Egypt and Syria, in order to maintain legitimacy with their own populations; any steps taken by the Arab world in support of Sadat or Asad would broaden the conflict strategically. Each dimension of the conflict influenced the political and military course of the 1973 Arab-Israeli war on the southern front.

DIPLOMATIC ESCALATION

During the operational pause on the southern front, Egyptian forces conducted probing attacks designed to expand their bridgeheads to Artillery Road;

the Israelis, for the most part, foiled these efforts. Little territory changed hands in these engagements, as each side played for time before receiving follow-on missions. Nonetheless, casualties continued to mount on both sides, and the diplomatic front began to experience significant movement.

Although Sadat had ordered an operational pause, General Command conducted one major attack, to rectify the only significant glitch in the crossing operation.[3] Operation *Badr* had called for the 1st Mechanized Infantry Brigade from the 6th Mechanized Infantry Division to cross the Suez Canal in the 19th Infantry Division's sector during the night of 6–7 October. On the morning on 7 October, the brigade was to have made a rapid push to Ras Misalla, some seventeen kilometers south of Third Army's southern bridgehead. Unfortunately for the Egyptians, the 19th Infantry Division experienced difficulties constructing its bridges across the Suez Canal, causing a forty-eight-hour delay in the 1st Brigade's crossing. The brigade reached the east bank during the night of 8–9 October, two days late. Rather than abort its mission, General Command decided to proceed with the attack.

At six in the morning of 10 October, the brigade moved out in three battalion-sized columns, using the coastal road to Sharm al-Shaykh. The Egyptians managed to occupy the undefended wells at Ayun Musa. Before sunset, however, Israeli aircraft, combined with ground forces in the area, stopped the Egyptian advance and forced a retreat back to Ayun Musa during the night of 10–11 October. During the operation, the brigade commander lost half his tanks, about fifteen, and a number of artillery pieces. The 1st Brigade's fate underscored the risk involved for the EAF in moving outside its bridgeheads to confront Israeli forces on open terrain.

Meanwhile, on the diplomatic front, Sadat, who clearly understood his own military's inferiority in a war against Israel, sought to garner support from the Arab world for his strategic aims. Already on 7 October, with the war not yet thirty-six hours old, Sadat had ordered several trusted officials to hold meetings on exploiting the oil weapon. On 10 October, Sadat pushed that button. A delegation headed by Sayyid Mari departed for the Gulf states to elicit economic support and to coordinate diplomacy with other Arabs as another influence on the United States to change its policy toward the Arab-Israeli conflict. From 10 to 16 October, Mari visited Saudi Arabia, Kuwait, Abu Dhabi, Qatar, Bahrain, and Oman. Discussions included raising oil prices and cutting production—moves that, if effective, would have global economic repercussions. Every Arab leader committed additional financial aid for the armed struggle and, in some cases, promised combat troops.[4]

As in the Arab world, diplomatic gears began slowly moving in Washington and Moscow. Although the Nixon administration had begun sending special military equipment to Israel on 7 October, during the first three days of the war, the United States expected a quick and easy victory, as had occurred in 1967, and consequently maintained a convenient distance from the conflict. That assessment changed dramatically as word reached Washington of staggering Israeli losses. In addition to the nuclear alert discussed in the previous chapter,

Israel's ambassador, Simcha Dinitz, reported forty-nine planes downed, including nineteen Phantoms, and some five hundred tanks destroyed, four hundred of them in the Sinai. Clearly, Israel was engaged in bitter war of attrition without a quick and easy victory in sight, and the United States needed to reassess its policy.

On 9 October, Nixon responded with a promise to replace all Israeli losses, with the understanding of a fast delivery schedule. The package included Phantoms, Skyhawks, and antitank TOW (tube-launched, optically guided, wire-linked command) missiles.[5] Some equipment reached Israel rapidly but secretly. On 11 October, for example, the IDF was already running a special course for training its soldiers on the use of the TOW missiles, some of which had been in country before the war.[6] Most likely, American military personnel traveled to Israel to provide assistance in the instruction. The IDF's employment of these antitank guided missiles surprised both the Egyptians and the Syrians and served to help defeat Arab armor during the remainder of the war.

Meanwhile, Moscow, like Washington, was moving slowly to support its Arab allies. Late in the evening on 7 October, Vinogradov informed Sadat that the USSR would begin resupplying Egypt and Syria within forty-eight hours.[7] The massive flow of weapons and equipment to Syria, however, commenced only on 10 October, with the arrival of some twenty Antonov-12s with two hundred tons of supplies. Egypt, for its part, received its first major shipment on 11 October. During the war, the Soviets airlifted about fifteen thousand tons of war material to both Arab countries; another sixty-three thousand tons arrived by sea from 30 October onward. Most of this aid went to Syria, whose military situation had begun deteriorating as early as 8 October.[8] Such aid raised concern in Tel Aviv and Washington.

On 12 October, without a public American commitment to match Soviet supplies to the Arabs, Israel's political leadership seriously considered, for the first time in the war, the possibility of a cease-fire in place. Several factors weighed heavily on the Meir government. Israel had suffered many casualties, and certain war materials were beginning to run short. There had been no major shipments of military supplies by the United States to Israel, while the Soviets were deeply engaged in delivering weapons and equipment to Syria and Egypt. On the positive side, Israel's military situation was much improved from that of the first few days of the war. The IDF had pushed the Syrians off the Golan Heights and had captured terrain east of the Purple Line. Israel could now bargain with territory seized from the Syrians for land captured by the Egyptians in the Sinai. Consequently, in the afternoon of 12 October the Meir cabinet instructed Abba Eban, the foreign minister, to broach the possibility of a cease-fire in place with the Nixon administration.[9]

Concurrent with Israel's move, Great Britain, with some nudging from the United States, considered sponsoring a UN resolution for a cessation of hostilities. On 13 October, the British ambassador in Cairo approached Sadat about such a prospect, but the Egyptian president refused to countenance a cease-fire unless Israel agreed to a withdrawal from occupied territories.[10] Israel would do nothing of the sort, closing the door for the moment to any further discussions on the subject. As subsequent events would show, Sadat had missed an excellent opportunity to end the war in a very favorable military position. But the effect on Egypt's standing in the Arab world would have been quite negative, as most Arabs would have perceived it as a clear sellout. Continuing the war made more sense politically.

Meanwhile, Washington could not sit idly and watch the Soviets continue rearming Syria and Egypt. American credibility would suffer serious damage if Washington's ally lost on the battlefield owing to material shortages. As noted by Kissinger later, the US had to "demonstrate that the military option backed by Soviet arms was an illusion; that diplomatic progress depended on American support."[11] On 13 October, therefore, the Nixon administration informed Israel that the United States would immediately commence a massive arms airlift, employing American military planes to ensure the arrival of shipments as quickly as possible. On 14 October, the first American cargo planes landed in Tel Aviv's airport before a crowd of senior Israeli officials and reporters. Golda Meir was moved to tears, the first she had shed since the outbreak of hostilities, greatly relieved at this visible sign of the firm US commitment to ensuring that the war ended favorably for Israel.[12]

National will received a major boost as well. Israel would no longer fight alone, with a restrained ally far in the background. The United States had openly placed its prestige behind Israel. The IDF could now wage war more aggressively, knowing that the United States would replenish its losses. The next thirty-three days would witness some 566 sorties of C-141s and C-5s bringing 22,395 tons of weapons, equipment, and supplies, while naval ships deposited another 33,210 tons in Israeli ports. Additionally, Washington delivered fifty-six A-4 Skyhawk and F-4 Phantom combat aircraft to prevent the Israel air force from reaching its red line.[13] A severe shortage in warplanes might have pushed Israel into seriously contemplating the use of nuclear weapons to ensure its dominance of the battlefield. Fortunately, Israel avoided that choice.

The American military aid was meant to outmatch that of the Soviets, which it easily did, but not without negative fallout for Washington. To provide Israel with a superiority in war material required the United States to strip its depots in Europe, creating much consternation within the North Atlantic Treaty Organization. It was to take several years for the Pentagon to replenish these stores to their pre–October 1973 levels. Given the Soviet military threat in Central Europe, Washington could ill afford a repetition of a major resupply of Israel in another Arab-Israeli war. Peace and stability in the Middle East served the national interests of the United States, and the war represented to some degree a failure in American foreign policy in this vital part of the world.

AN URGENT CALL FOR HELP

The Egyptian-Syrian coalition, despite all its advantages, brought burdens for Sadat. By entering into an alliance with Asad, the Egyptian leader had tied his country to events on the northern front, even though Egypt and Syria fought their fronts independently. Initially, the battle for the Golan went well for the Syrians, which served the EAF well, but then matters turned quickly for the worse on the northern front. In fact, on 11 October Syria's military situation had become quite desperate. By then, the IDF had gained the initiative, pushed the Syrians back to the Purple Line, and was advancing toward Damascus.[14]

Syria's military problems stemmed, in large measure, from the political instability that had plagued regimes in Damascus since the country's independence from France in 1945. Hafez al-Asad, as noted, had come to power in a military coup in November 1970, the tenth such change in government in twenty-five years. Each military coup had resulted in a purge of officers and the rapid promotion of others who were politically connected to the new leadership, a process that undermined professionalism in the officer corps.

To break the pattern of military coups, Asad, who himself belonged to the unpopular Alawite religious minority (some 11 percent of the population), devoted the first year or two of his reign to consolidating power and gaining legitimacy. During this period, he created a praetorian guard, called the Defense Companies, under his brother Rifaat. By the eve of the war, the Defense Companies, some five thousand strong and heavily dominated by Alawites, were receiving better equipment and higher pay than the regular army. When, for example, Syria received its first T-62 tanks from the USSR, Asad assigned them to Rifaat, for protecting Damascus. Sadat, on the other hand, allocated his T-62s to the 15th and 25th Independent Armored Brigades for the crossing operation.

In addition to being pampered, the Defense Companies reported directly to Asad, bypassing the normal chain of command through the defense minister, Major General Mustafa Talas. Syria thus entered the 1973 war with two separate armies, with only the regular army under the direct control of the defense ministry. Further complicating matters, the Syrian officer corps remained politicized, with loyalty (based in large measure on proper religious affiliation) emphasized over competence in determining promotions, especially into the senior command positions. Consequently, the SAF failed to prepare for war as well as did the EAF. Syria's air defense system, for example, was hastily completed just prior to the war; also, one of three infantry divisions assigned to the first-echelon attack was short of tanks and armored personnel carriers.[15] Finally, the Syrian military still depended on Soviet advisors, who remained in combat units throughout the war.[16] Egypt, on the other hand, having expelled its Soviet advisors in July 1972, had prepared since then to fight on its own. Syria thus entered the war with a political army, designed first of all to maintain a minority-based regime in power.

Egypt, in sharp contrast to Syria, had in the last six years witnessed relative political stability under two strong presidents and a loyal senior command. Therefore, Egypt's military reforms had had greater success in depoliticizing and professionalizing the armed forces after their disastrous defeat in 1967. Moreover, unlike the SAF, the EAF had waged the Three Years War. That combat had sharpened the military skills of the EAF, providing invaluable experience in preparing to refight the IDF. Thus, in terms of coalition warfare, the Egyptians took the lead in going to war, with the Syrians joining as junior partners. The SAF, however, faced a greater challenge—Israel would focus its main effort on the Golan Heights, where it lacked strategic depth. Moreover, Israeli reserve units would reach the northern front faster than they could the Sinai theater of operations. Syria thus presented the weak link in the coalition, threatening to compromise any Egyptian gains in the war.

By 10 October, Israel's Northern Command had accomplished its mission of pushing the Syrians off the Golan Heights. Now, Israel faced the important decision of what course to take next. Meir's war cabinet met late in the evening to discuss this important matter. Most present favored continuing the main effort against Syria, although a voice or two recommended halting operations for the purpose of launching a major offensive against Egypt. Political considerations carried great weight in deliberations. Gaining territory east of the Purple Line would strengthen Israel's diplomatic position after the war. Should the superpowers force a premature end to hostilities, Israel would thus be in possession of Syrian territory that could be bartered for lands already lost to Egypt in the Sinai.

Militarily, the situation seemed ripe for exploitation. Israeli military intelligence was reporting serious cracks in the SAF. Apparently, a mutiny had broken out in the Syrian 1st Armored Division; overall, the SAF was down to less than six hundred tanks. Failure to exploit this opportunity could haunt Israel later. An Iraqi armored division of some three hundred tanks was en route to help the Syrians, and its arrival might lead to a major Arab counterattack. In addition, the Soviets had commenced their massive resupply of Syria on 10 October. Senior Israeli officials thus expressed concern that within a short period the Syrians might initiate another offensive while the IDF was focused on the Sinai front.

Shortly before midnight on 10 October, after weighing all the arguments, the Israeli cabinet approved an offensive against Syria, scheduled to begin at 11:00 A.M. on 11 October. One military goal was to capture the town of Sasa, less than thirty-five kilometers from Damascus, well within artillery range. Such a threat to the Syrian capital, it was hoped, would convince Asad to accept an immediate cease-fire.[17]

Although tough fighting awaited the Israelis, Asad, no doubt, was becoming quite concerned that the tide of war had clearly turned against him. His army had lost close to a thousand tanks in six days of intense combat and had no terrain gains to show for it. Moreover, the IDF had commenced a drive toward Damascus. In the afternoon of 11 October, therefore, Asad dispatched a special emissary to Cairo to make a personal appeal to Sadat for a major attack toward the passes for the purpose relieving pressure on the Golan front.[18] The Syrian president informed the Soviet ambassador of his appeal. Mukhitdinov, in turn, wired Moscow, suggesting that Vinogradov meet with Sadat and urge a favorable response.[19] By now, Israeli forces were dangerously close to Damascus.

Asad's appeal presented Sadat with a difficult decision. To abandon Syria would have undermined Sadat's credibility in the Arab world after the war. Egypt relied too heavily on financial assistance from oil-producing countries like Saudi Arabia and Kuwait to risk such censure. Other Arab states were coming to the aid of Egypt and Syria. Iraq, for one, had already dispatched a second division and several air squadrons to the northern front. Sadat was compelled, out of both political and economic necessity, to demonstrate solidarity with his Arab brethren against Israel. He could not leave the Syrians to fend for themselves while his own army "hid" within secure bridgeheads, protected by an integrated air defense umbrella. Finally, a war of longer duration favored Sadat's aim of inflicting the greatest possible casualties on the IDF.

Whatever his exact motivations, Sadat decided to help Asad, a decision that adversely altered the course of the war for Egypt in the Sinai. In the early hours of 12 October, the Egyptian president ordered an offensive toward the passes, with the purpose of deflecting Israeli attention away from the Syrian front. Ahmad Ismail quickly transformed Sadat's order into an operational directive, for execution at 6:30 in the morning of 13 October.

Sadat's political decision sparked serious consternation at Center Ten and at both field army headquarters. Consequently, Ahmad Ismail decided to hold a high-level conference at Center Ten at six o'clock in the evening of 12 October. At the meeting, many senior officers voiced reservations about attacking toward the passes. Shazli and both field army commanders led the argument, attempting to convince the war minister that the time had passed for shifting to the offensive. But Ahmad Ismail had no choice but to obey his supreme commander; it was a political decision, he countered, outside his control. He did, however, agree to postpone the offensive twenty-four hours, to 6:30 A.M. on the 14 October, hoping a delay would enhance the plan's chance of success.[20] Twenty-four more hours failed to prevent the inevitable, and in fact the delay created its own problems.

Ironically, the northern front stabilized on 14 October, putting into question whether the Syrians truly needed Egyptian help. Israel's Northern Command had seized territory within Syria, but many Israeli units, which had been fighting for an entire week, were near exhaustion. Also, fresh Arab troops were arriving. The Iraqi armored division of three hundred tanks joined the battle on 12 and 13 October; a Jordanian armored brigade of four thousand men and 150 Centurion tanks entered the fighting on the 14th. These two Arab reinforcments helped prevent the IDF from reaching Sasa. But the SAF was too battered to launch a counterattack on 14 October in support of the Egyptian offensive. The IDF was thus already focusing its attention and air assets on defeating the EAF.

A TURNING POINT IN THE SINAI

As anticipated by many senior Egyptian officers, Egypt's attack on the 14 October proved an unmitigated disaster, attempted too late and with insufficient forces and little imagination. By the end of the day, the initiative had clearly passed to the Israelis. The IDF would then exploit the opportunity to establish its own bridgehead on the west bank of the Suez Canal, thereby taking away some of the luster of the EAF's accomplishments in the first part of the war.

In accordance with Sadat's strategic guidance, General Command identified three major goals for the offensive: to relieve pressure on the Syrian front by forcing the Israelis to withdraw units from the Golan; to establish defensive lines near or at the western entrances of the mountain passes; and to inflict as many casualties on the IDF as possible.[21] The five infantry divisions would not participate in the attack. Ahmad Ismail committed a limited force; only a portion of the armored and mechanized brigades in the operational reserve. Second Army transferred the 1st Armored Brigade and the 18th Mechanized Infantry Brigade from the 21st Armored Division to the east bank; Third Army did likewise with the 3d Armored Brigade from the 4th Armored Division.[22]

The operational plan called for four major axes of advance, involving five armored and two mechanized infantry brigades. In Second Army's sector, the 21st Armored Division would conduct the main effort, with its two armored and one mechanized brigade, to capture Tasa, while the 15th Armored Brigade moved from Qantara East to capture Baluza. These two thrusts would extend Second Army's bridgehead eastward to a line between Baluza and Tasa. Meanwhile, Third Army would launch the 11th Mechanized Brigade toward the Giddi Pass while the 22d and 3d Armored Brigades raced to the Mitla Pass (see Map 15).[23] The new Egyptian defensive positions would restrict Israel's opportunities to maneuver against the bridgeheads.

Ahmad Ismail's plan, no doubt reflecting Sadat's wishes, represented a half effort, doomed to defeat. Leaving all five infantry divisions in their bridgeheads made military sense; they were not designed to maneuver over open desert. But any serious offensive to the passes should have involved both armored and both mechanized infantry divisions, at least twelve brigades in all. Attacking with only two mechanized and five armored brigades on four axes provided the IDF with an excellent opportunity for a "turkey shoot," especially since the Israeli armored forces were prepared in defensive positions, expecting the assault. Israel would be highly satisfied with the results of the battle.

In addition to committing insufficient mechanized and armored forces, General Command failed to provide adequate air defense. Operation *Badr* had called for the transfer of five air defense brigades to the east bank for a major offensive to capture the passes. Fahmi, however, moved only nine battalions, less than two brigades, to the east bank, much to the consternation of field commanders involved in the attack. The Egyptian air defense commander felt that a half-hearted land effort required only minimal coverage, and he resisted all demands to transfer more brigades.[24] Clearly, the Egyptians had in mind a limited operation, largely a symbolic gesture, in support of Syria, not a serious military threat to the IDF.

The IDF, for its part, was prepared for the Egyptian offensive on 14 October. Apparently, the United States provided some useful intelligence to the Israelis. An American SR-71 spy plane had flown a reconnaissance mission over the Suez Canal on 13 October, and no doubt the Americans provided the Israelis with aerial photos of Egyptian troop dispositions. This intelligence was most likely not critical, but only reinforced Israel's own information, gathered from various sources. Many Egyptians, however, still believe today that the Americans provided the Israelis with intelligence of a decisive nature.

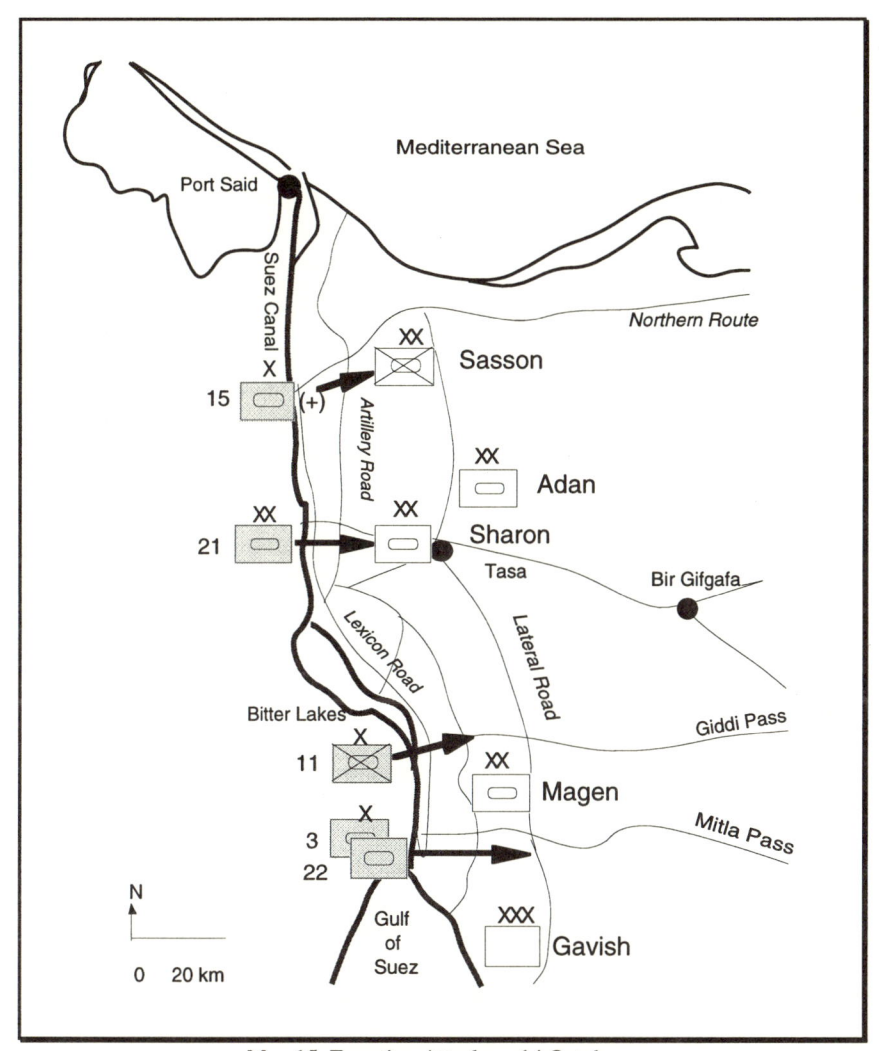

Map 15. Egyptian Attack on 14 October.
[Major General Gavish, commanded several brigades responsible for the Southern Sinai, a newly created command separate from that of Southern Command under Bar-Lev.]

Facing the attacking Egyptians were four Israeli divisions. Three were deployed forward: Sasson with two mechanized and one tank brigade in the north, Sharon with three tank brigades in the center, and Magen with two tank and one mechanized brigade in the south. Adan, with three tank brigades, constituted the front's reserve, with the mission of preparing for a possible countercrossing to the west bank of the Suez Canal.[25] By now, the Israelis also possessed TOW missiles.

Numerous mistakes, or questionable choices, plagued the Egyptian offensive. First, the attack began at a most inopportune time: at 6:30 in the morning, when the sun was in the eyes of Egyptian soldiers. This decision proved most unwise indeed. Second, the Egyptians advanced over open terrain without conducting proper reconnaissance. Third, the Egyptian air force flew only a limited number of sorties in support of the land operation. Fourth, the EAF abandoned the combined-arms approach it had used in its crossing operation for more tank-heavy formations, pitting some four hundred tanks against seven hundred on the Israeli side. Better integration of infantry and artillery might have helped the advance. Fifth, beside the use of smoke, deception formed little part of the plan; no surprises awaited the IDF. Compounding these problems, Major General Saad Mamun, the commander of Second Army, suffered a heart attack at 8:30, shortly after his forces had commenced their offensive. His chief of staff assumed command at ten o'clock, and subsequent events would find him wanting in leadership skills.[26]

All of this worked to the detriment of the EAF, especially since the IDF was aware of the impending offensive. In some sectors, Israeli armor units waited patiently behind ridgelines until the Egyptians were within a thousand meters before opening fire with devastating accuracy. Caught by surprise in open field, Egyptians became sitting ducks. By midafternoon, virtually all attacking Egyptian units were in full retreat back to their bridgeheads, leaving behind some 250 destroyed tanks, a figure that surpassed the 240 tanks lost through 13 October![27] Some losses were owed to friendly fire, as Egyptian units lost their way in the sun's glare, smoke, and dust.[28] The EAF never recovered operationally or tactically.

The losses can best be appreciated by concrete examples. The Egyptian 21st Armored Division began the war with approximately 280 tanks, 124 tanks in each of its two armored brigades and 31 in its mechanized infantry brigade. For the crossing operation, General Command had attached one armored brigade to the 16th Infantry Division; the remainder of the 21st Armored Division was in the operational reserve on the west bank. To conduct the 14 October offensive, General Command transferred that remainder to the east bank, with the mission of capturing Tasa. The plan of advance placed the 14th Armored Brigade north of the road to Tasa while the 1st Armored Brigade took the southern route; the 18th Mechanized Infantry Brigade trailed both brigades. Brigadier General Ibrahim al-Orabi, the division commander (later chief of the General Staff), also planned to transport by helicopter a commando company to help capture Tasa. To hide their movement, the Egyptians employed smoke, a tactic that backfired, causing confusion and loss of control within the division.

To face the Egyptian tank division, Sharon deployed his armored *ugdah* as follows: the Erez Armored Brigade blocked the Ismailiya Road, the Reshef Armored Brigade watched Akavish Road, and the Raviv Armored Brigade held Tasa, as the division's reserve. Both Egyptian tank brigades stumbled into prepared Israeli ambushes. By ten o'clock, the Egyptians had pulled back to regroup and attempt another assault in the afternoon. Neither Egyptian armored brigade made any headway, and by the end of the day the two brigades had retreated into their bridgeheads. Egyptian losses were heavy. The 1st Armored Brigade, which had experienced combat for the first time, had only sixty-six tanks left. The brigade commander, Colonel Muhammad Tawfiq Abu Shadi, was dead. For its part, the 14th Armored Brigade, already combat seasoned from the crossing operation, ended the day with only thirty-nine tanks. Fortunately for the division, the 18th Mechanized Infantry Brigade saw no action that day and thus managed to keep its full complement of thirty-one tanks. By the day's end, the 21st Armored Division had lost around 150 tanks, or approximately half its prewar strength. Sharon claims to have lost only five tanks.[29]

Egyptian Third Army fared no better. Wassel, its commander, faced Major General Kalman Magen's armored *ugdah*, with its 150 tanks. Magen had just taken command of the division on 13 October; its previous commander, Mandler, had been killed by an Egyptian artillery shell. The Avram Armored Brigade of approximately fifty tanks was positioned along the road to Giddi Pass. To the south stood a mechanized infantry brigade of some thirty "ancient" Super Shermans outfitted with the Israeli 105-mm gun. Blocking the road to Mitla Pass was the Shomron Armored Brigade, with sixty-five Patton tanks. One infantry battalion guarded the two strategic passes. Magen also possessed a paratroop battalion in the sector south of the Mitla Road; a second paratroop battalion at the south end of Artillery Road; and three battalions of 155-mm self-propelled artillery pieces south of the Mitla Pass.[30]

Wassel directed his main effort to the Mitla Pass. Here he committed the 22d Armored Brigade, attached to the 19th Infantry Division, and the 3d Armored Brigade, which had spent the first week of the war in relative calm on the west bank. As in other sectors, both Egyptian armored brigades drove into the waiting arms of the IDF. The 3d Armored Brigade lost sixty of its original 124 T-55 tanks and virtually all its artillery. Similar damaged occurred to the 22d Armored Brigade. By midafternoon, the two Egyptian brigades had retreated back into the shelter of Third Army's bridgehead. Among the Egyptians killed was Colonel Nur al-Din Abd al-Aziz, the commander of the 3d Armored Brigade.[31]

In the 14 October offensive, the Egyptians lost a total of 250 tanks, to twenty to thirty on the Israeli side. All this transpired for no gain in territory. At least two Egyptian brigade commanders were dead. Strategically, Sadat may have demonstrated his solidarity with the Arab cause, but operationally and tactically the Egyptians had lost much. Militarily, the Egyptians never fully recovered from this disaster. It now remained for the IDF to exploit this sudden turn of events.

The 14th of October, though it witnessed a major Israeli military success, had a painful side for Israel. After some procrastination, partly out of a desire not to alarm the public, Elazar finally authorized on that day the first official release of Israeli casualty figures: 656 known dead in the first eight days of fighting. By now, many Israelis on the home front had realized that all was not well in the war, but this first public acknowledgment of the numbers killed gave concrete form to the extent of the human tragedy so far. Moreover, military censors placed a hold on the publication of any obituaries submitted by bereaved families until the end of the war. Citing the need for secrecy at a news conference, Dayan admonished the nation to delay its mourning until the resolution of the armed struggle: "We are in the midst of war, and we can't give public expression at this time to our grief for the fallen."[32] His words underscored Israel's imperative to focus its national will on winning the conflict before directly confronting its human tragedy.

OPERATION STOUTHEARTED MEN

The sheer magnitude of the EAF's military defeat stunned and demoralized Egypt's General Command and energized the IDF. While Egyptian officers attempted to regain their composure and regroup their battered forces, senior Israeli commanders quickly grasped that the tide of war had shifted in their favor. The time for the IDF to exploit success was at hand.

Consequently, late in the evening on 14 October, Elazar requested the cabinet to approve a crossing to the western bank—an operation called Stouthearted Men. The confident chief of the General Staff gave Meir his assessment of the new strategic situation in the Sinai: "Golda, it will be all right. We are back to ourselves and they [the Egyptians] are back to themselves."[33] Buoyed by the fortuitous turn of events, the cabinet approved Elazar's request at thirty minutes past midnight on 15 October.[34] The operation would begin with high hopes of a quick victory on the battlefield; yet despite much reason for such optimism, Israel's political and military leadership would learn that the Egyptians had not completely reverted to their old selves. The EAF would once more demonstrate its newfound combat mettle.

The Egyptians needed to recover quickly from their defeat if they were to prevent the Israelis from exploiting the new military balance. At 1:00 P.M. on 14 October, even before the full extent of the disaster became known, Sadat visited Center Ten and ordered Shazli to the front to assess the day's damage. The chief of the General Staff arrived at Second Army's advance headquarters in Ismailiya at two o'clock. There he learned of Mamun's incapacity and ordered him to a hospital in Cairo. By eleven that evening, Shazli was back in Center Ten filing "a full report on our most calamitous day."[35] Military wisdom would have suggested that General Command reconstitute its operational reserve on the west bank by transferring units from the east shore. But Ahmad Ismail feared that pulling armor and mechanized units back from the east to the west bank might weaken morale and cause panic in the Egyptian army. Memories of commanders abandoning their units for the west bank in the Six Day War still haunted him.[36] Consequently, Ahmad Ismail refused to withdraw any forces to the west bank.

Egyptian forces on the west bank, however, were spread rather thin. In its operational reserve, Second Army possessed three mechanized infantry brigades: the 10th opposite Qantara East, the 118th around Ismailiya, and the 116th west of Deversoir. A commando group was located at Abu Suwayr Airport, while two battalions, one Kuwaiti and the other Palestinian, were stationed in the Deversoir area. Third Army relied on the 2d Armored and the 6th Mechanized Brigades from the 4th Armored Division, the 113th Mechanized Infantry Brigade from the 6th Mechanized Infantry Division, and a commando group (minus three battalions). The strategic reserve under General Command's direct control consisted of an armored brigade and a mechanized infantry brigade from the 3d Mechanized Infantry Division, two independent armored brigades, a paratroop brigade, two air assault brigades, and a commando group.[37] Only prompt and coordinated use of these forces could easily defeat an Israeli attempt to establish a lodging on the west bank.

While the Egyptians were attempting to recover from their debacle, the IDF prepared to cross the canal. Operation Stouthearted Men called for two Israeli armored divisions to cross at Deversoir, at the northern tip of the Great Bitter Lakes and encircle the Egyptian Third Army by surrounding Suez City, cutting off the Egyptians on the east bank from their supply bases. Israeli military intelligence had estimated that the Egyptians had only seven hundred tanks operational on both banks of the Suez Canal. Southern Command possessed roughly the same number divided into four divisions: Sharon 240, Adan 200, Magen 140, and Sasson 125.[38] However, the Israelis could concentrate their armor at the crossing site at Deversoir, where the Egyptians had positioned only the southern flank of the 16th Infantry Brigade.

In the crossing operation, Sharon would secure both sides of the Suez Canal and the two roads, Akavish and Tirtur, that led to the crossing site on the east bank. Adan would then cross over to puncture the Egyptian air defense system, thus allowing the Israeli air force to provide ground support and threaten Cairo. Meanwhile, part of the Magen Armored *Ugdah* would take control of the bridgehead, relieving Sharon. Adan would then race south to encircle Third Army, with Sharon providing flank protection for the dash to Suez City. To support this Blitzkrieg-type operation, Elazar planned to insert a paratroop force by helicopter to secure the key position of Gebel Ataka (see Map 16).

Based on the assumption as it was that the Egyptians had returned to their 1967 form, Operation Stouthearted Men was an optimistic plan, allotting one day for crossing the Suez Canal and another day or so for the lightning encirclement of Third Army. This timetable proved completely unrealistic. Again, the Egyptians exhibited unexpected resilience, even when confronted with units operating in the rear. Again, the Israelis would discover that they were not facing the Egyptian army of 1967.

Sharon, as noted earlier, had to secure the access routes and the crossing site. To draw Egyptian attention away from Deversoir, the Raviv Armored Brigade would launch a diversionary attack toward Missouri, a sand hill, and Hamutal. Meanwhile, the Reshef Armored Brigade, with the mission of securing

212   THE ALBATROSS OF DECISIVE VICTORY

the crossing site and the routes to it, would embark on a route south of Tirtur and Akavish roads. Once on Lexicon Road, Reshef planned to secure Deversoir with one force, push another force north and northeast to widen the crossing site, and send a third eastward to open Tirtur and Akavish roads. To facilitate the movement of troops and equipment across the Suez Canal, Southern Command hoped to capture some Egyptian bridges intact and to bring forward its own heavy bridge, pulled by a tank company.

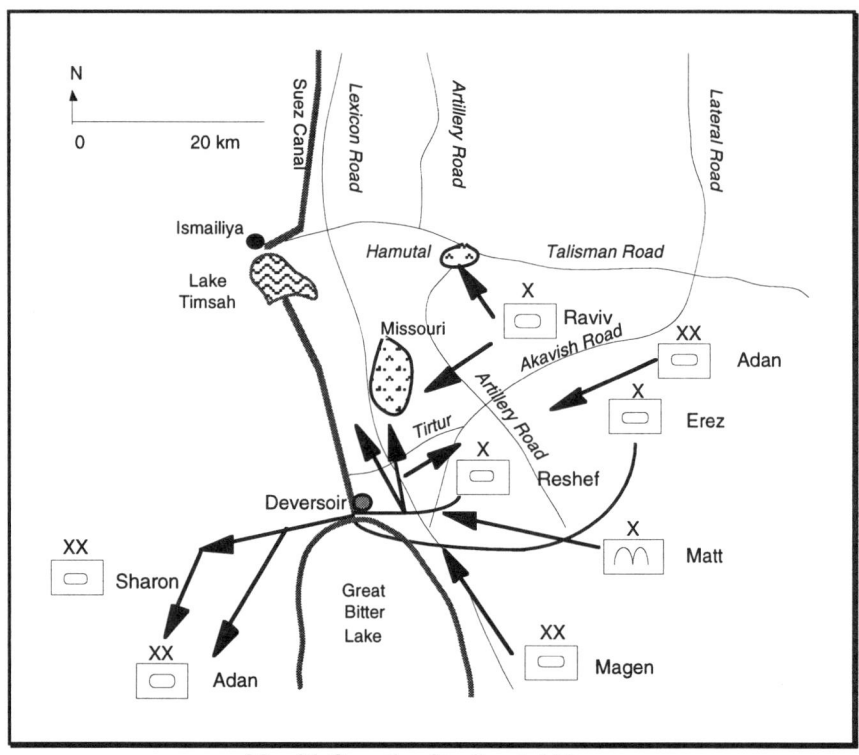

Map 16. Operation Stouthearted Men.

During the night of 15–16 October, after Reshef secured Deversoir, Colonel Danny Matt's six hundred paratroopers would cross to the west bank, supported by a tank company from the Erez Armored Brigade. Another tank company from that brigade would then tow a preconstructed bridge to Deversoir via Akavish Road. Once in place, the remainder of the Erez Armored Brigade would cross to secure the bridgehead on the west bank. Sharon's command and control would stretch from Raviv, east of Artillery Road, to Matt, west of Deversoir.

In Operation Stouthearted Men, terrain favored the defender. Two roads led to the area of Deversoir: Akavish, three and a half to four meters in width, was the only paved road, connecting Tasa with the Great Bitter Lake. Tirtur was a dirt track, north of Akavish, but it offered the most direct route to the crossing site at Deversoir. Key terrain features for the crossing operation were the Chinese Farm and Missouri, both held by the Egyptians. The Chinese Farm, a large agricultural area of crops and irrigation dikes four to six kilometers from the Suez Canal, offered ideal terrain for defensive positions. Both Akavish and Tirtur Roads passed through the Chinese Farm to reach the canal. The hill known as Missouri touched the northeastern portion of the Chinese Farm, providing the Egyptians with a dominating position.

The EAF faced challenges in resisting the Israeli countercrossing. Egyptian operational reserves were spread over a large area on the west bank. Egyptian commanders had to concentrate them quickly if they were to defeat the first Israeli forces crossing to the west bank. This required accurate and timely intelligence of enemy movements, and then a quick and appropriate response. General Command thus faced the formidable task of formulating a plan and coordinating a major counterattack by widely dispersed forces. The Israeli countercrossing would prove a test of how well the Egyptians had reformed their armed forces for the 1973 war.

ISRAEL'S ASSAULT

At 5:00 P.M. on 15 October, the tenth day of the war, the IDF kicked off its crossing operation with an artillery barrage all along the Egyptian front.[39] Simultaneously with this display of firepower, Raviv launched his diversionary probes toward Missouri and Hamutal, managing to draw Egyptian attention to himself. Brigadier General Abd Rab al-Nabi Hafez, the commander of the Egyptian 16th Infantry Division, committed part of his divisional reserve to prevent an Israeli penetration into his bridgehead.[40] This response weakened Hafez's ability to respond to an Israeli attack on Second Army's southern flank.

At seven o'clock, two hours after Raviv's attack, Reshef embarked on his critical mission with ninety-seven tanks. His reinforced brigade comprised four tank and three infantry-paratroop battalions on half-tracks, along with a small reconnaissance unit. After reaching Lexicon Road, forward elements of the brigade moved quickly to secure the Deversoir crossing site. No Egyptians were present to offer resistance, so this part of the operation went without a hitch. The Israelis had clearly hit an Achilles' heel in the Egyptian bridgehead.

In establishing defensive positions for the 16th Infantry Division, Hafez had failed to secure his southern flank properly. His bridgehead should have extended south of Deversoir to encompass the Israeli strong point at the northern tip of the Great Bitter Lake, but it did not. Instead, the 16th Infantry Brigade, under the command of Brigadier General Abd al-Hamid, located its southernmost defenses on a small ridgeline three or four kilometers north of Deversoir.[41] This tactical error was nearly fatal for the EAF. Reshef's line of advance south of the Chinese Farm and then north along Lexicon Road ensured the Israeli capture of the crossing site at Deversoir without combat. Here, the Egyptian army repeated its mistakes at the 1967 battles of Rafah and Abu Ageila, when local commanders had failed to secure a flank, which the attacking Israelis exploited as their main effort. In the Six Day War, these two blunders had set in motion a series of tactical events that led to the collapse of the entire army in the Sinai. Seven years later, however, the Egyptians would escape such a fate.

After reaching the crossing site, Reshef divided his armored brigade's attack into three prongs: the 7th Armored Battalion heading north along Lexicon, with the 42d Infantry Battalion and a couple of tank platoons trailing to mop up in its wake; the 18th Armored Battalion turning northeast to take Missouri from the rear; and the 40th Armored Battalion clearing Tirtur and Akavish Roads from west to east. Meanwhile, two paratroop companies and a reduced tank company would clear the area west of the Chinese Farm. Reshef held one paratroop battalion as his reserve.

Matters began positively for Reshef but quickly turned desperate. After seizing the Deversoir area, the Israeli 7th Armored Battalion moved north along Lexicon, managing to avoid any Egyptian resistance until some four kilometers north of Deversoir. Simultaneously, the Israeli 18th Armored Battalion, heading northeast, stumbled into an Egyptian administrative area, sparking alarms throughout the 16th Infantry Division. Within minutes, a major firefight broke out between Egyptian defenders and Israeli attackers. Much of the fighting took place at close quarters, and Reshef found himself, a brigade commander, having to fire his vehicle's machine gun to avoid capture. Egyptian soldiers with anti-tank weapons inflicted many casualties, forcing Reshef to order the 7th Armored Battalion back several kilometers to the south and to form a defensive line with the 18th Battalion.

At 4:00 A.M. on 16 October, after heavy fighting most of the night, Reshef's tanks had dwindled from ninety-seven to forty-one, or fifty-six tanks in a mere twelve hours—a loss comparable to those of the Egyptian 3d Armored Brigade on 14 October. Reshef also counted over 120 men, including some forty officers, killed, wounded, or missing. Over the next several days, each company would see its the original commander and his replacement killed in action. At six in the evening, Reshef's inventory increased to eighty-one tanks, as Sharon released a tank battalion from Erez's and Raviv's armored brigades, and Adan assigned one of his division's tank battalions to him as well.[42] The entire assault force would experience intense fighting and heavy losses in men and equipment for every kilometer of ground gained.

After the war, many Israeli participants found it difficult to describe the horrors of the close combat in the Chinese Farm area. Sharon provided a poignant account of the carnage on the battlefield: "It was as if a hand-to-hand battle of armor had taken place. . . . Coming close you could see Egyptian and Jewish dead lying side-by-side, soldiers who had jumped from their burning tanks and died together. No picture could capture the horror of the scene, none could encompass what had happened there. On our side that night [15th–16th] we had lost 300 dead and hundreds more wounded."[43] This battle of attrition served Sadat's purpose, even though from an operational perspective the initiative was passing to the IDF.

Stiff Egyptian resistance prevented Reshef from accomplishing all his missions, but seizing the crossing site, thanks to the lack of Egyptian defenses there, proved fairly easy. The crossing of the Suez Canal could, therefore, proceed as planned. At 1:35 A.M. on 16 October, Matt began moving his six hundred paratroopers to the west bank. At 6:43, the first of thirty tanks traversed the Suez Canal on rafts. By eight o'clock, Matt had established a small bridgehead on the west bank, after which time Israeli tanks fanned out from his sector to destroy Egyptian SAM batteries. By the late afternoon, Israeli tankers claimed to have destroyed several missile sites, one about twenty kilometers from the Suez Canal, before returning to their base virtually out of fuel.[44] According to Egyptian sources, most of the missile sites recorded by Israelis as destroyed from long-range hits were actually dummy installations.[45] Whatever the reality, the Israeli assaults tipped off the Egyptian air defenders to the presence of Israeli forces on the west bank.

Despite his having crossed to the African continent, the Israelis failed to secure a wide corridor on the east bank to support Matt. The Egyptian 16th Infantry Brigade, which had seen little combat until now, repelled Israeli attempts to open up either Tirtur or Akavish Road for the bridging equipment. The Egyptian division commander dispatched the 18th Mechanized Infantry and the 14th Armored Brigades to help block the roads. Egyptian resistance virtually cut off the Israelis on the west bank, causing Dayan to recommend the operation be aborted. For the thirty-seven hours after 11:30 A.M. on 16 October, no more Israeli tanks crossed the Suez Canal; Southern Command concentrated its resources on securing a route to Matt.

Israel tried to reap political benefit from the crossing. Ignoring the precarious nature of the situation during the afternoon of 16 October, Meir went before the Knesset and announced that an Israeli force had crossed into Africa.[46] From a military standpoint, this announcement compromised the operation, by drawing the world's, and especially Egypt's, attention to it. Meir felt compelled to raise the morale of the Israeli nation with some good news from the Sinai front; therefore, she took the risk of making Operation Stouthearted Men public. Still, her revelation, despite the prime minister's best intentions, placed additional pressure on Southern Command to defeat the EAF.[47]

While Meir gloated before the Knesset, Sadat was delivering his first address of the war to the People's Assembly, unaware of the Israeli countercrossing. After his speech, the Egyptian president learned of Meir's statement that Israeli tanks had crossed to the west bank of the Suez Canal, and he turned to Ahmad Ismail for information. The ever-faithful war minister, relying on initial reports from the field, told Sadat that only seven or eight tanks had actually crossed. Rather than threatening Egypt, it seemed, the Israeli government was merely seeking to raise national morale in wake of the announcement of casualties on 14 October. Ahmad Ismail confidently assured Sadat that the Israelis posed no serious threat. "Our estimate is that this type of war of nerves with tanks will end with the destruction of these forces, even if we have to begin burning all the farms which are hiding these tanks."[48]

Meanwhile, Egyptian and Israeli commanders were confronting the new realities of the battlefield. The unexpected Egyptian resistance at the Chinese

Farm forced Israel's Southern Command to change its plan.[49] By late morning on 16 October, Bar-Lev, anxious about the fate of the small force on the west bank, ordered Adan to commit his *ugdah* to help open Akavish and Tirtur Roads. To clear out the Egyptians dug into dikes in the Chinese Farm required more infantry; Southern Command turned to the paratroop battalion under Colonel Uzi Yairi, which had been at Ras Sudar since the first day of the war and ordered its immediate dispatch to Tasa.

Arriving at ten o'clock that evening by helicopter, Yairi felt pressured to go immediately into action and clear Akavish Road, even though Southern Command had not provided him adequate intelligence about his adversary's forces—their size, combat power, or location. The four companies of the paratroop battalion, under Lieutenant Colonel Yitzhak Mordechai, set out, groping in the dark. At 2:30, the advance company came into contact with Egyptian defenders at ranges as close as two hundred meters, too close for artillery support. Dawn revealed the paratroopers pinned down in the open with heavy losses. Yairi's first requests for help did not elicit a quick response from Southern Command. Later in the day an armored force finally came to rescue the paratroopers, but it ran into Egyptian mines and Sagger missiles, losing a number of tanks. After heavy fighting lasting most of the day, Mordechai finally managed to extricate his battalion. The paratroopers had lost forty killed and a hundred wounded. Some paratroopers were down to one or two bullets.[50]

But the paratroop battalion's bloody effort had not been in vain. Elements of the Egyptian 16th Infantry Brigade, low on ammunition after heavy fighting with the Israeli paratroopers, withdrew from the Chinese Farm during the night of 17 October; the Israeli battalion, aided by armor, had in fact helped open up Akavish Road. But the intense fighting and heavy casualties had taken a palpable emotional toll. Dayan, who met the brigade commander on 21 October, later described his touching encounter with Yairi:

I found him worn out. I knew he had lost a lot of men in combat, but I had not expected to find him so downcast. His face bore an expression of ineffable sadness, and his eyes, swollen from lack of sleep, were—what was worse—without luster. We talked about his battle to open the access road to the Canal. Chaim Bar-Lev, who was with me, said, "Uzi, you suffered heavy casualties, but you opened the road!" Uzi held to his own: "The road was opened not by me but by the armor. I would like to be able to say that my unit did it, but this was not so. We had suffered seventy casualties because we went into action too hastily, without proper intelligence on the enemy's defenses."[51]

Contrary to Yairi's personal assessment, the paratroopers certainly had played an important role in opening the access road, but their accomplishment seemed to pale before so many casualties. A period of "peace" can make people forget that war against a determined foe is very bloody business.

EGYPT'S INITIAL REACTIONS

Egyptian soldiers and officers demonstrated unexpected resolve in the face of emerging serious threat to their rear. Their combat heroism placed obstacles in the Israeli path, making each gain of a kilometer by the Israelis a bloody affair. In the end, however, Egypt's political and military leadership failed to thwart the Israeli effort to encircle Third Army. In some respects, the Egyptians did indeed return to their old selves of 1967 as Elazar had told Meir after the 14 October offensive—but not completely.

On 16 October, Second Army directed the first major Egyptian response to the IDF's countercrossing operation. The 21st Armored Division deployed its 1st Armored Brigade with thirty-nine tanks between Lexicon Road and the Suez Canal; the 18th Mechanized Infantry Brigade with thirty-one tanks to reinforce the 16th Infantry Brigade, holding the Chinese Farm and Missouri; and the 14th Armored Brigade between the 16th Infantry and 3d Mechanized Infantry Brigades, as a reserve. Egyptian armored counterattacks pushed Reshef southward on Lexicon Road for several kilometers, while the mechanized infantry helped secure the defensive positions in the Chinese Farm sector. On the west bank, a reinforced battalion from the 116th Mechanized Infantry Brigade attacked Matt's small force. The Israelis defeated the Egyptians quickly, with Colonel Husayn Ridwan, the Egyptian brigade commander, losing his life in the operation (see Map 17).[52]

Word of the Israeli countercrossing reached Center Ten. Second Army reported only seven to ten Israeli tanks on the west bank and promised to deal with this threat in a most expeditious manner. Despite the apparent small size of the Israeli force and the confident words, Shazli and Gamasi decided to dispatch the 23d Armored Brigade from the strategic reserve as a precaution. The tank brigade deployed west of Deversoir on 17 October, though General Command opted not to employ it in the attack of that day.[53] In addition, General Command appointed a new commander for Second Army to replace Major General Saad Mamun, who had suffered a heart attack at 8:30 in the morning of 14 October. Major General Abd al-Munim Khalil, previously the commander of the Central District (Cairo), reached Ismailiya that evening.[54] Meanwhile, General Command made plans for dealing with the Israelis the next day.

At Center Ten, concern grew steadily throughout the day as reports filtered in of Israeli forces on the west bank. Fahmi, the air defense commander, pressed General Command to take decisive action to defeat the threat to his SAM batteries. Obviously, many more Israeli tanks were operating on the west bank than had been reported by Second Army. At 11:00 P.M. on 16 October, Sadat visited Center Ten to discuss the situation. Shazli recommended the withdrawal of armored forces—mainly the 21st Armored Division and the 25th Tank Brigade—from the east bank to handle the Israeli crossing on the west bank where the terrain and the air defense umbrella favored the Egyptians. Sadat and Ahmad Ismail opposed this view and urged a major attack on the east bank. Both men feared that any withdrawal of troops from the east bank would weaken morale,

218   THE ALBATROSS OF DECISIVE VICTORY

that Egyptian soldiers would recall when officers abandoned their units in the Six Day War. The ghost of 1967 thus haunted the senior commanders, making many Egyptians prisoners of their past. Shazli failed to change their minds.[55]

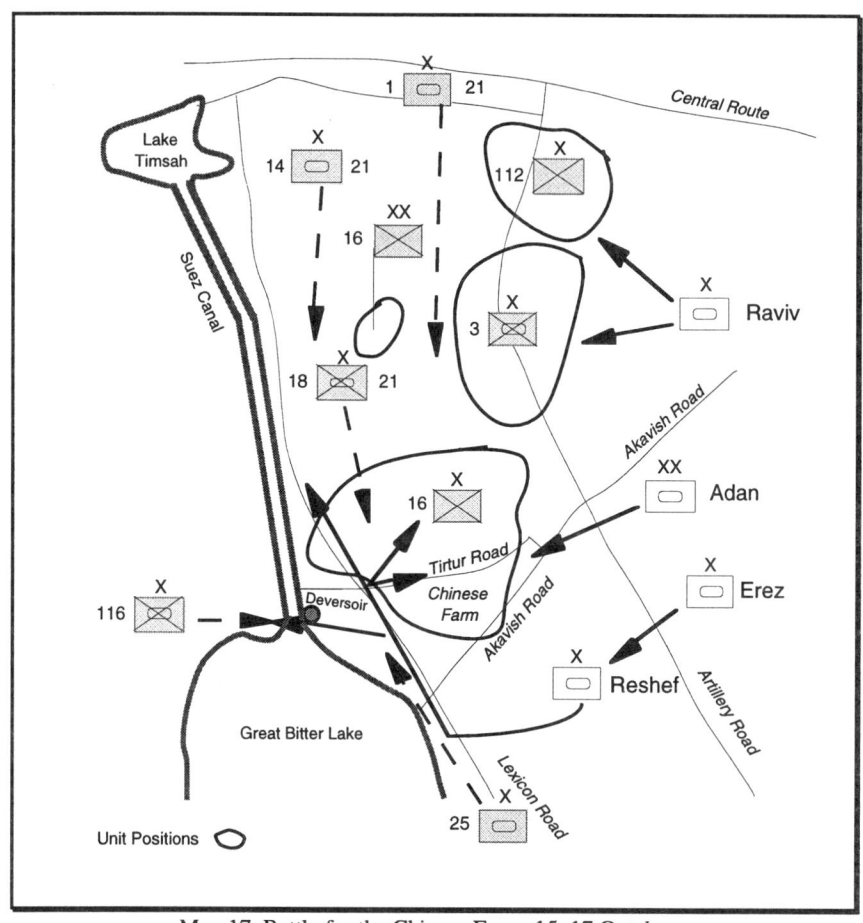

Map 17. Battle for the Chinese Farm, 15–17 October.

After his meeting with Sadat, Ahmad Ismail quickly developed his scheme of counterattack on the east bank. The remaining hundred tanks of the 21st Armored Division would attack the Deversoir crossing site, moving north to south. Meanwhile, the 25th Armored Brigade with its T-62s would strike south to north, from Third Army's sector. On the western side of the Suez Canal, a mechanized infantry battalion from the 116th Mechanized Infantry Brigade, supported by the 85th Paratroop Battalion, would assault the Israeli bridgehead. The war minister's decision to employ the 25th Tank Brigade on the east bank was highly questionable. In order to link up with the 21st Armored Division, the brigade had to move between the two field armies and outside the Egyptian bridgeheads. The route of advance was over thirty kilometers of terrain favorable for ambushes.

Israeli commanders responded quickly to intelligence of the Egyptian 25th Tank Brigade's movement.[56] Reshef stationed four tanks on Lexicon Road facing south. At 12:30, these tanks spotted advance elements of the Egyptian brigade and began firing on them. The Egyptians faithfully continued their slow advance to link up with the 21st Armored Division. Meanwhile, the Nir and Keren Armored Brigades established ambush positions along a ridgeline parallel to the Egyptian line of advance. At 2:45 in the afternoon, the Israelis suddenly sprang their trap, having held their fire until the Egyptians had unwittingly boxed themselves in. Reshef's tanks had assumed a blocking position in the north, with Nir taking the central position and Keren holding the southern part. By 5:15, the Egyptian brigade had been virtually destroyed.[57] Meanwhile, the 21st Armored Division stalled in its attack against the Israeli crossing site.

October 17 thus proved another defeat for the EAF. The 1st Tank Brigade lost twenty of its fifty-three tanks. Adan's ambush destroyed sixty-five of seventy-five T-62s of the 25th Tank Brigade; only ten tanks and seven armored personnel carriers managed to escape to safety. The battalion from the 116th Mechanized Infantry Brigade experienced similar destruction on the west bank; it redeployed in defensive positions to prevent an Israeli advance westward. A final setback befell the Egyptians. By the end of the day, as discussed in an earlier section, the Egyptian 16th Infantry Brigade pulled out of line to positions northward, thereby abandoning Akavish, though not Tirtur, Road to the Israelis.[58] The Egyptian defeat on October 17 would end the last good chance to defeat the Israeli countercrossing.

MORE ATTRITION BATTLES

Southern Command continued to focus on widening the narrow corridor on the east bank rather than on developing a main effort on the west bank. The burden of expanding the bridgeheads on both sides of the Suez Canal fell on Sharon. In the ensuing reconfiguration of missions, Sharon would no longer cross his division and then move southward to help Adan capture Suez City. Rather, Sharon was to advance northward on the west bank, three or four kilometers to block Egyptian bridges and, if possible, cut water and fuel pipelines to Second Army's bridgehead. On the east bank, the Reshef and Raviv Armored Brigades would attempt to seize Missouri and secure Akavish and Tirtur Roads.

Adan would cross with the Amir and Nir Armored Brigades during the night of 17–18 October, raising the number of Israeli tanks on the western shore to over a hundred. One brigade would head westward to destroy more Egyptian SAM batteries, while a second moved south to seize as much terrain as possible before the Egyptians regained their composure and occupied key positions. Only after these two missions were accomplished would Elazar allow the Reshef Armored Brigade to join Sharon on the west bank. Elazar also placed a gag on the IDF. Upset by Meir's public announcement of the initial countercrossing and by the increasing press coverage of tactical events, he ordered that no statements were to be made to the press about military operations unless coordinated with the IDF spokesperson.[59]

Sharon opposed these changes to the original plan. He wanted to garner his entire *ugdah* on the west bank, as the best way to destroy the Egyptian army on the east bank. For him, attempting to capture Missouri to widen the corridor was a waste of resources. Over the next several days, Sharon's efforts on the east bank would be half-hearted; instead, he concentrated his energies on the west bank. During this period, Bar-Lev, frustrated by this lack of cooperation, would request Sharon's firing, while Sharon would try to have plans changed by appealing to members of the cabinet, including Dayan. This command problem would receive much press coverage after the war.

Despite Sharon's opposition, Southern Command moved ahead with its new plan. During the night of 17–18 October, the Adan *ugdah*, minus the Keren Armored Brigade, finally crossed to the west bank, two days behind schedule.[60] The first unit set foot on African soil at 11:30 P.M. on 17 October; by the next morning, both Amir and Nir had moved their armored brigades to the west bank. Nir fanned out westward, while Amir headed southward. In addition to these two brigades, Israeli forces on the west bank included the Erez Armored Brigade, with thirty-eight tanks, and Matt's paratroop brigade, both under Sharon's command.

Matters continued to unravel for the Egyptians on 18 October. General Command drew upon its strategic reserves in an attempt to arrest the Israeli thrust on the west bank. While remnants of the 21st Armored and 16th Infantry Divisions attacked the Israeli bridgehead at Deversoir, the 23d Tank Brigade (from the 3d Mechanized Infantry Division) and the 85th Paratroop Battalion, both released from Cairo, and elements of the 116th Mechanized Infantry Brigade assaulted Sharon's and Adan's forces on the western shore of the Suez Canal. Again Israelis forces beat back the Egyptian attacks, inflicting heavy losses. Colonel Hasan Abd al-Hamid, commander of the 23d Tank Brigade, was wounded, forcing the chief of staff to assume command. The 85th Paratroop Battalion, for its part, suffered a hundred killed or missing, and it had to be withdrawn for reconstitution back to its base in Inshas, near Cairo.[61]

Though attacked from the west, Sharon still tried to advance northward along the western shore of the Suez Canal to cross the Sweet Water Canal, just south of Ismailiya, but Egyptian light infantry forces defeated his numerous attempts. Dense vegetation along the man-made waterway created excellent defensive terrain. In particular, the 170th Paratroop Brigade, from the strategic reserve, and 129th Commando Group used antitank weapons to block Sharon's attempt to push north and capture Ismailiya, a feat that would have threatened Second Army's logistical lifeblood. But the Egyptians paid a heavy price in men for their tactical success.[62]

Meanwhile, Adan was faring a little better than Sharon. Egyptian forces rallied at Tsach, preventing Adan from advancing westward. The Amir and Nir Armored Brigades managed to push south as far as the base of Gebel Geneifa, capturing Fayid airfield and destroying a number of Egyptian SAM sites so that the Israeli air force could begin providing air cover. With Egyptian resistance stiffer than expected, Adan requested the return of the Keren Armored Brigade, which Southern Command had commandeered as its operational reserve.[63]

At 1:05 in the afternoon on 18 October, Southern Command decided to reinforce the west bank. Bar-Lev released the Keren Armored Brigade from the front's reserve and returned it to Adan's command. During the night of the 18th-19th, Keren crossed with only two battalions, a total of forty to forty-five tanks, and linked up with Adan the next morning (19 October), raising the number of tanks in the *ugdah* to 170. Moreover, half of the Magen Armored *Ugdah*, some eighty tanks, received the order to cross that night as well. Finally, Yairi, of the Chinese Farm fame, was ordered to join his paratroopers to Sharon's *ugdah* on the west bank. As for Israeli forces left on the east bank, the Sasson *ugdah*, consisting of two brigades and a special task force of T-55 tanks, was deployed in the northern and central sectors; in the center, the Sharon *ugdah* had Reshef Armored Brigade in the Deversoir and the Chinese Farm areas, with the Raviv Armored Brigade facing Missouri; in the south, the remainder of the Magen *ugdah* regrouped as a task force under the command of Colonel Yisrael Granit.[64]

With additional forces on the west bank, Elazar made yet another adjustment to the operational plan. On 19 October, the IDF would have all of one *ugdah* and parts of two more on the west bank, some 250 tanks and over ten thousand men. Adan would head west of Gebel Geneifa and then toward Suez City. Meanwhile, Magen would follow Adan, protecting his flank. Sharon, for his part, would continue pushing northward to Ismailiya, while at the same time directing the capture of Missouri on the east bank. Much to Sharon's chagrin, Bar-Lev kept the Reshef Armored Brigade on the east bank, reinforced with additional tanks from other units (see Map 18).[65]

Absent in the new plan was the bravado of the earlier version, which had promised a quick and decisive defeat of the EAF. At nine o'clock in the evening of 18 October, while Magen was crossing with part of his division, Elazar appeared before the cabinet and provided a sober evaluation of the operation: "A battle is not being conducted according to the more optimistic model—the one that predicts the total collapse of the Egyptian army—but according to a realistic one. . . . The Egyptian army is not what it was in '67."[66] These words echoed those of Gonen uttered on 8 October.

Egyptian resistance had forced a change in Israeli thinking. A new factor now influenced the planning of operations: a concern for casualties, especially of elite infantry, which was always in short supply. Two weeks into the war, with the human losses growing daily, Israeli commanders began to assign greater weight to the factor of casualties when planning military operations.[67] A determined Egyptian foe continued to take a heavy toll of Israeli lives.

CRISIS IN EGYPT

Throughout the war, the Soviets, fearing an Arab defeat, tried to convince Sadat to end hostilities as quickly as possible. Finally, Brezhnev decided to make a more direct appeal. On 15 October, he ordered Premier Aleksei Kosygin to Cairo to seek an immediate cease-fire.

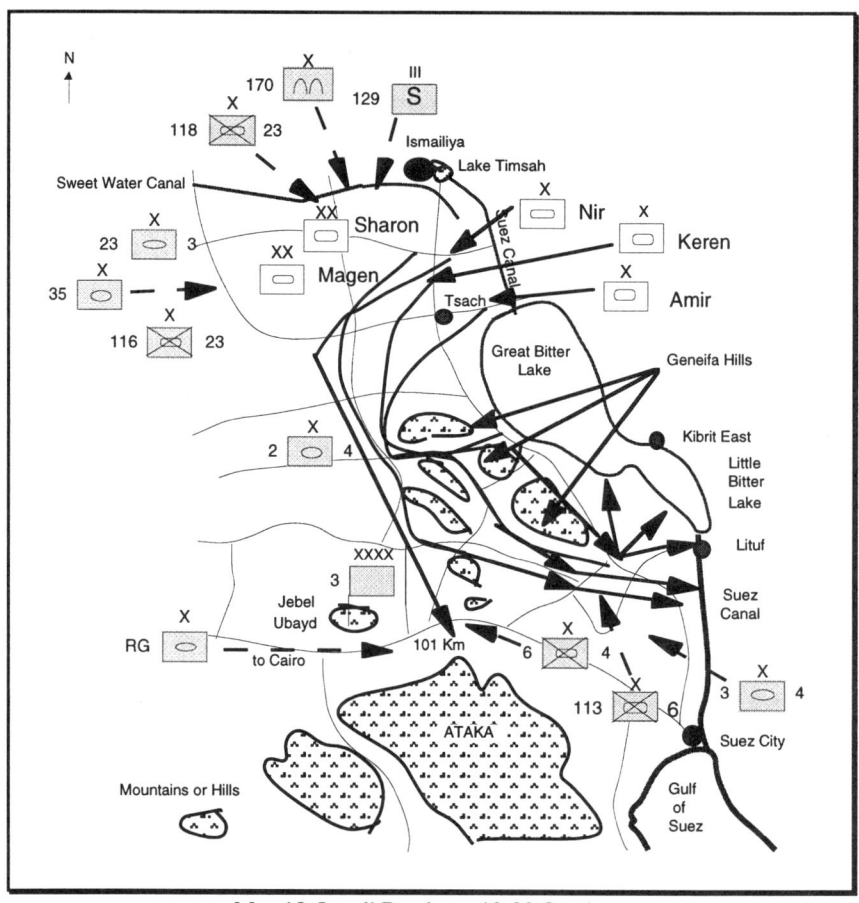

Map 18. Israeli Breakout, 19-22 October.

Kosygin arrived in Egypt on the evening of the 16th, and for the next three days (17–19 October) met with Sadat daily. The Soviet premier patiently tried to change Sadat's mind, but the Egyptian leader felt nothing would be gained unless he possessed some guarantee that Israel would withdraw from territories conquered in the Six Day War. On the 18th, Kosygin produced aerial photos showing the extent of the Israeli thrust on the west bank, but Sadat expressed confidence. Kosygin returned to Moscow somewhat dejected, having failed to obtain Sadat's assent to a cease-fire in place.[68]

On the 18th, the day before Kosygin's departure, Sadat decided to gain a better assessment of the war by personally visiting Center Ten, which he did at two in the afternoon. There the Egyptian president reversed his prohibition against the withdrawal of any forces from the east bank, giving permission for the recall of the 3d Armored Brigade to the west bank. Its new mission was to rejoin the 4th Armored Division to help prevent the Israelis from capturing the road from Cairo to Suez City. In addition to this redeployment, Sadat ordered Shazli to go to Ismailiya immediately and take command of Second Army, in the hope of defeating the Israelis on the west bank.[69]

Shazli faced an monumental task, for the Israelis on the west bank had gained the initiative. He arrived in Ismailiya at 5:30 and immediately took command of Second Army.[70] For the next forty-four hours, Shazli tried to defeat Israeli forces on both sides of the Suez Canal, but all his efforts proved for naught. Egyptian troops failed to seize either the IDF's crossing site on the west bank or the bridgehead on the eastern side. The EAF was even forced to abandon the Chinese Farm, thus opening up both Titur and Akavish Roads for Israeli use. On the positive side, however, a combined force of paratroopers and commandos prevented Sharon from reaching Ismailiya, and Missouri remained in Egyptian hands, a major obstacle to Israeli attempts to widen the crossing site on the east bank.

But General Command did not stop the Israeli advance to Suez City. Ahmad Ismail committed the entire 4th Armored Division, the 113th Mechanized Infantry Brigade, and the Republican Guard Tank Brigade, dispatched from Cairo. Unfortunately for the Egyptians, their counterattacks were delivered piecemeal and with insufficient numbers. The Egyptians often found themselves attempting to block Israeli advances instead of counterattacking. A lack of clear intelligence and slow command response hampered Egyptian operations.

Six days of intense fighting from 14 to 19 October finally took its toll on the Egyptian army. The 21st Armored Division was down to approximately forty tanks; the 16th Infantry Division's tank force had dwindled to around twenty from a prewar figure of 124.[71] Among the killed or wounded were two division (23d and 16th) and two brigade (116th and 23d) commanders. By 20 October, Egypt faced a critical situation on the battlefield.

After forty-four hours at Second Army's forward headquarters in Ismailiya, Shazli returned to Center Ten in the evening of 20 October and filed a pessimistic report, evaluating the military situation as critical. He insisted on the withdrawal of four armored brigades from the east to the west bank within twenty-four hours so as to prevent the Israelis from encircling the Egyptian forces on the east bank. Other senior commanders opposed such a transfer, some still fearing that withdrawing armored forces from the east bank might spark panic among the troops. Rather than overrule Shazli, who apparently had to co-sign key decisions, Ahmad Ismail called Sadat by telephone and requested his presence at Center Ten to make the critical decision.[72]

At 10:30 in the evening of 20 October, Sadat arrived at Center Ten to solve the impasse caused by Shazli's intransigence. The Egyptian president first met privately with his war minister, for close to an hour. Sadat then listened to the opinions of Gamasi, Mubarak (air force), Fahmi (air defense), Mahiy (artillery), and Nassar (military intelligence) at a general meeting. Each man, with the sole exception of Shazli, who chose to remain quiet throughout, provided an assessment of the situation. Years later, Gamasi and Fahmi would both claim that they opposed any pullback of main units, fearing that such a move would leave Egyptian forces on the east bank vulnerable to Israeli attacks. There was also concern about the effect on morale of such a move. After listening to his senior commanders, Sadat simply decided: "We will not withdraw a single soldier to the west."[73] With these few words, he promptly departed, not hinting what would be the next step

In one sense, this decision represented a change in Egypt's war strategy. Sadat had embarked on war more concerned with inflicting as many casualties on the IDF as possible than in capturing land per se. Now, well into the war, he and General Command were fixated on holding all territory captured on the east bank of the Suez Canal rather than on dealing with the threat posed by the IDF in the Egyptian rear. Wearing down Israeli forces should have remained the primary goal, and fighting the main effort on the west bank was the best way to do that. Concentrating forces in defensive positions to block the expansion of the Israeli bridgehead, rather than counterattacking against the crossing site as occurred on 17 October, made most sense in light of Sadat's strategy of bleeding Israel in battle. Moreover, the EAF's strength lay with the tactical defensive, not the offensive.

The Egyptian way of war emphasized the set-piece battle, meticulously planned and centrally controlled. For the crossing operation, General Command relied on combined arms, by which all other weapons systems assisted the infantry in its forward progress. Such a system experienced difficulty reacting quickly to the unexpected challenges produced by Operation Stouthearted Men. To launch counterattacks against advancing Israeli forces, Egyptian mechanized forces required careful planning and depended upon a methodical advance of all elements. Not blessed with time for these prerequisites, the Egyptians tended to respond in a dilatory, poorly coordinated, and piecemeal fashion. In this sense, the EAF resembled the French army trying to stop the German panzer divisions breaking through the Ardennes in May 1940.

The late meeting on 20–21 October troubled Sadat. Upon his return to Tahra Palace at 2:10 in the morning, Sadat called several senior advisors and informed them that he had decided to accept a cease-fire in place. As an explanation for this sudden change in a prior strategy of protracting the conflict, Sadat declared how his trip to the Center Ten had convinced him that the country and the armed forces were in grave peril and that the only option was to seek a cessation in hostilities, with the help of both superpowers.[74] Third Army's fate now rested squarely on diplomacy. But there was to be a bright side for Sadat in events on the diplomatic front.

WAR AND DIPLOMACY IN A FINAL RACE

In fact, diplomacy helped save the Egyptian Third Army from certain collapse. Soviet pressure and Arab oil, combined with Israel's military ascendance over both Egypt and Syria, convinced the Nixon administration to launch a diplomatic offensive in conjunction with the Soviet Union. By the end of the war, the United States had committed itself to work for peace in the Arab-Israeli conflict, exactly what Sadat wanted to accomplish by the war.

As Egypt's and Syria's fortunes declined on the battlefield, other Arab states rallied to help their brethren. On 17 October, the Arab oil-producing states raised the price of oil 70 percent, announced a 5 percent cut in production, and threatened to reduce output 5 percent every month until Israel withdrew from territories seized in the Six Day War. One day later, the Saudi government announced a 10 percent cut in output. Washington now made a rather unwise move. On 19 October, Nixon formally requested from Congress a $2.2 billion emergency aid package for Israel. Saudi Arabia promptly retaliated by placing an oil embargo on the United States; other Arab states quickly followed Riyadh's lead.

The military struggle between the Arabs and Israelis was now taking the added form of economic warfare. Arab announcements of price hikes and production cuts quickly shook stock markets around the world and heightened concern in Western Europe and Japan. As an oil crisis began unfolding, the Nixon administration, because of the Watergate scandal, moved on the diplomatic front to assert global leadership. On 19 October, Kissinger accepted a Soviet invitation to visit Moscow to discuss bringing hostilities to an end, departing just before the Saudis announced their oil embargo. The American delegation arrived in Moscow at 7:30 in the evening of 20 October.[75]

It was in this context that Sadat went to Center Ten late on 20 October to meet with his senior commanders, knowing that Washington and Moscow were both moving to end the armed conflict. Kissinger had used the secret channel to inform Hafez Ismail of his trip to Moscow.[76] This news definitely pleased Sadat, who had, after all, gone to war to elicit an American commitment to resolving the Arab-Israeli conflict. Hoping for a diplomatic breakthrough, the Egyptian president desperately wanted to keep all his bridgeheads intact, and it was for this reason that he remained adamant on not withdrawing any forces from the east to the west bank. In a phone conversation with his war minister before the meeting at Center Ten, Sadat expressed apparent hope of a political resolution: "Yes, Ahmad. Yes. We must take a chance and see what Kissinger will produce in Moscow."[77] Sadat needed a quick end to hostilities in order to be in a strong position after the war. On 21 October, the Egyptian president began desperate appeals to both the Americans and the Soviets for the quick implementation of a cease-fire.

The morning on 21 October found the IDF still debating the best course of action for the countercrossing operation. Elazar met again with Bar-Lev and Gonen at Southern Command's forward headquarters. Six days of heavy aerial and artillery bombardment had failed to dislodge the Egyptians from Missouri. Elazar remained adamant about widening the passage way to the west bank. Moreover, intelligence assessments indicated that the 16th Infantry Division had lost combat effectiveness and that the 21st Armored Division was down to a few tanks. The time thus appeared ripe for a major strike against Missouri. Sharon, however, advocated defeating Second Army by bypassing Ismailiya to the west and heading north for Qantara. He delayed action on any "suggestions" received to send forces back to the east bank.

To bring this maverick general in line, Bar-Lev flew by helicopter to Sharon's forward headquarters, intending in person to order an assault on Missouri. Aware of the possibility that a cease-fire loomed on the horizon, Southern Command felt compelled to seize a secure corridor to the west bank before foreign pressure halted offensive operations. Sharon had little choice but to comply with Bar-Lev's order to take Missouri, in conjunction with Sasson capturing Hamutal. With both the Reshef and Erez Armored Brigades on the west bank, Sharon relied on the Raviv Armored Brigade to act on the east bank

At 3:15, after experiencing delays in getting started, Raviv finally attacked with his forty tanks, supported by an additional five tanks from another unit. Meanwhile, a reduced armored battalion from Sasson attacked Hamutal and managed to capture and hold the eastern section of the hill, though not the western part. Raviv, however, failed to register any gains that day. He lost twenty-four men killed or missing, including eight officers, and more than twenty tanks, leaving less than twenty in the entire brigade. Missouri and the western part of Hamutal remained in Egyptian hands.[78]

That night, Elazar decided to try again to take Missouri and ordered Sharon to transfer the Reshef Armored Brigade back to the east bank for this purpose. Sharon resisted this order, instead arguing once again for a major effort on the west bank to surround Second Army. If Sharon and Adan could succeed in their missions, he was sure, both the Second and Third Armies would collapse, and Sadat's objective of seizing and holding territory on the east bank would be decisively defeated. Southern Command, however, saw matters differently. The Egyptians were threatening the narrow corridor to the west bank, and the Israelis needed to secure it before contemplating expanded missions on the west bank. Bar-Lev blamed Sharon for not supporting Raviv in his attempt to capture Missouri. Sharon, on the other hand, was livid, because he considered Raviv's attack unnecessary, he appealed above his superiors, to Dayan. The defense minister intervened and used his influence to persuade Elazar to call off any more attacks on Missouri.[79]

On the west bank, the Israelis fared a little better. By the end of 20 October, the IDF held a bridgehead extending twenty to twenty-five kilometers west of the Suez Canal and approximately sixty kilometers north to south. Some additional ground was gained on 21 October. Magen's *ugdah* remained in the center, essentially as a reserve. Sharon, for his part, seized a few more kilometers northward, when Amnon Reshef reached to the southern part of Lake Timsah. Adan, reinforced by an engineering and a paratroop battalion, the latter from the Golan front, had pushed south a little and was now in the plain south of Gebel Geneifa. Still, over thirty kilometers of tough terrain, filled with Egyptian camps and guarded by the 4th Tank Division, separated him from Suez City.

Meanwhile, on the diplomatic front, Kissinger reached an agreement on 21 October with the Soviets for a UN Security Council resolution calling for a cease-fire in place, to begin on 22 October at 6:52 P.M. A new sense of urgency now emerged in Israel when Meir received word of the Moscow agreement. Political wisdom dictated gaining as much ground from the Egyptians as possible for bargaining purposes after the war. Israeli operational plans for 22 October changed accordingly.

Sharon would extend his bridgehead westward and northward from the Suez Canal, with the aim of disrupting the flow of water and fuel to Second Army at the Sweet Water Canal. Meanwhile, Adan, instead of pushing south to reach Suez City, would now turn east and with all haste reach the Suez Canal at the southern tip of the Little Bitter Lake, opposite the Lituf strong point located on the east bank. In conjunction with Adan's mission, Force Granit would launch an attack on the east bank in order to capture Lituf, now held by Egyptian troops, and then establish a link with Adan on the west bank. This operation would give the IDF two supply routes for its forces on the west bank, one at Deversoir and the other at Lituf, thereby strengthening the Israeli bargaining position after the war. Meanwhile, Magen would dash toward the road from Suez City to Cairo in order to protect Adan's rear and allow him to concentrate on a east-to-west move toward the Suez Canal.[80] Diplomatic events were now directly influencing military objectives and operational tempo.

Adan, in accordance with his new orders, assigned missions to his brigades. Gabi Amir would continue pushing down the shoreline road along the Great Bitter Lake and then turn north to the point between the two lakes. Meanwhile, Aryeh Keren would stay on Amir's right with the aim of reaching the waterway south of Amir and opposite the captured Israeli strong point of Lituf. Natke Nir would shadow Keren, protecting his right flank.

To stop the Israeli advance southward, General Command possessed three armored and two mechanized infantry brigades. Of these forces, one tank and mechanized brigades had already suffered heavy losses; Third Army clearly needed additional forces. During the early hours of 22 October, Wassel ordered the 22d Tank Brigade, attached to the 19th Infantry Division, to transfer immediately a tank battalion to the west bank. Colonel Mustafa Hasan, the commander of the 22d Tank Brigade, would be killed in action on 22 October leading that battalion.[81]

Unfortunately for the Egyptians, Israeli ground forces had compromised Egypt's air defense umbrella. As later noted in a book published by three Egyptian major generals, the Israelis had driven "a deep bulge in [Egypt's] air defense system, which exposed the [Egyptian] forces holding the bridgehead of the Third Army to air attacks."[82] Throughout 22 October, the Israeli air force took advantage of this puncture. Israeli pilots provided ground support for advancing ground units and challenged Egyptian combat planes sent to bomb them.

Unable to defeat the advancing Israeli ground troops, Sadat decided to give Israel a warning of his long-range missile capabilities. On 22 October, the Egyptians launched two SCUDs against Deversoir, to demonstrate to Israel that Egypt could reach Israeli cities.[83] Unfortunately, the missiles missed their targets, demonstrating only their lack of precision. These SCUDs were controlled by Soviet crews, and only Moscow could have permitted their launching. Apparently the Soviet embassy in Cairo had failed to reach the foreign minister, Andrei Gromyko, for that green light, and the Soviet defense minister had given the approval.[84] Sadat no doubt took this action in a calculated attempt to strengthen his bargaining position after the war.

When the cease-fire finally came into effect at 6:52, Adan had failed to reach his objectives along the Suez Canal. Consequently, Israeli forces, rather than observe the UN resolution for an immediate cessation of hostilities, continued fighting into the night. Israeli brigade commanders pressed their units to reach their objectives. Keren especially felt pressure to reach the Suez Canal opposite Lituf; he ordered Lieutenant Colonel Elyashiv Shimshi, a tank battalion commander, to advance despite the cease-fire. Shimshi stumbled into an Egyptian camp and engaged in a fierce firefight during the night. Finally, he refused to continue unless he received additional infantry to fight through a greenbelt. Finally at one o'clock in the morning of 23 October, Keren backed down and gave him permission to withdraw. Shimshi abandoned nine of his eighteen tanks, each remaining tank having to transport two crews.[85]

On the east bank, Granit did no better than Keren. The Egyptians defeated all Israeli attempts to capture the Lituf and Botzer strong points. An Israeli armored battalion lost half its force, nine tanks, in an attempt to seize Lituf. Another force tried to seize Botzer, known as Kibrit East to the Egyptians, a strong point just north of Lituf. Kibrit East was isolated, separated from Third Army's bridgehead. Its bridgehead included remnants of the 603d Infantry Battalion from the 130th Marine Brigade, some ten tanks from the 25th Independent Tank Brigade (destroyed on 17 October), a 120-mm mortar battalion, and an engineering company. From 22 October on, this small garrison managed to resist all Israeli attempts to defeat it.[86] Obviously, the IDF lacked sufficient forces on the east bank to establish a second corridor to the west bank.

When dawn finally came on 23 October, Israel's military situation was far from perfect. Only a single avenue of supply through Deversoir connected Israeli forces on the two banks of the Suez Canal. Moreover, some twenty kilometers separated the Adan and Magen divisions from Suez City. Israeli artillery fire could easily interdict the Suez-City-to-Cairo road, but the Egyptians still could, albeit with great effort, resupply Third Army on the east bank. As Elazar noted on 23 October, "They [the Egyptians] seem to sprout up there, and no matter how hard you batter them, the next morning they have the same number of men."[87] But Israel was determined to finish off the Egyptian Third Army, despite the cease-fire.

THE ENDING OF HOSTILITIES

Upon receiving word of Kissinger's deal with the Soviets in Moscow, Meir extended to the secretary of state an invitation to visit Israel to discuss the details of the agreement. Kissinger arrived in Israel at one o'clock in the afternoon of 22 October to present his case. Meir accepted a cease-fire in place to begin that day but asserted that a couple days more would have allowed the Israelis to defeat the Arabs. Before departing, Kissinger told the Israeli leadership, "I would understand if there was a few hours' slippage in the cease-fire deadline while I was flying home."[88] Events on the battlefield would extend those few hours into a two days.

Fortunately for Israel, UN Resolution 338, which called for a cease-fire in place, failed to provide for a peacekeeping force to supervise its implementation. This omission provided Israel an opportunity to continue its advance southward. Consequently, in the evening of 22 October the Israeli cabinet formally approved continued military operations if the Egyptians failed to observe the cease-fire.[89] For their part, Israeli field commanders, frustrated because they could interdict the road from Suez City to Cairo only with artillery fire, looked for any excuse to resume offensive operations and surround Third Army. Adan, whose *ugdah* had borne the brunt of the advance south toward Suez City, put it this way: "It was with a heavy heart that I came to the decision that we would have to finish off the job the next day."[90] On the morning of 23 October, Meir, who also was anxious to encircle Third Army, gave her approval for the resumption of offensive operations.[91]

This green light from the prime minister brought results for Israel. While Adan drove toward Suez City, Magen moved on his western flank toward the port town of Adabiyya, some fifteen kilometers south of Suez City. Magen effectively surrounded Third Army by capturing Adabiyya at eleven o'clock in the evening of 23 October. Cairo was now unable to supply Third Army by land, sea, or air. Some forty thousand Egyptian troops and 250 tanks were surrounded on the east bank, held hostage by the Israeli force on the west bank.[92] But the Israelis were themselves in a difficult situation, with a tenuous logistical line. Throughout 23 October, however, Egypt's General Command seemed at loss what to do other than commit any available forces to defensive positions or small counterattacks. Third Army pulled back its forward command center to the main headquarters to the south of Gebel Ubayd, signifying the abandonment of Suez City. It now fell to local commanders to try to save a desperate tactical situation.

Israel saw an opportunity to defeat decisively Third Army. At 1:30 A.M. on 24 October, Southern Command gave Adan permission to capture Suez City "provided it does not become a Stalingrad situation."[93] At the time of the commencement of the October War, Suez City had been essentially a ghost town, with only five thousand residents—mainly government officials, police, local militia, and oil and cement workers. But capturing a deserted town can be costly.

Urban warfare favors the defender; it presents serious challenges to any attacker. Suez City's narrow streets and tall brick buildings offered Egyptian defenders excellent cover to establish lethal ambushes. Israeli armor forces, for their part, lacked adequate infantry trained to conduct combined-arms operations in an urban setting. The EAF sought to take maximum advantage of this Israeli weakness. To bolster his defenses, Brigadier General Yusuf Afifi, commander of the 19th Infantry Division, sent additional forces, especially antitank teams, into the city. These regular units, with the town's police force and local militia, organized a popular defense of the city. Overall, some five thousand military and police personnel prepared for the Israeli onslaught. The Mosque of Martyrs became the central point of the resistance. On 24 October, Brigadier General Adil Islam was appointed to defend the city.

Israeli military intelligence estimated the Egyptian forces in the city as a commando battalion, two mechanized infantry battalions, and remnants of other small units. Apparently, senior Israeli commanders had no notion of serious Egyptian resistance. Consequently, Adan made a highly controversial decision to enter the town with his *ugdah*, which now numbered some 175 tanks, about sixty in each of the three armored brigades. Most of his tank battalions supported reduced armored infantry companies, not enough foot soldiers for city fighting.

At 5:20 A.M. on 24 October, the Israeli air force, supported by two artillery battalions from Adan's division, commenced bombarding the city. After the fire preparation, Israeli ground troops cautiously moved into town. The bitter battle lasted until dawn the next day. The experience of Nahum's armored battalion from Keren's brigade typified the problems of Israeli units in urban warfare. At 10:15, Nahum moved into the city with twenty-one tanks, seven armored personnel carriers, and eight half-tracks. The city's narrow streets channeled the battalion into a column stretching two and a half kilometers. Suddenly, at an intersection, Egyptian troops opened fire. "Within minutes nearly all the commanders were hit. In the entire battalion only four officers were left who could function; all the rest were slouched over in their turrets, dead or wounded. Control of the battalion was lost, the radio net jammed by too many cries for help. Some of the hit tanks had come to a halt, and the others could barely get by them. Some of the tanks and armored personnel carriers turned down side streets, some made it back, others were never heard from or seen."[94] A paratroop battalion trailing the column managed to extricate the tank crews.

By the end of the day, Adan ordered a general pullout from the city. Trapped Israelis soldiers had to fight their way out under the cover of darkness. Nir lost his deputy brigade commander and half his staff officers. In its failed assault on the town, Adan's *ugdah* suffered at least eighty killed, 120 wounded, and forty destroyed tanks, too heavy a cost for no tactical gain. After the war, grieving Israeli families would question the wisdom of storming a city whose capture had clearly not been essential for defeating Third Army; the Egyptians, on the other hand, would turn 25 October into a holiday commemorating the Israeli pullout from the city.

The continued fighting after 6:52 P.M. on 22 October had meanwhile spawned a superpower crisis. On 23 October, Sadat met four times with Vinogradov in the hope of enlisting strong Soviet action to stop Israeli offensive operations.[95] In response to Sadat's protests of Israeli truce violations, Tel Aviv claimed that the Egyptians had fired on Israelis first, thereby provoking the attack to seal Third Army's fate. As the battlefield situation became desperate for the Egyptians, Sadat appealed to both the United States and the USSR to send troops to enforce the UN cease-fire.

On 24 October, Moscow took action that added stress to the situation. Apparently, the Politburo had crafted a communiqué, mild in tone, to Washington expressing concern over Israeli actions. But Brezhnev decided at the last minute to add tough language: the IDF had to cease and desist with its military operations; if not, the Soviets were willing to dispatch combat troops to the Middle East, unilaterally if necessary. Brezhnev's note caught Washington awash in the Watergate scandal. Not wanting to appear weak to either the international community or to the American public, the Nixon administration opted for a decisive response.

Late on 24 October, Washington ordered all its armed forces to Defense Condition III, the highest state of readiness in peacetime, the first such global alert since the Cuban missile crisis of 1962. The Nixon administration wanted to send a clear signal to Moscow of how serious its opposition was to the dispatch of Soviet troops. Soviet intelligence quickly detected the new level of conventional and nuclear readiness in the United States and around the world. Brezhnev, confronted with possible escalation, backed down from his threat, and the international crisis began to subside quickly.[96] But both superpowers had now become deeply immersed in helping resolve the 1973 Arab-Israeli war, and Sadat could find some satisfaction in these turn of events.

To save Third Army, Sadat withdrew his demand for a joint American-Soviet force and agreed to a UN peacekeeping force. On 25 October, the UN passed another resolution for a cease-fire, this time dispatching an international force to Egypt to ensure compliance from both sides. Israel, under pressure from the United States, eventually allowed nonmilitary supplies to reach Suez City and the isolated Third Army. On 29 October, the first supply convoy crossed to the east bank. The plight of the Egyptian Third Army, however, was to remain precarious until the lifting of the blockade in February 1974.

Although the battlefield had become desperate for the Egyptians, all was not lost for Egypt militarily. Despite the setbacks in the latter half of the war, the EAF continued to resist with determination. A combined Egyptian commando and paratrooper force, for example, registered a tactical victory of strategic import by stopping Sharon's repeated attempts to surround Ismailiya; Second Army's position thus remained secure on both the east and west banks. Moreover, regular troops, militia, police, and townspeople continued to prevent Israeli forces from capturing Suez City, inflicting heavy casualties in the process. Further, to the surprise of everyone, including Sadat and senior officers back in Cairo, surrounded Egyptian forces on the east bank maintained their combat integrity. Finally, and perhaps most important for Sadat's war strategy, the IDF had suffered high casualties throughout the countercrossing operation. Elazar's cautiousness before the cabinet on 18 October thus proved well founded.

The IDF had clearly gained the initiative, seizing Egyptian territory and defeating Egyptian troops. Its progress on the ground, however, lacked the lightning speed of 1967. Adan required five days of virtually continuous fighting (19–23 October) to encircle, but not seize, Suez City. This "dash" to Suez City averaged only twenty kilometers per day, a far cry from the Six Day War when Israeli armor had traversed 250 kilometers in four days, with the first day devoted to breakthrough assaults on fortified Egyptian positions.[97] But to its credit, the IDF held Third Army hostage on the east bank (see Map 19).

CONCLUSION

Despite the setbacks suffered in the first four days of the war, the IDF turned the tide of war in its favor after the EAF launched its ill-fated offensive on 14 October. Southern Command boldly tried to defeat the EAF on the west bank. Numerous problems and mistakes plagued the Egyptian military in the latter half of the war. First of all, Second Army, and later General Command, failed to respond in a timely fashion to the Israeli countercrossing. Piecemeal, uncoordinated, and dilatory counterattacks characterized the Egyptian responses. The EAF clearly suffered from an overly centralized command system, with a reaction time too slow for fighting the more agile IDF.

Despite Israeli operational and tactical successes, the last ten days or so of the war offered sobering combat experiences for Israel. During this final phase, the EAF exacted a heavy toll in Israeli blood and treasure. In this regard, Egyptian field officers and line troops made up for their senior command's seeming paralysis, by fulfilling Sadat's strategic objective of inflicting on the IDF the greatest possible losses in men and equipment. Furthermore, this new Egyptian combat staying power prevented the IDF from achieving a decisive military victory.

Yet, despite all the bright spots for the EAF, the IDF clearly gained ascendence on the battlefield in the second half of the war. In this respect, Israelis could claim, with deserved pride, a major military accomplishment. But a final evaluation of the war's significance had to await the political ramifications within Israel in the postwar period.

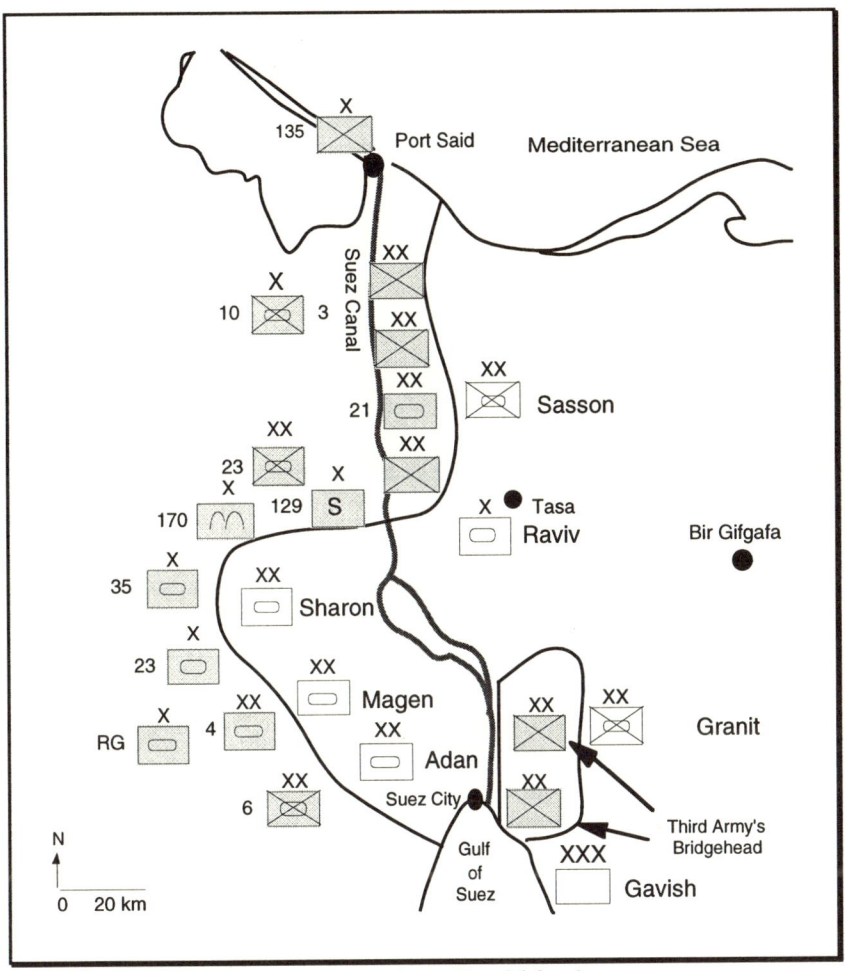

Map 19. Second Cease-Fire, 25 October.
[Note: Virtually all forces are seriously depleted in combat power.]

NOTES

1. Sun Tzu, *The Art of War*, translated by Samuel Griffith (London: Oxford University Press, 1963): 85.

2. Carl von Clausewitz, *On War*, translated by Michael Howard and Peter Paret (Princeton, NJ: Princeton University Press, 1983): 96.

3. Gamal Hamad, *al-Maarik al-Harbiyya ala al-Gebha al-Misriyya: Harb Oktobir 1973 al-Ashr min Ramadan* (Cairo: al-Zuhra lil-Ilam al-Arabi, 1989): 233–238, 759–778; Saad Shazli, *The Crossing of the Suez* (San Francisco: American Mideast Research, 1980): 241-242; and Chaim Herzog, *The War of Atonement, October 1973* (Boston: Little, Brown, 1975): 200.

4. Sayyid Mari, *Awraq Siyasiyah*, III (Cairo: al-Maktab al-Misri al-Hadith, 1979): 727–755; Muhammad Hasanyan Haykal, *Oktobir 1973: al-Silah wa al-Siyasat* (Cairo: al-

Ahram, 1993): 373; and Muhammad Hafez Ismail, *Amn Misr al- Qawmi fi Asr al-Tahaddiyat* (Cairo: Markaz al-Ahram lil-Targama wa al-Nashr, 1987): 325.

5. Henry Kissinger, *Years of Upheaval* (Boston: Little, Brown, 1982): 491–496; and William B. Quandt, *Peace Process: American Diplomacy and the Arab-Israeli Conflict, 1967–1976* (Washington, DC: Brookings Institute, 1993): 157.

6. Hanoch Bartov, *Dado: 48 Years and 20 Days* (Tel Aviv: Ma'ariv, 1981): 423. For the presence of TOWs in Israel before the war, James R. Schlesinger, brief conversation with author, 10 October 1998, Washington, DC.

7. Anwar Sadat, *In Search of Identity* (New York: Harper and Row, 1977): 253–254; Muhammad Hassanayn Haykal, *The Road to Ramadan* (New York: Quadrangle, 1975): 213–214; and Victor and Israelyan, *Inside the Kremlin During the Yom Kippur War* (University Park: Pennsylvania State University Press: 1995): 57.

8. Shazli, *Crossing the Suez*, 275; Hamad, *al-Maarik al-Harbiyya*, 502–505; and Israelyan, *Inside the Kremlin*: 58–61.

9. Abba Eban, *Abba Eban: An Autobiography* (New York: Random House, 1977): 514–515; Bartov, *Dado*: 444; Michael Brecher, *Decisions in Crisis: Israel, 1967 and 1973* (Berkeley: University of California Press, 1980): 214–215; Quandt, *Decades of Decision*: 180–183; and Ariel Sharon, *Warrior: The Autobiography of Ariel Sharon* (New York: Simon and Schuster, 1989): 310.

10. Sadat, *In Search of Identity*: 256–258; Kissinger, *Years of Upheaval*: 516–518; and Ismail, *Amn Misr al-Qawmi*: 326–327.

11. Kissinger, *Years of Upheaval*: 502.

12. Golda Meir, *My Life* (New York: G. P. Putnam's Sons, 1975): 431.

13. Trevor Dupuy, *Elusive Victory: The Arab-Israeli Wars, 1947–1974* (1978 reprint, Fairfax, VA: Hero Books, 1984): 567–569; and Julian Thompson, *The Lifeblood of War: Logistics in Armed Conflict* (London: Brassey's, 1991): 231.

14. For the struggle over the Golan Heights, see Jerry Asher and Eric Hammel, *Duel for Golan: The 100-Hour Battle That Saved Israel* (New York: Morrow, 1987); Dupuy, *Elusive Victory*: 436–469; Edgar O'Ballance, *No Victor, No Vanquished: The Yom Kippur War* (San Rafael, CA: Presidio Press, 1978): 119–146; and Herzog, *War of Atonement*: 78–145.

15. Material on the SAF comes from numerous sources: Alasdair Drysdale, "The Syrian Armed Forces in National Politics: The Role of the Geographic and Ethnic Periphery," in *Soldiers, Peasants, and Bureaucrats*, edited by Roman Kolkowicz and Andrej Korbonski (London, 1982): 52–76; Hanna Batatu, "Some Observations on the Social Root's of Syria's Ruling Military Group and the Causes for Its Dominance," *Middle East Journal* 35 (1981): 331–344; Mustafa Khalil, *Suqut al-Jawlan* (Cairo: Dar al-Itisam, 1980): 13–33; and Maoz Moshe, "Alawi Military Officers in Syrian Politics, 1966–1974," in *Military and State in Modern Asia*, edited by Harold Z. Schiffrin (Jerusalem, 1976): 277–297.

16. Israelyan, *Inside the Kremlin*: 73.

17. Moshe Dayan, *Moshe Dayan: The Story of My Life* (New York: William Morrow, 1976): 516–519; Bartov, *Dado*: 409–415; and Brecher, *Decisions in Crisis*: 211–213.

18. Muhammad Abd al-Ghani al-Gamasi, *Mudharikat al-Gamasi: Harb Oktobir 1973* (Paris: al-Munshurat al-Sharqiyya, 1990): 378; and Dupuy, *Elusive Victory*: 465.

19. Israelyan, *Inside the Kremlin*: 67.

20. Shazli, *Crossing of the Suez*: 246–247; Gamasi, *Mudharikat*: 385–386; Muhammad Abd al-Ghani Gamasi, interview with author, 25 June 1994, Cairo, Egypt; Haykal, *Oktobir*: 432; and Hamad, *al-Maarik al-Harbiyya*: 289–290.

21. Gamasi, *Mudharikat*: 402; and Adil Yusri, *Rihla al-Shaq al-Mualaqa: min Ras al-Ush ila Ras al-Qubra* (Cairo: Dar al-Muarif bi-Misr, 1974): 232.

22. Shazli, *Crossing of the Suez*: 243–246; Gamasi, *Mudhakirat*: 385, 405–406; and Haykal, *Oktobir*: 432.

23. Gamasi, *Mudharikat*: 402; Hamad, *al-Maarik al-Harbiyya*: 298, 306; and Talat Ahmad Musallam, interview with author, 10 October 1998, Washington, DC.

24. Muhammad Ali Fahmi, interview with author, 21 October 1996, Leavenworth, Kansas.

25. Avraham Adan, *On the Banks of the Suez* (Novato, CA: Presidio Press, 1980): 236. For the best information on Israeli forces at this point in the war, see Pierre Razoux, *La Guerre Israélo-Arabe d'Octobre 1973: Une Nouvelle Donne Militaire au Proche-Orient* (Paris: Economica, 1999): 146–149, 155–157.

26. This assessment of the 14 October offensive comes from various sources, including discussions with Egyptian officers attending the U.S. Army Command and General Staff College, Fort Leavenworth, Kansas. See Hamad, *al-Maarik al-Harbiyya*: 308–312, 829–832; and Hasan Mustafa, *Maarik al-Jabhah al-Misriyya fi Harb Ramadan* (Baghdad, 1982): 370–380.

27. Shazli, *Crossing of the Suez*: 244; and Gamasi, *Mudharikat*: 403.

28. Hamad, *al-Maarik al-Harbiyya*: 315; and Egyptian officer, interview with author, Fort Leavenworth, Kansas.

29. Egyptian material comes from Hamad, *al-Maarik al-Harbiyya*: 303, 373–374; Abd al-Munim Khalil, *Hurub Misr al-Muasirah fi Awraq Qaid Maydani: 1939–1945, 1956, 1962–1967, 1968–1970, 1973* (al-Qahirah: Dar al-Mustaqbal al-Arabi, 1990): 206; and Musallam, interview. For Israeli versions, see David Eshel, "The World's Great Tank Battles: October 14, 1973," *Born in Battle* 8 (January 1980): 32–34; and Sharon, *Warrior*: 310.

30. Eshel, "The World's Great Tank Battles": 36–37.

31. Hamad, *al-Maarik al-Harbiyya*: 282–289; and author's discussion with Egyptian officer from that brigade. I have been unable to find any figures on human casualties.

32. "Israel Reports 656 Killed in War," *New York Times*, 15 October 1973: 18.

33. Meir, *My Life*: 432.

34. Bartov, *Dado*: 469–472.

35. Shazli, *Crossing of the Suez*: 248–250.

36. Haykal, *Road to Ramadan*: 238.

37. Hamad, *al-Maarik al-Harbiyya*: 104, 359–360, 508–509; and Amin Huwaydi, *al-Furus al-Daia: al-Qararat al-Hasima al-Istinzaf wa Oktobir* (Beirut: Shirka al-Matbuat lil-Tawzi wa al-Nashr, 1991): 401–402.

38. Adan, *On the Banks of the Suez*: 252–254, 334; Bartov, *Dado*: 471, 476–479; Sharon, *Warrior*: 311–313; and Herzog, *War of Atonement*: 209–210.

39. Material for Israeli perspectives on the battle for Deversoir comes mainly from Herzog, *War of Atonement*: 210–222; Adan, *On the Banks of the Suez*: 263–273; Sharon, *Warrior*: 313–324; Amnon Reshef, interview with author, 30 June 1994, Tel Aviv, Israel; and Danny Matt, interview with author, 6 July 1994, Tel Aviv, Israel.

40. Colonel Darwish Hasan Darwish, interview with author, 29 April 1988, Fort Leavenworth, Kansas. Darwish was a company commander in the 16th Infantry Brigade during the battle.

41. Darwish, interview; Gamasi, interview, 25 June 1994; Khalil, *Hurub Misr al-Muasirah*: 197; and Hamad, *al-Maarik al-Harbiyya*: 343.

42. Reshef, interview. See also Adan, *On the Banks of the Suez*: 263–270, 276–278; Dayan, *Moshe Dayan*: 530; and Herzog, *War of Atonement*: 211–217.

43. Sharon, *Warrior*: 316.

44. Matt, interview; Adan, *On the Banks of the Suez*: 266–267, 271–273; Sharon, *Warrior*: 315; and Herzog, *War of Atonement*: 217–221.

45. Muhammad Ali Fahmi, interview with author, 21 October 1996, Leavenworth, Kansas; and discussions with Egyptian air defenders attending US Army Command and General Staff College, 1995–97.

46. Charles Mohr, "Israel Sends a Task Force behind the Egyptian Lines," *New York Times*, 17 October 1973: 1.

47. Bartov, *Dado*: 492–493.

48. Haykal, *Oktobir*: 466–467; and *Road to Ramadan*: 230–231.

49. Adan, *On the Banks of the Suez*: 274–297; Herzog, *War of Atonement*: 223–230; and Bartov, *Dado*: 482–495.

50. Giora Eyland, interview with author, 6 July 1994, Tel Aviv, Israel. During the war, Eyland was a young officer in the paratroop battalion; at the time of the interview, he commanded the Infantry and Paratroop Corps. See also Adan, *On the Banks of the Suez*: 280, 284–295; Bartov, *Dado*: 488, 496–499; and Ze'ev Schiff, *October Earthquake: Yom Kippur 1973* (Tel Aviv: University Publishing Projects, 1974): 242–244; and Herzog, *War of Atonement*: 225–226.

51. Dayan, *Moshe Dayan*: 534–535. For a similar assessment, see Bartov, *Dado*: 159.

52. Hamad, *al-Maarik al-Harbiyya*: 345–348, 360–364, 373–375, 425–430.

53. Gamasi, *Mudhakirat*: 411–416.

54. Khalil, *Hurub Misr al-Mu'asirah*: 13–15.

55. Shazli, *Crossing the Suez*: 253–255; Haykal, *Oktobir*: 473–474; and Khalil, *Hurub Misr Al-Muasirah*: 205–206.

56. Bartov, *Dado*: 493.

57. Aryeh Keren, interview with author, 4 July 1994, Israel; Adan, *On the Banks of the Suez*: 301–307; and Herzog, *War of Atonement*: 227–228.

58. Shazli, *Crossing the Suez*: 256–260; Gamasi, *Mudhakirat*: 416–417; Khalil, *Hurub Misr al-Muasirah*: 206; and Hamad, *al-Maarik al-Harbiyya*: 396–413, 426–437.

59. Bartov, *Dado*: 503–507; Adan, *On the Banks of the Suez*: 298–299: and Sharon, *Warrior*: 326–329.

60. Israeli sources on the last part of the war include Adan, *On the Banks of the Suez*: 308–438; Bartov, *Dado*: 505–579; and Herzog, *War of Atonement*: 234–250.

61. Shazli, *Crossing the Suez*: 260; Khalil, *Hurub Misr al-Muasirah*: 209–210, 230; and Hamad, *al-Maarik al-Harbiyya*: 437, 470–473, 481–482.

62. Herzog, *War of Atonement*: 238–239; and Hamad, *al-Maarik al-Harbiyya*: 474–479, 482, 601.

63. Adan, *On the Banks of the Suez*: 318–326; Herzog, *War of Atonement*: 242–243; and Hamad, *al-Maarik al-Harbiyya*: 490–492.

64. Bartov, *Dado*: 511; Keren, interview; and discussions with Israeli officers attending US Army Command and General Staff College.

65. Bartov, *Dado*: 514–515, 518–519; and Adan, *On the Banks of the Suez*: 327–328, 345.

66. Bartov, *Dado*: 515.

67. Adan, *On the Banks of the Suez*: 368. See also Bartov, *Dado*: 557.

68. Israelyan, *Inside the Kremlin*: 89–114; Sadat, *In Search of Identity*: 258–259; and Haykal, *Road to Ramadan*: 235.

69. Shazli, *Crossing of the Suez*: 262–63.

70. The following discussion of the EAF's actions is the result of a careful sifting of often conflicting information. Khalil, *Hurub Misr al-Muasirah*: 187–188, 212–216, 223, 230; Hamad, *al-Maarik al-Harbiyya*: 484–486, 489–494, 497–501, 623, 679–681; Shazli, *Crossing of the Suez*: 260–267; and Haykal, *Oktobir*: 486–517.

71. Hamad, *al-Maarik al-Harbiyya*: 674–677.

72. Shazli, *Crossing of the Suez*: 265–267; Gamasi, *Mudhakirat*: 419–421; Gamasi, interview, 25 June 1994; Muhammad Ali Fahmi, interview with author, 22 June 1994, Cairo; Hamad, *al-Maarik al-Harbiyya*: 641–642, 665; and Haykal, *Oktobir*: 501. In their accounts, Shazli and Haykal wrongly describe the meeting as taking place on the night of 19/20 October.

73. Gamasi, interview, 25 June 1994; Fahmi, interview, 22 June 1994; Shazli, *Crossing of the Suez*: 265–267; and Gamasi, *Mudhakirat*: 419–421.

74. Haykal, *Oktobir*: 511, 518, 523–528; and Ismail, *Amn Misr al-Qawmi*: 344–346.

75. For a discussion of the diplomatic developments, see Kissinger, *Years of Upheaval*: 532–568; Quandt, *Peace Process*: 166–171; Dayan, *Moshe Dayan*: 537–538; and Donald Neff, *Warriors against Israel: How Israel Won the Battle to Become America's Ally* (Brattleboro, VT: Amana, 1988): 241–274.

76. Haykal, *Oktobir*: 500–501, 812.

77. Haykal, *Road to Ramadan*: 237; and *Oktobir*: 503.

78. For the day's events on the east bank, see Bartov, *Dado*: 534–542; Adan, *On the Banks of the Suez*: 372–375; and Sharon, *Warrior*: 329–330.

79. Bartov, *Dado*: 547; Adan, *On the Banks of the Suez*: 375–377; and Sharon, *Warrior*: 330–331.

80. Adan, *On the Banks of the Suez*: 379–383; Bartov, *Dado*: 549; and Herzog, *War of Atonement*: 245–246.

81. Hamad, *al-Maarik al-Harbiyya*: 683.

82. Hasan al-Badri, Taha al-Magdub, and Muhammad Ziya al-Din Zohdi, *The Ramadan War, 1973* (New York: Hippocrene Books, 1978): 112.

83. Sadat, *In Search of Identity*: 265.

84. Israelyan, *Inside the Kremlin*: 143–145.

85. Material for the events of 22 October comes from Elyashiv Shimshi, interview with author, 7 July 1994, Tel Aviv, Israel; Keren, interview; Gabi Amir, interview with author, 6 July 1994, Tel Aviv, Israel; and Adan, *On the Banks of the Suez*: 379–399.

86. Hamad, *al-Maarik al-Harbiyya*: 413, 839–841; Bartov, *Dado*: 549, 551; and Herzog, *War of Atonement*: 246.

87. Bartov, *Dado*: 557.

88. Kissinger, *Years of Upheaval*: 569.

89. Dayan, *Moshe Dayan*: 538–539.

90. Adan, *On the Banks of the Suez*: 401–402.

91. Brecher, *Decisions in Crisis*: 173, 223–224.

92. Shazli, *Crossing the Suez*: 270; and Hamad, *al-Maarik al-Harbiyya*: 542.

93. For treatments of the battle for Suez City from different perspectives, see Adan, *On the Banks of The Suez*: 409–425; Hamad, *al-Maarik al-Harbiyya*: 535–586; and Glenn F. Rogers, "The Battle for Suez City," *Military Review* (November 1979): 27–33.

94. Adan, *On the Banks of the Suez*: 414.

95. Israelyan, *Inside the Kremlin*: 154.

96. Kissinger, *Years of Upheaval*: 568–611; Quandt, *Peace Process*: 171–177; Barry M. Blechman and Douglas M. Hart, "The Political Reality of Nuclear Weapons: The 1973 Middle East Crisis," *International Security* 7 (Summer 1982): 132–156; and Israelyan, *Inside the Kremlin*: 168–191.

97. Adan, *On the Banks of the Suez*: 437.

8

ASCENT OF THE DOVE

> The history of the twentieth century suffices to remind us that there are many ways to win a war, that the various ways are not equivalent, and that the final victory does not necessarily belong to the side that dictates the conditions of peace.
> —Raymond Aron[1]

> The gap between expectations of the Israeli Defense Forces and the way in which the war was actually conducted—being prolonged and with many casualties—caused a deep crisis. . . . The common expectations from the IDF were that any future war would be short with few casualties.
> —Avraham Adan[2]

As the violence drew to a close with the implementation of the second cease-fire under UN supervision, it was difficult to forecast the future of the Arab-Israeli conflict. Though caught off guard by the outbreak of hostilities, the IDF had reasserted its military power to take the initiative from the EAF and surround the Egyptian Third Army on the east bank. Israel had gained a major strategic advantage for postwar negotiations. Sadat, for his part, could claim successes in the war as well. Militarily, his army had crossed the Suez Canal and captured the Bar-Lev Line. Moreover, the EAF had inflicted heavy casualties on the IDF throughout the war. Diplomatically, the United States had been forced to help broker the cease-fire.

Egypt and Israel could claim their own versions of victory. Now it remained to see exactly what impact the war would have on Israel and the United States. In the end, Sadat would gain the return of the Sinai through diplomatic means alone. To that degree, Sadat's war strategy thus proved successful.

DISENGAGEMENT OF FORCES

On 28 October, a peacekeeping force under the command of General Ensio Siilasvuo, a Finn, established checkpoints between the opposing forces. That same day, Egyptian and Israeli military representatives commenced disengagement talks, under UN auspices, in a tent located at Kilometer 101 on the Suez City to Cairo road. Any serious progress, however, depended on US involvement. Recognizing that, both belligerents made pilgrimages to Washington shortly after the second cease-fire. Egypt took the lead in this regard; Ismail Fahmi, the acting foreign minister, met with Nixon and Kissinger on 29 October. Meir did the same two days later. These meetings set in motion a five-and-a-half-year peace process.

Operation Stouthearted Men had clearly and unequivocally compromised Egypt's bargaining position after the war. It did not matter that Israel had violated the first cease-fire to encircle Suez City and Third Army; few Americans would quibble about how the Israelis achieved their military objective. By holding the first echelon of Third Army hostage on the east bank, Israel had placed Sadat in a desperate situation after the war; he could ill afford the humiliation of having to surrender forty thousand troops and 250 tanks. Thus, Egypt had to start its postwar negotiations with a demand for the immediate end to the encirclement of Third Army and the IDF's return to the battle lines of 22 October. Although initially Israel refused to budge on either demand, Washington pressured it to allow, under UN and Israeli supervision, the passage of nonmilitary supplies to the reinforced Egyptian 7th and 19th Infantry Divisions on the east bank.

Israel, despite a bargaining position stronger than that of Egypt by the mere fact of having surrounded Third Army, had its own vulnerabilities. Israeli negotiators wanted a quick resolution of two important issues: the return of all Israeli prisoners of war and the lifting of Egypt's naval blockade of Bab al-Mandab, at the entrance to the Red Sea.[3] Life was precious in Israel, and Israelis were especially sensitive over the fate of missing Israeli soldiers; some were dead, but there was hope that others were merely in captivity. The return of captives became a priority in disengagement talks at Kilometer 101. Egypt's blockade, of secondary importance in the short term, posed an economic burden and undermined Israel's right to unbridled use of international waters over the long term. Egypt thus possessed two items with which to barter in negotiations with Israel.

Washington, for its part, was determined to play the central role in any discussions between Israelis and Arabs, and Sadat desired such a serious American involvement. But the United States proved unable to assume the role of honest broker, for American national interests in the Middle East were based on maintaining Israel's dominant position in the region. This tenet of American foreign policy provided Israel a clear advantage in any negotiations involving the United States as a mediator. Sadat had to be fully cognizant of this reality and formulate policies and actions accordingly.

After Fahmi's and Meir's respective visits to Washington at the end of October, the United States moved to demonstrate its new resolve to bring progress to the Arab-Israeli conflict. On 6 November 1973, Kissinger arrived in Cairo to begin step-by-step diplomacy. Sadat, anxious to build a working relationship with the United States, wanted to appear conciliatory and reasonable in his discussions with the American secretary of state. Surprises, however, awaited all involved in the negotiations. The Egyptian president retreated from his insistence on the immediate pullback of Israeli forces to positions held at the time of the first cease-fire, that of 22 October. More importantly, Sadat agreed to return all Israeli prisoners of war, even though the IDF still held Egyptian Third Army hostage. Although this gesture of goodwill removed an important leverage over Israel, Sadat was determined to show flexibility and gain trust rather than haggle over specific details.

The above two concessions paved the way for Sadat and Kissinger to reach an agreement rapidly. It had six points:

- The scrupulous observance of the cease-fire
- The commencement of discussions for a return to the lines of 22 October and the separation of opposing forces
- The daily supply of water, food, and medicine to Suez City and the evacuation of all wounded civilians from the town
- No impediment of nonmilitary supplies to the east bank, with Israeli officers inspecting the cargo for weapons and ammunition prior to their crossing
- The replacement of Israeli checkpoints on the Suez-Cairo Road with United Nations soldiers
- Upon the implementation of the above point, the exchange of all prisoners of war, including the wounded.

The two men accomplished much in the first round of discussions after the 1973 war. The Meir government, spurred by the promise of a quick return of captured Israeli soldiers, gave its approval to the six-point agreement on 9 November. On 11 November, Israeli and Egyptian representatives signed the appropriate papers at Kilometer 101.

Sadat clearly wanted to break the diplomatic logjam as quickly as possible, but his main target was the United States, not Israel. Upon reaching his agreement with Kissinger, Sadat reportedly remarked to him: "Never forget, Dr. Kissinger. I am making this agreement with the United States, not with Israel."[4] The Egyptian leader was intent on establishing formal diplomatic relations with Washington, which would finally take place on 28 February 1974. In the interim, Egypt and the United States would exchang ambassadors in interests sections. In 1973, Sadat was clearly hoping that Washington would apply sufficient pressure on Israel for the return of occupied Arab lands.

Kissinger, after meeting with Sadat in Cairo, visited Amman and Riyadh. Washington assigned great importance to Saudi Arabia, because of the kingdom's vast oil reserves as well as its influence among the Arab Gulf states. The

Nixon administration wanted King Faysal's endorsement of a step-by-step approach to the Arab-Israeli conflict as well as his assistance in ending the oil boycott. King Faysal, despite his strong revulsion toward Zionism, gave his approval to Kissinger's strategy, promising to ease the oil embargo upon proof of concrete progress in Israel's withdrawal from conquered territories.[5] Kissinger's quick visit to the Middle East in the aftermath of the October War reflected Washington's nascent commitment to a resolution of the Arab-Israeli conflict. This policy stood in marked contrast to the fallout from the Six Day War, when Johnson had preferred to let the Arabs and Israelis solve their own problems, with as little American participation as possible.

The initial postwar negotiations took place against a backdrop of a low-level war of attrition on both northern and southern fronts. By one count, approximately 450 artillery and small arms exchanges occurred in the Sinai and on the west bank from the end of October 1973 to early February 1974. During this period, Egyptian sources claimed to have killed 187 Israeli soldiers, destroyed forty-one tanks, and downed eleven planes.[6] Dayan, on the other hand, admitted to a toll of only fifteen killed and sixty-five wounded on the Israeli side.[7] The Golan front experienced its share of incidents: at least thirty-seven Israeli soldiers were killed and 158 wounded between March and May 1974 alone.

Neither Meir nor Sadat could easily afford another war of attrition like the one that had occurred on the Sinai front after the Six Day War. After the six-point agreement in November, Kissinger continued his shuttle diplomacy, this time focusing on a disengagement of forces. Success came first on the southern front, after Kissinger had traveled back and forth between Egypt and Israel for a week, from 11 to 17 January 1974. On the 18th, both sides signed a disengagement agreement. Israel agreed to withdraw all its forces from the west bank to fifty kilometers east of the Suez Canal. Sadat, in turn, consented to recalling the bulk of the Second and Third Field Armies to the west bank. On the east bank, in zone of six to ten kilometers in width, Sadat agreed to limit Egyptian forces to seven thousand troops, six batteries of short-range 122-mm artillery pieces, and thirty tanks. Israel consented to the same troop limitations in its zone. Neither side would deploy weapons capable of downing planes conducting reconnaissance flights over these zones; nor would they deploy any surface-to-surface missiles capable of reaching the other side. A UN buffer zone thirty kilometers wide would separate the armies. To monitor compliance, the United States promised to conduct regular intelligence overflights, making the results available to both parties.

Agreement on the Egyptian-Israeli front left two important issues requiring immediate attention: normalization of the northern front and the lifting of the oil boycott. Sadat promised to help the United States on both matters. In the second week of February, he attended an Arab summit in Algiers, but the other Arab leaders refused to lift the embargo until a settlement was reached between Israel and Syria. Despite this initial setback for Sadat, most Arab oil producers decided on 18 March to resume oil shipments, with the understanding that Syria and Israel would reach an agreement in the near future. Kissinger continued his shuttle diplomacy with great energy, learning rather quickly that Asad was not as easy to work with as Sadat. Syria eventually reached a disengagement agreement with Israel, on 31 May 1974. While diplomats worked to achieve meaningful progress, Meir faced a political battle at home as a direct result of the war.

IMPACT IN ISRAEL

The 1973 war had ended on a positive military note for Israel. The IDF had recovered from its initial shock to gain the initiative on both fronts. In the Sinai, the encirclement of Suez City and Third Army had undermined Sadat's strategic position and put the Israeli government in a strong bargaining position after the war. On the northern front, the IDF had counterattacked to regain all territory lost on the Golan and even penetrated twenty kilometers into Syria, to within forty kilometers of Damascus. In light of these Israeli operational and tactical achievements on both fronts, many Western observers unabashedly awarded Israel a military victory in 1973. In sharp contrast to foreign evaluations, however, many Israelis assessed the 1973 Arab-Israeli war in more negative terms, even though the conflict ended with the IDF having the upper hand.[8]

Decisive victory had definitely eluded the Israeli army on both fronts. The IDF had failed to destroy either the Egyptian or Syrian armed forces, minimizing any sense of a clear military victory in Israel, even though the country's leadership maintained an aura of self-confidence for world consumption. To add to the wounds to its pride, Israel had depended on US military assistance to finish the war. By 23 October, for example, the Israeli air force had lost at least 102 airplanes, approximately one-fourth of its entire arsenal. To avoid reaching its red line, Israel received forty Phantoms and thirty-two Skyhawks from the United States, a resupply that proved critical for maintaining the high number of sorties for control of the air and support of ground operations.[9] Requesting a major arms resupply under the duress of war with rising casualties was a bitter pill for a proud nation to swallow.

More such pills surfaced after the war's conclusion. The second cease-fire gave Israelis time to contemplate on how ill prepared their army had been for the war. The outbreak of hostilities had surprised virtually everyone in Israel. Worse, no one had expected three weeks of intense fighting with such heavy casualties. During the war, there were moments of great uncertainty and anguish among the Israeli people. When the fighting finally ended, Israelis could now confront their national grief.

Israeli losses were staggering for a small country that had come to expect decisive victory with few casualties in short wars. Over 2,800 Israelis had been killed, at least 8,800 had been wounded, and some five hundred were prisoners of war or missing in action. Equivalent losses for the United States in the Vietnam War would have been two hundred thousand Americans killed—a figure four times the actual number but inflicted in the span of only three weeks. Arab losses were heavy as well. Egypt lost five thousand killed and twelve thousand wounded; Syria suffered over three thousand dead and six thousand wounded.

Tank losses stood at 840 for Israelis (many repaired during the war), 1,100 for the Egyptians, and 1,200 for the Syrians. Airplane destruction was also high: 102 (some sources claim figures closer to two hundred) for Israel, 223 for Egypt, and 118 for Syria.[10] Clearly, the IDF inflicted more death and destruction on Arab armies than the Arabs did on it, but this fact provided little consolation to the Israeli people.

Many Israelis regarded the war as a Pyrrhic victory. As Yaël Dayan, Moshe Dayan's daughter, noted through a character in her novel on the 1973 war, it was difficult to feel elated about the final outcome: "People didn't know what to believe anymore. The loss was heavier than the gain. The loss was measured by lives, the gain—square miles."[11] In military parlance, the tactical and operational successes had failed to translate into a clear strategic triumph, making the human losses more painful. A better-prepared IDF could have avoided some of the initial casualties suffered during the surprise attack on both fronts, especially in the Sinai, where Israeli units heroically attempted to reach strong points to save their beleaguered brethren.

The 1973 conflict brought a new anguish to the Israeli experience of war. Unlike its past wars, two generations came together in this conflict. Fathers and sons, both in uniform, participated in the same conflagration. Each followed the other's progress closely. Fathers lost sons, and sons lost fathers, forcing one to leave the battlefield to bury the other. The 1973 conflict thus became known in Israel as "the War of Fathers and Sons."[12]

There was the problem of the missing in action. Many Israelis were unsure of the fate of family members. Over three hundred Israeli soldiers found themselves in captivity, but no one knew the exact number, nor the identity of the captives. Israel had not suffered so many captured in war, a reality that added to the national sense of loss and agony. The public clamored for the return of Israeli prisoners before any negotiations took place with the Arabs.

As discussed, Sadat complied rather quickly with the prisoner-of-war issue, exchanging 241 Israelis for 8,031 Egyptians over the period between 15 and 22 November 1973. (Most of the Egyptian soldiers were rear-area troops captured on the west bank during the last week of the war.) On the Golan front, however, matters moved at what seemed to Israelis to be a snail's pace. Only on 27 February 1974 did the Syrians provide Kissinger a list of sixty-five captives, promising to allow a visit by Red Cross representatives. The information brought instant relief to some families; others experienced great sorrow at omission of their loved ones. Elazar, as he read the list, broke down and cried in the presence of Kissinger.[13] Meir, for her part, held a grudge over what to her was an agonizing delay: "I personally shall never forgive the Egyptians or the Syrians . . . for withholding that information for so many days. . . . I thought to myself that torture by our enemies is worse than death."[14] The issue of Israeli prisoners of war underscored the country's lack of preparedness for war.

Israelis also incurred a new type of casualty. For the first time in its history, the IDF suffered a high incidence of combat shock, something for which the medical corps had failed to prepare adequately. Until 1973, few psychiatric cases resulting from battle situations had been reported in Israel, in large measure because previous conflicts—with the sole exception of the first Arab-Israeli war—had been quick victories with relatively few casualties. In 1973, however, Israeli soldiers fought in a lethal, intense, and a prolonged war. Ariel Sharon, one Israel's most experienced warriors, pointed out this unique aspect of this armed conflict: "I have been fighting for twenty-five years, and all the rest were just battles. This was a real war."[15]

The intense fighting in 1973 produced a high ratio of psychiatric cases, with figures ranging from as low as 12.3 to as high as 23.1 percent of all nonfatal casualties. Unprepared to treat such wounds on the spot, the IDF tended to pull these casualties quickly from the battlefield to rear areas. Such evacuation made recovery much harder. Without enough time to assess critically its procedures in war, the IDF had to develop its doctrine for treating battle stress *after* the conflict. This involved, for example, the assignment of professional psychiatric teams to medical battalions at division level.[16]

The 1973 conflict was not a short war by Israeli standards, especially in light of the time that elapsed before Israeli reservists could return to civilian life. Many reservists served much longer than three weeks. In 1967, the IDF had begun demobilizing major units two days after the cessation of hostilities; in 1973, however, Israel faced a very different kind of war termination. The EAF and the SAF had escaped military defeat. Both armies remained intact, and though badly battered, they were still capable of launching limited offensive operations against Israeli forces. And the IDF could not redeploy to more defensible positions. Israel's political leaders wanted to keep all the territory seized on both fronts for negotiations with Egypt and Syria.

This political decision placed a major burden on the IDF. On the southern front, the Israeli bridgehead stretched a hundred kilometers north and south and twenty to twenty-five kilometers west of the Suez Canal. A similar bulge existed on the northern front. Owing to the indecisive end of the 1973 war, coupled with the existence of vulnerable salients on both fronts, Israel had to maintain many reservists on active duty for several months.

Numerous steps were taken to return as many reservists to civilian jobs or university classes as possible and as quickly. The Armor School, for example, moved from the Negev to Bir Gifgafa in the Sinai so as to be nearer the front. Reorganized after the Six Day War to form an armored brigade from its instructors and students in the event of hostilities, the school now constituted a front reserve while training armor units. Although classes resumed quickly, both instructors and students were acutely aware of the distinct possibility of a sudden deployment into combat.[17]

Despite such steps, the IDF was forced to keep many reserve units on active duty in the Sinai as late as April 1974. Many families of these civilian soldiers suffered economic hardships. Small businesses went bankrupt without their main breadwinners at home, and the economy suffered serious strain from the huge financial burden of keeping reserve units mobilized for so long. This painful state of affairs added to the people's anger over the IDF's lack of preparedness for war.

A RECKONING IN ISRAEL

The months after hostilities brought much consternation in Israel. Israelis quickly became obsessed with the question of what had gone wrong. Myriad voices called for accountability, demanding an impartial inquiry to investigate what became known as the *Mechdal*, or the Great Blunder—that is, the failure of the government and the army to avoid the surprise attack and its consequences. A growing avalanche of protests finally compelled Meir to agree to the formation of such a body.

On 18 November 1973, the Israeli cabinet set the commission's mandate. First, the commission would investigate the intelligence information, assessments, and decisions made prior to the outbreak of the war. Second, it would examine the army's deployment, preparedness, and actions up until the IDF contained the Arab forces. On 21 November, the august board convened under the chairmanship of the Dr. Shimon Agranat, the American-born president of Israel's supreme court. The other esteemed members of what became known as the Agranat Commission were also well-respected figures: two former chiefs of the General Staff, a supreme court justice, and the state comptroller. Proceedings began on 25 November 1973.

Even before the Agranat Commission's formation, a number of Israeli generals initiated a public debate by criticizing each other's performances, spawning what became known as "the war of the generals." Sharon opened Pandora's box on 11 November 1973, in an interview with a correspondent from the *New York Times*. In it, the reserve general criticized his superiors for delaying the crossing of a second armored division to the west bank for thirty-six hours, thereby losing an opportunity to defeat rapidly the Egyptian army.[18] Chief of the General Staff David Elazar and former front commander Haim Bar-Lev responded in kind, chastising Sharon for making his personal feelings public.[19] Charges and countercharges continued for several months. This acrimonious public debate tarnished the image of several generals and revealed cracks in the IDF.

While generals publicly fired salvos at each other, soldiers wrote letters to newspapers offering their own complaints and criticisms. Many veterans of the war joined protest demonstrations against the government, in particular singling out Golda Meir and Moshe Dayan.[20] Never before had the IDF experienced such public criticism and soul-searching.

Mottie Ashkenazi, a reserve captain in command of Budapest, the only strong point in the Sinai not to surrender to the Egyptians, became an overnight symbol of national frustration and disappointment. He began his protests with a sit-in before the defense ministry, demanding Dayan's resignation. In the hope of reaching some understanding, Dayan met personally with Ashkenazi, an encounter that lasted past midnight. After the long and strenuous session, the defense minister found little good to say about his critic.

He kept criticizing and sniping at others without mercy, while heaping encomiums upon his head. In nothing he said did I find a spark of trust, of faith, of anything constructive. All was nihilistic. It was not by Mottie Ashkenazi and people like him that Israel had been built, and not through them that Israel would grow and prosper.[21]

Dayan could easily ignore the protests of one man, but not of the many. As Meir later noted in her memoirs, "Much of the outcry was genuine. Most of it, in fact, was a natural expression of outrage over the fatal series of mishaps that had taken place."[22] The Israeli cultural attitude of *ein breira* (no alternative) had produce a public unready to forgive those responsible for the *Mechdal*.

The national turmoil directly affected politics. In late December, Israel held national elections, originally scheduled for 30 October but postponed owing to the outbreak of war. Golda Meir and the Labor Party returned to power, but with a loss of five seats, dropping from fifty-six to fifty-one seats out of a total of 120 in the Knesset. Labor received only 39.6% of the vote, a substantial drop from the 46.2% in the last election. More importantly, Menachem Begin and his Likud Party gained 31% of the vote, presenting the first serious challenge to Labor since independence. Weakened by the election results, Meir took until 10 March 1974 to form her coalition cabinet. But this achievement proved short-lived, for on 2 April 1974, after holding 140 meetings and hearing fifty-eight witnesses, the Agranat Commission presented an interim report, in large measure to provide a demanding public some concrete answers. The initial revelations proved damaging enough to cause an earthquake throughout Israeli society and its armed forces.

Commission members castigated Israeli military intelligence for failing to assess accurately available information that had clearly pointed to a high probability of war.[23] Senior intelligence officers had discovered their error too late and had failed to fulfill their contract of a forty-eight-hour advance warning. The report recommended the termination of the careers of the director of military intelligence, his assistant in charge of research, the head of the Egyptian research section, and the chief intelligence officer for Southern Command. All these senior officers—one major general, one brigadier general, and two lieutenant colonels—quickly left military service.

The Agranat Commission also found David Elazar seriously negligent in several areas. The chief of the General Staff had suffered from "an overconfidence in the I.D.F.'s ability to repulse under any circumstances an all-out attack by the enemy on two fronts."[24] Consequently, the IDF lacked a "detailed" plan based on realistic assessment of its adversaries' capabilities in the event of a surprise Arab attack. Moreover, the commission concluded that Elazar should have ordered a partial mobilization by the morning of 5 October as a precautionary measure, given the unusually large number of Arab troops massing on both the northern and the southern fronts. Finally, the high command had erred in failing to provide clear instructions for deployment according to war plans once it became certain the Arabs would attack that day. While recognizing the chief of the General Staff's invaluable leadership during the war, the commission still recommended that Elazar resign. Elazar, shocked by this part of the report, left the military with bitter feelings. Many say that it was of a broken heart that he died in 1976 while writing his memoirs to vindicate himself.

The Agranat Commission's other major casualty was the commander of the Sinai front. Shmuel Gonen had emerged a hero from the Six Day War as commander of the elite 7th Armored Brigade, which had led ground forces in their lightning advance across the Sinai. In only four days, his brigade had captured Rafah and al-Arish on the northern route, then pushed through Egyptian defenses in the Bir Gifgafa area before reaching the Suez Canal. In the 1973 war, however, fortune failed to shine on Gonen, now a major general. During the first few days of the war, he proved ineffective in command and suddenly found himself relieved on 10 October, remaining as deputy to the new front commander. After the commission's negative evaluation of his performance, Gonen left the army in disgrace, eventually going into self-imposed exile.

In addition to recommending the dismissal of key senior officers, the Agranat Commission highlighted the need for constitutional reform of the national command authority. Since independence, Israel had been functioning without a clear delineation of powers, responsibilities, and obligations of the cabinet, the defense minister, and the chief of the General Staff in security matters. The Agranat Commission advocated addressing this deficiency, in light of the national furor to assess blame for the *Mechdal*. In response, "The Basic Law: The Army" was passed in 1976 in an attempt to clarify the exact relationship between the prime minister, the minister of defense, and the chief of the General Staff.[25]

For all its critical assessment, the Agranat Commission's report did not indict the country's political leadership. This omission sparked outrage and protests throughout the country. The Israeli public, already reeling from high casualties and upset by revelations of the army's failings, felt that the commission had made the senior military leaders into scapegoats for the politicians. Golda Meir and Moshe Dayan should have borne responsibility for the military's unpreparedness. News leaks describing Dayan's erratic behavior during the war ignited a powerful wave of criticism, fueled by intellectuals, the press, and opposition parties. Dayan's refusal to step down when confronted with calls for his resignation sparked a major crisis for Meir's new coalition government.

Rather than adopt a siege mentality, Meir bowed to the growing furor and resigned on 11 April 1974. On 3 June, Yitzhak Rabin, the chief of the General Staff in the Six Day War, became Israel's fifth prime minister and the first native-born Israeli to hold the position. The Labor Party thus managed to retain the reins of government, but the ruling elite had suffered a serious blow. The 1977 elections would usher in a new era in Israeli politics, bringing Begin and the Likud Party to power and ending Labor Party's continuous reign since the establishment of Israel in 1948. Ironically, Begin, a former guerrilla organizer and hard-liner toward the Arabs, would sign the peace treaty with Egypt in 1979.

As the political landscape changed in Israel, the IDF also underwent significant changes as a direct result of the 1973 war.[26] Israeli doctrine had to make allowances for the possibilities of strategic surprise and of greater attrition of men and material in a longer war. A prewar plan to cut the length of national service was dropped. Instead, the government increased the size of the standing force, from 115,000 in 1973, to 164,000 in 1977, and to 170,000 in 1982. The size of the reserve grew during this period from 300,000 to 540,000, as Israelis learned the importance of quantity, and not just quality, in conventional warfare. Israel also increased its war stocks, based on the expenditure of material in 1973.

Additionally, Arab tactical successes with antitank and surface-to-air missiles had exposed a serious doctrinal flaw in the IDF. Israeli ground forces had proven weak in combined-arms warfare. Consequently, the General Staff now lessened its emphasis on armor and strengthened other combat branches, in particular the artillery. Training exercises lay greater stress on the tank in cooperation with paratroopers, infantry, artillery, and engineers. To facilitate maneuver through suppressive firepower, the Artillery Corps increased the number of self-propelled artillery pieces, thereby reducing the reliance of the ground forces on the air force as flying artillery. Moreover, new military budgets provided funds for the purchase of modern armored personnel carriers, American-made M-113s, equipped with TOWs, to protect paratroopers, infantry, and engineers on the more lethal battlefield.

Despite the new stress on combined arms, tanks remained central to the Israeli way of war. To help suppress Arab infantry armed with antitank missiles, the Armor Corps mounted .30- and .50-caliber machine guns on its tanks. Moreover, Blazer reactive armor was added to increase protection from missile impact. In addition to improving existing technology, the Armor Corps, drawing upon the 1973 war experience, made changes to pre-war plans for its own tank. By 1982, the IDF was operating the *Merkava* (Chariot), a unique weapons system with special features that emphasized survivability over firepower and maneuver.

The Israeli air force, for its part, also underwent major changes as a result of the 1973 war. To enhance its ability to gain air superiority in the next conflict, it devoted more attention to the air defense threat. New tactics to destroy missile batteries from the air, based in part on lessons learned during the war, became standard for training programs. Moreover, Israel purchased the Airborne Warning and Air Control System (AWACS) from the United States and manufactured its own drone planes; together the systems were to be instrumental in destroying the Syrian SAM system in the Bekaa Valley in 1982. The Israeli air force also addressed the problem of ground support. Better communications equipment and procedures were implemented to make the pilots more responsive to ground forces. The command and control system remained centralized in the hands of the air force commander, who would ensure that primary attention was given to attaining air superiority.

Overall, the 1973 war shattered two articles of faith in Israel: the infallibility of the intelligence community and the invincibility of the armed forces. Both beliefs had drawn sustenance in large measure from the Blitzkrieg-type victory of the Six Day War. In 1973, that triumph came to haunt the IDF, like an albatross: any less-than-stellar performance would fail to meet Israeli society's high expectations. The shock, uncertainty, and peril that had ripped through the armed forces and society during the first days of the war became indelibly ingrained in the national psyche. Arab armies had proven that they could generate the combat power necessary to inflict heavy casualties and to wage a prolonged war. The overall experience of the 1973 war humbled the Israelis, altered the Israeli political landscape, and taught them a hard lesson. A clever opponent can gain political capital by developing an astute policy commensurate with his own military capabilities, even against a foe superior in the critical areas of intelligence, airpower, and armored warfare.

SADAT'S ROAD TO PEACE WITH ISRAEL

By mid-1974, Sadat could derive much satisfaction from Egypt's war effort. Israeli forces had completely withdrawn from the west bank, and the EAF occupied six to ten kilometers of the Sinai on the east bank of the Suez Canal. Moreover, the war had caused much turmoil in Israel, no doubt much more than ever expected by Sadat. The war of words among Israeli generals, the findings of the Agranat Commission, the firings of senior military figures, and the fall of the Meir government had undermined Israel's theory of security. The United States, for its part, had demonstrated a commitment to the Arab-Israeli conflict through Kissinger's shuttle diplomacy of the six months after the war. Egypt could be proud of its battlefield accomplishments.

But Sadat made miscalculations. He overestimated how much influence Washington could exert over Israel. Shortly after the October War, Sadat stated publicly that the United States held 99 percent of the cards in the Arab-Israeli conflict. In line with such reasoning, Egyptian foreign policy focused on wooing the United States at the expense of straining relations with the USSR. Gradually, Sadat lost the ability to use the Soviets for leverage with the Americans. Also, contrary to his calculations, Israel exerted significant influence in Washington; American presidents often balked at applying pressure on Israel, in large measure because of Jewish money and votes in the United States. Often, Washington had to pay dearly for major concession.

One such example stands out in particular—the second Egyptian-Israeli disengagement agreement of 1975. In return for a twenty-to-forty-mile Israeli withdrawal to the passes, President Gerald Ford, who had replaced Nixon as a result of the Watergate scandal, committed the United States to a secret sixteen-point memorandum of understanding with Israel. Among other items, Washington promised increased economic aid; the delivery of vast quantities of new sophisticated weapons, including the F-15 and F-16 attack fighters and Pershing intermediate-range ballistic missile; compensation for the loss of oil in the Sinai; the promise of no recognition of the Palestinian Liberation Organization (PLO) until its acceptance of Resolutions 242 and 338; and a pledge to refrain from any diplomatic moves in the Middle East without prior consultation with Israel. Some Israelis privately hailed this document as a second Balfour Declaration, strengthening Israel's bargaining position with the other Arabs.

Sadat also seemed to underestimate Israel's stubborness. Despite the October "Earthquake" in Israel, no Israeli leader rushed into negotiations for the return of captured Arab lands in 1967, even in the Sinai. Negotiations dragged on; at times they stalled. In some instances, Sadat looked to the Americans to nudge Israel; other instances saw Israeli officials urging Washington to badger Egypt. Sometimes, the Egyptians and Israelis dealt directly with each other, without the presence of American officials. Both parties even held secret discussions, unbeknowest to Washington. Despite all the efforts, however, most Israeli officials were skeptical of Sadat's sincerity.

Israel and the United States were not the only problems facing Sadat. Each step in the peace process generated controversy and resistance within both Egypt and the Arab world. Some Egyptian officials resigned in protest over Sadat's decisions and actions; others were fired for their criticisms. Sadat once summarized the obstruction presented by his own armed forces thus: "My army! First I had trouble convincing them to go to war. Now I have trouble persuading them to make peace."[27] By one count, Sadat went through seven prime ministers (twice holding that position himself), eight foreign ministers, seven war/defense ministers, and eight chiefs of the General Staff from 1971 to 1979, as he dragged Egypt into conformance with his policies.[28] In addition to resistance on the home front, Sadat grew impatient with the criticism from other Arab leaders, who readily attacked him whenever it appeared he was willing to reach some accomodation with Israel on his own. (Only Hasan II of Morocco and Hussein of Jordan offered support, albeit discreetly.)

Each step along the peace route required moral courage on Sadat's part. But in November 1977, Sadat decided on a truly courageous move. He offered to visit Jerusalem and address the Israeli people directly on their soil. In war, Sadat had targeted Israeli society, causing it to feel the pain of war as much as possible, through heavy casualties and prolonged conflict. Now he sought to speak to individual hearts and generate trust in the name of peace. Israelis were caught completely off guard by this historic move, including the intelligence community. As noted by then Defense Minister Ezer Weizman, "Sadat's peace offensive of 1977 was almost as unexpected as the Yom Kippur onslaught."[29]

On 19 November 1977, Sadat arrived in Israel by Egyptian Air to be met by a gathering of Israeli dignitaries, among them his former adversary, Meir. The next day, he addressed the Knesset in forceful language. The content of the address differed little from previous Egyptian demands; what had changed was that an Arab leader was delivering the message in Israel itself. There would be no separate peace and no interim agreements. Peaceful relations would come if only Israel withdrew behind the line of 4 June 1967 and addressed the Palestinian problem. Most Israelis were taken aback, wondering what to make of Sadat's visit and speech.

By this bold act, Sadat broke a psychological barrier in Israel. For the first time since Israel's establishment, an Arab head of state had spoken to the Israeli nation about peace. Sadat's historic trip touched a chord in Israeli society. Within a few months, Israel witnessed the birth of a dovish movement, *Shalom Ahshav*, or Peace Now. Also, on 8 March 1978, 348 reserve officers and noncommissioned officers, apparently all combat veterans, presented the Israeli government with a letter widely published in daily newspapers. The Officers' Letter urged the cabinet "to chose the road of peace" rather than establish more settlements or hide behind notions of a Greater Israel. By the end of May, more than a hundred thousand Israeli citizens had added their signatures to the letter.

Then came an invitation from President Jimmy Carter that Sadat and Begin join him at Camp David for a marathon summit to produce an agreement. On 2 September 1978, the day before the Israeli delegation's departure to Camp David, some hundred thousand Israelis demonstrated in Tel Aviv, calling upon Begin to return with a peace agreement.[30] Public opinion polls showed that Israeli passions had been aroused for peace. A good portion of the Israeli nation was urging its leadership to make every effort to achieve a treaty with Egypt.

Thus, on the eve of the Camp David summit, Egypt and Israel seemed pulled in opposite directions politically. Sadat appeared more willing to take risks in reaching an agreement with Israel than were his immediate advisors or even his people. Most Egyptians were generally opposed to reaching a separate peace treaty with Israel, in large measure out of attachment to the Arab world. Begin, on the other hand, took a hard line stance, tougher than that of his advisors and a majority of his nation. From 5 to 17 September, in the tranquil Camp David setting, Carter, Sadat, and Begin would confront the volatile issues of the Arab-Israeli conflict, issues that had caused four wars (five, if one counts the Three Year border war) in thirty years.[31] The marathon summit eventually bore fruit. On 17 September 1978, at eleven in the evening in the East Room of the White House, Sadat, Begin, and Carter signed the Camp David Accords. This agreement provided a framework for a peace treaty to be signed within three months.

In the accords, each side agreed to respect the other's existence and pledged to resolve all problems without war. Israel agreed to withdraw all its armed forces from the Sinai, returning the peninsula to Egypt's sovereignty. Egypt, meanwhile, promised to allow Israel the right of free passage of ships through the Gulf of Suez, the Suez Canal, the Strait of Tiran, and the Gulf of Aqaba. The accords placed limitations on the stationing of troops: Egypt could deploy only one mechanized or infantry division in an area up to fifty kilometers east of the Suez Canal; Israel, for its part, was limited to four infantry battalions in the area three kilometers east of its international border with Egypt in the Negev. UN forces would patrol the area between. Finally, the agreement addressed the Palestinian problem, calling for a five-year transitional period for the

West Bank and Gaza to full autonomy for its inhabitants. No mention was made of Jerusalem's status. Everything seemed in place for the final details to be worked out within three months.

Nonetheless, hard work awaited the three parties before the signing of a separate treaty between Egypt and Israel. Begin found opposition back in Israel. Hard-liners verbally attacked the agreements; in one incident, zealots attacked his car with tomatoes and other debris, breaking a windshield. Fortunately for Begin, Israel's democratic form of government allowed the prime minister to defer the final decision to a vote of the Knesset. All 120 members participated in the tally: eighty-four voted in favor, nineteen opposed it, and seventeen chose to abstain. Ironically, most of those who voted in the negative or preferred not to vote came from either Begin's own party or the National Religious Party. Labor thus provided Begin with the necessary votes.

Challenges also forced Sadat upon his return to Egypt. Foreign Minister Muhammad Ibrahim Kamel had already tendered his resignation at Camp David, before the summit's conclusion. To strengthen his position at home, Sadat implemented wholesale changes in his government. He appointed a new prime minister, speaker for the People's Assembly, war minister, and chief of the General Staff. The war ministry's name changed to the defense ministry to symbolize the military's new focus on maintaining Egypt's current borders.

A rude shock awaited Sadat from the Arab world, however. Disappointed with Sadat's decision to make a separate agreement with Israel rather than seek a comprehensive solution, the Arab League met in Baghdad and on 5 November threatened to move its headquarters from Cairo if Sadat signed a peace treaty with Israel. Calls were made for Sadat to abrogate the Camp David Accords. Libya and Iraq, joined by the PLO, tried to create a rejectionist front against Egypt's solitary drift toward a deal with Israel.

The Baghdad summit incensed Sadat, who now seemed determined to chart his own course. Yet, the last steps toward the peace treaty proved hard indeed. More snags developed over interpretations of the accords. Among the thorny issues were the linkage of a peace treaty between Egypt and Israel to the Palestinian question; Egypt's treaty obligations with other Arab states; the establishment of diplomatic relations and the exchange of ambassadors; and the timetable for the phased Israeli withdrawal from the Sinai. Especially troublesome was Israel's decision to expand its settlements on the West Bank and Gaza in the interim. Three months passed without the signing of the peace treaty.

Only a major effort by the United States could push the parties to agree on a final document: Carter personally traveled to both countries. His tireless efforts eventually brought success, if almost three months behind schedule. The Israeli cabinet gave its final approval on 14 March. On 20 March, after ten hours of discussion, the Knesset ratified the treaty: ninety-five voted for and eighteen against, two abstained, and three refused to participate in the process.

Finally, on 26 March 1979, Sadat and Begin signed at the White House a peace treaty, officially ending a state of war between the two countries. Israel agreed to withdraw to a line east of al-Arish and Ras Muhammad within nine months. Egypt would regain the entire Sinai by March 1982. In one regard, the United States purchased this agreement, by providing huge material incentives for each side, for Israel more so than for Egypt. For Israel, abandoning the Sinai meant leaving two military airfields and uprooting Israeli settlers. The Carter administration committed, as compensation, over three billion dollars for the construction of new airfields in Negev and for the transfer of sixteen civilian settlements. Egypt, meanwhile, received a promissory note of $1.5 billion in military aid over the next three years.

Egyptians, however, also paid a price for this agreement. Sadat had opposed a separate treaty with Israel, but he ended up signing one without any firm guarantees of linkage to the other problems in the Arab-Israeli conflict. Outstanding issues included the return of all Arab lands seized in the Six Day War, the Palestinian problem, and the status of Jerusalem. In fact, Sadat reversed himself on the Palestinian issue. At the Rabat Conference held in January 1974, Egypt had supported an Arab resolution to recognize the PLO as the sole representative of the Palestinian people. Now Sadat agreed to Jordan representing the Palestinians in future negotiations with Israel.

Sadat apparently had expected other Arab states to follow his lead, despite their public statements to the contrary. Instead, on 31 March 1979, less than a week after the signing of the treaty, the Arab League made good on its threat uttered in Baghdad. It transferred the league's headquarters to Tunis and imposed a political and economic boycott on Egypt. Ostracism by Arab brethren proved a bitter pill for many Egyptians to swallow. By this time indifferent to Arab criticism, Sadat revealed his thoughts on the subject to one of his diplomats:

I do not wish to underestimate the magnitude of the problems and worries that Egyptian diplomacy is facing. But all these problems and worries pale in comparison with this land we have regained. They are not worth one square meter of this land, which we have regained without spilling the blood of my children. . . . I don't want to belittle the efforts you are making, but I assure you that a square meter of this Egyptian land is far more important than your diplomatic difficulties.[32]

Sadat had become firmly committed to regaining his Sinai without further Egyptian blood. For him, peace with Israel was worth the price.

CONCLUSION

Although the IDF had redeemed itself in the last ten days or so of the 1973 war, Israeli citizens, accustomed to voicing their opinions freely, demanded a full accountability for the first half of the conflict. Battle-hardened reservists led the charge. Combined Egyptian and Syrian combat power had revealed weaknesses and errors in Israeli strategic thought, war doctrine, and force structure. The flaws could not be glossed over; neither could the controversial decisions escape public debate. The findings of an impartial board of inquiry resulted in the fall of a government and the sudden termination of promising military careers.

But Sadat proved unable to translate these developments into an Israeli withdrawal from all Arab lands captured in the Six Day War. Israeli mettle in combat translated into political stubbornness on the diplomatic front, as a "diplomacy of attrition" wore down any Egyptian hope of quick progress. Sadat found himself maneuvered into accepting a separate peace treaty with Israel. But he made that choice willingly. His decision to give peace a chance in return for the Sinai significantly influenced the course of the Arab-Israeli conflict. As a result of his moral courage, Sadat earned a place in history as a peacemaker and statesman. In 1978 he, like Begin, received the Nobel Peace Prize.

NOTES

1. Raymond Aron, *Peace and War: A Theory of International Relations* (New York: Doubleday, 1966): 577.
2. Avraham Adan, *On the Banks of the Suez* (Novato, CA: Presidio Press, 1980): viii–xii.
3. Henry Kissinger, *Years of Upheaval* (Boston: Little, Brown, 1982): 615; and Abba Eban, *Abba Eban: An Autobiography* (New York: Random House, 1977): 530–531.
4. Kissinger, *Years of Upheaval*: 643.
5. For the first diplomatic moves after the war, see William B. Quandt, *Decade of Decisions: American Policy Toward the Arab-Israeli Conflict, 1967–1976* (Berkeley: University of California Press, 1977): 200–218; and Kissinger, *Years of Upheaval*: 616–666.
6. Mahmud Riyad, *Mudhakirat Mahmud Riyad I: al-Bahth an al-Salam wa al-Sina al-Sharq al-Ust* (Beirut: al-Muessah al-Arabiyya lil-Dirasat wa al-Nashr, 1987): 477.
7. Moshe Dayan, *Moshe Dayan: Story of My Life* (New York: William Morrow, 1976): 566.
8. For a recent analysis of this paradoxical situation, see Charles S. Lieman, "The Myth of Defeat: The Memory of the Yom Kippur War in Israeli Society," *Middle Eastern Studies* 29 (July 1993): 399–418.
9. Hanoch Bartov, *Dado: 48 Years and 20 Days* (Tel Aviv: Ma'ariv, 1981): 545, 559.
10. Trevor N. Dupuy, *Elusive Victory: The Arab-Israeli Wars, 1947–1974* (1978 reprint, Fairfax, VA: Hero Books, 1984): 609; and Edgar O'Ballance, *No Victor, No Vanquished: The Yom Kippur War* (San Rafael, CA: Presidio Press, 1978): 301. Such figures are always controversial, often varying greatly from one source to another.
11. Yaël Dayan, *Three Weeks in October* (New York: Delcorte Press, 1979): 149.
12. Israeli literature is filled with this theme. See as examples: Bartov, *Dado*: 363, 367, 559, 568; Golda Meir, *My Life* (New York: G. P. Putnam's Sons, 1975): 432; and Ariel Sharon, *Warrior: The Autobiography of Ariel Sharon* (New York: Simon and Schuster, 1989): 320.
13. Kissinger, *Years of Upheaval*: 962.
14. Meir, *My Life*: 436.
15. Insight Team (*Sunday Times*, London), *Insight on the Middle East War* (London: Times Newspaper, 1974): 228.

16. Reuven Gal, *A Portrait of the Israeli Soldier* (Westport, CT: Greenwood Press, 1986): 209–219; and Reuven Gal, Interview with author, 3 July 1994, Israel. Gal served for five years as chief psychologist in the IDF, including the period under discussion.

17. Gabi Amir, interview with author, 6 July 1994, Tel Aviv, Israel. Then a colonel, Gabi Amir commanded the Armor School.

18. Charles Mohr, "Israeli General Tells How Bridgehead across the Suez Canal Was Established," *New York Times*, 12 November 1973: 20.

19. "Bar-Lev Disputes Sharon on Suez Attack," *New York Times*, 12 November 1973: 20.

20. Eric Marsden, "Israel's Battle of the Generals Hots Up," *Sunday Times*, 10 February 1974: 7.

21. Moshe Dayan, *Moshe Dayan*: 599.

22. Meir, *My Life*: 449.

23. For a published version in English, see "The Agranat Report: The First Partial Report," *Jerusalem Journal of International Relations* 4/1 (1979): 69–90 and 4/2 (1979): 95–128; and "Excerpts from Israeli Report and Elazar Letter," *New York Times*, 4 April 1974: 12.

24. "Excerpts from Israeli Report": 12.

25. For detailed studies of this complex subject, see Yehuda Ben Meir, *Civil-Military Relations in Israel* (New York: Columbia University Press, 1995); and Yoram Peri, *Between Battles and Ballots: Israeli Military in Politics* (Cambridge: Cambridge University Press, 1983).

26. International Institute for Strategic Studies, *The Military Balance 1972–1973* (London: International Institute for Strategic Studies, 1972): 31–32; International Institute for Strategic Studies, *The Military Balance 1974–1975* (London: International Institute for Strategic Studies, 1972): 34–35; Anthony H. Cordesman and Abraham R. Wagner, *The Lessons of Modern War, I: The Arab-Israeli Conflicts, 1973–1989* (Boulder, CO: Westview Press, 1990): 109–114; Gunther E. Rothenberg, *The Anatomy of the Israeli Army: the Israel Defence Force, 1948–1978* (New York: Hippocrene Books, 1979): 213–224; and Martin van Creveld, *The Sword and the Olive: A Critical History of the Israeli Defense Force* (New York: Public Affairs, 1998): 245–267.

27. Kissinger, *Years of Upheaval*: 836.

28. Muhammad Fawzi, *Istratijiyyah al-Musliha: al-Giza al-Sani min Mudhakirat al-Fariq Awwal Muhammad Fawzi* (Cairo: Dar al-Mustaqbal, 1986): 291.

29. Ezer Weizman, *Battle for Peace* (New York: Bantam, 1981): 386.

30. Mordechai Bar-On, *In Pursuit of Peace: A History of the Israeli Peace Movement* (Washington, DC: United States Institute for Peace Press, 1996): 97–112.

31. For a discussion of Camp David and the subsequent peace treaty by the participants themselves, see Quandt, *Camp David*: 206–339; Jimmy Carter, *Keeping Faith: Memoirs of a President* (New York: Bantam Books, 1982): 273–429; Cyrus Vance, *Hard Choices: Critical Years in America's Foreign Policy* (New York: Simon and Schuster, 1983): 219–255; Weizman, *Battle for Peace*: 340-390; Moshe Dayan, *Breakthrough: A Personal Account of the Egypt-Israel Peace Negotiations* (New York: Knopf, 1981): 149–284; Avraham Tamir, *A Soldier in Search of Peace: An Inside Look at Israel's Strategy* (New York: Harper and Row, 1986): 31–66; and Muhammad Ibrahim Kamel, *Camp David Accords: A Testimony* (London: KPI, 1986): 294–382.

32. Boutros Boutros-Ghali, *Egypt's Road to Jerusalem: A Diplomat's Story of the Struggle for Peace in the Middle East* (New York: Random House, 1997): 282.

9

CONCLUSION

Israel's decisive military victory in the Six Day War spawned an albatross for the IDF. Israeli Jews came to expect that their clearly superior armed forces would win the next war as they had won the last one: quickly, decisively, and with few casualties. And the IDF itself, encouraged by the Israeli public's expectations, believed that it could repeat its stellar performance of 1967. After all, the Israeli army enjoyed the advantages necessary to win: a marked superiority in intelligence, airpower, and armored forces, three major pillars of modern conventional warfare. The IDF also possessed a distinct advantage in quality of men and weapons. Moreover, the military victory in 1967 provided Israel with more-defensible borders and greater strategic depth on all three fronts. Given such clear advantages, it is no wonder that virtually every Western military expert assumed that the IDF would easily defeat any Arab army or coalition of armies, and that Israelis held the same view. The 1973 war, however, demonstrated the folly of excessive faith in superior military power to win conventional wars.

Israelis should have acted on the truism that history does not repeat itself. In May 1967, the Arab world had been unprepared for war with Israel. Egypt had been embroiled in a five-year struggle in Yemen that in May was tying down between thirty to forty thousand troops. This conflict had put Cairo and Riyadh in competition for influence in the Arab world. Syria, for its part, had witnessed increasing domestic unrest, owing to the leftist policies of a radical regime in power since only 1966. Jordan, meanwhile, was the pariah state of the region, having strained relations with both Egypt and Syria. In such a divided and polarized Arab world, Israel saw little likelihood of the Arabs contemplating war in the near future. Rather suddenly, a series of Arab decisions escalated tensions in the region to the point where the Arabs stumbled into war against what should have been their better judgment.

In the three weeks of escalating tensions before the outbreak of the 1967 hostilities, Nasser practiced a dangerous form of brinkmanship, attempting to gain political advantage during the crisis but without initiating hostilities. Meanwhile, the EAF suffered from unclear political direction, a politicized senior command, and general ill-preparedness for war against Israel. Adding salt to its own wounds, General Command made several bad decisions in May, including the replacement of most division commanders and their chiefs of staff, the unexpected creation of a front command, the forward deployment of too many Egyptian troops, and the positioning of forces away from the Israeli main effort. All these changes predisposed the EAF for a major defeat. Because neither Jordan nor Syria provided serious help to Egypt, the IDF was able take advantage of interior lines and focus on defeating the EAF first; then it conveniently defeated the other two Arab armies piecemeal.

The IDF, unlike the EAF, used the prewar crisis productively. In particular, the Israeli General Staff moved from limited terrain objectives, meant for barter after the conflict, to defeating the EAF decisively. The last two weeks before war worked to Israel's benefit, providing adequate time with which to prepare for such a fast-pace campaign. This "waiting" proved critical, because the bulk of IDF consisted of reservists, who greatly benefited from time to prepare themselves physically and emotionally for war. By the eve of hostilities, the IDF was ready to wage a blitzkrieg against the dysfunctional EAF.

Israel also gained some diplomatic leverage during the nearly three weeks between the beginning of tensions and the outbreak of war. On the strategic level, much of the Western world had grown sympathetic to Israel's plight, threatened by hostile statements and actions by Arab leaders, in particular Nasser. The Israeli cabinet thus unleashed its military power at a most opportune moment. Meanwhile, international opinion encouraged Nasser to accept the first strike.

While Israeli pilots destroyed Egyptian warplanes on the tarmac, IDF ground forces moved quickly to win the first land battles in the Sinai. In flank attacks from unexpected directions, both the Tal and Sharon divisions, each task organized for its particular mission, punctured rapidly through Egyptian forward defenses at Rafah and Abu Ageila. Meanwhile, an armored (reserve) brigade from the Yoffe *ugdah* silently infiltrated between Tal and Sharon for the major thrust into central Sinai. Operational audacity followed on the heels of tactical successes as three Israeli divisions fanned out over the entire peninsula, racing to the passes like an expanding torrent. Amer's fatal error of ordering all his forces to withdraw from the Sinai in one night helped cause their rout. In a mere four days, the IDF destroyed the EAF, capturing the entire Sinai in the process.

Such military victories occur infrequently in warfare. In particular, Israel's blitzkrieg resulted from a fortuitous confluence of the IDF's military preparedness, the EAF's serious blunders, and a strategic setting favorable to Israel. The odds were against Israel being as fortunate in the next conflict; however, no senior Israeli official seriously attempted to disabuse the public about a repeat performance. Instead, Israeli society and its armed forces preferred to bask in the reality of the Six Day War: the Israeli army had won a lightning victory against three Arab armies.

Conditions, however, differed markedly in 1973. Unlike in 1967, the EAF and SAF had by then prepared to wage a war of attrition against the IDF. Egypt led the way in this regard. Its political and military leadership had improved the many weak areas of 1967. Specifically, the Egyptians strengthened civilian control of the military, to enhance unity of political purpose; restructured the General Command, to harmonize effort within the armed forces; implemented rigorous and realistic training programs, to improve tactical performance in combat; and integrated Soviet air defense and antitank weapons systems, to inflict as much damage on the IDF as possible. Israel's military establishment underestimated the cumulative effect of all these improvements; consequently, the Egyptians did not conform to its expectations. The IDF's surprise was not just the combined Egyptian-Syrian offensive on 6 October but also the combat mettle of both Arab armies, especially that of the Egyptians. During the war, Israeli commanders would have to learn again and again that they were not fighting the Egyptian army of 1967, a costly lesson in the midst of armed confrontation.

By merely starting the war, Egypt and Syria exposed cracks in Israeli doctrine and preparedness. Israeli ground forces were weak in combined arms, dependent on the plane and tank for rapid maneuver, and short on artillery and infantry well-trained for attrition battles in the forward tactical area. The Egyptians, by possessing the initiative, shaped the character and tempo of the war's first phase in favor of Egyptian strengths and Israeli weaknesses. Israeli field commanders unexpectedly found themselves having to fight attrition battles to stall Egyptian advances.

Complicating matters further, Israel's air force and ground forces had to fight concurrently for control of their respective battlefields. Senior Israeli commanders faced difficult operational decisions in terms of resource allocation, and they experienced problems in coordinating joint operations. Fighting simultaneously for control of the air and the ground, with the Egyptians possessing the initiative, increased the fog and friction of war and placed greater stress on Israeli officers and soldiers. Much of this transpired precisely because the Arabs had initiated the armed conflict. Israeli improvisation, an asset in 1967, now failed to derail the Egyptian crossing of the Suez Canal and the capture of the Bar-Lev Line.

War derives its purpose from policy, and Sadat had wisely crafted a strategy based on a realistic assessment of the EAF's capabilities. Israel's undisputed superiority in air and armored forces precluded any Egyptian chance of a clear military victory; rather, his intent was to avoid losing and hope for a favorable stalemate on the battlefield. In line with this reasoning, Sadat's strategic directive of 5 October 1973 avoided identifying traditional military objectives—the defeat of the enemy's army or the capture of strategic terrain. Rather, Ahmad Ismail took as his military objective the inflicting of the greatest damage possible in men and material, in a campaign limited to the establishment of bridgeheads up to fifteen kilometers east of the canal. The psychological shock of the EAF's ability to cause suffering and anguish in Israel would, Sadat hoped, force the Israeli leadership and society to soften their obduracy on the return of captured territories in the Six Day War. In light of Sadat's guidance, the EAF planned a strategic offense that quickly turned into a tactical defense.

Though he put careful thought and preparation into starting another conflict, Sadat discovered that war never follows even the best-laid plans and strategies. The Egyptian leader naturally focused his main effort on the diplomatic front. Here, he sought to entice the United States to become involved in resolving the Arab-Israeli conflict. Unfortunately for him, Washington proved dilatory in responding, an American strategy that gave Israel time to regain the initiative on both fronts. Syrian inability to seize the Golan Heights forced Sadat to order a supporting Egyptian offensive to the Sinai passes. This political decision fundamentally changed the course of the war on the battlefield; the Egyptian army never recovered from the October 14 offensive.

In response to the Israeli countercrossing of the Suez Canal, Sadat made two questionable decisions. Rather than maintaining a focus on inflicting casualties, he now became fixated on maintaining all the bridgeheads intact as evidence of the EAF's successes against the IDF; therefore, he opposed the transfer of Egyptian armored forces to the west bank to defeat the Israeli bridgehead there. On the diplomatic front, when Washington's first major diplomatic step in the war was a massive resupply of Israel, Sadat, to avoid alienating the Nixon administration, spurned all Soviet efforts to sponsor a cease-fire, even a personal visit by Kosygin. Soviet sponsorship of a cease-fire through the auspices of the United Nations, however, would not have necessarily jeopardized Sadat's goal of drawing the United States into the role of an honest broker after the war. Kissinger's departure for Moscow luckily coincided with the increasing danger to the Egyptian Third Army on the east bank; timing could not have been better for Sadat in this regard.

Sadat managed to reap a number of political benefits from the October War. The United States awakened to the importance of Egypt for stability in the Middle East, and eventually Washington nudged Israel toward accommodating Sadat's demand for the gradual return of the Sinai. But no one could have predicted the exact political repercussions in Israel from the IDF's failure to produce another decisive military victory. The 1973 war ended the careers of a number of senior Israeli officers and helped bring down the government; Israeli society indeed experienced the great shock planned by Sadat.

Sadat was a resourceful and determined leader, who used war as an extension of policy by other means according to Clausewitz's theory. In particular, the Egyptian case of 1973 offers a compelling example of a limited war waged successfully against a militarily superior foe, one who even possessed nuclear weapons. The EAF embarked on war not to defeat the IDF or seize strategic terrain but to discredit the IDF's deterrent power by inflicting an unacceptable level of casualties. A tactical defense would quickly follow a strategic offense, along a broad front. Military objectives were carefully formulated within the Egyptian army's capabilities and were intended to enhance the chances or probability of success for Ahmad Ismail and the EAF.

On the political level, Sadat intended that the effects of the war's violence be felt in Israel both during and after the war. The cumulative effect would cause a change in Israeli policy and attitudes toward the Arabs. His target was the Israeli government and people. He also sought to break the diplomatic stalemate in the Arab-Israeli conflict by drawing the United States away from its strong support of Israel and into a working relationship with Egypt. To accomplish this feat required skillful diplomacy before, during, and especially after the war. In postwar negotiations, Sadat eventually captured the West's attention by his courageous actions and ultimately gained the return of the Sinai through peaceful means.

Israel's experience should give serious pause to the United States. Its armed forces decimated the Iraqi military in a thirty-nine-day air assault followed by a hundred-hour land campaign. Desert Storm resembled, in many respects, the Israeli victory in 1967. The American blitzkrieg has spawned similar expectations within American society and the military: the new standard of excellence is to achieve a decisive victory, in a short time, with few casualties. To achieve such a triumph, the US armed forces have come to rely on superiority in information (intelligence) warfare, airpower, and maneuver forces, the same advantages the IDF possessed over Arab armies in 1973. Moreover, to avoid attrition battles in the tactical area in favor of a lightning thrust into the enemy's operational rear, the US Army has recently committed itself to the digitization of the battlefield. Because of these haunting parallels with the IDF and Israeli society, the United States stands to gain much from a examination of the 1973 Arab-Israeli war, in the light of the Six Day War.

Sadat's strategic success should prove a sobering reminder for Western armies confident in their superiority over armed forces in other parts of the world. In this light, a military should avoid the paradigm of a short war, decisive victory, and few casualties as its standard of excellence in conventional warfare. Nor should government or people take such a performance by its armed forces for granted. A smart adversary can force attrition battles in the tactical and operational areas, thereby accentuating the bloody nature of war. Substantive political advantage can be gained by the weaker opponent. Limited war thus offers numerous possibilities for a head of state to conduct a war against a militarily superior adversary for political advantage.

SELECT BIBLIOGRAPHY

UNPUBLISHED SOURCES

Adan, Avraham. Interview with author. 30 June 1996, Tel Aviv. Chief of Staff in Yoffe's division in 1967 and commanded 252d Armored Division in 1973.

Amir, Gabi. Interview with author. 6 July 1994, Tel Aviv. Commanded Armor School's armored brigade in the Sinai during the 1973 war.

Darwish, Darwish Hasan. Interview with author. 29 April 1989, Fort Leavenworth. Commanded infantry company in the Egyptian 16th Infantry Brigade during the battle for the Chinese Farm.

al-Dessouki, Murad Ibrahim. Interview with author. 28 June 1994, Cairo. Egyptian commander of mechanized infantry battalion in 1973 war.

Dvir, Yuval. Interview with author. 4 July 1994, Israel. Deputy commander of reconnaissance battalion in the Sinai during the 1973 war.

Eyland, Giora. Interview with author. 6 July 1994, Tel Aviv. A lieutenant in the Israeli paratroop battalion in the battle for the Chinese Farm.

Fahmi, Muhammad Ali. Interviews with author. 22 June 1994, Cairo; 28 September and 21 October 1996, Leavenworth, Kansas. Commander of Egyptian air defenses, 1968--1974.

al-Gamasi, Muhammad Abd al-Ghani. Interviews with author. Cairo, 31 October 1993 and 25 June 1994. Egyptian director of operations in the 1973 war.

Gareev, Makhmut. Interviews with author. 12 and 14 September 1995, Moscow, Russia. Chief of staff for Soviet military mission in Egypt, 1970--1972.

Keren, Aryeh. Interview with author. 4 July 1994, Israel. Commanded an armored (reserve) brigade in the Sinai during the 1973 war.

Matt, Danny. Interview with author. 6 July 1994, Tel Aviv. Commanded an Israeli paratroop brigade in the 1967 and 1973 wars.

Michelsohn, Colonel Benny. Letter correspondence to author, March 1990. Chief, Department of Military History, IDF.

Musallam, Talat Ahmad. Interviews with author. 9 and 10 October 1998, Washington, DC. Commanded the 18th Mechanzied Infantry Brigade in the Egyptian 21st Armored Division during the 1973 war.

Nir, Natke. Phone conversation with author. 5 October 1987. Commander of independent armored battalion at battle of Abu Ageila.

264 SELECT BIBLIOGRAPHY

Official Egyptian Military Sources. Military briefing given by Egyptian officers to author in October 1986.

Orren, D. Elhannon. Letter correspondence with author, 28 March 1991. Department of Military History, IDF.

Reshef, Amnon. Interview with author. 30 June 1994, Tel Aviv. Commanded an armored brigade in the Sinai during the 1973 war.

Schlesinger, James R. Brief conversation with author. 10 October 1998, Washington, DC. American secretary of defense during the 1973 war.

Sharon, Ariel. Interview with author. 7 July 1994, Tel Aviv. Israeli divisional commander in the 1967 and 1973 wars.

Shemshi, Elyashiv. Interview with author. 7 July 1994, Tel Aviv. Commanded armored (reserve) battalion in the Sinai during the 1973 war.

Sion, Dov. Interview with author. 2 November 1986, Tel Aviv. Liaison officer between Southern Command and Sharon's *ugdah* in 1967 war.

Spector, Iftihar. Interview with author. 7 July 1994, Tel Aviv. Commanded air squadron in 1973.

ARABIC SOURCES

Abd al-Hamid, Muhammad Kamal. *Maaraka Sina wa Qanat al-Suways* [The Battle of Sina and the Suez Canal]. Cairo: al-Wa'y al-'Arabi, 1960.

Abu Fadl, Abd al-Fattah. *Kuntu Naiban lil-Rais al-Mukhabarat* [I Was a Deputy to the Chief of Intelligence]. Cairo: Dar al-Harriya, 1986.

Ali, Kamal Hasan. *Mudarrabun wa Mufawwadun* [Warriors and Negotiators]. Cairo: al-Ahram, 1986. Commander of 2d Armored Brigade in 1967 war and commandant of Armor Corps in 1973 war.

Azmi, Mahmud. *al-Quwwat al-Mudarraa al-Israiliyya Abr Arbaa Hurub* [Israeli Armored Forces through Four Wars]. Beirut: Munazzama al-Tahrir al-Filatiniyya, 1975.

al-Badri, Hasan. *al-Taawun al-Askari al-Arabi al-Mushtarak: Madihu, Hadirhu, Mustaqbalhu* [Combined Arab Military Balance: Its Past, Its Present, Its Future]. Riyad: Dar al-Mariyya, 1982.

al-Badri, Hasan, Taha al-Magdub, and Muhammad Zia al-Din Zohdi. *Harb Ramadan: al-Gawla al-Arabiyya al-Israiliyya al-Rabia, Oktobir 1973* [The Ramadan War: The Fourth Arab-Israeli Conflict, October 1973]. Cairo, 1974.

al-Baghdadi, Abd al-Latif. *Mudhakirat Abd al-Latif al-Baghdadi* [The Memoirs of 'Abd al-Latif al-Baghdadi]. Volume II. Cairo: al-Maktab al-Misri al-Hadith, 1977. Original member of the Revolutionary Command Council of 1952 who daily visited general headquarters during the 1967 war.

Farag, Izz al-Din. *al-Quwwat al-Musallaha wa Maaraka al-Bina* [The Armed Forces and the Battle for Reconstruction]. Cairo: Dar al-Qawmiyya, 1964.

Fawzi, Muhammad. *Harb al-Thalath Sanawat 1967–1970* [The Three Years War, 1967–1970]. Beirut: Dar al-Wahda, 1983). Egyptian chief of the General Staff in the 1967 war and then commander in chief from 1967 to 1971.

___. *Istratijiyyah al-Musaliha: al-Giza al-Sani min Mudhakirat al-Fariq Awwal Muhammad Fazwi* [Strategy of Peace: The Second Part of the Memoirs of General Muhammad Fawzi]. Cairo: Dar al-Mustaqbal, 1986.

al-Gamasi, Muhammad Abd al-Ghani. *Mudhakirat al-Gamassi: Harb Oktobir 1973* [The Memoirs of Gamasi: The War of October 1973]. Paris: al-Munshurat al-Sharqiyya, 1990). Egyptian chief of staff for the front command in the 1967 war and director of operations in the 1973 war.

al-Hadidi, Salah al-Din. *Harb Oktobir fi al-Mizan al-Askari* [The October War in the Military Balance]. Cairo: al-Nashr Maktabah Madbuli, 1974. Commandant of the Nasser Higher Academy and commander of the Central Military District, Cairo.

___. *Shahid ala Harb 1967* [Witness to the 1967 War]. Cairo: Dar al-Shuruq, 1974.

___. *Shahid ala Harb al-Yaman* [Witness to the Yemeni War]. Cairo: Maktaba Madbula, 1984.

Hamad, Gamal. *Min Sina ila al-Golan* [From Sina to the Golan]. Cairo: al-Zuhra lil'I'lam al-'Arabi, 1988.

___. *al-Maarik al-Harbiyya ala al-Gebha al-Misriyya: Harb Oktobir 1973 al-Ashr min Ramadan* [Military Battle on the Egyptian Front: The October War of 10 Ramadan]. Cairo: al-Zuhra lil-Ilam al-Arabi, 1989.

Haykal, Muhammad Hasanayn. *1967: al-Infijar* [1967: The Explosion]. Cairo: Markaz al-Ahram, 1990. Nasser's and Sadat's close confidant.

___. *Oktobir 1973: al-Silah wa al-Siyasat* [The October War: Weapons and Politics]. Cairo: al-Ahram, 1993.

Huwaydi, Amin. *Adwa ala Ashab Naksa wa ala Harb al-Istiznaf* [Insight into the Reasons for the Setback of 1967 and the War of Attrition]. Beirut: Dar al-Taliah, 1975. Egyptian war minister immediately after 1967 war.

___. *al-Furas al-Daia: al-Qararat al-Hasima fi Harbi al-Istinzaf wa Oktobir* [Lost Opportunities: Decisive Decisions in the War of Attrition and October War] Beirut: Shirka al-Matbuat Lil-Tawzi wa al-Nashr, 1991.

___. *Maa Abd al-Nasir* [With Abd al-Nasir]. Cairo: Dar al-Mustaqbal, 1985.

Ismail, Muhammad Hafez. *Amn Misr al-Qawmi fi Asr al-Tahaddiyat* [Egypt's National Security in the Age of Limitations]. Cairo: Markaz al-Ahram lil-Targama wa al-Nashr, 1987. Sadat's national security advisor before and during the 1973 war.

Khalil, Abd al-Munim. *Hurub Misr al-Muasirah fi Awraq Qa'id Maydani: 1939–1945, 1956, 1962–1967, 1968–1970, 1973* [Wars of Contemporary Egypt According to the Papers of a Field Commander]. Cairo: Dar al-Mustaqbal al-Arabi, 1990. Commanded forces at Sharm al-Shaykh in the Six Day War and assumed command of the Second Field Army on 17 October 1973.

Mari, Sayyid. *Awraq Siyasiyah* [Political Papers]. Three volumes. Cairo: al-Maktab al-Misri al-Hadith, 1979. Senior Egyptian official in both the Nasser and Sadat regimes.

Murad, Mahmud. *Muharib lil-Kull al-Usur: Dirasa Tarihiyya an al-Insan al-Misri al-Mugatil* [Warriors through the Centuries: Historical Study on the Fighting Egyptian Man]. Cairo: al-Haia al-Misriyya al-Umm lil-Kuttab, 1972.

Murtagui, Abd al-Mohsen Kamil. *al-Fariq Murtagui Rawiya al-Haqaiq* [General Murtagui Discusses the Facts]. Cairo: Dar al-Watan al-Arabi, 1976. Egyptian front commander in 1967 war.

Mustafa, Hasan. *Harb Haziran 1967* [The War of 1967]. Volume I. Beirut: al-Mu'assasa lil-Dirsat wa al-Nashr, 1973.

___. *Maarik al-Jabhah al-Misriyya fi Harb Ramadan* [Battles on the Egyptian Front in the Ramadan War]. Baghdad: no publisher, 1982.

Mustafa, Khalil. *Suqut al-Jawlan* [The Fall of Golan]. Cairo: Dar al-Itisam, 1980. Major Mustafa was a Syrian military intelligence officer for Golan before the 1967 war.

Ramadan, Abd al-Aziz. *Harb Oktobir fi Mahkama al-Tarih* [The October War in the Judgment of History]. Cairo: Madbuli, 1984.

———. *Tahtim al-Aliha: Qissa Harb Yunyo 1967*. Volume II. [Destruction of the Goddess: The Story of the War of June 1967]. Cairo: Maktaba Madbuli, 1986.

Riyad, Mahmud. *Mudhakirat Mahmud Riyad 1948–1978, I: al-Bahth an al-Salam wa al-Sira al-Sharq al-Awst* [Memoirs of Mahmud Riyad 1948-1978, I: The Search for Peace and the Struggle in the Middle East]. Beirut: al-Mu'essah al-'Arabiyya lil-Dirasat wa al-Nashr, 1987. Egypt's foreign minister, 1964–1972.

Sabri, Musa. *Wathaiq al-Harb Oktober* [Documents of the October War]. Cairo: al-Maktab al-Misri, 1974.

Shalabi, Ahmad. *Harb 1967–1973* [War of 1967–1973]. Cairo: no publisher, 1975.

Subh, Ahmad Ismail. *Ubur al-Mihna* [Crossing the Barrier]. Cairo: al-Hai'a al-Misriyya al-'Umma lil-Kitab, 1976. Egyptian eyewitness to the battle for Suez City in 1973.

al-Tantawi, Husayn. *Butulat Harb Ramadan* [Heroes of the Ramadan War]. Cairo: Dar al-Sha'ab, 1975.

Yusri, Adil. *Rihla al-Shaq al-Mualaqa: min Ras al-Ush ila Ras al-Qubra* [Journey of the Cut Leg: From Ras al-'Ush to the Bridgehead]. Cairo: Dar al-Muarif bi-Misr, 1974. Egyptian brigadier general in command of the 112th Infantry Brigade in the 1973 war.

OTHER LANGUAGES

Abdel-Malek, Anouar. *Egypt: Military Society*. New York: Random House, 1968.

Adan, Avraham. *On the Banks of the Suez*. Novato, CA: Presidio Press, 1980. Israeli armor division commander in the 1973 war.

"The Agranat Report: The First Partial Report." *The Jerusalem Journal of International Relations* 4/1 (1979): 69–90 and 4/2 (1979): 95–128.

Ajami, Fuad. *The Arab Predicament: Arab Political Thought and Practice Since 1967*. Cambridge: Cambridge University Press, 1981.

Allon, Yigal. *The Making of Israel's Army*. New York: Universe Books, 1970.

Amos, John W. *Arab-Israeli Military/Political Relations: Arab Perceptions and the Politics of Escalation*. New York: Pergamon Press, 1979.

Ansari, Hamied. *Egypt, the Stalled Society*. New York: State University of New York Press, 1986.

Armstrong, G. P. "Egypt," in *Fighting Armies: Antagonists in the Middle East*, edited by Richard A. Gabriel. Westport, CT: Greenwood Press, 1983, 147–165.

Aron, Raymond. *Peace and War: A Theory of International Relations*. New York: Doubleday, 1966.

Aronson, Shlomo, with Oded Brosh. *The Politics and Strategy of Nuclear Weapons in the Middle East: Opacity, Theory, and Reality, 1960–1991, An Israeli Perspective*. New York: State University of New York Press, 1992.

Asher, Jerry and Eric Hammel. *Duel for the Golan: The 100-Hour Battle That Saved Israel*. New York: William Morrow, 1987.

Avidor, Gideon. "From Brigade to Division." *Military Review* 58 (October 1978): 64–71.

al-Badri, Hasan, Taha al-Magdub, and Muhammad Zia al-Din Zohdi. *The Ramadan War, 1973*. New York: Hippocrene Books, 1976.

Baker, Raymond William. *Egypt's Uncertain Revolution under Nasser and Sadat*. Cambridge, MA: Harvard University Press, 1978.

Barakat, Halim. *Days of Dust.* Translated by Trevor Le Gassick. Wilmette, IL: Medina University Press International, 1974.
Bar-Joseph, Uri. "Rotem: The Forgotten Crisis on the Road to the 1967 War." *Journal of Contemporary History* 31 (July 1996): 547–566.
Barkai, Mordekhay. "The Battle of Kuti's Infantry Brigade." *Ma'arachot* 187 (1967): 12–24.
___ (ed.). *Written in Battle: The Six-Day War as Told by the Fighters Themselves.* Tel Aviv: Le'Dory Publishing House, [1967].
Barnett, Michael N. *Confronting the Costs of War: Military Power, State, and Society in Egypt and Israel.* Princeton, NJ: Princeton University Press, 1992.
Bar-On, Mordechai. *In Pursuit of Peace: A History of the Israeli Peace Movement.* Washington, DC: United States Institute of Peace Press, 1996. Member of the Knesset and activist in Peace Now.
Bar-Siman-Tov, Ya'acov. "The Bar Lev Line Revisted." *Journal of Strategic Studies* 11 (June 1988): 149–176.
___. *Israeli-Egyptian War of Attrition, 1969–1970: A Case Study in Limited Local War.* New York: Columbia University Press, 1980.
Bartov, Hanoch. *Dado: 48 Years and 20 Days.* Tel Aviv: Ma'ariv, 1981.
Bar-Zohar, Michael. *Embassies in Crisis: Diplomats and Demagogues behind the Six-Day War.* Englewood Cliffs, NJ: Prentice-Hall, 1970.
Beattie, Kirk J. *Egypt during the Nasser Years: Ideology, Politics, and Civil Society.* Boulder, CO: Westview, 1994.
Beaufre, André. "Une Guerre Classique Moderne: La Guerre Israëlo-Arabe," *Strategie* (July–August 1967): 7–25.
Ben Elissar, Eliahu, and Ze'ev Schiff. *La Guerre Israelo-Arab: 5–10 Juin 1967.* Paris: Julliard, 1967.
Ben Meir, Yehuda. *Civil-Military Relations in Israel.* New York: Columbia Press, 1995.
Blechman, Barry M., and Douglas M. Hart. "The Political Reality of Nuclear Weapons: The 1973 Middle East Crisis." *International Security* 7 (Summer 1982): 132–156.
Bondy, Ruth, et al. *Mission Survival: The People of Israel's Story in Their Own Words: From the Threat of Annihilation to Miraculous Victory.* New York: Sabra Books, 1968.
Boutros-Ghali, Boutros. *Egypt's Road to Jerusalem: A Diplomat's Story of the Struggle for Peace in the Middle East.* New York: Random House: 1997. Egypt's minister of state for foreign affairs during Sadat's visit to Jerusalem and the discussions at Camp David.. Later became UN secretary general.
Brecher, Michael, with Benjamin Geist. *Decisions in Crisis: Israel, 1967 and 1973.* Berkeley: University of California Press, 1980.
Burdettt, Winston. *Encounter with the Middle East: An Intimate Report on What Lies behind the Arab-Israeli Conflict.* New York: Atheneum, 1969.
Carter, Jimmy. *Keeping Faith: Memoirs of a President.* New York: Bantam Books, 1982.
Churchill, Randolph S., and Winston S. Churchill. *The Six Day War.* Boston: Houghton Mifflin, 1967.
Clausewitz, Carl von. *On War.* Translated by Michael Howard and Peter Paret. Princeton, NJ: Princeton University Press, 1984.
Cohen, Avner. "Cairo, Dimona, and the June 1967 War." *Middle East Journal* 50 (Spring 1996): 190–210.

Cohen, Eliezer. *Israel's Best Defense: The Full Story of the Israeli Air Force.* New York: Orbis, 1993.
Cohen, Eliot A., and John Gooch. *Military Misfortunes: The Anatomy of Failure in War.* New York: Vintage Books, 1991.
Cordesman, Anthony H., and Abraham R. Wagner. *The Lessons of Modern War, I: The Arab-Israeli Conflicts, 1973–1989.* Boulder, CO: Westview Press, 1990.
Dawisha, A. I. *Egypt in the Arab World: The Elements of Foreign Policy.* New York: John Wiley & Sons, 1976.
Dawisha, Karen. *Soviet Policy toward Egypt.* New York: St. Martin's Press, 1979.
Dayan, David. *Strike First! A Battle History of Israel's Six-Day War.* New York: Pitman, 1967.
Dayan, Moshe. *Breakthrough: A Personal Account of the Egypt-Israel Peace Negotiations.* New York: Knopf, 1981.
___. *Moshe Dayan: The Story of My Life.* New York: William Morrow, 1976.
Dayan, Yaël. *Israel Journal: June 1967.* New York: McGraw-Hill, 1967. Israeli military correspondent assigned to Sharon's *ugdah* in 1967 war.
___. *Three Weeks in October.* New York: Delcorte Press, 1979.
Dekmejian, R. Hrair. *Patterns of Political Leadership: Egypt, Israel, Lebanon.* Albany: State University of New York Press, 1975.
Dishon, David (ed.). *Middle East Record,* III: *1967.* Jerusalem: Keter Publishing, 1971.
___. *Middle East Record,* IV: *1968.* Jerusalem: Israel Universities Press, 1972.
___. *Middle East Record,* V: *1969-1970.* Jerusalem: Israel Universities Press, 1973.
Dupuy, Trevor. *Elusive Victory: The Arab-Israeli Wars, 1947–1974.* 1978, reprint Fairfax, VA: Hero Books, 1984.
Eban, Abba. *Abba Eban: An Autobiography.* New York: Random House, 1977. Israeli foreign minister in 1967.
El Hussini, Mohrez Mahmoud. *Soviet-Egyptian Relations, 1945–85.* New York: St Martin's Press, 1987.
Eshel, David. *Chariots of Fire: The Story of the Israeli Armor Corps.* London: Brassey's, 1989.
___. "Counterattack in the Sinai: 8 October 1973." *Military Review* (November 1993): 54–66.
___. "The World's Great Tank Battles: October 14, 1973." *Born in Battle* 8 (January 1980): 32–47.
Fahmi, Ismail. *Negotiating for Peace in the Middle East.* Baltimore: John Hopkins University Press, 1983. Egypt's foreign minister 1973–1977.
Farid, Abd al-Majid. *Nasser: The Final Years.* Reading, UK; Ithaca Press, 1994. Nasser's personal secretary from 1959 to 1970.
Gal, Reuven. *A Portrait of the Israeli Soldier.* Westport, CT: Greenwood Press, 1986. Served for five years as chief psychologist in the IDF, including the period under discussion.
Gavish, Yeshayahu. "The Southern Front in the 1967 War." *Safra Sayfa* 4(1981): 45–52 (in Hebrew). Israeli front commander on the Sinai during 1967 war.
Gawrych, George W. "Combat Engineering: Egyptian Engineers in the Crossing Operation." *Combined Arms in Battle since 1939*, edited by Roger J. Spiller (Fort Leavenworth, KS: US Army Command & General Staff College Press, 1992): 43–49.
___. "The Egyptian High Command in the 1973 War." *Armed Forces and Society* 13 (Summer 1987): 535–546.

___. "The Egyptian Military Defeat of 1967." *Journal of Contemporary History* 26 (1991): 277–305.
___. *Key to the Sinai: The Battles of Abu Ageila in the 1956 and 1967 Arab-Israeli Wars.* Fort Leavenworth, KS: Combat Studies Institute, 1990.
___. *The 1973 Arab-Israeli War: The Albatross of Decisive Victory.* Fort Leavenworth, KS: Combat Studies Institute, 1996.
Gazit, Mordechai. "Egypt and Israel-Was There a Peace Opportunity Missed in 1971?" *Journal of Contemporary History* 31 (1997): 97–115.
Glanz, Harding A. "Abu Ageila: Two Battles, Part II." *Armor* 83 (July–August 1974): 15–21.
Glassman, Jon. *Arms for Arabs: The Soviet Union and War in the Middle East.* Baltimore: Johns Hopkins University Press, 1975.
Golan, Galia. *Yom Kippur and After: The Soviet Union and the Middle East Crisis.* Cambridge: Cambridge University Press, 1977.
Haddad, Yvonne. "Islamists and the 'Problem of Israel': The 1967 Awakening." *Middle East Journal* 46 (Spring 1992): 266–285.
Handel, Michael. *Israel's Political-Military Doctrine.* Cambridge, MA: Harvard University Press, 1973.
Harkabi, Yehoshafat. "Basic Factors in the Arab Collapse During the Six Day War." *Orbis* 11 (Fall 1967): 677–691.
Haykal, Muhammad Hassanayn. *The Cairo Documents.* New York: Doubleday, 1973.
___. *The Road to Ramadan.* New York: Quadrangle, 1975.
___. *The Sphinx and the Commissar: The Rise and Fall of Soviet Influence in the Middle East.* New York: Harper and Row, 1978.
___. "The Strategy of Attrition," in *The Arab-Israeli Reader,* edited by Walter Laqueur and Barry Rubun. 4th ed. New York: Facts on File, 1985, 414–427.
Henriques, Robert. *A Hundred Hours to Suez: An Account of Israel's Campaign in the Sinai Peninsula.* New York: Viking Press, 1957.
Hersh, Seymour M. *The Samson Option: Israel's Nuclear Arsenal and American Foreign Policy.* New York: Random House, 1991.
Herzog, Chaim. *The Arab-Israeli Wars: War and Peace in the Middle East from the War of Independence through Lebanon.* New York: Vintage Books, 1984.
___. *The War of Atonement, October 1973.* Boston: Little, Brown, 1975.
Hofstadter, Dan. *Egypt and Nasser, III: 1967–1972.* New York: Facts on File, 1973.
Horowitz, Dan. "Flexible Responsiveness and Military Strategy: The Case of the Israeli Army." *Policy Sciences* 1 (1970): 191–205.
Howard, Michael, and Robert Hunter. *Israel and the Arab World: The Crisis of 1967.* London: Institute for Strategic Studies, 1967.
Insight Team. *Insights on the Middle East War.* London: *Sunday Times,* 1974.
International Institute for Strategic Studies. *The Military Balance 1972–1973.* London: International Institute for Strategic Studies, 1972.
___. *The Military Balance 1974–1975.* London: International Institute for Strategic Studies, 1972.
Israel Defense Forces. *Commanders of the Six Day War and Their Battle Reports.* Tel Aviv: IDF, 1967.
Israeli, Raphael. *The Political Diary of President Sadat.* Three volumes. Leiden: Brill, 1978–1979.

___. "Sadat: The Calculus of War and Peace." In *The Diplomats, 1939–1979*, edited by Gordon Craig and Francis L. Loewenheim (Princeton, NJ: Princeton University Press, 1994): 436–458.

Israelyan, Victor. *Inside the Kremlin During the Yom Kippur War*. University Park: Pennsylvania State University Press, 1995. Soviet diplomat and member of special four-man task force formed to assist the Politburo in handling the 1973 Arab-Israeli war.

Kahalani, Avigdor. *The Heights of Courage: A Tank Leader's War on the Golan*. New York: Praeger, 1992. Israeli commander of 77th Tank Battalion on the Golan in the 1973 war.

Kamel, Muhammed Ibrahim. *The Camp David Accords: A Testimony*. London: KPI, 1986. Egypt's foreign minister 1977–79.

Karawan, Ibrahim A. "Sadat and the Egyptian-Israeli Peace Revisited." *International Journal of Middle East Studies* 26 (1994): 249–266.

Katz, Samuel M. *Soldier Spies: Israeli Military Intelligence*. Novato, CA: Presidio, 1992.

Kerr, Malcolm. *The Arab Cold War*. Oxford: Oxford University Press, 1978.

Khalidi, Ahmed. "The War of Attrition." *Journal of Palestinian Studies* 3 (1973): 60–87.

Kissinger, Henry. *White House Years*. Boston: Little, Brown, 1979.

___. *Years of Upheaval*. Boston: Little, Brown, 1982.

Korn, David A. *Stalemate: The War of Attrition and Great Power Diplomacy in the Middle East, 1967–1970*. Boulder, CO: Westview Press, 1992.

Liddell Hart, Basil. *Strategy*. New York, 1974.

___. "Strategy of a War." *Encounter* 30 (February 1968): 16–20.

Liebman, Charles S. "The Myth of Defeat: The Memory of the Yom Kippur War in Israeli Society." *Middle Eastern Studies* 29 (July 1993): 399–418.

Luttwak, Edward N., and Dan Horowitz. *The Israeli Army*. New York: Harper and Row, 1975.

Marshall, S. L. A. *Sinai Victory*. New York: William Morrow, 1958.

Meir, Golda. *My Life*. New York: G. P. Putnam's Sons, 1975. Israel's prime minister in the 1973 war.

Meital, Yoram. *Egypt's Struggle for Peace: Continuity and Change, 1967–1977*. Gainesville: University Press of Florida, 1997.

Mor, Ben D. *Decisions and Interaction in Crisis: A Model of International Behavior*. Westport, CT: Praeger, 1993.

Movshovitz, Yoram and Dan Petreanu. "The Artillery Corps—1948 to the Present." *IDF Journal* 4 (Fall 1987): 17–20.

Mutawi, Samir A. *Jordan in the 1967 War*. Cambridge: Cambridge University Press, 1987.

Narkiss, Uzi. *The Liberation of Jerusalem: The Battle of 1967*. London: Valentine Mitchell, 1983. Then a major general, Narkiss was in charge of Israel's Central Command (facing Jordan) in the 1967 war.

Nassif, Ramses. *U Thant in New York 1961-1971: A Portrait of the Third UN Secretary-General*. New York: St. Martin's Press, 1988. U Thant's press spokesperson.

Neff, Donald. *Warriors against Israel: How Israel Won the Battle to Become America's Ally*. Brattleboro, VT: Amana, 1988.

___. *Warriors for Jerusalem: The Six Days That Changed the Middle East*. New York: Linden Press, 1984.

Nixon, Richard. *RN: The Memoirs of Richard Nixon*. Two volumes. New York: Warner Books, 1978.

O'Ballance, Edgar. *No Victor, No Vanquished: The Yom Kippur War.* San Rafael, CA: Presidio Press, 1978.

___. *The Third Arab-Israeli War.* Hamden, CT: Archon Books, 1972.

Owen, Roger. "The Role of the Army in Middle Eastern Politics—A Critique of Existing Analyses." *Review of Middle Eastern Studies* 3 (1978): 63–81.

Pa'il, Meir. *The IDF Campaign against Abu Ageila in Three Wars.* Tel Aviv: IDF, n.d.

Parker, Richard B. *Politics of Miscalculation in the Middle East.* Bloomington: Indiana University Press, 1993. Political counselor of the American embassy in Cairo during the 1967 war and officer in charge of Egyptian affairs in the Department of State during the war of attrition.

___ (ed.). *The Six-Day War.* Gainesville: University Press of Florida, 1996.

Peri, Yoram. *Between Ballots and Bullets: Israeli Military in Politics.* London: Cambridge University Press, 1983.

Peters, Rudolph. *Islam and Colonialism: The Doctrine of Jihad in Modern History.* The Hague: Mouton, 1979.

Pry, Peter. *Israel's Nuclear Arsenal.* Boulder, CO: Westview Press, 1984.

Quandt, William B. *Decade of Decisions: American Policy toward the Arab-Israeli Conflict, 1967–1976.* Berkeley: University of California Press, 1977. Member of National Security Council during the 1973 war.

___. "Lyndon Johnson and the June 1867 War: What Color Was the Light?" *Middle East Journal* 46/2 (Spring 1992): 198–228.

___. *Peace Process: American Diplomacy and the Arab-Israeli Conflict since 1967.* Washington, DC: Brookings Institute, 1993.

Rabin, Yitzhak. *The Rabin Memoirs.* Boston: Little, Brown, 1979. Israeli chief of the General Staff in the 1967 war.

Rabinovich, Abraham. "First Strike," *Jerusalem Post International Edition,* 13 June 1992: 10–11.

Rahmy, Ali 'Abd al-Rahman. *The Egyptian Policy in the Arab World: Intervention in Yemen, 1962–1967.* Washington, DC: University Press of America, 1983.

Razoux, Pierre. *La Guerre Israélo-Arabe d'Octobre: Une Nouvelle Donne Militaire au Proche-Orient.* Paris: Economica, 1999.

Riad, Mahmud. *The Struggle for Peace in the Middle East.* New York: Quartet Books, 1981. Egyptian foreign minister 1964–71.

Rikye, Indar Jit. *The Sinai Blunder: Withdrawal of the United Nations Emergency Force Leading to the the Six-Day War of June 1967.* London: Frank Cass, 1980. An Indian general who commanded UN troops in Egypt before the 1967 war.

Rogers, Glenn F. "The Battle for Suez City." *Military Review* (November 1979): 27–33.

Rothenberg, Gunter E. *The Anatomy of the Israeli Army: The Israel Defence Force, 1948–1978.* New York: Hippocrene Books, 1979.

Rubinstein, Alvin Z. *Red Star on the Nile: The Soviet-Egyptian Influence Relationship since the June War.* Princeton, NJ: Princeton University Press, 1977.

Sachar, Howard M. *An History of Israel: From the Rise of Zionism to Our Time.* New York: Alfred A. Knopf, 1976.

Sadat. Anwar. *In Search of Identity.* New York: Harper and Row, 1977.

Sadat, Jehan. *A Woman of Egypt.* New York: Pocket Books, 1987. Anwar Sadat's wife.

Schiff, Zeev. *A History of the Israeli Army: 1874 to the Present.* New York: Macmillan, 1985.

Seale, Patrick. *Asad of Syria: The Struggle for the Middle East.* Berkeley: University of California Press, 1988.

Seguev, Samuel. *La Guerre de Six Jours*. Paris: Calmann-Levy, 1967.

Sharon, Ariel. *Warrior: The Autobiography of Ariel Sharon*. New York: Simon and Schuster, 1989. Commanded *ugdot* in 1967 and 1973 wars.

al-Shazli, Saad. *The Crossing of the Suez*. San Francisco: American Mideast Research, 1980. Egyptian chief of the General Staff in the 1973 war.

Shemshi, Elyashiv. *Storm in October* (in Hebrew). Tel Aviv: Maarachot, 1986.

Sherman, Arnold. *In the Bunkers of the Sinai*. New York: Sabra Books, 1971.

___. *When God Judged and Men Died: A Battle Report of the Yom Kippur War*. New York: Bantam Books, 1973.

Springborg, Robert. *Mubarak's Egypt: Fragmentation of the Political Order*. Boulder, CO: Westview Press, 1990.

Stein, Janice Gross, and Raymond Tanter. *Rational Decision-Making: Israel's Security Choices, 1967*. Columbus: Ohio State University Press, 1976.

Strategic Survey, 1970. London: Institute for Strategic Studies, 1971.

Sun Tzu. *The Art of War*, translated by Ralph D. Sawyer. Boulder, CO: Westview Press, 1994.

Tamir, Avraham. *A Soldier in Search of Peace: An Inside Look at Israel's Strategy*. New York: Harper and Row, 1986. Retired Israeli major general and participant at the Camp David summit.

Telhami, Shibley. *Power and Leadership in International Bargaining: The Path to the Camp David Accords*. New York: Columbia University Press, 1990.

Teveth, Shabtai. *The Tanks of Tammuz*. New York: Viking Press, 1968. Israeli press official in Tal's *ugdah* in 1967 war.

Thompson, Julian. *The Lifeblood of War: Logistics in Armed Conflict*. London: Brassey's, 1991.

Tibi, Bassam. *Conflict and War in the Middle East 1967–1991: Regional Dynamic and the Superpowers*. New York: St. Martin's Press, 1993.

Ulanoff, Stanley M., and David Eshel. *The Fighting Israeli Air Force*. New York: Arco, 1985.

van Creveld, Martin. *Command in War*. Cambridge, MA: Harvard University Press, 1985.

___. *The Sword and the Olive: A Critical History of the Israeli Defense Force*. New York: Public Affairs, 1998.

Vance, Cyrus. *Hard Choices: Critical Years in America's Foreign Policy*. New York: Simon and Schuster, 1983. Secretary of state under President Carter and participant at Camp David.

Vatikiotis, P. J. *Nasser and His Generation*. New York: St. Martin's Press, 1978.

Vitan, Ariel. "The Soviet Military Presence in Egypt 1967–1972: A New Perspective." *The Journal of Slavic Military Studies* 8 (September 1995): 547–565.

Wakebridge, Charles. "The Syrian Side of the Hill." *Military Review* (February 1976): 20--30.

Wald, Emanuel. *The Wald Report: The Decline of Israeli National Security since 1967*. Boulder, CO: Westview Press, 1992.

Waterbury, John. *The Egypt of Nasser and Sadat: The Political Economy of Two Regimes*. Princeton, NJ: Princeton University Press, 1983.

Weizman, Ezer. *Battle for Peace*. New York: Bantam, 1981. Israeli director of operations in 1967 war and defense minister at the Camp David summit.

___. *On Eagles' Wings*. New York: Macmillan, 1976.

Weller, Jac. "Infantry and the October War: Foot Soldiers in the Desert." *Army* (August 1974): 21–26.
Whetton, Lawrence L. *The Canal War: Four-Power Conflict in the Middle East.* Cambridge, MA: MIT Press, 1974.
Yonay, Ehud. *No Margin for Error: The Making of the Israeli Air Force.* New York: Pantheon Books, 1993.
Yost, Charles. "The Arab-Israeli War: How It Began." *Foreign Affairs* 46 (January 1968): 304–320.

NEWSPAPERS AND MAGAZINES

al-Ahram
The Egyptian Gazette
al-Nasr
New York Times
Newsweek
Washington Post

INDEX

Adan, Avraham
    Bar-Lev Line 104–105
    battle for Suez City, 229–230
    counterattack on 8 Oct., 183–187, 189–190
    countercrossing, 211, 216, 219, 220, 221
    dash to Suez City, 226–227, 232
    imperative of victory, 144, 235
    prisoners of past, 175
    reaction to Arab attack, 173
    relationship with Gonen, 193
    67 war, 55
Agranat Commission, 246, 247–248, 250
Alawite minority rule in Syria, 4, 203
Ali, Ahmad Ismail
    appointed war minister, 134
    commander of both fronts, 149, 151, 166–167
    disagreement with Shazli, 136–137, 223–224
    Director of General Intelligence, 128, 134–136
    final strategic guidance, 147
    Islam, 85
    Israeli countercrossing, 210, 215, 217–218
    offensive to passes, 205–206
    operational pause 191, 193
    professionalism, 136, 137
    tactical changes to *Badr*, 153–154

Amer, Abd al-Hakim
    Israeli deception, 44, 56, 66
    firing and suicide, 73
    general withdrawal order, 58–59, 258
    micro-management 67 war, 58
    operational control of armed forces, 15, 16–17, 18
    politicalization of the army 12–13, 34, 73, 78, 79
    Yemeni Civil War, 128
Amir, Gabi
    counterattack on 8 Oct., 184, 186, 187, 189
    countercrossing, 219–220, 227
    deployment to Sinai, 168, 174, 175
Arafat, Yassar, 121
Aron, Raymond, vi, 1, 71, 239
Asad, Hafiz
    appeal to Sadat, 204–205
    coordination with Sadat, 149–150, 165, 167, 170, 180, 191
    seizure of power, 149, 203
    war strategy, 167, 179, 181–182, 193, 199, 202–205, 243
Ashkenazi, Mottie, 246–247

Badran, Shems al-Din, 8, 13, 73, 77–79, 89
Baghdad Summit, 253
Bar-Lev, Haim

276 INDEX

appointment as Sinai commander, 194
construction of Bar-Lev Line, 104–105
countercrossing, 216, 220, 225–226
post-73 war, 246
Three Years War, 119
Bar-Lev Line, 104–106, 121, 141–142, 144, 170
Battles, 1967 war
Abu Ageila: 48–56, 258
air war, 39–42, 58, 60, 63, 64, 65
Bir Gifgafa, 63
Bir Lahfan, 54–56, 57–58
Gebel Libni, 58
Giddi Pass, 62
Golan Heights, 60, 64–65
Jordanian front, 60
Mitla Pass, 60–62
Nakhl, 62–63
Rafah and Giradi Pass, 42–48
Romana, 63–64
Battles/Special Operations, 1967–70
air war, 110, 114, 116–117, 119–120
Green Island, 110–111
Nag Hamadi, 103–104, 110
Ras al-Ush, 100
Ras Gharib, 113–114
Ras Zafrana, 111–113
Shadwan Island, 115–116
sinking of *Eilat*, 101
Battles, 1973 war
Chinese Farm, 213–219, 221, 223
Egyptian commando strikes, 176–177
Egyptian crossing of the Suez, 170–179
Egyptian offensive on 14 Oct., 205–210
Golan Heights, 168, 181–182, 202–205
Israeli breakout to Suez City, 225–229
Israeli counterattack on 8 Oct., 183–190
Israeli countercrossing, 210–221
operational pauses, 190–194
Suez City, 229–230
Begin, Menachem, 247–248, 252–253, 255
Ben-Gurion, David, 3, 28
Brezhnev, Leonid, 99, 115, 132–133, 179, 222, 231
Britain, 2, 14, 24, 201–202

Camp David Accords, 252–253
Carter, Jimmy, 252–254
Clausewitz, Carl von, vi, xii, 39, 95, 163, 199, 260

Dayan, Moshe
actions 6–8 Oct., 178, 181, 182–183,
actions on before 73 war, 140, 142, 144
appointed defense minister in 67, 11, 12, 30
changes to 67 war plan, 30–31, 33, 34
countercrossing, 215, 216, 226
delay on publishing casualty list, 210
post-73 war, 242, 244, 246–248, 255
recollections of 6 Oct., 173
67 war, 47, 57, 60, 65, 67
Three Years War, 103, 110, 117
de Gaulle, Charles, 8, 95
Dimona Nuclear Reactor, 6, 11, 18
Dome of the Rock, 84

Eban, Abba, 9, 11, 173
Egyptian Armed Forces, 1967
air defense, 14
air force, 14
command changes, 18
intelligence, 14, 19–21, 22, 27
ground forces, 15, 20, 21–22
Plan *Fajr*, 18
Plan *Qahir*, 15–19, 21, 43
politicalization, 12–14
reserves, 21

training, 14, 21
Egyptian Armed Forces, 1967–70
    air defense, 82–83, 115, 118, 119, 120–121
    air force, 102, 107, 109
    critical thinking, 87–91
    combat leadership, 79–81
    conscription policy, 82–83
    Coptic Christians, 86–87
    depoliticalization, 74–75, 76–77, 80
    General Command, 76–79
    ground forces, 82, 102, 107
    intelligence, 89, 90–91
    Islam, 84–87, 230
    national will, 83–87
    Soviet aid, 75–76, 115–117
    training, 83
Egyptian Armed Forces, 1973
    air defense, 141
    air force, 140
    General Command, 135–138
    ground forces, 153–157
    Plan *Badr*, 152–156, 170–171, 189–190, 192, 200, 206
    Soviet aid 133, 135
Eisenhower, Dwight D., 8, 95
Eitan, Raful, 45–48, 57, 65, 119
Elazar, David
    67 war, 65
    counterattack on 8 October, 183–184, 186, 190
    countercrossing, 210, 211, 219–220, 221, 226, 228
    eve of 73 war, 164, 166, 168–170, 174,
    firing Gonen, 193–194
    first days of 73 war, 175, 178–179, 182,
    operational pause, 193
    post-73 war, 244, 246–248
Erez, Haim, 193, 208, 212, 214, 220, 226
Eshkol, Levi,
    background, 3–4
    May Crisis (1967), 5, 7, 9 , 11, 28, 30, 33, 34
    67 war, 65

Three Years War, 98, 101, 104, 106

Fahmi, Muhammad Ali, 83, 137–138
Fawzi, Muhammad
    before 67 war, 6, 7, 13–14, 16
    67 war, 59
    reconstruction after 67 war, 73–77, 79–80, 88, 92
Faysal, King of Saudi Arabia, 82, 100, 150, 242. See also Saudi Arabia
France, 2, 5–6, 14, 97
Ford, Gerald, 250

Gamasi, Muhammad al-Ghani, 42, 92, 123, 137–138, 194, 217, 224
Gavish, Yeshayahu,
    67 war, 31, 33, 54–55, 57, 60, 65, 67
    73 war, 207
    Three Years War, 103, 105
German Blitzkrieg of 1940, 96–97, 224
Gonen, Shmuel
    actions 6–9 Oct., 174, 175, 182, 183–184, 187, 189–190
    Agranat Commission, 248
    fired as Sinai commander, 193–194
    67 war, 45–48, 57–58, 64–65

Hasan II, King of Morocco, 251
Haykal, Muhammad Hasanayn
    descriptions of senior officers, 76–77, 136, 137
    limited war concept, 108–109, 146–147
    mistakes in 67 war, 89
    oil as a weapon, 150
    operational pause, 191
Hod, Mordechai, 25, 26, 40
Hofi, Yitzhak, 33, 164
Holocaust Syndrome, 23, 97
Hussein, King of Jordan, 10, 23, 121, 150, 167, 251. *See also* Jordan

Iraq, 10, 23, 87, 99, 150, 204, 205, 253

Ismail, Muhammad Hafez, 148, 180, 225
Israel Defense Forces, 1967
　air force, 24–26
　command in war, 24, 26–27, 34
　ground forces, 26–27, 32–33
　intelligence, 6, 7, 26, 27
　military culture, 22–24
　Plan *Kilshon*, 27–28, 29
　Plan *Moked*, 40
　Plan *Nahshonim*, 30–33, 54, 57
　reserves, 23, 26–27
Israel Defense Forces, 1973
　air force, 97–98, 109, 114, 140
　arms industry, 98
　Bar-Lev Line, 142–143
　ground forces, 141–142
　intelligence, 139–140, 140–141
　Plan Dovecote, 143, 174
　Plan Rock, 143,
Izzat, Suleyman, 13, 137

Jadid, Salah, 4, 149
Jerusalem, 47, 84, 95, 97, 252–253, 254
Johnson, Lyndon Baines, 2, 9 11, 66, 96, 99, 242
Jordan
　civil war, 121,
　May Crisis (1967), 6, 10, 23, 35
　post-67 war, 84, 96, 98, 100, 123
　post-73 war, 251, 254
　67 war, 42, 67
　73 war, 149, 167

Keren, Aryeh
　counterattack on 8 Oct., 184, 186, 187,
　countercrossing, 219, 220, 221,
　drive to Suez City, 227, 228, 230
Khartoum Conference, 100, 101
Kissinger, Henry
　cease-fire, 225, 227, 229, 260
　détente, 132
　first communique with Sadat in 73 war, 180–181
　pre-war strategy, 132, 148,
　secret channel to Egypt, 148, 149, 151, 179
　shuttle diplomacy, 241–243, 244, 250
Kosygin, Aleksei, 8, 116, 222

Liberty, sinking of, 66
Liddell Hart, Basil, 127

Magen, Kalman
　counterattack on 8 Oct., 184, 186, 187
　countercrossing, 212, 221, 226
　dash to Suez City, 227, 228
　defense on 14 Oct., 209
Maginot Line, 105
Mahmud, Muhammad Sidqi, 13, 14, 25, 88–89, 137
Mamun, Saad, 138, 208, 210, 217
Mandler, Avraham, 56, 174, 182, 183, 184, 209
Masada Complex, 23
Matt, Danny, 51, 103, 212, 215, 217, 220
Mechdal, 246, 247, 248
Meir, Golda
　American air supply, 202
　appointment as prime minister, 98
　attack into Syria, 204
　cease-fire proposal, 201
　countercrossing, 215, 219
　disengagement agreement, 241–242
　fall of government, 246–248, 250
　mobilization of reserves, 166, 168–170
　nuclear weapons, 192–193
　Operation Oz, 143–144
　personality, 106–107
　prisoners-of-war, 244
　Sadat's 1971 initiative, 130, 131
　Sadat's trip to Jerusalem, 251
　surprised by Arab attack, 172–173
　terrorist act in Austria, 164

Three Years War, 114, 116–117, 120
violation of first cease-fire, 227, 229
Mohsen, Salah al-Din, 14–15, 17, 56, 90
Mubarak, Hosni, 137–138, 224
Mukhitdinov, Nuritdin, 167, 179, 204
Murtagui, Abd al-Mohsen Kamil, 14, 17, 21, 41, 56–59, 90

Napoleon Bonaparte, 97
Nassar, Uthman, 56–58, 89
Nasser, Gamal Abdul
    background, 2–3
    cease-fire in 1970, 118, 120
    evacuation of the Canal area, 101
    health and death, 111, 121–122
    Khartoum Conference, 100–101
    legacy to Sadat, 127–128, 134, 135
    new air defense system, 119–120
    reconstruction of the army, 74–79, 81–84, 86–92
    resignation and return, 72–73
    severance of diplomatic relations with US, 99
    67 war, 42–44, 57, 59, 65, 68
    Soviet combat troops, 115, 118
    steps to 67 war, 5–6, 7, 8, 10, 12–15, 17, 18. 22, 33, 34
    strategy of attrition, 107–109, 111–113
Nir, Natke
    battle of Abu Ageila, 50–51, 53–55
    counterattack on 8 Oct., 177, 184, 186, 189
    countercrossing, 219–220, 227, 230
Nixon, Richard, 120, 132–133, 201, 225, 240, 250. *See also* United States
Nuclear Weapons
    factors in Asad's and Sadat's war strategies, 181–182
    Israel making operational, 192–193, 200–201
    67 war, 5–6, 11–12, 18 181

Oil as a weapon, 150, 205, 225, 242

Palestinians/PLO, 18, 43, 121, 250, 251, 253, 254
Peace Now, 252
Purple Line, 164, 182, 201, 203–204

Rabin, Yitzhak
    ambassador to US, 248
    67 war, 6–7, 28, 30, 47, 65
    73 war, 173
    Three Years War, 114, 120
Raviv, Tuvia, 193, 209, 211–214, 219, 221, 226
Reshef, Amnon, 98, 174, 193, 212–214, 217, 219, 221, 226
Riyad, Abd al-Munim, 10, 73, 77, 81, 92, 103, 148, 157, 255

Sadat, Anwar
    Arab support for war, 200
    Asad, coordination with, 149–150, 165, 167, 170, 179–180, 191
    background, 128
    consolidation of power, 128–129
    diplomacy during 73 war, 163, 180–181, 191, 222, 225
    edging to war, 131–135, 165–166
    expulsion of Soviet advisors, 133
    Israeli countercrossing, 215, 217–218, 222–223
    King Hussein, 150
    launching of SCUDs, 228
    Nasser era, 5, 74–75, 79, 81, 83, 86, 87
    offense to passes. 202–203, 205, 209
    oil as a weapon. 150, 156, 166
    operational pause, 191–193
    orientation toward the US, 129
    peace with Israel, 239–244, 250–255
    rejection of cease-fire, 201–202

significance in art of war, 259–261
trip to Jerusalem, 251–252
Three Years War, 111, 115–116, 123
war strategy, 140, 142, 145–151, 151–157, 191, 259–261
Sadiq, Muhammad, 115, 128, 131–134, 151
Saudi Arabia
oil embargo, 225
support to Sadat, 150–151, 156, 200, 205
Yemeni Civil War, 3, 82, 100
Sasson, Yitzhak, 53, 207, 211, 221, 226
Sharon, Ariel
counterattack on 8 Oct., 183, 184, 187, 189
countercrossing, 211–212, 214, 219–221, 226–227, 231
defense on 14 Oct., 207, 208–209
insubordination, 193, 226
observations of 7 Oct., 182
67 war, 31, 50–55, 60, 63
Three Years War, 105–106, 121, 123
post-73 war, 245–246,
Shazli, Saad al-Din,
career, 136
command crisis, 223–224
Crossing Command, 155
Operation *Badr*, 151, 152, 153
operational pause, 191, 192
opposition to 14 Oct Offensive, 205
67 war, 18, 19, 43–44, 56–57, 59, 64
Syrian alliance, 151
tensions with Ahmad Ismail, 136–137
Shimshi, Eliashiv, 187, 188, 228
Shomron, Dan, 174, 182, 184, 209
Soviet Union
advance warning of 73 war, 167
aid to Egypt after 67 war, 75–76, 79, 83, 115, 118, 119, 122
aid to Egypt before 73 war, 135
aid during 73 war, 203

cease-fire attempts in 73 war, 179–180, 222, 225, 227, 231
combat troops in Egypt, 115, 116–117, 120
May Crisis (1967), 5, 8–9
relations with Nasser after 67 war, 95, 98, 99–100, 106
Sadat's expulsion of Soviet advisors, 133
Sadat's launching of SCUDs, 228
67 war, 57
Sun Tzu, 127, 199
Syria
alliance with Egypt, 149–151, 156, 166–167
armed forces in 73 war, 149, 203
border clashes in 1967, 4–5
Islam, 4
post-67 war, 87, 89, 100
post-73 war, 242–243
67 war, 10, 42, 60
73 war, 163–165, 173, 180, 181–182, 192, 199, 201, 202–205

Ta'ozim, 144
Tal, Israel
Bar-Lev Line, 105–106
67 war, 31, 44–47, 50, 53, 55, 57–58, 60, 64–65
Thant, U, 7, 102
TOW missiles, 201, 208

United Nations
disengagement of forces, 240, 242
May Crisis (1967), 5, 7
Security Council Resolution 242, 102, 120, 130
67 war, 59
73 war, 181, 227, 228, 229, 231
Three Years War, 100
United States
aid to Israel during 73 war, 178, 193, 200–202, 225
Defense Condition III, 231
détente, 132–133

disengagement agreements after 73 war, 240–243
indifference to Sadat, 129, 130–131, 133
May Crisis (1967), 8, 9, 11, 23
peace treaty between Israel and Egypt, 253–254
Sadat's letter on 7 Oct, 180
67 war, 65
secret channel to Sadat, 148–149
sixteen point memorandum with Israel, 250–251
SR-71 spy plane, 206–207
Three Years War, 95, 97–98, 106, 114, 117–120

Vietnam War, 9, 96, 145–146, 243
Vinogradov, Vladimir, 167, 179–180, 192, 201, 204, 231

Wassel, Abd al-Munim, 58, 138, 209, 227
Watergate Scandal, 225, 231, 250
Weizman, Ezer, 28, 65, 110, 133, 251

Yaguri, Assaf, 187–188, 189
Yariv, Aharon, 27, 28
Yemeni Civil War, 2, 3, 5, 6, 14, 15, 21, 27, 82, 100
Yoffe, Avraham, 19, 31, 54–55, 58, 60–61

Zeira, Eliyahu, 139, 141, 164, 166, 168, 173
Zippori, Mordechai, 50–51, 53, 63

About the Author

GEORGE W. GAWRYCH is Historian on the faculty of the U.S. Army Command and General Staff College, a position he has held since July 1984. He taught at the University of Hawaii, the University of Kansas, and the School of International Studies at Fort Bragg, North Carolina. His publications on modern Middle East history include articles in academic journals and two short monographs published by the U.S. Army. In November 1989, he received the Turkish Studies Association's biennial prize for the best published article in Turkish Studies.